*Cambridge studies in medieval life and thought*

Edited by WALTER ULLMANN, LITT.D., F.B.A.
*Professor of Medieval Ecclesiastical History
in the University of Cambridge*

*Third series vol. 5*

# LAW AND SOCIETY
# IN THE VISIGOTHIC KINGDOM

# CAMBRIDGE STUDIES IN
## MEDIEVAL LIFE AND THOUGHT
## THIRD SERIES

# LAW AND SOCIETY
## IN THE
# VISIGOTHIC KINGDOM

### P. D. KING
*Lecturer in Medieval History*
*in the University of Lancaster*

CAMBRIDGE
AT THE UNIVERSITY PRESS
1972

Published by the Syndics of the Cambridge University Press
Bentley House, 200 Euston Road, London NW1 2DB
American Branch: 32 East 57th Street, New York, N.Y.10022

© Cambridge University Press 1972

Library of Congress Catalogue Card Number: 77-179163

ISBN: 0 521 08421 0

Printed in Great Britain
at the University Printing House, Cambridge
(Brooke Crutchley, University Printer)

# CONTENTS

*TO MY MOTHER*

# PREFACE

The Visigothic kingdom was born from the moribund body of the Western Roman Empire: it met its death nearly two and a half centuries later by the sword of Islam. Its lifespan extended therefore over an epoch of consuming fascination: a twilight age, sub-antique, from one point of view; a gestation period, early medieval, from another. One would confidently expect to find in the history of Visigothic Spain and Septimania during this time material which would help to furnish answers to some of the basic questions asked by classicists and medievalists. To what extent did the Roman world live on in the West after its political demise? What were the fundaments of the Western civilisation which emerged from the commixture of Roman experience and sophistication, Germanic immaturity and vigour and the new teachings of Christianity? In what degree were the characteristics of the later medieval world foreshadowed in those of the late Empire? It is the more difficult, in view of the quite crucial significance of these matters, to account for the remarkable historiographical aversion from study of the Visigothic kingdom. It may be that the transitional character of the age in which it flourished has in fact served as a deterrent to some classicists and medievalists, unable to feel themselves at home in a world abundant with unfamiliar features. But Merovingian Gaul has had its fair share of historians. More important, no doubt, has been the absence of the powerful impetus to investigation which has been provided for the historians of other countries by keen interest in national evolutionary developments. While the early kingdom of the Franks metamorphosed into the France and Germany of the Middle Ages proper, the Visigothic power knew only sudden extinction in 711: in any case, the lack of concern with later Spanish medieval history – a phenomenon largely explicable in terms of linguistic difficulties and cultural prejudices – is itself striking. The Arab conquest has also been responsible for what is perhaps the most considerable factor making for neglect, the assumption that Visigothic history is remote, cut off from the later European Middle Ages as a whole. In fact, one has only to think of Pseudo-Isidore's employment of the Visigothic conciliar sources and of the invocation of Visigothic monarchical practices by the anti-papal writers of the eleventh century to recognise the influence exercised upon the succeeding ages. This influence will unquestionably appear the greater once historians of the later period operate with a more intimate knowledge of the Visigothic kingdom.

That such a knowledge is not easily attainable itself constitutes a barrier to study. Whatever the reasons for neglect in the past, the result has been a scarcity of those earlier learned papers and monographs which, however much they may now be scorned, provide the essential foundations upon which modern researchers into the histories of other areas and peoples can build. There is a case for simple antiquarianism with respect to the Visigoths. Most of what has been written is by Spanish scholars and not only sometimes difficult to obtain but sadly often of little value or even accuracy when access is finally achieved. Historians like Sánchez-Albornoz in South America, Orlandis Rovira in Spain and E. A. Thompson in this country have done much to rectify the deficiencies, but it remains the fact that the inquirer into some or other aspect of early medieval history is more often than not obliged to tackle the Visigothic sources direct without even an effective guide to these, let alone a significant body of auxiliary literature. The apparent aridity of these sources, overwhelmingly legal and conciliar, presents itself as a further deterrent to examination, as Professor Thompson has justly observed.

The aim of this book is to provide an account of what the most important single block of source material, the great legal compilation issued by King Ervig in 681, has to tell us about the structure and ethos of Visigothic society as the kingdom drew near to its end. I have not attempted to write a general history of the kingdom about the year 681, a task which would have meant – to take two instances – the payment of much greater attention to political events and the devotion of a lengthy section to the Church and its organisation. But I have gone backwards – and occasionally forwards – in time when it seemed useful or appropriate to do so, and have frequently introduced material from other sources, particularly the acts of the councils, in order to illustrate, to explain or to expand certain points.

## Preface

Limitations of space have forbidden the regular citation of Roman, Germanic and Romano-barbarian legal and juristic texts or of biblical and patristic sources which stand in close relation with the Visigothic laws, but references have been made when they seemed especially valuable. Those interested will find parallels and precedents in the footnotes to Zeumer's edition of the Visigothic codes, in his articles in the *Neues Archiv* for 1899 and 1901, and throughout the work of Alvaro d'Ors on the earlier Eurician code. Moreover, I am no lawyer: when I have found it necessary to examine the law itself rather than the society which it reflects I have done so with trepidation and, I hope, humility. It seemed essential, for example, to include a chapter on the administration of justice, but my account is a frankly tentative step into a field where legal historians have feared – or at any rate neglected – to tread. Here as elsewhere the dearth of secondary literature has obliged me to lengthier justifications of the positions I have adopted than would be ideal. Nevertheless, the notes have been savagely pruned – on occasions, I fear, over-pruned.

The dangers in the historical use of legal material, especially when there is no sizeable body of non-legal sources yielding direct information upon the reality of the situation, are notorious: it is insidiously easy to translate legal precept into social practice, to slip from the fact of a measure's existence to the assumption of its enforcement, to attribute relevance to provisions illustrating long-past conditions, and it would no doubt be wishful thinking to believe that I have always successfully escaped these snares. But the rewards are peculiarly valuable. No other source has the evidential merit possessed by law as the mirror of the aspirations and ideals of the society which produces it – or, at least, of the governing circles of that society. It is precisely for this reason that one cannot but concur with Gibbon's *dictum* that the laws of a nation form the most instructive portion of its history. But the laws of Ervig's code permit far more than our recognition of the direction in which he and kings before him attempted to steer Visigothic society. They offer also a wealth of information bearing upon the institutions of the kingdom and upon the day-to-day life enjoyed or endured by its inhabitants, for the raw stuff of the laws was necessarily the features of society as it existed, even if the legislative goal was sometimes to emend these. The subject-matter of the laws is so diverse that practically no aspect of life is left untouched. The laws shed light upon the financial and administrative systems, upon the execution of justice, upon the military organisation, upon the economy; they deal with marriage and guardianship, slavery and manumission, the aristocracy and the Church; they illustrate the relationship of king and people, of Roman and Goth, of patron and client, of landlord and tenant; they regulate sales and donations, loans and testaments. Topics range from murder to the castration of animals, from treason to grave-robbing, from rape to prostitution. In short, the laws reflect in the most comprehensive fashion the internal organisation and social conditions of the Visigothic kingdom; they constitute a vast storehouse of information, a repository which cannot be overestimated in importance.

The editions used of original sources are not indicated in the footnotes but will be found in the bibliography. References to the conciliar sources are given thus: XII Tol. *Tomus*, 3 (Twelfth Council of Toledo, Royal Address and canon three), Mer. 17 (Council of Merida, canon seventeen) and so on. The edition in volume eighty-four of J. P. Migne, *Patrologia latina*, is consistently used, and I sometimes add the column number in parentheses to make location easier. The Visigothic laws are cited thus: VI. 2. 1, 3, 3. 4 (VI. 2. 1, VI. 2. 3, VI. 3. 4), and in all cases according to the overall numbering in bold type in Zeumer's edition. I have used the shorter forms of the names of Spanish authors in the footnotes (for example, R. d'Abadal), but have indicated the full forms in the bibliography (for example, R. d'Abadal i de Vinyals) when they are known to me.

With the exception of one chapter, virtually the whole of this book has been written during the first sixteen months of my tenure of a Research Fellowship at the University of Leicester. I am profoundly grateful to the Research Board of the University, both for the opportunity this Fellowship has permitted me and for the financial assistance which has allowed me to travel to libraries around the country. I have further to express my thanks to the Managers of the Frederick William Maitland Memorial Fund for the generous grant which I received while still a schoolmaster at Dulwich College in 1969. My debt to Professor Walter Ullmann, whose enthusiasm and learning have been an inspiration to me since I was an undergraduate, is immense and irredeemable. But the last word must be reserved for my wife, who has responded to my neglect with a forbearing stoicism and to my crises of confidence with an encouraging cheerfulness. *Dux femina facti.*

*Market Harborough*                                                              P.D.K.
*May 1971*

It is now the most agreeable of obligations further to thank the Managers of the Frederick William Maitland Memorial Fund, who have made a most handsome contribution towards the cost of publication.

*Yealand Conyers*                                                                P.D.K.
*February 1972*

# ABBREVIATIONS

| | |
|---|---|
| *AEA* | *Archivo español de arqueología* |
| *AHDE* | *Anuario de historia del derecho español* |
| *AST* | *Analecta Sacra Tarraconensia* |
| Barc. | Council of Barcelona |
| *BFD* | *Boletim da Faculdade de Direito* (Universidade de Coimbra) |
| *BRAH* | *Boletín de la Real Academia de la Historia* |
| *Carm.* | *Carmen* |
| *CE* | *Codex Euricianus* |
| *CEB* | *Codicis Euriciani leges ex Lege Baiuvariorum restitutae* |
| *CEH* | *The Cambridge economic history of Europe*, 2nd edn |
| *CH* | *Continuatio Hispana* |
| *CHE* | *Cuadernos de historia de España* |
| *CR* | *Codex revisus* (of Leovigild) |
| *CT* | *Codex Theodosianus* |
| CUA | Catholic University of America |
| *DEO* | Isidore, *De ecclesiasticis officiis* |
| *DVI* | *De viris illustribus* |
| *EHR* | *The English historical review* |
| *Ep.* | *Epistola* |
| Esp.; esp. | España, Espagne; español, espagnol |
| *ET* | *Edictum Theoderici* |
| *Etym.* | Isidore, *Etymologiae* |
| EV | Estudios visigóticos |
| *EW* | *Epistolae Wisigoticae* |
| *FV* | *Formulae Visigothicae* |
| Gesch. | Geschichte |
| *HF* | Gregory of Tours, *Historia Francorum* |
| *HG* | Isidore, *Historia Gothorum* |
| hist. | history, histoire, historia, história, historical, historique, histórico, historisch |
| *HJ* | *Historisches Jahrbuch* |
| *HS* | *Hispania Sacra* |
| *HW* | Julian of Toledo, *Historia Wambae regis* |
| IRMAE | Ius romanum medii aevi |
| *LB* | *Lex Burgundionum* |

xiii

| | |
|---|---|
| LO | *Liber Ordinum* |
| LRB | *Lex Romana Burgundionum* |
| LRV | *Lex Romana Visigothorum* |
| LRV.CT | *Lex Romana Visigothorum, Codex Theodosianus* |
| LRV.PS | *Lex Romana Visigothorum, Pauli Sententiae* |
| MA | Middle Ages, Moyen Âge, Mittelalter |
| Mer. | Council of Merida |
| MGH | *Monumenta Germaniae Historica* |
| MGH.AA | *Monumenta Germaniae Historica, Auctores Antiquissimi* |
| MGH.Epp. | *Monumenta Germaniae Historica, Epistolae* |
| MGH.LL | *Monumenta Germaniae Historica, Leges* |
| MGH.SSM | *Monumenta Germaniae Historica, Scriptores Rerum Merovingicarum* |
| MIÖG | Mitteilungen des Instituts für österreichische Geschichtsforschung |
| NA | *Neues Archiv der Gesellschaft für ältere deutsche Geschichtskunde* |
| Narb. | Council of Narbonne |
| PL | J. P. Migne, *Patrologia latina* |
| Reg. | Pope Gregory I, *Registrum epistolarum* |
| REL | *Revue des études latines* |
| RET | *Revista española de teología* |
| RPH | *Revista portuguesa de história* |
| RSDI | *Rivista di storia del diritto italiano* |
| Sar. | Council of Saragossa |
| SDHI | *Studia et documenta historiae et iuris* |
| Sent. | Isidore, *Sententiae* |
| Sett. | *Settimane di studio del centro italiano di studi sull'alto medioevo* |
| Tol. | Council of Toledo |
| VPE | *Vitae sanctorum patrum Emeretensium* |
| VSF | *Vita sancti Fructuosi* |
| Zeumer, XXIII, XXIV, XXVI | References thus are to Zeumer's various articles in the indicated volumes of the *NA*: see bibliography for details |
| Zeumer, LV | Zeumer's edition of the *Leges Visigothorum* |
| ZRG.GA/ KA/RA | *Zeitschrift der Savigny-Stiftung für Rechtsgeschichte, Germanistische Abteilung/Kanonistische Abt./Romanistische Abt.* |

Chapter 1

# INTRODUCTION

The historical career of the Visigothic kingdom as a *de iure* autonomous political unit began in that same decade which witnessed the deposition of the last Roman Emperor in the West. When the redoubtable Euric seized royal power in 466 the area under Visigothic domination was little larger than that originally assigned to the barbarians by the treaty which Constantius, chiefly concerned to counter the threat of the *Bacaudae*, had concluded with King Wallia in 418 and by which the Goths had received land in southern Gaul in return for a promise of their federate services.[1] The new king determined upon expansion and opened his offensive in Spain in 468 and in Gaul in the following year. His breach of treaty was attended by outstanding success. When peace was made with the Eastern Emperor in 475 Euric was recognised as the sovereign master of a vast kingdom whose northern boundary was formed by the Loire and whose southern was near, if it had not reached, the straits of Gibraltar: to this was added in 477 Provence, ceded by Odovacer after Visigothic occupation in the previous year.[2] Thereafter, renowned and feared, Euric enjoyed the role of the mightiest ruler of the West, to whose court at Toulouse there flocked ambassadors and suppliants of many races.[3] It was an imposing legacy which he left his successor when he died in 484.

[1] On the significance of the *Bacaudae* see E. A. Thompson, 'The settlement of the barbarians in southern Gaul', *Journal of Roman studies*, XLVI (1956), 65–75, whose case is not met by B. S. Bachrach, *Traditio*, XXV (1969), 354–8. But the single stone of the settlement threatened to kill several dangerous birds: see J. M. Wallace-Hadrill, *The long-haired kings and other studies in Frankish hist.* (London, 1962), pp. 26–9. On the fortunes of the *foedus* after 418 see A. Loyen, *REL*, XII (1934), 406–15, and on the division of lands below, pp. 204–6.

[2] Details in K. F. Stroheker, *Eurich, König der Westgoten* (Stuttgart, 1937), pp. 8off., though for the expansion see also R. d'Abadal, *Del reino de Tolosa al reino de Toledo* (Madrid, 1960), pp. 39–47.

[3] Sidonius, *Ep.* VIII. 9, Ennodius, *Vita Epifani* 80, 86, 90, Cassiodorus, *Variae* III. 3.

The independent kingdom thus created owed its existence to what may best be termed the 'nationalist' party among the Visigoths. Throughout the turbulent century since the panic-stricken flight from the Huns and crossing of the Danube into the Empire in 376, there had been apparent a basic divergence of policy towards Rome within the barbarian ranks.[1] Already in 382, we are told, two Gothic chieftains drew their swords after an argument at the dinner-table of Theodosius: the one desired nothing but the extinction of the Empire, the other friendship and alliance between Goth and Roman.[2] The dichotomy was maintained during the following years. Alaric I fluctuated between the two attitudes.[3] Athaulf began by holding to the first but was later won over to the second and allegedly because of this murdered in 415.[4] His successor, Sigeric, was also a man of peace: it was for this reason that he too was disposed of after a short reign.[5] In his place the Goths chose Wallia with the deliberate intention of breaking the peace: only force of circumstances compelled him to preserve it.[6] His successor, Theodoric I,[7] pursued throughout his lengthy reign a policy characterised by constant hostility towards the Empire to which the Goths were theoretically bound as federates: only once, and then as the result of a direct threat posed to his own dominions by the invading Huns, did he fight loyally alongside his

[1] See R. Gibert, 'El reino visigodo y el particularismo esp.', *EV*, I (Rome–Madrid, 1956), 17–24 (with references also to the pre-entry period), and E. A. Thompson, 'The Visigoths from Fritigern to Euric', *Historia*, XII (1963), 105–26 (though I do not agree that the two sides were the optimates and the rank and file).

[2] Eunapius, *Frag.* 60, cit. in L. Schmidt, *Gesch. der deutschen Stämme bis zum Ausgange der Völkerwanderung*, I: *Die Gesch. der Ostgermanen* (Berlin, 1910), p. 188.

[3] Thompson, 'Fritigern to Euric', p. 111.

[4] Orosius, *Historiae adversum paganos* VII. 43. 4–6. But Orosius may have assumed the responsibility of anti-Roman feeling for Athaulf's death on the basis of later developments: other sources, though conflicting, show personal motives (see J. Orlandis, *El poder real y la sucesión al trono en la monarquía visigoda*, EV, III (Rome–Madrid, 1962), 61–2) and Athaulf's successor followed a policy of peace.

[5] Orosius, VII. 43. 9. On the slightly different version of *HG* 20 see H. Messmer, *Hispania-Idee und Gotenmythos* (Zurich, 1960), p. 117.

[6] Orosius, VII. 43. 10: 'Ad hoc electus a Gothis, ut pacem infringeret, ad hoc ordinatus a Deo, ut pacem confirmaret'. Cf. *HG* 21. The terrestrial agent of the divine ordinance was Constantius, who held the Goths in an economic stranglehold: see Thompson, 'Settlement', p. 67.

[7] I retain the traditional nomenclature, although the king's name is correctly Theodorid: see K. A. Eckhardt, 'Die Nachbenennung in den Königshäusern der Goten', *Festgabe Harold Steinacker* (Munich, 1955), p. 36, n. 3.

Roman 'allies'.[1] A similarly anti-Roman policy was followed by his eldest son and successor, Thorismund, and was responsible for his death at the hands of his brothers Theodoric and Frederic.[2]

The thirteen years from 453 to 466 constitute the period when the influence of the 'peace' party among the Visigoths was at its zenith. Hidatius's designation of Theodoric II in 456 as 'fidus Romano ...imperio' might be applied to him at almost any time of his reign: only during the brief episode of the *coniuratio Marcelliana* and the subsequent war against Majorian does the Gothic–Imperial alliance appear to have been broken, and certainly this does not indicate Theodoric's hostility to the Empire as such.[3] In 454, 456, 457 and again in 462 Theodoric was to be found fighting in support of the Romans: he was even responsible for the elevation of Avitus to the Imperial title in 456 and for his protection thereafter.[4] No doubt Theodoric thought also in terms of gaining territorial advantage for his Goths: he would in any case have been compelled so to think by the 'war' party among them. But everything that we know about the king demonstrates his satisfaction with a state of continued political dependence on the Empire, an attitude reflected in the words put into his mouth by Sidonius:

Roma...nil te mundus habet melius...Romae sum te duce amicus, principe te miles.[5]

The murder of Theodoric by his bellicose brother Euric was inspired, then, by political discontent as much as by personal ambition, for the attacks almost immediately launched against the surrounding territories, as well as other aspects of Euric's reign, show the new king to have belonged to that group among the Goths who

---

[1] Details in Schmidt, *Gesch.*, pp. 233–48. The Goths fighting with the Romans in 446 were probably mercenaries – 'ad depraedandum', says Hidatius, *Continuatio chronicorum Hieronymianorum* 134.

[2] Prosper Tiro, *Epitoma chronicon* 1371: cf. *HG* 30 and Thompson, 'Fritigern to Euric', p. 124.

[3] Hidatius, 170. For plot and war see C. E. Stevens, *Sidonius Apollinaris and his age* (Oxford, 1933), pp. 40–51, 181–5; further, K. F. Stroheker, *Der senatorische Adel im spätantiken Gallien* (Tübingen, 1948), pp. 55ff.

[4] Hidatius, 158, 173, 186, 217 etc., *HG* 31ff. Details of the reign in Schmidt, *Gesch.*, pp. 252–9. It was during the campaign of 462/3 that the Goths occupied Narbonne at Imperial invitation and that Frederic was killed.

[5] Sidonius, *Carm.* VII. 501–12: cf. ib. XXIII. 70–1 where Theodoric is 'decus Getarum, Romanae columen salusque gentis'.

3

favoured war and who looked forward to the day when they would no longer be subject to even nominal Roman control.[1] Such an attitude had its roots in the national self-consciousness of the Goths, in their awareness of themselves as a people separate and quite distinct from the Romans among whom they lived. The obvious racial division, visibly and aurally expressed in dress and language,[2] was reinforced by the confessional. There can be no doubt of the strength of the Goths' adherence to the Arianism which they had adopted between 382 and 395,[3] and characteristic of the first part of Euric's reign was his championship of the heresy and suppression, determined if not bloody, of orthodox Catholicism.[4] According to Sidonius, the king hated the very sound of Catholic: he appeared more the leader of his sect than of his people. The churches were abandoned, the bishoprics left vacant, and the bishop of Clermont considered that the task had become to keep bound to Rome in faith those territories which had been lost politically.[5] Such evidence leaves little doubt of Euric's oppression.[6] That this was primarily motivated by political considerations serves only to confirm the national character of the credal cleavage.[7] It was precisely because the Goths were Arian that the Roman resistance movement was led

[1] See, among many, Stroheker, *Eurich*, pp. 4–7, E. Stein, *Hist. du bas-empire*, I (Paris–Brussels–Amsterdam, 1959), 388–9, and K. Schäferdiek, *Die Kirche in den Reichen der Westgoten und Suewen bis zur Errichtung der westgotischen katholischen Staatskirche* (Berlin, 1967), pp. 12–13. For Theodoric's murder see Orlandis, *Poder real*, p. 66.

[2] For the skin-clad Visigoths see Claudian, *De bello pollentino sive gothico* 481–2, and Sidonius, *Ep.* I. 2, and for language C. Sánchez-Albornoz, 'Pervivencia y crisis de la tradición jurídica romana en la Esp. goda', *Sett.*, IX (1962), 143–4, and literature cit. there. Ennodius, 89, 90, shows Euric using an interpreter in the peace negotiations of 475.

[3] On the conversion and its date see E. A. Thompson, *The Visigoths in the time of Ulfila* (Oxford, 1966), pp. 78–93, though I see no reason to reject the report of Jordanes, *Getica* 131, that the Goths promised in 376 to adopt Christianity, even if *Getica* 132 is unreliable.

[4] On Euric and the Catholics see above all Stroheker, *Eurich*, pp. 37ff., and Schäferdiek, pp. 18–31.

[5] *Ep.* VII. 6. But Euric was not in fact interested in proselytism: see below in text.

[6] *HF* II. 25 is to be disregarded: Stroheker, *Eurich*, pp. 40ff. Note that Euric, like Constantine before him and Clovis and Sisebut (see *EW* 9) afterwards, regarded his faith as responsible for his successes: Sidonius, *Ep.* VII. 6.

[7] The political motivation is frequently stressed: see, e.g., G. Yver, 'Euric, roi des wisigoths', *Études d'hist. du MA dédiées à Gabriel Monod* (Paris, 1896), pp. 43ff., K. Voigt, *Staat und Kirche von Konstantin dem Großen bis zum Ende der Karolingerzeit* (Stuttgart, 1936), p. 131, E. A. Thompson in *Nottingham mediaeval studies*, IV (1960), 9.

*Introduction*

by the clergy: equally, it was precisely among these clergy that the Catholic Franks were later to find support.[1] It is difficult to avoid the conclusion that the Goths, living in a predominantly orthodox world, clung so stubbornly to their Arianism in large part because the heresy represented an essential mark of their distinctiveness as a people from the native Romans.[2] It is hardly likely, anyway, that they maintained their faith as a matter of conviction after due reflection on the relationship of the Persons of the Trinity: the sophistication of thought which characterised those Visigothic scholars at Toulouse capable of arguing the niceties of their belief certainly cannot be attributed to the Goths as a whole.[3] Significantly, the Romanophil Theodoric II is reported to have been lukewarm in his Arianism, an adherent 'pro consuetudine potius quam pro ratione'.[4] The detestation of the heresy displayed by the Catholic Romans could only have strengthened the Goths in it.[5] Since Arianism belonged to *Gothia*,

[1] Especially so, as many of the Gallo-Roman nobility had entered the Church, which had therefore become a 'Rückzugsstellung des Romanentums' (Stroheker, *Eurich*, p. 51). On the aristocratic background of the fifth- and sixth-century episcopate see idem, *Senatorische Adel*, passim. In my view Stroheker considerably underestimates the influence of religion on the Romans of the time. Sidonius would not have stressed the anti-Catholic character of Euric so strongly unless such an emphasis had corresponded to sentiment among the Romans, at least of his circle. It was religious influence – encouragement by the priest Constantius and the introduction of the rogations of Bishop Mamertus of Vienne – which inspired the resistance of Clermont to the Goths: see Sidonius, *Epp.* III. 2, VII. 1, Stroheker, *Eurich*, pp. 72–3. Similarly, it was the anti-Arian writings of Faustus of Riez which led to his exile after Euric's conquest of Provence: Stroheker, *Eurich*, p. 58, though doubtful is Schäferdiek, pp. 30–1. In truth, one cannot clearly or profitably distinguish between the political and religious aspects of the struggle. This applies equally to the later Gothic–Frankish conflict.
[2] See J. Orlandis, 'El cristianismo en la Esp. visigoda', *EV*, 1 (Rome–Madrid, 1956), 4: 'Para los visigodos...el Arrianismo...había llegado a ser uno de los factores constitutivos de su personalidad'. Catholics were called simply 'Romans' by the Goths, according to Gregory of Tours, *Liber in gloria martyrum* 24, 79. Naturally, some Romans in the West were Arians: Salvian, *De gubernatione Dei* v. 14.
[3] For Visigothic revisions of the Gothic Bible see Salvian, v. 5ff., and Thompson, *Visigoths in the time of Ulfila*, pp. 149–53. Note also the theological dispute mentioned in Sidonius, *Ep.* VII. 6.
[4] Idem, *Ep.* I. 2. For a papal letter describing Frederic, Theodoric II's brother, as *filius noster*, see *Epistolae Arelatenses genuinae* 15, and on the circumstances evoking it, Schäferdiek, pp. 11–12.
[5] See Wallace-Hadrill, pp. 45–6, and for an example of Catholic hostility Ennodius, 92. Inadmissible is *Vita Viviani* 6, for the life is a sixth-century product based upon the *V. Epifani*: see P. Courcelle, *Hist. littéraire des grandes invasions germaniques*, 3rd edn (Paris, 1964), pp. 339ff.

5

Catholicism to *Romania*, Euric was naturally disinclined to 'Arianise' the occupied territories.[1] The kingdom which Euric created was the result, then, of Gothic pride and national sentiment, but, paradoxically, its very establishment threatened the continued coherence of the Goths as a people. Dispersed now over a much greater area than before and settled among a subject population by whom they were outnumbered fifty or a hundred to one,[2] the danger of submersion in the Roman mass was acute. Given this background, it is understandable that Euric should have maintained in force the harsh prohibition of intermarriage between Roman and barbarian standing in the *Codex Theodosianus*[3] and that he should have found it desirable to issue a code of laws, the so-called *Codex Euricianus*, for the regulation of his scattered Goths and of their relations with the Romans.[4] Although Isidore tells

[1] See Schäferdiek, pp. 28–9. The 'national heresy' thesis was certainly overstated by E. L. Woodward, *Christianity and nationalism in the later Roman Empire* (London, 1916), passim: see A. H. M. Jones in *Journal of theological studies*, new series, x (1959), 280–98 (though cf. idem, *The later Roman Empire, 284–602* (4 vols, Oxford, 1964), II, 965). But one does not have to project modern nationalist notions back into the past or to underestimate the passions engendered by doctrinal controversies to recognise the likelihood that political hostility to Rome acted as a considerable psychological factor in persuading people of the truth of a certain deviant form of the Roman religion.

[2] See Stroheker, *Eurich*, p. 109 with n. 81, W. Reinhart, 'La tradición visigoda en el nacimiento de Castilla', *Estudios dedicados a Menéndez Pidal*, I (Madrid, 1950), 537. The mass settlement in Spain (in any case restricted to Old Castile) probably took place after Euric's reign, but garrisons had to be provided, governors appointed and so on.

[3] See below, p. 14 with n. 1, and Stroheker, *Eurich*, pp. 119–21.

[4] I defend the traditional view of the *CE* as a 'national' Gothic code (and that of the later *LRV* and *CR* as 'national' codes for the Romans and Goths respectively) and argue against the distinct territorialist theses propounded by A. García Gallo, 'Nacionalidad y territorialidad del derecho en la época visigoda', *AHDE*, XIII (1936–41), 168–264 (maintained still in idem, *Curso de hist. del derecho esp.*, 7th edn, I (Madrid, 1958), 54–5) and A. d'Ors, 'La territorialidad del derecho de los visigodos', *EV*, I (Rome–Madrid, 1956), 91–124 (earlier in *Sett.*, III (1956), 363–408), in my 'The character of Visigothic legislation' (unpublished doctoral dissertation: University of Cambridge, 1967), passim. The territorialist notions have received little support outside the peninsula (for which see, most recently, R. Gibert, *Hist. general del derecho esp.* (Granada, 1968), pp. 10ff. (*pro*), L. G. de Valdeavellano, *Curso de hist. de las instituciones esp. de los orígenes al final de la edad media* (Madrid, 1968), p. 177 (*contra*)): but see P. S. Leicht, *RSDI*, XVII–XX (1944–7), 203–7, W. Reinhart, 'Über die Territorialität der westgotischen Gesetzbücher', *ZRG.GA*, LXVIII (1951), 348–54 (see also idem, *AHDE*, XVI (1945),

us that the Goths had previously been ruled by customary law alone, this is certainly an exaggeration:[1] an Eurician law expressly referred to a provision of Theodoric I,[2] and Sidonius, writing about 470, was able to contrast what he termed the *leges Theodoricianae* with the laws of the Theodosian code.[3] But this collection was probably small and composed in the main of measures concerning the division of lands and perhaps some aspects of the internal Gothic regime.[4] In the new circumstances this was no longer adequate.

The *Codex Euricianus*, described by one whose authority in the field is unrivalled as 'the best legislative work of the fifth century',[5] was Euric's second great achievement. Probably issued about 476,[6]

704–11), H. Mitteis, *ZRG* cit., pp. 531–2, W. Rocls, *Onderzoek naar het gebruik van de aangehaalde bronnen van Romeins recht in de Lex romana Burgundionum* (Antwerp, 1958), p. 9, n. 25, and A. Guarino, *Storia del diritto romano*, 4th edn (Naples, 1969), pp. 611–12. Especially important in criticism are A. Schultze, *Über westgotisch-spanisches Eherecht, mit einem Exkurs: 'Zur Gesch. der westgotischen Rechtsquellen'*, Berichte über die Verhandlungen der Sächsischen Akad. der Wissenschaften zu Leipzig, philologisch-hist. Klasse, xcv (1943), part iv, pp. 105–30, P. Merêa, *Estudos de direito visigótico* (Coimbra, 1948), pp. 199–248, and Sánchez-Albornoz, 'Pervivencia', pp. 128–99.

1 *HG* 35. A possible explanation is that Isidore knew that the *CE* was the first comprehensive body of written laws ruling the Goths (the sense of 'Gothi legum instituta scriptis habere coeperunt') and assumed the sole previous rule of customary law: see Zeumer, xxiii, 440, and for *lex*, *mos* and *consuetudo*, *Etym.* ii. 10. 1–3, with A. García Gallo, 'San Isidoro, jurista', *Isidoriana*, ed. M. C. Diaz y Diaz (Leon, 1961), pp. 137–9. On the whole matter of the pre-Eurician regime see King, pp. 1–25.

2 *CE* 277: cf. *CE* 275, 276, and A. d'Ors, *El código de Eurico. Edición, palingenesia, índices*, EV, ii (Rome–Madrid, 1960), 196ff.

3 *Ep.* ii. 1. But I cannot think that the *ll. Theod.* formed a collection comparable to the *CT*, as does F. Beyerle, 'Zur Frühgesch. der westgotischen Gesetzgebung', *ZRG.GA*, lxvii (1950), 5: irony, indeed, cannot be ruled out, as Wallace-Hadrill, p. 40, n. 2, observes. That they constituted a *lex Romana* (thus K. von Amira, *Germanisches Recht*, 4th edn by K. A. Eckhardt, i (Berlin, 1960), 20ff.) is unlikely.

4 *CE* 327 refers to a *prior lex* concerning intestate succession which is not Roman, despite García Gallo, 'Nacionalidad', pp. 201–4: see Merêa, *Estudos*, pp. 209–20, King, pp. 65–70. I am certainly not convinced by the view of G. Vismara, expressed most recently in *Edictum Theoderici*, IRMAE, part i, 2b *aa* α (Milan, 1967), passim (elaborating earlier remarks in *Sett.*, iii (1956), 409–63 = *EV*, i (Rome–Madrid, 1956), 49–89), that the *ET* is identifiable with the *ll. Theod.*: see in criticism P. Merêa, *BFD*, xxxii (1956), 315–24, Sánchez-Albornoz, 'Pervivencia', p. 155, n. 66, and B. Paradisi, *Bullettino dell'Istituto di Diritto Romano*, 3rd series, vii (1965), 1–47, although F. Merzbacher, *HJ*, lxxxix (1969), 6–10, declares himself in favour.

5 E. Levy, *Gesammelte Schriften*, i (Cologne–Graz, 1963), 209.

6 See A. d'Ors, 'Varia Romana', *AHDE*, xxvii/xxviii (1957/8), 1164–5.

it was a lengthy compilation of some 350 clauses, arranged under separate chapter headings.[1] Its sole remains, unfortunately, are clauses 276 to 336 of the original, little more than a sixth therefore, and many of these clauses are in fact almost totally illegible or so fragmentary as to be unintelligible, so deplorable is the state of preservation of the palimpsest which contains them, while others are lacking altogether.[2] Although some missing laws have been reconstituted on the basis of the closely allied texts of the *Lex Baiuvariorum*,[3] and although a recent attempt has been made to supply others from a study of the obviously early laws incorporated in the later Visigothic compilations,[4] the code as it originally existed must for the most part remain sadly unknown to us. From what survives, however, it is abundantly clear that the Goths had adopted many of the principles and provisions of Roman law.[5] This is wholly understandable, for of all the barbarian peoples they had been longest in contact with Roman civilisation, and the influence of Roman private law had doubtless had its effect upon them, as the

[1] Stroheker, *Eurich*, p. 95, n. 24, puts the number of clauses at between 350 and 400, although d'Ors, *Código*, p. 50, considers 350 a maximum figure. Three chapter headings are extant, and two others clear enough from the surviving fragments: others, conjectured and justified by d'Ors, *Código*, passim, are listed on his pp. 54–5.

[2] On the palimpsest see E. A. Lowe, *Codices latini antiquiores*, v: *France, Paris* (Oxford, 1950), p. 31, and for its discovery and early use R. de Ureña, *La legislación gótico-hispana* (Madrid, 1905), pp. 27–31. It was the work of, above all, Zeumer, XXIII, 434–64, to establish that it contained Eurician law.

[3] Zeumer, *LV*, pp. 28–32. *CE* 274 and 275 are also reconstructed with the help of the Bavarian law.

[4] D'Ors, *Código*, passim.

[5] There is virtual unanimity on the highly Romanised character of the *CE* and the view of E. Heymann, *ZRG.GA*, LXIII (1943), 363, that the Roman elements are 'nur Modifikationen und Ergänzungen des Gotenrechtes' (cf. now also O. Perrin, *Les burgondes* (Neuchâtel, 1968), p. 48, speaking of customary laws) is assuredly to be rejected. But this Roman impregnation is not an argument in favour of territoriality, as Levy, *Schriften*, p. 307, points out: see also King, pp. 47–9. On Roman elements in the (national) *Lex Burgundionum* (*LB*) see A. von Halban, *Das römische Recht in den germanischen Volksstaaten*, part I, Untersuchungen zur deutschen Staats- und Rechtsgesch., ed. O. Gierke, LVI (Breslau, 1899), pp. 284ff. They were not entirely absent from Frankish law: see J. Gaudemet, 'Survivances romaines dans le droit de la monarchie franque du V^ème au X^ème siècle', *Tijdschrift voor rechtsgeschiedenis*, XXIII (1955), 149–206, especially 161ff. (legal sources), 177ff. (practice), 205. Visigothic hostility to Rome was political, not cultural, and even Theodoric I had his son, the future Theodoric II, taught Roman law and literature by Avitus: Sidonius, *Carm.* VII. 495ff. Roman jurists, of course, produced the *CE*: for Leo of Narbonne and Marcellinus see Beyerle, pp. 6–8.

result of the activity of Roman traders, even before the entry of 376,[1] and much more so since then.[2] But the Roman character of the code can easily be exaggerated,[3] particularly since most of the extant provisions deal with transactions – precisely the field where Roman models are most likely to have been followed.[4] The notions of vulgar Roman and Germanic law not infrequently coincided, so that the discovery of a Roman parallel to an Eurician measure is not necessarily the discovery of the law's source.[5] At the same time there were certain Eurician laws which were exclusively Germanic,[6] and others again which, although not Germanic, departed radically from the current Roman law found in the *Codex Theodosianus* and in the writings of the jurists.[7] The law of the Eurician code was, in fact, *sui generis*.

Euric's achievements were highly impressive, and it may be that in the hands of a strong successor the kingdom would have maintained its predominant position and even have expanded to the north. But this must be very doubtful, for its abiding weakness was

[1] For the concern of the pre-entry Visigoths with Roman trade see Thompson, *Visigoths in the time of Ulfila*, pp. 14–16, 19–20, 34–43, who (p. 39) points out that Latin had already made its mark on the Gothic language by the middle of the fourth century, largely through the influence of traders.

[2] See Stroheker, *Eurich*, pp. 101–2, Levy, *Schriften*, pp. 202–3, 213.

[3] See King, pp. 169–233.

[4] Levy, *Schriften*, pp. 203–4, 218.

[5] See C. Frh. von Schwerin, 'Notas sobre la hist. del derecho esp. más antiguo', *AHDE*, I (1924), 42ff., Levy, *Schriften*, pp. 204–6, and King, pp. 172–4. Not enough attention is paid to the influence of Germanic practice itself on the vulgar law: but see J. Gaudemet, *La formation du droit séculier et du droit de l'église aux IVe et Ve siècles* (Paris, 1957), pp. 130–1, and Levy, *Schriften*, pp. 173ff., 206ff., 216–17.

[6] See E. Levy, *West Roman vulgar law. The law of property* (Philadelphia, 1951), pp. 125–6, and the comments of Sánchez-Albornoz, 'Pervivencia', pp. 167ff. Important as is the matter of the origin of those Germanic elements which appear in the law of the post-Visigothic period, it cannot be discussed here. Earlier literature will be found in E. Wohlhaupter, 'Das germanische Element im altspanischen Recht und die Rezeption des römischen Rechtes in Spanien', *ZRG.RA*, LXVI (1948), 135–210, and there is a useful account of the views of García Gallo and others in R. d'Abadal, 'À propos du legs visigothique en Esp.', *Sett.*, V (1958), 562–70.

[7] G. Braga da Cruz, 'A sucessão legítima no código Euriciano', *AHDE*, XXIII (1953), 769, rightly speaks of the 'formação dum sistema sucessório deveras original': see also Levy, *Schriften*, p. 216, though differently d'Ors, *Código*, p. 248. I devote most of the last chapter of my dissertation to an examination of the striking contrasts between the provisions of the *CE* (and *Antiquae* of the *CR*) and those of the *CT/ LRV* in the matters of succession and matrimonial property: these contrasts furnish the most powerful of arguments against both the territorialist theses.

the disunity which Euric had done so much to foster.[1] A first price was to be paid in 507.[2] In the preceding years a formidable threat to the kingdom of Toulouse had arisen beyond the northern frontier. The expansionist policy of the Catholic Clovis menaced the Goths with what was allegedly proclaimed by the Franks as a holy war against the Arians.[3] Negotiations failed, and Alaric II was obliged eventually to take up arms. Gregory of Tours reports much sympathy for the Franks in the period before hostilities broke out,[4] and the Catholic bishops in particular seem to have been inspired to treasonable activity. Caesarius, bishop of Arles and acknowledged leader of the Church, was exiled on the grounds of conspiracy to deliver his city to the Burgundians, allies of Clovis, and other bishops suffered a similar fate for similar behaviour.[5] But in 506 Alaric changed his tune. In September Caesarius presided over the first-ever assembly of the Catholic clergy of the kingdom, the Council of Agde,[6] and just seven months previously the king had published for the use of the native Romans the *Lex Romana Visigothorum*, or Breviary, a code wholly Roman in content and consisting of a series of texts – many of them accompanied by explanatory *Interpretationes*, themselves the work of an earlier age – taken from the *Codex Theodosianus*, from later Novels and from certain juristic works, notably those of Paulus and Gaius.[7] The Breviary was to remain in force in the Visigothic kingdom for nearly 150 years and to exercise an enormous influence outside its confines.[8] Both the circumstances

---

[1] Only two revolts, both in Spain, are known from this period, however (*Chron. Caesaraug. reliquiae* ad aa. 496, 497, 506), and the Burdunelus who figured in the first may be thought, from his name, to have been a Goth.

[2] For the following see E. F. Bruck, 'Caesarius of Arles and the *Lex Romana Visigothorum*', *Studi in onore di Vincenzo Arangio-Ruiz*, 1 (Naples, 1953), 201–17. Wholly different is the view of Schäferdiek, pp. 32–55.

[3] In *HF* II. 37 Clovis is alleged to have declared: 'Valde molestum fero, quod hi Arriani partem teneant Galliarum'.

[4] *HF* II. 35.

[5] See Schmidt, *Gesch.*, p. 274, Courcelle, p. 241. But note now the comments of Schäferdiek, pp. 34–9.

[6] On the council see Schäferdiek, pp. 55–67.

[7] On all aspects of the *LRV* see J. Gaudemet, *Le Bréviaire d'Alaric et les Epitome*, IRMAE, part 1, 2b *aa* β (Milan, 1965), passim.

[8] For possible references to the *LRV* in the seventh-century councils, see A. Larraona and A. Tabera, 'El derecho justinianeo en Esp.', *Atti del Congresso Internazionale di Diritto Romano, Bologna II* (Pavia, 1935), pp. 96, 106 with n. 77. The references are wrongly denied by García Gallo, 'Nacionalidad', pp. 235–41: see Schultze,

of 506, however, and the obvious speed with which the code was produced argue that its promulgation was a last-minute attempt by Alaric to show his concern for the Roman provincials and thus to win their support in the imminent struggle.[1] But although some Romans did fight with the Visigoths at Vouglé in 507, the battle was lost and Alaric killed. The twin policies of expansion and 'separateness' led directly to the loss of the Gallic territories, with the exception of Septimania, preserved by the intervention of Theodoric the Ostrogoth. Henceforth it was to be Spain which constituted the major stage upon which Visigothic history was played out.

That history was a stormy one in the period following Vouglé,[2] and the kingdom was fortunate indeed to discover in the person of Leovigild, who came to share the kingship with his brother in 568 or 569 and became sole ruler in 572, a monarch whose qualities enabled him not merely to arrest the process of disintegration but to perceive and tackle the root causes of the malaise, so setting the state on a new path.[3] Only one sixth-century king had died peacefully before Leovigild's accession: indeed, between 531 and 555 no less than four successive monarchs had been murdered by discontented factions. Separatism was rife, particularly in Baetica, where the city of Cordova had been in rebellion since the early years of Agila (549–555).[4] During the years since Vouglé the Byzantines had

*Eherecht*, pp. 109–13 (though often exaggeratedly), King, pp. 119–36. Definite allusions occur in II Sev. 1 and 3 and highly probable ones in ib. 8 and IV Tol. 46, while *LRV.PS* I. 1. 2(4) is cited word for word in a dispute heard before VI Tol. in 638: see *Exemplar judicii inter Martianum et Aventium episcopos* C3. Note further that the one version of the *LRV* emanating from Spain (on the palimpsest see Ureña, p. 43) also – and alone – contains a law promulgated by Teudis in 546 and concerning judicial costs. Generally on the career of the *LRV* see A. de Wretschko in the *Prolegomena* to the Mommsen edn of the *CT*, pp. cccvii–ccclx.

[1] 'Emergency measures', says Bruck, 'Caesarius', p. 205: for the same view see already F. Dahn, *Westgothische Studien* (Würzburg, 1874), pp. 4–5. For signs of speed in the production of the code see Bruck, 'Caesarius', pp. 209, 215 etc. Differently on all this, Schäferdiek, pp. 42–5.

[2] Details in E. A. Thompson, *The Goths in Spain* (Oxford, 1969), pp. 7–19.

[3] For this view, in which I wholly concur, of Leovigild's reign see K. F. Stroheker, 'Leovigild', in idem, *Germanentum und Spätantike* (Zurich–Stuttgart, 1965), pp. 134–91 (originally published in *Die Welt als Gesch.*, V (1939), 446–85), an article of great value for all aspects of the reign.

[4] See Thompson, *Goths*, pp. 60–3 and, for Cordova, pp. 321–3, rejecting the usual view of Byzantine occupation. For comments, frequently undeveloped, on separatism see generally Gibert, 'Particularismo', pp. 24–45.

Law and society in the Visigothic kingdom

established themselves in force in the south-east,[1] and the Sueves still maintained an independent kingdom in Galicia: both powers, and the Franks also, were the more dangerous for their adherence to Catholicism in a period when orthodoxy was on the offensive.[2] Leovigild's greatness was shown not least in his successful defence of the realm's territorial integrity. By 578 the revolts which he inherited or which sprang up had been suppressed, and later threats, of internal or external origin, were all triumphantly met.[3] Towards the end of his reign he was even able to expand his boundaries by the conquest and absorption of the Sueve kingdom.[4] What was most impressive about Leovigild, however, was not his military prowess, essential as that was, but his recognition of the need both to break down the internal divisions of the kingdom and to enhance the status of the monarchy, itself the paramount unitive element.[5] In the second respect he appears to have followed a deliberate policy of imitation of Byzantium.[6] First among Visigothic kings he clad himself in royal garments and seated himself upon a throne;[7] first he

[1] For the Byzantine conquest see Thompson, *Goths*, pp. 320–9, modifying the account of Stroheker, *Germanentum*, pp. 209–16.

[2] See J. Fontaine, 'Conversion et culture chez les wisigoths d'Esp.', *Sett.*, xiv (1967), 91–101, for some illuminating remarks on this offensive.

[3] See Thompson, *Goths*, pp. 60–4, 74–6, and for the revolt of Hermenegild below, in text. Both *HF* iv. 38 and *HG* 51 report Leovigildian purges.

[4] The last years of the Sueve kingdom are the subject of a paper by C. Torres, 'Mirón, rey de suevos y gallegos, y los últimos monarcas suevos', *Cuadernos de estudios gallegos*, xiv (1959), 165–201.

[5] Quite correctly Stroheker, *Germanentum*, p. 190, declares: 'Schon Leowigild und nicht erst Rekkared I. ist der Schöpfer des westgotisch-spanischen Einheitsstaates': for Leovigild and the theme of unity see also J. L. Romero, 'San Isidoro de Sevilla. Su pensamiento históricopolítico y sus relaciones con la hist. visigoda', *CHE*, viii (1947), 21–6, and Schäferdiek, pp. 189–92. Differently, Thompson, *Goths*, p. 108, denying that Leovigild had any 'quixotic wish' to unite Goths and Romans. Why 'quixotic'?

[6] For Byzantine influence on Leovigild see Stroheker, *Germanentum*, pp. 229–33. A tiny but significant indication of its extent is shown by the Greek name Reccopolis given to one of the cities the king refounded. There will be plenty of examples in the pages which follow of the constant Byzantine influence in practically every walk of Visigothic life.

[7] *HG* 51. Leovigild was also perhaps the first Visigothic king to wear a crown, but the only evidence is from the coinage (see G. C. Miles, *The coinage of the Visigoths of Spain: Leovigild to Achila II* (New York, 1952), p. 48) and the dependence of this upon Byzantine models renders it of doubtful value: see P. E. Schramm, *Herrschaftszeichen und Staatssymbolik*, i (Stuttgart, 1954), 137, who, pp. 133–6, shows the Goths to have used head-bands as a form of decoration already in their pre-entry

issued an independent regal coinage;[1] first, perhaps, he organised his *comites* into an established palatine *officium*.[2] Already in 573, in an attempt to secure continuity of government as well as perpetuation of his dynasty, he associated his two sons with him on the throne.[3]

Leovigild also took the first steps towards removal of the barriers separating Goth from Roman. His policy in this respect was not, and could not be, thoroughgoing. The distinctions of Euric's time still survived, even if a century of contact had doubtless served to bring the two peoples closer together.[4] Leovigild left the system of separate legal regimes undisturbed, contenting himself with the production of a revised version of Euric's code, the so-called *Codex Revisus*, many of the provisions of which appear as 'old laws', *Antiquae*, in later compilations.[5] But he closely concerned himself with two other aspects of disunity. The ban on miscegenation now disappeared,

days. Coronation is not certain for any period. *HG* 52, 'regno est coronatus' (of Reccared), is by no means conclusive, and the *Via Regia* relied upon by C. Sánchez-Albornoz, 'La *ordinatio principis* en la Esp. goda y postvisigoda', *CHE*, xxxv (1962), 8, is not admissible as a Visigothic source according to J. Scharf, *Deutsches Archiv für Erforschung des MAs*, xvii (1961), 351, who cites an unpublished MS of P. E. Schramm. But cf. p. 24, n. 2, below for the formula *Regi a Deo vita*.

[1] First, that is, among legitimate kings, for it is the view of P. Grierson, cit. from an unpublished MS by J. N. Hillgarth, 'Coins and chronicles: propaganda in sixth-century Spain and the Byzantine background', *Historia*, xv (1966), 506–7 – who himself concurs – that the 'regal' coins of Hermenegild, Leovigild's rebellious son, preceded the Leovigildian second 'mintless' series. On the types of Leovigildian 'national' coins see Miles, pp. 175–98, with the comments of P. Grierson, 'Visigothic metrology', *Numismatic chronicle*, 6th series, xiii (1953), 81, 84, 86–7.

[2] Below, p. 56, n. 3.

[3] John of Biclar, *Chronica* 573. 5 ('consortes regni'). On *HF* iv. 38, referring to an actual division of the kingdom, see Orlandis, *Poder real*, pp. 4–6. Isidore says nothing of the matter, though he earlier noted (*HG* 48) the joint rule of Leovigild and Liuva I.

[4] Indeed, the races were still distinguished in some texts after the introduction of territorial law: see ix Tol. 13, 14, and ix. 2. 9 (of Ervig), with d'Abadal, 'Legs visigothique', pp. 556–8.

[5] *HG* 51, and for the identification of *Antiquae* and untitled texts in the later codes with laws of the *CR*, Zeumer, xxiii, 426–33. Against the view of Ureña, pp. 323ff. – followed by Stroheker, *Germanentum*, pp. 162–5, and also by Schäferdiek, p. 190 – that Leovigild's code was the first territorial compilation, see King, pp. 112–18. I have been unable to trace R. Gibert, *El código de Leovigildo* (Rome–Madrid, 1965), cit. in Stroheker, *Germanentum*, p. 158, n. 3, but not available to him, and suspect that it may in fact not yet be published: cf. the reference to Gibert's plan for such a work in *Índice histórico esp.*, lii (Barcelona, May–August, 1968), 267 (no. 69764).

explicitly abrogated by law.[1] Even if the ban had in fact been ignored in past years,[2] it is impossible to understand Leovigild's reasons for removing it, rather than attempting to ensure its enforcement, unless he had rejected the view that the separation of Goth and Roman was right and proper.[3] Similarly inspired by the hope for unity was the king's religious policy.[4] Made grimly aware of the dangers of two religions in a single state by the Catholic revolt led by his son Hermenegild,[5] Leovigild aimed at religious unification under the creed of a modified Arianism. His tactics were to make concessions so that transition would be less difficult for Catholics while threatening the obdurate, particularly those Goths who had

[1] III. I. I. The view of García Gallo, 'Nacionalidad', pp. 197–201, 221–4, that this *Antiqua* was Eurician and that the *prisca lex* which it abrogated was *CT* III. 14. 1, is rightly rejected by, e.g., Schultze, *Eherecht*, pp. 123–5, Merêa, *Estudos*, pp. 231–48: see King, pp. 54–63. The *prisca lex* may have been *LRV.CT* III. 14. 1, with *Interpretatio*, but is more likely to have been a lost Eurician provision: see Zeumer, XXIII, 88, and XXIV, 574, Stroheker, *Eurich*, p. 120, with n. 130, Sánchez-Albornoz, 'Pervivencia', pp. 160–1, and King, pp. 63–4.

[2] A common view: see, e.g., d'Ors, 'Territorialidad', p. 104, and Thompson, *Goths*, p. 59 with n. 1. See also P. Lombardía, 'Los matrimonios mixtos en el derecho de la iglesia visigoda', *AHDE*, XXVII/XXVIII (1957/8), 81ff. But the only certain example of pre-Leovigildian intermarriage is that of Teudis (Procopius, *History of the wars* v. 12. 50) who, as military commander in Spain (and in any case an Ostrogoth), was a law unto himself. The marriage of the parents of that Sinticio who died a sexagenarian in 632 and whose epitaph (J. Vives, *Inscripciones cristianas de la Esp. romana y visigoda*, 2nd edn (Barcelona, 1969), no. 86) describes him as 'paterno traens linea Getarum' may have taken place after the repeal: but in any case the mother may have been Frankish or Sueve, for the Roman form of the name is not decisive. See also Merêa, *Estudos*, p. 248.

[3] See d'Ors, loc. cit. (who yet considers the earlier prohibition 'theoretical'), Stroheker, *Germanentum*, pp. 160–2, 233. Differently Thompson, *Goths*, pp. 58–9, holding that repeal came because the ban was unenforceable. The wording of III. I. I does not in my view support this. And how does repeal, for whatever reason, square with Leovigild's alleged wish to keep the distinction between Goth and Roman 'sharp and clear-cut' (ib., p. 107)? For the possible connection of repeal with Leovigild's religious policy, see Zeumer, XXIII, 477, n. 4, and the contribution of J. Orlandis to the discussion at Spoleto in 1955, printed in *Sett.*, III (1956), 231–2.

[4] See Stroheker, *Germanentum*, pp. 166, 172–82. Thompson, *Goths*, pp. 105–9, is strongly opposed, but see Schäferdiek, p. 174, n. 138.

[5] Particularly valuable on the revolt and its significance are Messmer, pp. 121–33, Hillgarth, 'Coins and chronicles', pp. 483–501 (developing remarks in *AST*, XXXIV (1961), 21–46), Schäferdiek, pp. 140–57, 204, and Thompson, *Goths*, pp. 64–78: see also Orlandis, *Poder real*, pp. 3–12. For the Arian-Catholic crisis of which the revolt was the precipitation see Fontaine, 'Conversion', pp. 91–108.

been converted to orthodoxy, with a degree of persecution.[1] At an Arian council held at Toledo in 580 the earlier insistence upon the rebaptism of converts from Catholicism was dropped: henceforth the simple imposition of hands, promise of acceptance of communion and profession of the Arian doxology would suffice.[2] The measure, coupled with financial inducements, was successful in bringing large numbers of converts.[3] Two years later Leovigild went even further by denying the central dogma of Arianism: he now conceded the equality of Father and Son, holding only to the inferiority of the Holy Ghost.[4] This drastic change of view also had its effect: indeed, Gregory of Tours, though doubtless exaggerating, went so far as to say that there were 'few' Catholics left in Spain.[5] A similar policy underlay the later reintroduction of Arianism into the conquered Sueve kingdom, Catholic since 560.[6] To dismiss the venture as doomed to inevitable failure is to judge with the benefit of hindsight: Leovigild's policy had been in force for only six years (assuming its beginning at Toledo in 580) when he died, and in Galicia it had in fact had remarkable success in just a single year.[7] In any case, he had pointed out the goal to his successor.

Reccared I (586–601), his son, was not slow to reach it, even though

[1] On the persecutory measures see above all Schäferdiek, pp. 157–9, 165–79, and Thompson, *Goths*, pp. 78–83, who convincingly shows that they did not antedate Hermenegild's revolt but in my view underestimates their extent. I see no reason to discount the evidence of *HG* 50, for Isidore was probably an eye-witness.

[2] See John of Biclar, 580. 2 (where Leovigild is made to call Arianism 'nostram catholicam fidem'), Stroheker, *Germanentum*, pp. 173–5, and Schäferdiek, pp. 159–64. The decisions of the council were inscribed in what III Tol. *Fidei confessio* 16 (347c) denounced as a 'libellum detestabilem'.

[3] John of Biclar, loc. cit., *HG* 50, Schäferdiek, pp. 179–82.

[4] *HF* VI. 18. This position amounted to Macedonianism: see Stroheker, *Germanentum*, pp. 175–6, and, for its condemnation, III Tol. *Fide confessio* 10. Note that in 584 a Visigothic envoy to Gaul was even prepared to declare his belief that Father, Son and Holy Ghost were the *virtutes* of one God and to attend a Catholic service (though not to take communion): *HF* VI. 40, though cf. Schäferdiek, pp. 186–8. So too did Leovigild ('novo nunc ingenio'!) worship at Catholic shrines and in Catholic churches: *HF* VI. 18. It is perhaps precisely to this time that should be attributed the document discussed by M. C. Diaz y Diaz, 'Un document privé de l'Esp. wisigothique sur ardoise', *Studi medievali*, 3rd series, I (1960), 52–71, and assigned by him to the Arian period 560–590 on the grounds that the oath it contains is sworn on the Father and the Son but not on the Holy Ghost.

[5] *HF* VI. 18.          [6] See Thompson, *Goths*, pp. 88–90.

[7] See ib., p. 90, and John of Biclar, 587. 5, III Tol. *Tomus* (343c). For the east coast see p. 205, n. 6, below.

he followed a different path. There is no reason to doubt his personal sincerity when, within a year of his father's death, he was received into the Catholic fold.[1] But this is not to say that he did not also realise the immense advantages which he, succeeding monarchs and the kingdom at large would enjoy once unity of faith had been achieved. In 589, at the Third Council of Toledo, the Gothic and Sueve peoples, in the persons of their higher clergy and *seniores*, solemnly anathematised the errors of Arianism and embraced the dogmas of Rome.[2] Some Arian opposition had already flared up, but had been suppressed without undue trouble:[3] the *fides Gothica*, its strength no doubt weakened rather than made greater by the concessions of Leovigild, was brought surprisingly easily to the end of its career, for it presented no problem in the seventh century.[4] The tremendous significance of the conversion of 589 will be touched upon more than once in the pages which follow: here it will suffice to point out that the unity of all Christians in one Visigothic *ecclesia* became a powerful force operating in favour of unity of law. Reccared himself in fact issued laws binding upon all the inhabitants of the kingdom, and was followed in this by Sisebut (612-621),[5] but more important in fostering the notion of territorial law was certainly the universal character of the provisions emanating from the series of general councils, beginning with the Third Council itself, in which the Visigothic Church found its institutional expression. Not a few historians, misled by the presence of laymen at many of these gatherings, by the regular treatment there of matters regarded as predominantly secular and by the authoritative tone of the language of the canons, have chosen to regard these councils as national

---

[1] See Schäferdiek, pp. 194-6.
[2] Generally on the council, Schäferdiek, pp. 205-33.
[3] Details in Schäferdiek, pp. 198-203, Thompson, *Goths*, pp. 101-4.
[4] Below, p. 130. But Witteric's murder of Liuva II in 603 may have been connected with an Arian reaction, despite the lack of evidence. On the process of conversion before the council see Schäferdiek, pp. 196-8. The attitudes of the various source-authors towards the conversion and the preceding events are discussed by Fontaine, 'Conversion', pp. 108-23.
[5] See below, p. 17, n. 2 (Reccared), and XII. 2. 13, 14 (Sisebut). The *lex Teudi* of 546 was already territorial: see Zeumer, XXIII, 80ff., against whom I find Thompson, *Goths*, pp. 13-14, unconvincing. The view that a legal compilation was made by Reccared, exploded already by Zeumer, XXIII, 441-50, nevertheless reappears now in E. N. van Kleffens, *Hispanic law until the end of the MA* (Edinburgh, 1968), pp. 73, 75.

legislative assemblies, forerunners of the Cortes. This they were only in a very limited sense. Their main functions were in fact to support and to protect royal interests, actions and laws, to regulate certain matters of constitutional significance and, most frequently, to establish the norms of ecclesiastical government.[1] Conciliar measures did not have the character of civil law, were not enforceable by the judges of the kingdom, except when – as happened only at the Third Council in the whole of the period before Ervig – they were confirmed by the king, who provided penalties for their breach.[2] The only applicable sanctions were those of ecclesiastical discipline.[3] But these sanctions applied to all, for the Church saw, not Goths and Romans, but Catholics alone. There existed after 589, in other words, a considerable body of territorial and regional law in the form of conciliar law.

By the time of the seizure of the throne by Chindasvind in 642, the process of unification had been taken a step further by the expulsion of the Byzantines during the reign of Svintila (621–631).[4] With the exception of the Basques and Cantabrians in their northern fastnesses,[5] all the inhabitants of the peninsula now recognised the

[1] Numerous illustrations of these functions will appear below. For reason of simple convenience I have spoken throughout of the bishops as responsible for the production of conciliar decrees, despite the attendance of laymen at the councils.

[2] For III Tol. see the *Edictum regis*. All three surviving laws of Reccared – III. 5. 2, XII. 1. 2 and XII. 2. 12 – have some connection with canons of III Tol. – cc. 10, 18 and 14 respectively. *Re* III Tol. 14, note also Gregory the Great's reference to a *constitutio* of Reccared in *Reg.* IX. 228. The canons of XII Tol., although confirmed, were not included in Ervig's code issued later in the same year, but those of XIII Tol. (of 683) were introduced by XII. 1. 3. Laws in support of particular canons – and *vice versa* – are not rare.

[3] The euphoria induced by the conversion explains the behaviour of the bishops (in any case given considerable governmental responsibility by Reccared) who at Narbonne in 589 took it upon themselves to order fines and lashings to be paid to, or administered by, the city count (cc. 4, 9, 14: cf. c. 15). Later provisions where the bishops acted *ultra vires* – as, e.g., IX Tol. 10, ordering the enslavement of a child born to a cleric and a freewoman involved in an illicit union – were perhaps intended to galvanise the kings into action.

[4] On *HG* 62, describing Svintila as first to hold the 'totius Spaniae...monarchiam regni', and on Isidore's geographical rather than racial viewpoint, see R. Buchner in *Historische Zeitschrift*, CCVII (1968), 568–9.

[5] On whom see the excellent article of M. Vigil and A. Barbero, 'Sobre los orígenes sociales de la Reconquista: cántabros y vascones desde fines del imperio romano hasta la invasión musulmana', *BRAH*, CLVI (1965), 271–337 (with maps on pp. 338–9), where pp. 301ff. deal with the Leovigildian and later periods.

rule of Toledo;[1] with the exception of the Jews and of a few convinced pagans and heretics, all the king's subjects now accepted the
authority of the Catholic Church of which the king was the head.[2]
In many ways it is remarkable that unification of law had not also
been achieved during this period. The personal law system was quite
out of harmony with the prevailing emphasis on unity and corpora-
tional notions of society.[3] Both the repeal of the marriage prohibition
and the religious unification must, moreover, have gone a long way
towards destroying the mystique of racial separateness upon which
the system depended: it is no coincidence that traditional Gothic
art forms and dress were abandoned after the conversion.[4] From
a purely practical point of view also, only advantage could have
come from the abolition of a regime which must have presented
inconveniences at every turn.[5] Probably the concern with campaigning in the early years of the century and the internal troubles
of the 630s were responsible for the lack of reform.[6] But the energetic
Chindasvind turned immediately to the task and in 643/4 promulgated the first territorial code of the Visigothic kingdom.[7] Sadly, it
no longer survives as an entity, but it could not have been a satisfactory affair, for some years later – probably in 654[8] – Reccesvind
(649/53-672), Chindasvind's son and successor, published a revised

1 On Toledo as the capital see E. Ewig, 'Résidence et capitale pendant le haut MA',
   *Revue hist.*, CCXXX (1963), 31–6, but note Zeumer, XXIII, 101–2, for Teudis. *Urbs
   regia, civitas regia, praetorium* etc. appear as designations.
2 See below, chapter 5. The first major onslaughts upon the Jews took place precisely
   in this period.
3 A similar incongruity in the Frankish empire later inspired the well-known protest
   of Agobard against the personal law system: *Liber adv. legem Gundobadi* 4.
4 See Thompson, *Goths*, pp. 108–9.
5 But I persist in thinking with Zeumer, XXIII, 82–3, that the judicial system was
   early unified, despite Thompson, *Goths*, p. 14, n. 1, and pp. 212–15, who argues that
   a single judicial organisation was introduced with territoriality. It will have to
   suffice here to point to Narb. 4 and 14 which required Romans and Goths alike to
   suffer punishment at the hands of the city count – in Thompson's view (*Goths*,
   pp. 139–40) a judge for the Goths alone.
6 Details of the period 601–642 in ib., pp. 157–89.
7 This opinion is startlingly out of line with the traditional view of the development
   of Visigothic legislation which I have otherwise adopted. The arguments for it
   appear in King, pp. 146–66, but cannot be summarised or even indicated here,
   since they depend on close textual analysis. I hope to deal with the matter elsewhere
   before very long.
8 See VIII Tol. *Tomus* (414a), Ureña, pp. 458–61.

18

compilation.[1] Structurally, the new code had the same form as did the later one of Ervig. The majority of its laws had been contained already in the *corpus* issued in the reign of Leovigild, but some 200 others were the work of named kings since that time – nearly all, in fact, of Chindasvind and Reccesvind.[2]

Unity of law had therefore been achieved by the aged Chindasvind and confirmed by his son.[3] But the remarkable development of Visigothic legislation was not yet at an end. What led Ervig (680–687) to undertake so soon after his accession to the throne in October 680 the production of a new code is not known. But on 9 January 681 the king opened the proceedings of the Twelfth Council of Toledo – called with the primary object of gaining public sanction and guarantee of his position from the ecclesiastical and lay dignitaries of the kingdom, for the old king, Wamba (672–680), had lost the throne in strange circumstances[4] – and in the written address, or *Tomus*, which in customary fashion he presented to the gathering, he expressed the wish that those present would examine his laws so that by their common judgement those measures which were absurd or unjust might be corrected. None of the conciliar provisions made

[1] On the part of Braulio see Braulio, *Epp.* 38–41, and C. H. Lynch, *Saint Braulio, Bishop of Saragossa (631-651). His life and writings* (Washington D.C., 1938), pp. 136–40. But it is my view that the *codex* which Braulio revised was that of Chindasvind's compilation. For editions of Reccesvind's and Ervig's codes, see Ureña, pp. 45–108.

[2] Ureña, p. 146. I have been unable to consult the translation of the laws by S. P. Scott, *The Visigothic code* (Boston, 1910).

[3] In the view of Thompson, *Goths*, pp. 210–17, the reigns of Chindasvind and Reccesvind also saw a thoroughgoing reform of the administration. But I am less sure than is he that the administrative laws of the *LRV* are admissible evidence for the situation pertaining towards the middle of the seventh century. There is nothing else that I know of which supports the thesis. The unique view of E. Mayer, *Hist. de las instituciones sociales y políticas de Esp. y Portugal durante los siglos V a XIV*, I (Madrid, 1925), 14–15, with n. 19, that a personal law system continued even after the publication of Reccesvind's code is to be rejected out of hand on the evidence of II. 1. 5, 10 and 11.

[4] See on the matter F. X. Murphy, 'Julian of Toledo and the fall of the Visigothic kingdom in Spain', *Speculum*, XXVII (1952), 1–27. Although the story of how a potion was given to Wamba by Ervig so that, feeling death near, he would become a penitent and thereby lose the throne in accordance with the ruling of VI Tol. 17 dates from two centuries later (*Crónica de Alfonso III* 3), I remain deeply suspicious of Ervig – and of Julian of Toledo: see also F. Kern, *Gottesgnadentum und Widerstandsrecht im früheren MA*, 2nd edn by R. Buchner (Münster–Cologne, 1954), pp. 344–5, and Thompson, *Goths*, pp. 229–31. See further below, p. 124, n. 2.

any reference to this request, although the assembly dutifully dealt with the other matters mentioned in the *Tomus*. The result was rather to be seen some time later when a new code of laws, priced at twelve *solidi*, double the value put on Reccesvind's,[1] was promulgated. With the exception of the already issued anti-Jewish laws, confirmed at the Twelfth Council, its provisions were to take effect from 21 October 681.[2]

The code so swiftly produced was well organised.[3] It was divided into twelve books, which were subdivided into chapters, the number in each book varying from a minimum of two in the first to a maximum of seven in the fifth. Each book bore a brief inscription which gave a broadly accurate indication of its contents: the sole exception was the first book, where the rubric *De instrumentis legalibus* was quite inapposite, since the clauses the book contained were in fact concerned with legal philosophy – the duties of a legislator, the qualities of true law and so forth.[4] The inscriptions which introduced the separate chapters were regularly to the point. Each chapter was composed of a number of individually titled clauses, or laws, with thirty-one the maximum in any one chapter. In all the code contained 559 distinct *capitula*. By no means, however, were most of these laws new. A mere thirty-four were Ervig's own measures, and of these no less than twenty-eight dealt with the single topic of the Jews. Rather, Ervig's contribution took the form of a more or less careful revision of earlier laws, some of which he omitted altogether, but others of which he amended, sometimes simply in the interests of clarity, sometimes with a view to making quite drastic alterations in the law. Some eighty laws of the code show the signs of Ervigian correction. Three others were the work of Wamba. But even then it remains the case that something like eighty per cent of the code was constituted by laws which had already appeared in the code of Reccesvind. And *Antiquae*, dating back to the time of Leovigild and even to that of Euric, continued to form a majority of the laws overall.

---

[1] V. 4. 22.  [2] II. I. I.
[3] Generally on the code, editions etc., see Zeumer, XXIII, 496–500, Ureña, cit. in n. I, p. 19 above.
[4] For some comments on this first book, with reference to the scornful opinions of Zeumer and Dahn and the more appropriate attitude of Guizot, see A. K. Ziegler, *Church and State in Visigothic Spain* (Washington D.C., 1930), pp. 70–3.

# Introduction

Ervig's revision brought decided improvements, but he did not succeed in clearing away all the ambiguities and contradictions in the laws. With a few exceptions, the early laws were impressive in their clarity of thought and language, but later legislation, especially that of Chindasvind, was sometimes marred by a woeful obscurity,[1] and the predilection of Reccared and his successors for prolegomenary passages where they might express the piety, wrath or whatever which had led them to issue a legal pronouncement was too often responsible for a painfully baroque turgidity of style.[2] Montesquieu's well-known verdict on the Visigothic laws is not justified, however.[3] 'Pleines de rhétorique... gigantesques dans le style' they may often be – although the elaborate language in which the laws are clothed is in fact of major historical value, for it exposes to us the mind and aspirations of the legislator as more down-to-earth law does not[4] – but, as Gibbon recognised,[5] they are a long way from being 'vides de sens, frivoles dans le fond'. The law is, generally speaking, good law. By comparison with that of the other barbarian kingdoms, indeed, especially that of *Francia*, it is excellent law, and an accurate and revealing reflection of the extent to which the civilisation which begat it was, for all its numerous and grave faults, in advance of any other of Western continental Europe.

It is the Ervigian code of 681 which will be the primary object of examination in the pages which follow, not the amendments which it later underwent.[6] But it is worth noting here that despite what has just been said there are not a few indications in the code that the

---

[1] See, e.g., the Chindasvindian laws II. 1. 12, 19, 3. 9.

[2] The supreme example of empty and prolix rhetoric is IV. 2. 17 – wisely omitted by Ervig.

[3] *De l'esprit des loix*, 28. 1.

[4] The comments of H. Fichtenau, *Arenga. Spätantike und MA im Spiegel von Urkundenformeln* (Graz–Cologne, 1957), pp. 8–10, rejecting the remarkably frequent assessment of the terms of documentary preambles as 'öde Gemeinplätze', apply equally to the Visigothic laws. See also R. M. Honig, *Humanitas und Rhetorik in spätrömischen Kaisergesetzen* (Göttingen, 1960), pp. 23ff.

[5] *Hist. of the decline and fall of the Roman Empire*, 6th edn by J. B. Bury (7 vols, London, 1925), IV, 144, n. 132. There is a useful account of other appreciations of the code in Ziegler, pp. 83–8.

[6] For the legislation of Egica (hostile to Ervig) and probably Wittiza, see Zeumer, XXIII, 505–11, who shows that Egica did not issue a new code: *contra*, Ureña, pp. 503–36. For the career of the code after 711 see the brief account of R. Altamira, 'Spain', *The continental legal hist. series*, I: *General survey* (London, 1912), pp. 607ff.

kingdom was already in military, administrative and moral decline from that 'certain splendour' which it had attained during the seventh century,[1] and that those laws added by Ervig and his successors strengthen the impression of crisis. The sole Ervigian addition was a law published in 683 which confirmed the canons of the Thirteenth Council, among them the conciliar recognition of the first general remission of taxes known in the seventh-century kingdom.[2] Of the fifteen laws of Egica (687–702) and probably Wittiza (700/702–710), the last dated measure, of 702, is a revealing confession of the abundance of escaped slaves to be found throughout the land and of the futility of the governmental action taken to cope with the problem.[3] Another law – probably of Wittiza and later in date[4] – introduces into the courts the ordeal by boiling water and shows by this radical and primitive departure from the comparatively sophisticated rules of evidence operative beforehand how in another respect the situation was deteriorating. It lies outside the scope of this book to examine the import of this and other evidence of economic, social and political crisis in the closing years of the kingdom's existence – the plague, the famine, the further remission of taxes under Egica, the prohibition on Jewish trade, the later enslavement of all Spanish Jews on a blanket charge of treason, the poor state of the currency, the disputed succession of Roderick and so on[5] – for the question of the fall of the Visigothic power or to discuss the reasons why Tāriq's success in a single battle was virtually as decisive for the Visigoths as the Conqueror's was to be for the Anglo-Saxons.[6] But it is difficult not to believe that the Arabs' triumph was due less to their own strength than to the feebleness of their prey and difficult not to see in the conquest of 711 something of a *coup de grâce* for a demoralised and disintegrating kingdom bent on self-destruction.

---

1  The phrase is that of J. M. Lacarra, 'La península ibérica del siglo VII al X. Centros y vias de irradiación de la civilización', *Sett.*, XI (1964), 234.

2  XII. 1. 3.                    3  IX. 1. 21.

4  Thus Zeumer, XXIII, 511, of VI. 1. 3.

5  See the *Index* for page references below. For famine see *CH* 49. Roderick is the centre-point of the article of C. Sánchez–Albornoz, 'El senatus visigodo. Don Rodrigo, rey legítimo de Esp.', *CHE*, VI (1946), 5–99.

6  T. de Sousa Soares, 'Essai sur les causes économiques de la ruine de la monarchie wisigothique d'Esp.', *RPH*, VI (1955), 453–61, is disappointing. One regrets that no explanation of Arab success is attempted in the new *Cambridge hist. of Islam*, I (Cambridge, 1970), 86–7, 94–5.

Chapter 2

# THE KING AND THE LAW

The king portrayed in the Ervigian code has almost entirely escaped from his historically populist origins.[1] However fragile his position may often have been as a matter of historical fact, the theory of kingship which emerges from the laws is unashamedly theocratic. That is not to say that the exalted status of the monarch, his special character as head of the unitary body of society, his rights and responsibilities as God's terrestrial agent, are hammered home in the laws in the same emphatic fashion as they are in the conciliar records. Theocratic elements are almost wholly absent from that majority of laws which was issued before the conversion to Catholicism, and by no means present in most of the laws issued after that time. But the seventh-century kings not infrequently took advantage of the occasion of the promulgation of some new measure to employ language which reflected or bore relevance to their claims – and understandably so, for as the vehicle of propaganda calculated to underline the gulf between all-powerful ruler and dependent people,

[1] On the pre-settlement chieftains (not kings: see Jordanes, *Getica* 134, and on *HG* 2, version A, Messmer, 112–13), see Thompson, *Visigoths in the time of Ulfila*, pp. 43ff. I know of no evidence of sacral notions among the Visigoths: the naming of children after dead monarchs (see Eckhardt, 'Nachbenennung', pp. 34–55) indicates no more than the persistence of ideas of reincarnation (ib., pp. 40, 54) and not of ancestor-worship (on which see Thompson, *Ulfila*, pp. 59–60). On the Anses of *Getica* 78 see O. Höfler, 'Der Sakralcharakter des germanischen Königtums', *Das Königtum. Seine geistigen und rechtlichen Grundlagen*, Vorträge und Forschungen, III, ed. T. Mayer (Lindau–Constance, 1954), 85–8, and H. Wolfram in *Festschrift für Otto Höfler* (Vienna, 1968), pp. 479ff., but that the Visigoths had no particular veneration for the Amals who were these Anses (*Getica* 79ff.) is clear from their rejection (though later reversed) of the dead Alaric II's legitimate son, despite his maternal Amal blood, in favour of a bastard. On the *Balthi* as a *stirps regia* see the sceptical comments of P. Grierson, 'Election and inheritance in early Germanic kingship', *Cambridge hist. journal*, VII (1941), 11–12. But a clear tendency to succession based on blood was early apparent: the descendants of Theodoric I (himself the son-in-law of Alaric I: Sidonius, *Carm.* VII. 505) ceased to rule only in 531. During this period popular participation often took the form of acclamatory confirmation of an established situation: see Orlandis, *Poder real*, pp. 64–7.

23

the laws could hardly be excelled: they were, in this respect, the written counterparts of the visible aids introduced under Byzantine influence from Leovigild's time onwards, and culminating in the uniquely Visigothic institution of royal unction, to popularise and buttress the concept of theocratic kingship.[1] Coinage apart, it is difficult to imagine an influence of more pervasive and effective impact than that of the laws.[2] Used in conjunction with the extensive material of the conciliar acts, these legal references allow the composition of a detailed picture of the notional standing of the king.

The ideological basis of the king's position was the divine sanction attached to his rule. Although the Visigothic state is renowned for its elective monarchy, the fact is that few seventh-century rulers came to the enjoyment of royal power solely as the result of an elective process *stricto sensu*: it is more accurate to speak of an occupative throne, for prior association, designation and simple usurpation all played significant roles.[3] But by whatever practical means a king's accession might have been accomplished, it was the heavenly *fiat*

---

[1] For the Byzantine background see B. Rubin, *Das Zeitalter Iustinians*, I (Berlin, 1960), 125ff., where pp. 146–68 deal with the laws as a propaganda weapon. Some Byzantine parallels with the Visigoths are drawn by E. Ewig, 'Zum christlichen Königsgedanken im Frühmittelalter', *Das Königtum*, pp. 25ff.

[2] For propaganda and the coinage see Ewig, 'Königsgedanke', pp. 25–6. The formulas *Regi a Deo vita* and *Cum Deo* on Hermenegild's and Leovigild's coins are discussed by Hillgarth, 'Coins and chronicles', pp. 501–8: generally on the formulas etc. see F. Mateu y Llopis, 'Las fórmulas y los símbolos cristianos en los tipos monetales visigodos', *AST*, XIV (1941), 75–96. Idem, 'El arte monetario visigodo. Las monedas como monumentos. (Un ensayo de interpretación)', *AEA*, XVIII (1945), 53–4, holds that the figure of Christ appeared on some late coins: see also Miles, pp. 52–3.

[3] 'Occupative' is the term of Grierson, 'Election and inheritance', p. 14. Generally on the methods of accession from Liuva I's time onwards see Sánchez–Albornoz, 'Senatus', pp. 74–94, and, especially, Orlandis, *Poder real*, pp. 80–102, who concludes that election was employed only when a new king was not determined upon by claims of blood or designation. In fact, of the eighteen kings beginning with Leovigild and ending with Roderick (I exclude Hermenegild and Ricimer), eight – Leovigild, Reccared, Liuva II, Reccared II, Tulga, Reccesvind, Egica and Wittiza – followed relatives (all but Leovigild and Egica their fathers), and of these eight, six are known to have been previously associated or designated. Hereditary claim is particularly apparent in the case of Reccared II, who succeeded though only a *parvulus*. A ninth king, Ervig, was designated but in any case immediately anointed. Four others were usurpers. Little is left of an elective monarchy proper. For the Church's attitude see below, p. 50, n. 1.

which was considered the predestinative force behind the political reality. The notion is implicit in the words of an Egican law:

Cum divine voluntatis imperio principale caput regnandi sumat sceptrum[1]

and explicit in, for example, the terms of the votive mass said for the king:

[Deus] qui eum ante secula prescrivit et in seculo principari constituit.[2]

Understandably, therefore, the kings spoke of God as Himself responsible for their elevation to the highest pinnacle of earthly glory:

Excellentia nostri vigoris *a* virtutum *Deo fuerit* terrene glorie *sublimata* culminibus,

said Reccesvind,[3] confessing a debt later given concise expression by the author of the anonymous *Iudicium* in his designation of Wamba as 'electum a Deo regem nostrum'.[4] The kingdom was granted as the result of heavenly favour: it was conceded to the king, committed to him, by God,[5] and rightly characterised therefore as an *honor*.[6] 'Suintila *gratia divina* regni suscepit sceptra', declared Isidore.[7] Just as God created the head at the very summit of the human body so that it might rule over the *subdita membra*, so for the same purpose He set the king at the head of the body of society.[8] The king thus

---

[1] II. 1. 7.

[2] *LO* 294. See also XII Tol. 1: 'Quem...divinum judicium in regno praeelegit' and XVI Tol. 9. Kings were called to rule – 'regere sunt vocati' – according to VIII Tol. *Decretum judicii* (430c), where the Pauline notion of divine responsibility rather than Isidorian etymology should be seen as influential.

[3] XII. 2. 1: cf. his words at VIII Tol. (411c, 415b): 'Summus auctor rerum me...in regni sedem subvexit...Mihi divina pietas regimen fidelium dedit'.

[4] *Iudicium* 1. Cf. also III. 5. 2: 'Universis provinciis *Domino ordinante* ad regni nostri dicionem pertinentibus' and XII Tol. *Tomus*.

[5] See XII. 2. 14: 'Nostras a Deo conlatas regiones'. Conciliar references abound: see III Tol. *Tomus* (342c): 'Gentibus a Deo nobis creditis', v Tol. 1: 'In cuncto regno a Deo sibi [sc. regi] concesso', XVI Tol. *Praef.* (527b): 'Commissa sibi regni gubernacula...et commissos sibi populos' etc.

[6] XII Tol. 1: cf. XVI Tol. 10, II. 5. 19 (Egica).

[7] *HG* 62. The phrase *rex Dei gratia* nowhere appears, but Isidore's passage is its conceptual equivalent.

[8] It is worth quoting the important II. 1. 4 at length: 'Bene Deus...disponens humani corporis formam, in sublimen caput erexit adque ex illo cunctas membrorum fibras exoriri decrevit...formans in illo et fulgorem luminum, ex quo prospici possent, quecumque noxia concurrissent, constituens in eo et intelligendi vigorem, per

stood on high, above those divinely cast down beneath his sway:[1] they were his *subiecti, subiugati, subditi,* while he correctly termed himself 'Our Highness'.[2] But the lofty pre-eminence of the monarch, serene and glorious,[3] involved no justification of arbitrariness in his rule. Visigothic attitudes fell entirely within the ideational context of that general stock of notions flowing from the contemporary concept of government as a remedial device instituted by God for the prevention and correction of the consequences of the sin which had beset mankind since the Fall.[4] Kings owed their being to the workings of supernal mercifulness, as Reccesvind acknowledged when he spoke of *divina pietas* as the source of his royal rule,[5] but the objective of this *pietas*

quem conexa et subdita membra vel dispositio regeret vel providentia ordinaret. Hinc est et peritorum medicorum precipua cura, ut ante capiti quam membris incipiat disponi medella...quia si salutare caput extiterit, ratione colligit, qualiter curare membra cetera possit. Nam si arcem molestia occupaverit capitis, non potuerit in artus dirivationes dare salutis, quas in se consumserit iugis causa langoris. Ordinanda ergo sunt primo negotia principum, tutanda salus, defendenda vita, sicque in statu et negotiis plebium ordinatio dirigenda, ut dum salus conpetens prospicitur regum, fida valentius teneatur salvatio populorum'. The anthropomorphic metaphor employed here was of too general a currency for much weight to be given to the suspicion of Lynch, p. 140, n. 70, based on the grounds of 'Braulio's exceptional love of the dogma of the Mystical Body', that the bishop was the author of the law.

[1] See, e.g., VIII Tol. *Praef.*: 'Ea quae in me totius regiminis transfusa jura reliquit [Chindasvindus] ex toto divina mihi potentia subjugavit', XVII Tol. *Tomus*: 'Quos ditioni nostrae superna pietas subdidit'. Interesting is the contrast in VIII Tol. *Decretum judicii* (430d): 'Nam nunquid...ab *aequalibus* illi [sc. reges] potuerunt rerum coacervatione ditari, nisi *subjectis* glorioso apice potuissent attolli?' Cf. also II. 1. 1, XII. 2. 1 etc.

[2] Cf. II. 1. 5 (not in Ervig's code): 'Nostri culminis fastigium', II. 1. 6: 'Eminentie celsitudo terrene', IX. 2. 9: 'Principalis sublimitas' etc.

[3] 'Serenity' was a frequent royal designation: see II. 1. 1, 30, VII Tol. 1, *EW* 13 etc. Both this and *tranquillitas* (II. 1. 29, IX. 2. 8, XVII Tol. *Tomus* (553b), *EW* 10 etc.) were Imperial appellations: see Ewig, 'Königsgedanke', pp. 17, 27 with n. 78, Fichtenau, pp. 69ff., and Stroheker, *Germanentum*, p. 230. *Gloriosissimus* appears already in the *Commonitorium* to the *LRV* of 506 (Zeumer, *LV*, p. 466) while Reccesvind and later kings were regularly *gloriosus* in the headings of their laws. The designation extended to the queen (e.g., III Tol., *subscriptio* of Baddo) and even to the royal head and senses (XVI Tol. *Praef.* (527b); II. 1. 1). On the term see Fichtenau, p. 72. The councils abound in similar designations – *excellentissimus, praecelsus, perspicuus, clarissimus, invictissimus, inclytus* and so on.

[4] Sir R. W. and A. J. Carlyle, *A hist. of mediaeval political theory in the West,* 2nd edn, I (Edinburgh–London, 1927), 125ff., remains a valuable account.

[5] See above, p. 25, n. 3. Similarly Egica at XVII Tol. (above, n. 1).

was the amelioration of the wretched condition to which rejection of the divine law had brought the human race. The realm was granted to the king by God not for the gratification of his own desires but for the benefit of those over whom he reigned: in Reccared's words:

Deus omnipotens *pro utilitatibus populorum* regni nos culmen subire tribuerit,

or in Ervig's, nearly a century later:

Regnum fautore Deo *ad salvationem terrae et sublevationem plebium* suscepisse nos credimus.[1]

It was precisely this notion which was expressed by the writer of the anonymous extension to Isidore's chronicle when he spoke of Egica's guardianship, *tutela*, of the kingdom.[2] The king and his government, in other words, were the God-ordained means to a God-ordained end. The ruler's position was functional, for he acted as the *minister Dei*, as the delegated governor of God.[3] He held the kingdom, as the bishops said, *iure vicario*,[4] and it does not surprise to find Chindasvind expressly linking his legislative activity with the exercise of a vicariate role on behalf of the divine *principatus*.[5] It was through the king that God worked: *divina celsitudo* ordered the bishops to assemble at the Third Council of Saragossa, for example, but 'ex jussu...Egicani'.[6] For 'the king's heart is in the hand of the Lord...he turneth it

[1] III Tol. *Tomus* (342c); XII Tol. *Tomus* (468b).
[2] *CH* 53.
[3] At IV Tol. the proceedings opened with thanks to God and 'ministro ejus excellentissimo et glorioso regi'. See also 'ministerium regni presentis' in LO 295 and on the concept of *ministerium* H. H. Anton, *Fürstenspiegel und Herrscherethos in der Karolingerzeit* (Bonn, 1968), pp. 61, 404–6. But I do not think the second *ministerium* in XII Tol. *Tomus* (469b) ideologically significant. For delegation see VI Tol. 14, below, p. 32, n. 3.
[4] Below, p. 42, n. 3. Cf. Reccared's words in III Tol. *Tomus* (344d): 'Hae gentes quarum *in Dei nomine* regia potestate praecellimus'.
[5] IV. 2. 19: 'Divini principatus quodam modo peragimus vicem, cum necdum genitis misericordie porrigimus opem'. Why should H. Aubin, 'Stufen und Formen der christlich-kirchlichen Durchdringung des Staates im Frühmittelalter', *Festschrift für Gerhard Ritter* (Tübingen, 1950), p. 84, say that the vicariate is 'rein bildlich gemeint'?
[6] III Sar. *Praef.* Cf. VIII Tol. *Praef.*: 'Nos omnes divinae ordinatio voluntatis... principis serenissimo jussu...ad sacrum synodi coegisset aggregari conventum'.

whithersoever he will'.[1] As the divinity's agent, the king stood in a special relationship with God, and it was natural that he should have been held to personify the divine virtues. The terminology of the laws and canons, although very often non-Christian in its origins, must be seen, given the Christian background, as reflecting and propagating this characterisation.[2] The monarch designated himself 'nostra clementia';[3] his predecessors were 'dive memorie' and 'reverende memorie';[4] his law was 'divalis' and 'sacra'.[5] To the bishops at the Third Council of Toledo and at the Second Council of Saragossa, indeed, Reccared was *sanctissimus*,[6] and although the appellation was employed of no later ruler the councils were never at a loss to coin new expressions by which they might draw attention – realistically or not – to the orthodoxy and devoutness of the kings.

As the representative of God, Whom he strove to please,[7] the Visigothic monarch had as his all-embracing duty the direction of the Christian society placed in his charge towards the goal dictated by God: the methods and particular aims of his rule were wholly conditioned by this teleological consideration. The essential in-

[1] Proverbs 21. 1 was cited by the bishops in Mer. 8 (where the rearrangement of diocesan boundaries by the king was the result of the divine–royal link). Understandably, the king's wisdom was 'divinitus...concessa' (Mer. 23). See also below, p. 37, n. 4.

[2] Thus also in Byzantium: Rubin, pp. 127–9.

[3] II. 4. 8 (Egica), v. 7. 12, IX. 2. 8 etc. *Pietas, mansuetudo, miseratio* and *misericordia* all also appear in the code and all usages are common in the canons. For *pius* (as well as *iustus, felix* and *inclitus*) on the coins, see Mateu y Llopis, 'Fórmulas y símbolos', pp. 78–81.

[4] II. 1. 5, 8, XII. 2. 15 etc. Thus also the councils (e.g. Egara, VIII Tol. *Praef.* (411b) etc.), where not only the memory but also the person of the dead king is *divus*, as in XV Tol. *Tomus* (511b) – of Ervig, by Egica! Imperial influence is clear here, as it is in the designation *sacratissimus*, applied to the king (VIII Tol. *Praef.*) and even to the fisc (XVI Tol. 1): for the Christian Empire see the many examples in W. Ensslin, *Gottkaiser und Kaiser von Gottes Gnaden*, Sitzungsberichte der Bayerischen Akad. der Wissenschaften, philosophisch-hist. Abteilung (Munich, 1943), no. 6, pp. 71ff.

[5] XII. 2. 14; XIII Tol. *Lex in confirmatione* (505a). The royal office was also *divalis*: II. 4. 8 (Egica).

[6] III Tol. *Praef.*, II Sar. 1.

[7] Cf. III. 4. 18: 'Et nos ponere finem inlicitis ausibus rite conpellimur; quoniam et ipsi divinis nutibus devotissime placere conamur'. As Reccesvind said in VIII Tol. *Tomus*: 'Omnes reges terrae serviunt et obediunt Deo'. Note also Braulio, *Ep.* 32, where Chindasvind writes to the bishop: 'Quia aliud quam quod Deo est placitum, non credas me posse facturum...'!

strument of the king in this task was the law, by which the aspirations, ideals and practical decisions of government are in any society expressed in formulated rules binding upon the generality. It was a necessary consequence of the king's vice-gerential and functional status that the definition and propagation of the norms by which the community was to live in order that the God-decreed end might be attained should be in the royal hands alone. On the one hand, the laws of the Visigothic code were the product of the king's decisions and took their force from royal authority:[1] on the other, no laws other than those of the authorised code were admissible in the courts of the kingdom.[2] The origin of law lay no longer in the custom of the people but rather in the will of the king who, accepting the commandment of God, translated divine justice into legal *dicta* and gave these to his subjects.[3] They obeyed the law through the necessity created by royal command, the king himself through his own voluntary submission.[4] As the direction of society was the function of the king, so from him also emanated the law which made possible the fulfilment of his gubernatorial role. Governmentally speaking, the king and his law were indistinguishable.

The ultimate objective of the monarchical endeavours was the *salus populi*. It goes without saying that the highest 'health' for the Christian was that state of purity and grace which would bring him salvation, and as we shall see later the Visigothic kings – quite logically, given the God-based postulates of their rule – conceived themselves, and were viewed by others, as supremely responsible for the spiritual welfare of their subjects – though not, of course, individually possessed of the sacramental capacities of the *sacerdotes*. But the terrestrial *salus* of his people was no less the aim of the

---

[1] See Ervig's promulgation edict, II. I. I: 'Et ideo harum legum correctio vel novellarum nostrarum sanctionum ordinata constructio...in cunctis personis ac gentibus nostre amplitudinis imperio subiugatis innexum sibi *a nostra gloria valorem obtineat*', II. I. 2, II. I. 5 (Reccesvind's promulgation decree), II. I. 6 etc. Laws issued in the future would similarly have the king as their source: II. I. 13, 14. The *plurale maiestatis* is frequent in individual laws.　　　　　　　　[2] Below, p. 101.

[3] II. I. 2: 'Omnipotens rerum dominus...discere iustitiam habitatores terre... imperabit...Quapropter si obediendum est Deo, diligenda est iustitia...Gratanter ergo iussa celestia amplectentes, damus modestas simul nobis et subditis leges'. The comment of W. E. Brynteson, *Speculum*, XLI (1966), 423, that *Etym.* v. 3. 1–4 and ib. v. 5. 20 'reveal that custom was not the only form of law known in the period and that it may even have been regarded as a secondary form' is sadly inadequate.

[4] II. I. 2: see below, pp. 44ff.

## Law and society in the Visigothic kingdom

monarch. Without the *pax* and *quies* which this involved, religion could not flourish, as the bishops acknowledged,[1] but man's worldly well-being was in its own right an aim of the divinity when He created governments so that corruption and evil might not reign triumphant. The restraint of the depravity of man by means of the law is a theme, indeed, which runs throughout the code.[2] Law was called forth by the compulsion which the king felt to act against evil in order to hold it in check.[3] Reason demanded the production of laws, said the anonymous compiler of the first book:[4]

Ut earum metu humana coerceatur inprobitas, sitque tuta inter noxios innocentium vita, atque in ipsis inprobis formidato supplicio frenetur nocendi presumptio.[5]

Legal coercion was necessary to deal with that which polluted the right order of living:[6] wrong-doers had to be punished so that they and others might be deterred by fear.

Quorumdam seva temeritas severioribus penis est legaliter ulciscenda,

declared Chindasvind in a law providing for retaliation in kind,

ut, dum metuit quisque pati quod fecerit, saltim ab inlicitis invitus abstineat.[7]

---

[1] Cf. vi Tol. 16: '[Rex] cujus regimine habemus securitatem', vii Tol. 1, with reference to the 'utilitati publicae, sine qua quieti non vivimus', xiv Tol. 12: 'Sub cujus [sc. regis] pace pax servatur Ecclesiae' etc. For *pax*, note also ii. 1. 1, where 'una et evidens pax' embraces all the peoples of the kingdom.

[2] Thus, in the last book of the code Reccesvind was able to say (xii. 2. 1): 'Actenus per arduas culparum semitas iudiciorum cautos direximus gressos et per humane adinventionis precipites et inmoderatos excessos ordinate gravitatis emisimus cursus'.

[3] iii. 2. 7: 'Resistendum est pravorum ausibus, ne pravitatis amplius frena laxentur': cf. already iii Tol. (350b/c): 'Totis nitendum est viribus humanis moribus modum ponere et insolentium rabiem regia potestate refrenare'.

[4] It is true that the provisions of this first book, based in part on Isidorian sources, 'bewegen sich ganz in diesseitiger Gedankenführung der antiken Naturrechtslehre', but surely missing the point to say that the book 'weist im Ausdruck kaum eine Bezugnahme auf Gott auf' and that it 'steht...inhaltlich nicht anders' (Aubin, p. 81). The old Stoic notions had survived precisely because they were susceptible of, and had in fact received, Christian interpretation. For Braulio as the possible author of the book, see Lynch, pp. 139–40.

[5] i. 2. 5: cf. *Etym.* ii. 10. 5, v. 20. For the prince and the terror of the laws see also *Sent.* iii. 47. 1, 48. 5, 50. 4 and on these texts, Anton, pp. 56–8.

[6] iii. 3. 11.

[7] vi. 4. 3. Great stress was laid upon punishment: see iii. 5. 4, vi. 2. 1 etc. But the aim was deterrence: cf. iii. 4. 13: 'Si perpetratum scelus legalis censura non reprimit,

The king acted:

Et dissuadere, quod male suasum irrite libet, et proibere, quod turpe non decet, et auferre, quod male actum decus honestatis aborret,

and in this task his weapon was the *legalis censura*.[1] But although law appeared here in a negative, repressive role, its final function was positive, beneficent, for not only did it stand as a protective bulwark between the *populus* and the unmitigated miseries inseparable from the forces of evil, but it also constituted the means by which might be actively implemented and inculcated the principles of justice to which the king was committed as God's lieutenant. In either capacity law was health-giving – hence, 'salutifera remedia', 'salubre decretum'[2] – and for this reason rightly seen as the effluence of the mildness, *mansuetudo*, of the ruler,[3] just as government itself stemmed from the divine *pietas*:

Regalis pietas pro salute hominum suarum legum dignata est ponere decreta,

declared the bishops at Merida.[4] The solicitous concern which was of the very essence of the monarch's tutelary status found its supreme practical expression in the promulgation of laws by which the *utilitas* – which was merely another way of saying *salus* – of society might be assured:

Sollicita cura in principem esse dinoscitur, cum pro futuris utilitatibus beneficia populo providentur.[5]

sceleratorum temeritas ab adsuetis vitiis nequaquam quiescit' and VI. 5. 16: 'Quatenus, dum malorum pravitas conspicit constituta sibi supplicia preterire non posse, vel metu saltim territus a malis abstineat'. Deterrence was explicitly the motive for the public floggings ordered in III. 3. 4 ('ut hoc alii conmoniti terrore formident') and VIII. 1. 3 ('ad aliorum terrorem') and for the blinding decreed in Chindasvind's version of VI. 5. 16: it was no doubt also partly responsible for the provision that executions be in public (VII. 4. 7). See also VI. 2. 4: 'Ducentenis flagellis publice verberentur et decalvati deformiter decem convicinas possessiones circuire cogantur inviti, ut eorum alii corrigantur exemplis', Mer. 15 etc.

[1] XII. 2. 1.
[2] XII. 2. 14; X. 1. 4.
[3] I. 2. 6. For the characteristic term *moderamen* see Anton, pp. 63–4.
[4] Mer. 15. Cf. VIII Tol. *Epil.* (427c/d).
[5] III. 1. 1, a Leovigildian law. For *utilitas* see also I. 2. 4: 'Lex erit...*utilis*...in qua previdendum est ex utilitate', II. 1. 1: 'Sicut legum evidentia populorum est excessibus utilis...' etc.

The king was the divinely sanctioned steward of the kingdom in the *felicitas* of which his subjects found their defence:[1] what was more in keeping with his numinous character than to stretch out over his realm the hand of benevolence and assistance by the creation of legal remedies for the ills which his subjects suffered?[2]

It was society in its collective entirety with which the king was concerned in the promulgation of law, just as it was the government of all which had been delegated to him by God.[3] In terms of the unitary, organological concept of society which was reflected so powerfully in the Visigothic sources,[4] the king was the head of the public body and as such possessed both of the eyes with which to search out what was noxious and of the mind to reach decisions by which the dependent and subject parts might be ruled.[5] It was by his judgement that the diseases of the body were diagnosed and by his action that the appropriate neutralising medicines were administered.[6] The touchstone of efficacious and salutary law was therefore its contribution to the interests of the generality: as Reccesvind put it:

Quod utilitati multorum est congruum, non est nostre legis decreto pretermittendum.[7]

[1] Cf. xii. 1. 2: 'Omnes, quos regni nostri felicitate tuemur'.
[2] Ib.: 'Quid est enim iustitie tam proximum vel nobis familiare, quam piam fidelibus manum porrigere et iuste hos, quos regimus, in diversis negotiis adiubare?' Cf. *Nov. Val.* 1.
[3] vi Tol. 14: 'Cui *omnium gubernatio* superno constat *delegata* judicio'. Generally on the notion of the common good in the barbarian kingdoms – a notion present in the Roman, Germanic and Christian traditions – see W. Merk in *Festschrift Alfred Schultze* (Weimar, 1934), pp. 453–72.
[4] See, e.g., xiii Tol. *Tomus*, where the words are Ervig's: 'Quod *divulsam* per tyrannidem *nostri corporis partem* in societatis nostrae gremio conamur reducere' and viii Tol. *Decretum judicii*: 'Omnia certe totius *plebis membra subjecta* dum ad *principale caput* relevant...obtutum', ib., *Praef.* (411c), and xvi Tol. 10 (opening words). Generally on the concept as fundamental to the medieval world see Lecture 1 in W. Ullmann, *The individual and society in the MA* (London, 1967), especially pp. 36ff.
[5] ii. 1. 4.
[6] Cf. ii. 1. 29: 'Tranquillitatis nostre uno medicamine concedimus duo mala sanare', xii. 2. 1: 'Propriis membris confecto medicamine salutari'.
[7] ii. 4. 10. For a long statement of this theme see the beginning of ii. 1. 6 and the associated texts of viii Tol. 10 and *Decretum judicii* and on all these H. Beumann, 'Zur Entwicklung transpersonaler Staatsvorstellungen', *Das Königtum*, pp. 215ff., and Anton, pp. 64–5.

The notion that law might serve the interests of individuals rather than those of the body of society was rejected: the legislator was to act 'nullo privatim commodo, sed omnium civium utilitati communi'.[1] Asked by Egica to resolve the problems created by his swearing of two conflicting oaths, the bishops at the Fifteenth Council cited St Paul in their support of the claims of the generality and declared:

Nunquid paucorum salus erit exstinctio plurimorum? Aut nunquid tantum valere debet privatae rei commodum quam generalis relevatio populorum? Absit.[2]

The exhortation to the legislator to show his paternal love in the creation of the law so that he might gain the love of all was only another way of urging him to attend to the interest of the many.[3] But as law was devoted to the end of the *salus* of society as a whole, it followed that the subject of its sway was necessarily the whole community, without distinction of condition, age or sex: the law ruled learned and ignorant, city-dweller and countryman, Goth and Roman.[4] It further followed that the whole health of society consisted in obedience to its dictates:[5] it was law 'que summum salutis

---

[1] I. I. 3 (= *Etym.* II. 10. 6, v. 21). For practical expressions of the principle see VIII. 4. 29, concerned with the blocking of rivers: 'Nullus...contra multorum conmune commodum sue tantumodo utilitati consulturus...' and XII. I. 2: 'Nihil aliut eorum [sc. subiectorum] utilitatibus consulentes...iubemus, ut nullis indictionibus [etc.] comes [etc.] pro suis utilitatibus populos adgravare presumant'. For *publica utilitas* see below, p. 63, n. 1.

[2] xv Tol. (521c): I Cor. 10. 33 is cited in 521d. The full episcopal discussion extends over two and a half columns of Migne (cols 520a–522c). One of Egica's oaths had been sworn to Ervig before his marriage to the king's daughter and had provided that he would champion Ervig's children (probably sealing an agreement between two opposed factions: see R. d'Abadal, *Dels visigots als catalans*, I (Barcelona, 1969), 84–6): the other, also to Ervig, had bound him to swear before his own accession to do justice to the people.

[3] I. I. 8: 'Erit [artifex legum] quecumque sunt publica patrio recturus amore...ut hunc universitas patrem...habeat...sicque diligatur in toto'. Note Isidore's designation of Svintila (*HG* 64) as 'non solum princeps populorum, sed etiam pater pauperum vocari...dignus'.

[4] I. 2. 3: 'Lex regit omnem civitatis ordinem, omnem hominis etatem, que sic feminis datur ut maribus [etc.]', II. I. I. This is not to say, of course, that it did not rule different parts of the body in different ways: see below, chapter 6. We may note, however, that equality of treatment of men and women within a particular estate was provided for in several individual laws (e.g. III. 3. 11, VI. 2. 5, 4. 3) and may be taken as the general rule. For the lesser value put on a woman's life before Ervig's time, however, see below, p. 261, n. 6. [5] I. I. 9.

principum hac populorum culmen obtinet'.¹ This *salus* found expression in internal peace and security, but had its further temporal effects, for when all evil had been cut away the state of healthy *concordia* between the parts of the body which was society would allow victory over the enemies of the people.² Both the militant reality of the contemporary world and the concrete practicality attributed to notions which one might be tempted to believe remained in the realm of the abstract are evidenced in this promise of military success as the consequence of right order within the corporate body.

Since it was law which established the norms of correct behaviour, either negatively, by what it prohibited, or positively, by what it permitted or encouraged,³ it is understandable that it should have been conceived – again in terms of the anthropomorphic metaphor – as the distinctive force, the governing principle, the rational soul, of the public body – as, in a succinct phrase, the 'anima totius corporis popularis'.⁴ It is small wonder therefore that ignorance of the law was considered no less heinous than its breach and that no other law than that duly authorised by the head of the body could be admitted:⁵ there is no more room in a single body for two souls than there is for two heads. The designation of law as the soul of the public body was in fact the neater for its nicely precise reflection of the duality of the nature of law. The soul of man was of divine origin and eternal, but it inhabited an earthly frame and functioned within the world as the directive force of the individual: the soul existed, so to speak, on two planes, the worldly and the other-worldly. So too did law as the *anima* of the community. Certain characteristics were necessary to the law in order that it might fulfil its temporal function as the *gubernaculum civitatis*.⁶ It had to be possible;⁷ it had to be suited to the time and place of its promulgation;⁸ it had to be clearly expressed, so that there was no danger of ambiguity⁹ – especially so, since one of

¹ I. 2. 3. *Salvatio* in I. I. 2, II. I. 4, XII Tol. *Tomus* etc. is the equivalent of *salus*.
² I. 2. 6. For ecclesiastical concern with military success see Mer. *Praef.* and c. 3 (below, p. 58, n. 7) and III Sar. *Epil.* (where also peace at home). For the special prayers said when the king set out on campaign and returned, see *LO* 149–55.
³ And which was thus characterised as the 'fons disciplinarum...magistra vite' (I. 2. 2).      ⁴ I. 2. 2. See on the notion Ullmann, *Individual*, pp. 46ff.
⁵ Below, p. 101.      ⁶ The phrase of I. 2. 2.
⁷ I. I. 3.      ⁸ I. 2. 4.
⁹ I. I. 6: cf. I. 2. I, II. I. I etc.

its prime roles was the removal of doubt and obscurity.[1] These were particular attributes of practical and necessary importance, and dictated by the facts of the worldly situation of those to whom it was addressed. But far greater emphasis was placed upon those properties of the law which reflected its eternal nature. The Visigothic code was a product of its time, and it was a commonplace of contemporary thought that above all men ruled the immutable natural law, that body of principles of justice which were the expression of reason and of the nature of God Himself: these ideal norms constituted the exemplar upon which human laws should be modelled and therefore the yardstick against which they might be measured.[2] The qualities of the divine law – purity, honesty, truth, fairness, reasonableness – were accordingly the qualities which it was considered Visigothic law should embody and which in fact were frequently presented as the motivating bases of individual measures.[3] On the one hand, therefore, law was conditioned by the worldly surroundings in which it exercised its rule, was grounded in reality: on the other, it was characterised by the justice from which it sprang, was engendered in ideality. Behind the law stood divine, natural justice: law was – the phrase has Stoic echoes – the messenger of justice, the 'iustitie nuntia'.[4] As this justice was itself the justice of God – indeed, *was* God[5] –

[1] Cf. III. 4. 12: 'Quia...sepe iudices dubitare contingit, ideo specialiter decernere necessarium extitit, ut...', III. 1. 5, 3. 8, IV. 2. 17 (omitted from Ervig's code) etc. The theme is present in the promulgation edict II. 1. 1 itself.

[2] 'Lex erit...secundum naturam' in I. 2. 4 expresses this notion of the correspondence of law with the natural – as opposed to vitiated, since the Fall – order of things.

[3] See I. 1. 1: 'Cuius [sc. artificis legum] artis insigne ex hoc decentius enitere probabitur, si...*ex veritate* format speciem sanctionis...[et] *puris honestisque preceptis* modeste statuat articulos legis', I. 2. 4: 'Lex erit...*iusta et equabilia* prescribens, *congruens, honesta et digna*', and as examples of the many particular laws II. 5. 6: 'Et *honestas* hoc habet, et *iustitia* hoc adfirmat', V. 5. 5: '*Iustum* est enim', V. 7. 12: 'Quia indignum nostra pensat clementia', IX. 1. 11: '*Equum* est enim', X. 1. 17: 'Providentissime *iustique* iuris est, ut formam inveterate censure, que *ab equitatis ratione dissentit*, novellis etiam sanctionibus emendemus'. Reccesvind's promulgation decree, II. 1. 5, declared that he had rejected those laws 'quas non equitas iudicantis, sed libitus inpresserat potestatis'.     [4] I. 2. 2.

[5] See IV. 5. 6 (Wamba): 'Deus iudex iustus, qui iustitiam intemporaliter diligit, non vult servire iustitiam tempori, sed tempora potius equitatis lege concludi. Ipse igitur Deus iustitia est' and II. 4. 8 (Egica): 'Iustitia, que Deus est'. Thus, the *inlicita* of III. 4. 18 are those things displeasing to God and the *remedia* of XII. 1. 1 *Deo placita*. Note also II. 1. 9: 'Ut devotius servare probemur iustitiam Dei', III. 5. 3, 7 (Egica), 6. 2 ('tale nefas fieri nequaquam inter christianos oportet') etc.

it is not surprising that the law was revered as proximate to divinity, as 'emula divinitatis, antestis religionis'.[1]

It was justice, then, which the law existed to express in society, which created the law rather than was created by it.[2] Given this view, it is understandable that the maxim *Nullum crimen sine lege* could find no place in Visigothic legal philosophy.[3] To act in an unjust fashion was in itself an offence, even when no breach of the terms of an individual law was involved.[4] It was this notion which made the provision of retrospective law a matter of ease.[5] At the same time it saved the Visigothic legislators from the need to talk in Germanic terms of the 'discovery' of law.[6] As new offences against justice came to light, so new laws, as particular and utilitarian offshoots of that justice, were created.[7] Once created, of course, they could be rightly deemed of eternal validity,[8] precisely because they gave

[1] I. 2. 2. For reverence see II. I. 2, X. I. 4 etc.
[2] References to justice as the source of individual laws are relatively frequent: see, e.g., II. 5. 6 (n. 3, p. 35 above), V. 7. 13: 'Iustitia suadente' etc. Note the relation of justice and nature in IV. 2. 9 (cit. p. 248) and cf. X. I. 17: 'Si enim filius ab utroque parente gignitur et creatur, cur idem ad conditionem tantum pertineat genetricis, qui sine patre nullatenus potuit procreari? Hac rationabiliter nature lege conpellimur agnationem ancille, que servo alieno coniuncta peperit, inter utrosque dominos equaliter dividendam'.
[3] For its absence also from Roman law see F. H. Schulz, *Principles of Roman law* (Oxford, 1936), pp. 173ff.          [4] Cf. VI. 4. 5.
[5] Cf., for Roman law, G. Broggini, *The Irish jurist*, new series, I (1966), 168: 'The principle of non-retroactivity finds its limits in natural law, in the fundamental rules of justice which are timeless'. See King, pp. 154ff., for the view that Reccesvind's code as a whole was retroactive. II. I. 6, 8, 4. 8 (Egica) and IV. 5. 7 are in part explicitly retrospective: cf. also III. 5. I. But all the laws of Ervig's code were retrospective to the extent that the king ordered their application to all unfinished cases: II. I. 14. Cf. also XII Tol. 7 (below, p. 77, with n. 2).
[6] The Roman usages *legem condere* and *legem ponere* both occur in the code (e.g., I. I. I, 2; II. I. 6, III. 3. 8): note further *innovare* (II. I. 5), *inducere* (I. I. 3), *dare* (II. I. 2), *dedere* (II. I. 6) *leges*. These usages are characteristic of the theocratic-descending theme of government: see W. Ullmann, 'The Bible and principles of government in the MA', *Sett.*, X (1963), 209–10. But *legem ferre*, although histori-cally associated with the populist-ascending theme, is not, so far as I can see, etymologically bound to that, and in the code both *legislator* (title to I. I) and *lator iuris* (I. I. 4) appear. For *artifex legum* see I. I passim.
[7] Cf. VII. 5. 7: 'Quorundam sepe calliditas exigit, ut nove sanctionis constituamus edictum, dum eorum nova et aborrenda fraudis molimina...cognoscimus', V. 4. 17, X. I. 17 etc. Note also V Tol. 3: 'Inexpertis et novis morbis novam decet invenire medelam'. It was natural therefore that provision be made for royal additions to the code 'si iusta novitas causarum exegerit': II. I. 14.
[8] Cf. III. I. I, 5, IV. 5. 3, VII. 5. 7 etc.

expression to justice, which was itself eternal. In other words, the conception of law in terms both of the other world and of this allowed the composers of the laws to have the best of both.[1]

While the recognition of things noxious to the community was the responsibility of the king, then, the particular laws which he produced as a result had their ultimate origin in God Himself and His divine justice. An essential precondition of the formation of law was therefore knowledge of the norms of justice. But these were readily discoverable. There was the Bible, for the revealed Word of God was in necessary harmony with His eternal justice. Scriptural foundations for particular provisions are far from rare in the code.[2] There was reason, for through this universal human faculty all men could recognise the rational ordering which was the natural law. A glance through the pages of the code will reveal the regularity with which the later legislators in particular prefaced the constitutive parts of their laws with preambles explicative of their motives – a practice in contrast to that of other barbarian legislators, whose laws were usually solely, and starkly, informative of offence and consequence. There was conscience, for men, it was held, had inherent knowledge of the divine principles written in their hearts.[3] There was divine inspiration.[4] And there were the *mores* of good men, living or dead,[5] for through their examples could be held to be expressed the principles of justice which, by conscience or other

[1] It is a matter for regret that the Visigothic sources do not figure largely in the excellent article of R. Sprandel, 'Über das Problem neuen Rechts im früheren MA', *ZRG.KA*, LXXIX (1962), 117–37.

[2] A good example is provided by VI. 5. 1: 'Quicumque nesciens hominem occiderit et nullum contra eum odium habuerit, iuxta Domini vocem reus mortis non erit. Non enim est iustum, ut...'. See also II. 1. 9, IV. 2. 15 (cf. already *CE* 323), VI. 5. 8, XII. 2. 8 etc. The most extreme influence is to be found in IV. 2. 13\*, a Novel of Wamba, excluded by Ervig, in which Zeumer, ad loc., notes eight distinct citations of the O.T. and where Wamba's amendment of the existing law is therefore 'Domino ordinante': note also 'sicut fas est iustitie et sacra scriptura docet'. For an invented biblical reference see VI. 5. 21, which is in my view post-Visigothic.

[3] Cf. I. 1. 5, cit. below, p. 38, n. 3. Romans 2. 15 is basic.

[4] The source of II. 1. 6: cf. also XII. 2. 13: 'Deo adiubante', XII. 2. 14: 'Autore Domino' etc. At V Tol. the king presented the bishops with their programme 'divina inspiratione' (*Praef.*). But God was of course necessarily the author of all good actions: XIII Tol. 13.

[5] Thus I. 2. 2: 'Lex est...boni mores inveniens adque conponens'. Note also the 'nobilium inlustriumque gentium mores' and the 'sanctissimorum quoque patrum...regulas...et exempla' relied upon in XII. 2. 1.

means, they had perceived. The statement in I. 2. 4 that law should be according to custom – 'secundum consuetudinem civitatis' – was only another way of saying this, for that *consuetudo* should mean custom whatever its character and however uninformed by the principles of Christian justice is both in itself unthinkable and in flat contradiction to the occasional abrogations of established law, to which men had presumably conformed, which can be found in the code.[1] The idea that the norms of justice will be found in the common feeling of the people means that there is no case for adducing the witnessed association of the more important subjects with the king in the publication of law as possible evidence of the survival in constitutional theory of old Germanic populist notions – even if it was in fact no doubt the case that the king was obliged to take the opinions of these men into significant account.[2] The idea was rather that the public welfare would be better served by seeking the counsel of all.[3] This in no way detracted from the position of the king as finally responsible both for the recognition of things illicit and for the provision of fitting remedies: it simply meant that he would be able more easily to govern to the advantage of all.

If the production of just laws was the prime task of the Christian king, it is important nevertheless to note the role of mercifulness as a royal virtue.[4] *Clementia* was a traditional attribute of the good ruler,[5] but it is clear that the Visigothic king's self-appellation 'nostra

[1] E.g., III. I. I, IV. 5. I, X. I. 4 etc. It is better to correct the errors of past rulers than to err with them, says V. 4. 13.

[2] Association is witnessed in II. I. 5 (Reccesvind's promulgation decree), XII. 2. 14 and some MSS of II. I. I.

[3] The notion is expressed in I. I. 5: 'Erit [legislator] in adventione Deo sibique tantummodo conscius, consilio probis et parvis admixtus, adsensu civibus populisque conmunis, ut aliene provisor salutis commodius ex universali consensu exerceat gubernaculum, quam ingerat ex singulari potestate iudicium'. Cf. also XIII Tol. *Tomus*: 'Neque enim fas est quemquam, etiamsi bonus sit opus, sine consilio agere, cum tamen multum prosit bona cum consilio bonorum egisse'. There is no need to think that the *consensus* mentioned in II. I. 5 was constitutive.

[4] One should recall *Etym.* IX. 3. 5: 'Regiae virtutes praecipuae duae: iustitia et pietas. Plus autem in regibus laudatur pietas; nam iustitia per se severa est'. It is clearly the notion of justice as 'malum pro malo' (*Sent.* III. 50. 3) which rules here: for this and the other concept of justice in Isidore, proper Christian behaviour, see Anton, p. 59. Note also *LO* 295: 'Te [Deus] quoque eius pectori presidente, sic in cunctis exequatur iustitiam, ut pietatem et clementiam non amittat'.

[5] See now T. Adams, *Clementia principis* (Stuttgart, 1970), and for the *CT*, Honig, pp. 114ff.

clementia' gained a special significance by virtue of his position as God's vice-gerent on earth.[1] The king's mercifulness and paternal feeling – *pietas* – were held, as we have seen, to be displayed in the very creation of remedies for the distressful condition of mankind.[2] But mercy in the more usual sense of moderation or clemency towards the guilty was also characteristic of the king's activity.[3] The severity of the law must be tempered by the exercise of mercy, particularly in cases concerning the poor: such was the instruction of Chindasvind to his judges. If the letter of the law was in every event adhered to, the virtue of clemency would be abandoned.[4] We must assume a general right of reprieve as a basic royal prerogative, although we shall see later that some restrictions did exist.[5]

Quite in keeping with the Christian ethos and telos of Visigothic society was the inducement held out to the king to act as a true ruler and legislator should do. Personal *salus* in the shape of heavenly bliss would be his reward for the assumption of the duties of Christian kingship. At the end of his life the just and merciful ruler would put off the emblems of earthly glory and don in their stead the crown of everlasting life: the royal steward of the divine *principatus* was encouraged to his task by the allurement of that most desirable of prospects, salvation.[6] In every aspect of his activity, in short, the king was directed by the principles and tenets of the Christian religion.

Given the crucial role of the king in the governance of society, it is perfectly natural that his person and especial interests should have received particular attention in the laws. Society itself stood to profit from the protection afforded by the law to the king, for it was upon the health of the head that that of the body depended. Just as the principal concern of physicians was for the head, so the affairs of the king were to be dealt with before those of his subjects. His health and

---

[1] In VI. I. 7, e.g., it is the 'divina miseratio' which impels the king himself to mercy.
[2] Note also Ervig's introductory remarks to his edict of tax-remission at XIII Tol.:
    'Magnum pietatis est praemium quo removentur gravedines pressurarum, quia illud semper ante Dei oculos perfectae miserationis sacrificium approbatur, quo fit relevatio miserorum et ex hoc salvatio inducitur terrae per quod pressurae subvenitur humanae'.
[3] Quite in accordance with I. I. 7.
[4] XII. I. I: cf. VIII Tol. *Tomus* (414b). For mitigation see p. 94, n. 5, below.
[5] For particular references to reprieve see II. I. 8, VI. I. 7, XII. 3. 27 etc.
[6] I. 2. 6: cf. XII. 2. I, *in fine*.

life were to be defended in order that the salvation of the people dependent upon him might be assured. For if the head was ill the members could not be well.[1]

While such notions had no necessarily Christian content, in the circumstances of the Visigothic kingdom they can hardly be seen outside the context of the Christian-theocratic theme. What is remarkable is that the peculiar numinous character of the king remained the implicit rather than expressed premiss of those laws directly touching the royal person and activities. Undoubtedly chief in importance amongst these was Chindasvind's famous treason law, II. I. 8.[2] A supreme opportunity would appear to have offered itself here for the king to assert the theocratic thesis in terms similar perhaps to those adopted by the bishops at the Fourth Council of Toledo. That he did not do so was perhaps due to his recognition of the incongruity of employing such language when he himself had usurped the throne from the rightful king, Tulga. Nevertheless, the theme was implicit. Various acts were placed together and treated identically: travelling abroad, or intending to travel abroad, for the purpose of acting 'contra gentem Gothorum vel patriam', attempting or even desiring to stir up trouble within the kingdom 'in contrarietatem regni nostri vel gentis' and trying to bring about the death or deposition of the king or any one of his successors.[3] Two separate notions appeared here. On the one hand was the Germanic,

[1] II. I. 4 (cit. p. 25, n. 8, above): cf. VIII Tol. *Praef.* (411c): 'Regendorum membrorum causa salus est capitis, et felicitas populorum non nisi mansuetudo est principum'. A similar notion early in IV Tol. 75.

[2] The origins of this in the particular events of Chindasvind's accession need not concern us here. On them, and on the law in general, see Zeumer, XXIV, 57–69 – discussing also the possibility of an earlier Eurician provision (differently d'Ors, *Código*, p. 57), conciliar concern with the law in VII Tol. I, allied texts and later amendments – and Thompson, *Goths*, pp. 191–4. For an apparent preventive application of the law against Fructuosus – who escaped all punishment, despite VII Tol. I – see *VSF* 17 and E. A. Thompson, 'Two notes on St. Fructuosus of Braga', *Hermathena*, XC (1957), 58–63. The influence of the law and canon in the post-Visigothic period is the theme of Orlandis, *Poder real*, pp. 125–36 (= *AHDE*, XV (1944), 644–58).

[3] The mandatory penalties of either death or blinding (with in either case forfeiture of property) were not enforced against Paul in 673 despite the invocation of the law (and IV Tol. 75): see *Iudicium* 7, *HW* 27. Ervig introduced alternative corporal penalties – *decalvatio*, flogging, exile and perpetual enslavement to the fisc: for the last cf. XVI Tol. *Tomus* (530b), 10, and the doubtless connected *CH* 59. For Egica's later extension of treason to cover unlawful oaths (against anyone!) see II. 5. 19.

populist concept of treason against the people or land, *Landesverrat.*[1] That this concept still had strong and independent existence is shown by the limitation upon the king in the matter of the reprieve of traitors *contra gentem vel patriam*: supplicants were forbidden to approach the king on behalf of such men, and although he might reprieve them he should act only with the agreement of the bishops and *maiores palatii.*[2]

But there were no such restrictions when the treasonable activity had been directed against the king – 'in necem vel abiectionem nostram sive subsequentium regum'.[3] The notion here was the Roman one of treason against the ruler who stood on high, of high treason, for which Germanic society knew no precedents.[4] To be sure, the characteristic Roman term *maiestas* does not appear in II. I. 8 or elsewhere in the code:[5] to be sure, also, there ruled the practice of requiring the populace to swear an oath of allegiance, in terms of the breach of which the bishops, at least, often viewed offences against the king.[6] But the oath bears no implication of contractualism which might lead us to believe that simple deferential allegiance was not always called for.[7] Neither the original nor the

[1] On which see H. Brunner, *Deutsche Rechtsgesch.*, II, 2nd edn by C. Frh. von Schwerin (Munich–Leipzig, 1928), 881ff.

[2] VI. I. 7.

[3] Ib. The distinction of procedure was not denied by XII Tol. 3: 'Remissio talium qui contra regem, gentem vel patriam agunt...in potestate solum regia apponitur cui et peccasse noscuntur', x Tol. 2, XVI Tol. 10 etc., for mercy was in all cases a unique royal prerogative. But the cited text shows the potential comprehensiveness of *Hochverrat*, for 'royal power' was a virtually unlimited concept, given the theocratic premises. Cf. already the *Antiqua* VI. I. 4, where actions, or intended actions, 'contra *regnum*, gentem vel patriam' are referred to. On the different meanings of *regnum* see Sánchez-Albornoz, 'Senatus', p. 52. See also below, p. 129, n. I.

[4] See W. Ullmann, *Principles of government and politics in the MA*, 2nd edn (London, 1966), pp. 136–7.

[5] But both IV Tol. 31 and VI Tol. 11 use the term in relation to treason ('majestatis obnoxios' and 'pro capite regiae majestatis'): note also 'majestas nostra' in the *Decretum Gundemari* (at the end of the acts of XII Tol.) and HG 64: 'Regiae maiestatis virtutes', as well as the less significant *Etym.* v. 26. 25.

[6] See IV Tol. 75, VIII Tol. 2 (420a), x Tol. 2, XII Tol. I, XVI Tol. 9, 10. But note the absence of the oath from the canons of V and VI Tol., both concerned to protect the king and his family.

[7] Differently F. S. Lear, 'The public law of the Visigothic code', *Speculum*, XXVI (1951), 3–11: see also idem, 'Contractual allegiance vs. deferential allegiance in Visigothic law', *Treason in Roman and Germanic law* (Austin, 1965), pp. 123–35 (where pp. 136–64 carry a reprint of 'Public law'). But note that the oath was one of fidelity to people and country, as well as to king: IV Tol. 75, x Tol. 2, XVI Tol. 10, *Iudicium* 6.

Ervigian version of II. 1. 8 even mentioned the oath,[1] let alone defined in terms of its breach the offences with which they dealt,[2] and although the bishops at the Fourth Council relied heavily upon it, the references in the very same canon to the king as the Lord's Anointed indicate another point of view altogether.[3] In fact, it was quite understandable that the kings should have sought to buttress their position by the employment of an oath which at one and the same time would translate the Roman concept of allegiance into Germanic terms of personal fidelity,[4] would bring home individually and in concrete fashion to each subject the obligations of his status,[5] and would procure for the king the further protection afforded by the spiritual sanction which threatened the sacrilegious perjurer.[6] The super-additional character of the oath appears clearly in an Egican law where blame was attached to the man who neglected to take it precisely because it was by God's will that the king had assumed the

[1] Though Chindasvind obliged the important men of the kingdom to swear to carry out its terms (VII Tol. 1). VIII Tol. *Tomus* (413b), however, speaks of the whole people as having taken the oath: cf. ib. c. 2, where the bishops indulge their biblical and patristic erudition in agonised soul-searching as to whether the oath solemnly undertaken in God's name should be broken at the king's request – and do not surprise when they convince themselves that it should. Further, Thompson, *Goths*, pp. 199–201.

[2] Lear, 'Public law', p. 6, himself notes that II. 1. 8 'comprehends precisely the range of offences, from *perduellio* to high treason, that are embraced under the caption of majesty in Roman law'.

[3] c. 75. The bishops at XVI Tol. clearly found nothing incongruous about referring to the oath and the royal *ius vicarium* in the same sentence: 'Bonum est post Deum regibus, utpote jure vicario ab eo praeelectis, fidem promissam...servare' – where they go on to talk of the Lord's Anointed (c. 9). A meaningful contractual oath really cannot co-exist with a theocratic, anointed monarch. Cf. also XII Tol. 1, *Iudicium* 1.

[4] I do not, of course, mean to imply that the oath of allegiance was in itself of Germanic origin: see, e.g., C. Sánchez-Albornoz, *En torno a los orígenes del feudalismo*, I: *Fideles y gardingos en la monarquía visigoda* (Mendoza, 1942), p. 56, n. 73 (with earlier literature), for the view that its origins were specifically Roman. On the connection of the *Untertaneneid* and the development of the theocratic theme, see Ullmann, *Principles*, pp. 132–3.

[5] Note XI Tol. 10 (requiring an oath in another connection): 'Solet enim plus timeri quod singulariter pollicetur quam quod generali innexione concluditur'. No doubt the kings were particularly concerned to counteract the centrifugal forces of patronage and to prevent connections with a local lord taking precedence over allegiance to themselves.

[6] See IV Tol. 75: 'Sacrilegium quippe est, si violetur a gentibus regum suorum promissa fides' and *Iudicium* 6: 'Sub divini numinis sponsione testati'.

headship of society.[1] The punishment, we may note, was the exceptionally severe one of delivery of the offender and all his property into the power of the king, to be treated at the royal pleasure. It is perfectly natural that treason against the king should have been regarded as one of the most heinous of crimes. If the king possessed the character of a divine lieutenant, how could action against him not have been construed as disobedience to God Himself? The fault of the rebel Paul, in the eyes of the author of the *Iudicium*, was precisely that he seized the kingdom 'contra Dei voluntatem'.[2] And not only action was treated as a matter of the utmost gravity: by a Reccesvindian law, based on biblical authority, the imputation of crime to the king or even the speaking of evil against him placed the ordinary freeman wholly at the royal mercy and brought the confiscation of half the property of a man of higher standing. Even dead kings were protected by the law, with fifty lashes the penalty for their defamation.[3] A further law forbade the consultation of diviners about the king's health or future death, for trouble could easily arise from alarmist or seditious reports.[4] The exalted position of the monarch was the starting-point of other laws also. Wilful refusal to obey the king's command was a serious matter:[5] it was in keeping with this that judges who made unjust decisions on the orders of the king or in fear of him were in no way proceeded against.[6] It was the stature of the king which led Reccesvind to ordain that the monarch should be represented rather than appear in person in court cases in which he was involved: not only would it be insulting for the king to be opposed by a person of more humble estate but who, asked Reccesvind, would dare to stand up to deny a royal claim?[7] The same view of the special status of the king underlay the provision that

[1] II. I. 7. This law contains the only reference to the oath in the code and shows that it was administered to the people at large by *discussores iuramenti*.
[2] *Iudicium* 2.
[3] II. I. 9, on which see Zeumer, XXIV, 69–70. Ecc. 10. 20 and II Peter 2. 10 may be added to the sources cit. in Zeumer's notes to the text. Cf. also V Tol. 5, VII Tol. 1. Penalties for speaking ill of a dead bishop were provided by Mer. 17.
[4] Below, p. 147.
[5] II. I. 33: cf. XIII Tol. 8.
[6] II. I. 29 (but see below in text): cf. II. 5. 12, *in fine*. How II. I. 29 and 33 (last note) can lead Lear, 'Public law', p. 5, to the conclusion that 'the subject's allegiance is binding only so long as the king does right under the law' passes my understanding.
[7] II. 3. I, which applied also to the bishop.

the falsification of documents and counterfeiting of seals be more severely punished when royal *scripturae* were tampered with or when a copy of the royal seal was produced.[1] The supreme position of the monarch was thus both implicit in and protected by the laws. But at the same time these imposed certain limitations upon him. One such, concerning reprieves, has already been noted: we may refer also to the laws providing that both a transaction made in favour of the king, but under duress because as a result of royal extortion, and an unjust judicial decision made at the royal command were invalid,[2] and to Ervig's denial of the royal power to pardon more than once an offender against the anti-Jewish laws.[3] The effectiveness of these restrictions is bound up with the whole question of the rule of law over the king. It is understandable that the king, acting in his capacity as God's terrestrial agent and translating the norms of divine justice into the terms of human law, should have considered his decrees of permanent and universal applicability. Indeed, Reccesvind, in a law which remained in Ervig's code, declared the obligation of kings and people alike to obey the laws he gave:

Damus modestas simul nobis et subditis leges, quibus ita et nostri culminis clementia et succedentium regum nobitas adfutura una cum regimonii nostri generali multitudine universa obedire decernitur hac parere iubetur.[4]

By the law, therefore, kings were subject to the laws: God's law, expressed in the royal laws, bound all.[5]

On the other hand, while necessity, in the shape of royal power, obliged the people to obey the law which was imposed upon them, the king's obedience was voluntary:

Subiectos ad reverentiam legis inpellat necessitas, principis [*leg.*: principes] voluntas.[6]

---

[1] Below, p. 111: d'Ors, *Código*, p. 72, points out that Roman law had known no special treatment of official documents.
[2] II. 1. 6; II. 1. 29. But the first admits that justice may have to wait until after the death of the royal beneficiary!
[3] XII. 3. 27.
[4] II. 1. 2.
[5] Quite in accordance with *Sent.* III. 51. 1 ('Justum est principem legibus obtemperare suis'), etc.
[6] II. 1. 2. The point is apparently overlooked by F. H. Schulz, 'Bracton on kingship', *EHR*, LX (1945), 163.

No law, after all, has efficacy *per se*, but only through its enforcement, and enforcement was precisely the responsibility of the king. If he chose to disregard the laws of his predecessors – or his own – who had the right to say him nay?[1] He was the guardian of the kingdom, the father of his people, the steward of God: he was, in a thoroughly meaningful sense, sovereign.[2] If the divinely sanctioned king elected to amend the existing laws or to ignore them, what justification could be found for effective objection?[3] The problem was one which Reccesvind faced. Intent on protecting for the future the interests of those upon whom he would bestow land which he himself stood to acquire by virtue of a retroactive law, he seized upon the device of the oath as the answer. All future kings were to swear before their accession to uphold the law in question.[4] The move was a skilful one. In the first place, the part of the law requiring the oath to be taken would be enforced not by any king but by those responsible for the appointment of the new monarch, and Reccesvind strove to ensure that the constitutional proprieties upon which the effectiveness of the oath depended would be observed by declaring anathema upon anyone who sought unlawfully to seize the throne and upon those who helped him or gave him spiritual comfort.[5] In the second place,

[1] We may note here a basic inconsistency in the theocratic theme itself. On the one hand the king's legislative sovereignty – under the divine law – was accepted, since he alone was considered competent to issue laws in interpretation of the divine law. On the other it was rejected, since his laws were considered to have the same permanent validity as their ultimate source, the divine law, and thus to bind his successors' freedom of action. Monarchical legislative sovereignty was asserted when a king amended the laws of his predecessors, but by binding his successors to his own law he denied the very basis of his own action. Note, e.g., Egica's abrogation in x. 2. 5 of x. 2. 4, where Reccesvind had said: 'Valitura sanctionis huius eternitate decernitur'!

[2] For the sense of sovereign here see W. Ullmann, 'Der Souveränitätsgedanke in den mittelalterlichen Krönungsordines', *Festschrift P. E. Schramm*, i (Wiesbaden, 1964), 72–89 – though without reference to the Visigoths.

[3] The famous second canon of xiii Tol. (made law by Ervig: see xii. 1. 3) which insists that the king accord open trial by their peers to accused bishops and members of the *officium palatinum* (cf. already iv Tol. 75) reflects the reality of royal arbitrariness. For some preliminary comments on this aspect of the king's character see H. Grassotti, 'La *ira regia* en León y Castilla', *CHE*, xli–xlii (1965), 7–11.

[4] ii. 1. 6: more on this important measure below, p. 63. Reccesvind looked after both the present and the future by threatening palatine officers who murmured against the law with loss of office and half their property and with seclusion from the court.

[5] Ib.: cf. viii Tol. 10 in confirmation and already iv Tol. 75, v Tol. 3 and vi Tol. 17, 18, for conciliar anathemas against usurpers and rebels. 'Tyranny' is the term regu-

the king would after his accession be bound by the solemnity of an oath which he might disregard only at the peril of his soul. The aim therefore was to hold the royal *voluntas* in check by the threat of spiritual sanction. The same motive underlay the conciliar requirement that the intending king swear not to permit Jewish violations of the faith and maintain his oath on pain of anathema.[1]

But these oaths, and those others which the king had to swear before his accession,[2] were not contractual in the sense that their later breach gave justification for constitutional action against an offending king:[3] indeed, once a candidate became king his authority was – one must stress, in theory – wholly unfettered.[4] He sometimes owed his throne to direct election by the *sacerdotes* and *maiores palatii*, it is true,[5] and the bishops laid down in the conciliar acts the qualifications which a suitable candidate must possess.[6] But none of this implied control over the king, once king, any more than does – say – the election by the cardinals of a suitable individual as pope imply their right later to govern him. On the contrary, election meant

larly used in the Visigothic sources for the exercise of power without legitimate authority: see the illuminating article of Orlandis, 'En torno a la noción visigoda de tiranía', *Poder real*, pp. 13–42 (previously in *AHDE*, XXIX (1959), 5–43).

[1] VI Tol. 3.

[2] On these see Sánchez-Albornoz, 'Ordinatio principis', pp. 9–12. VI Tol. 3 makes it clear that such oaths existed already before 638 and concerned various subjects ('inter reliqua conditionum sacramenta'). For a pre-accession oath by Egica see above, p. 33, n. 2. According to *HW* 4 Wamba swore faith 'ex more' to the people before unction.

[3] The parallel often drawn (e.g. M. Martins, *Correntes da filosofia religiosa em Braga dos séc. IV a VII* (Oporto, 1950), pp. 309–11, A. Esteves, *Bracara augusta*, XXI (1967), 266–8, and J. Pérez de Urbel, ib., XXII (1968), 229–30) between the alleged royal-popular agreement and the monastic *pactum* of St Fructuosus, which provided for obedience by the monk, justice by the abbot, is inexact, if for no other reason because the monk had the possibility of recourse to the bishop or count, but the subject to no-one, for the king was supreme.

[4] Generally on the absence in the theocratic scheme of things of any right of deposition of the monarch, see Ullmann, 'Souveranitätsgedanke', pp. 75–6.

[5] VIII Tol. 10: it was this body which was the *senatus* of *CH* 68 according to Sánchez-Albornoz, 'Senatus', pp. 94–9. Earlier, the nobility as a whole ('primatus totius gentis') had had the right of participation with the *sacerdotes* in the appointment: cf. IV Tol. 75 (384c), V Tol. 3.

[6] The throne was forbidden to those whom 'nec origo ornat nec virtus decorat' (V Tol. 3), the meaning of which is shown by VI Tol. 17: 'Genere Gothus et moribus dignus'. Those who had been tonsured or had suffered *decalvatio* and those of servile extraction were also excluded by VI Tol. 17.

nothing more than the provision of an individual qualified in a particular fashion for an office, the powers and rights of which existed from God, not from the electors, and the possession of which, once lawfully gained, could not therefore be lost at their will.[1] The bishops might hold forth on the norms of behaviour which the good king should follow:[2] they might threaten evil kings with anathema.[3] But they never ventured to talk of deposition.[4] The numerous canons in which the councils hedged around the quasi-divinity of the king with threats of the supreme spiritual penalty for traitors both bear abundant witness to the reverence in which the king was held as God's earthly governor and illustrate, by their total failure to talk of justified rebellion, the lack of any ecclesiastical claim to binding control over the king's actions.[5] The famous Isidorian remark, 'rex eris, si recte facias: si non facias, non eris', did not metamorphose from an etymological statement into a declaration of constitutional

---

[1] Generally on this view of election see Ullmann, *Principles*, pp. 145–7. The characteristic usage 'electus in regem' has its Visigothic parallel in VIII Tol. 10: 'Erunt in regni gloriam praeficiendi rectores'. Cf. also XII Tol. 1: 'Qui [sc. rex] ante tempora in occultis Dei judiciis praescitus est regnaturus, nunc manifesto in tempore generaliter omnium sacerdotum habeatur definitionibus consecratus' and the revealing *HW* 2: 'Wamba princeps, quem digne principari Dominus voluit, quem sacerdotalis unctio declaravit, quem totius gentis et patriae communio elegit'.

[2] Cf. particularly the well-known VIII Tol. *Decretum judicii* (431a/b), where the high moral tone appears less commendable when one discovers that the clergy and *maiores palatii* who together drew up the document really required that royal virtue find expression in their own material aggrandisement. For other references to desirable royal qualities see IV Tol. 75 (385c–386a), VIII Tol. 10.

[3] IV Tol. 75 (386a), VI Tol. 3, VIII Tol. 10 etc.

[4] It might be thought that in Egica's reign they did so talk: cf. XVI Tol. 10: 'Si quis sane regum succedentium cunctas hujus constitutionis nostrae definitiones custodire aut adimplere distulerit, omnis linea generationis ejus perpetim condemnata depereat, et insuper ex divino judicio rebus omnibus et honore praesenti in saeculo careat, atque Christo judicante cum diabolo ejusque sociis ad interitum gehennae perveniat'. But both the context and 'ex divino judicio' indicate rather that they were leaving to the divinity the business of removing the king from his position and his goods from the king. It is clear, in any case, that the canon is concerned to safeguard the dispositions of the existing king.

[5] Relevant canons are IV Tol. 75, V Tol. 2, 7, VI Tol. 18, VII Tol. 1, X Tol. 2, XII Tol. 1 and XVI Tol. 10. (For the later use of the canons of IV and VI Tol. at Hohenaltheim – via Pseudo-Isidore – see W. Ullmann, *The Carolingian Renaissance and the idea of kingship* (London, 1969), p. 130.) For a judgement – on Sisbert of Tol. – in accordance with the canons see XVI Tol. 9 and ib. *Decretum judicii*. Note also IV Tol. 30, 45, V Tol. 4, 5, VI Tol. 12, 17, and cf. VIII Tol. 2, XIII Tol. 1 and XVII Tol. 8. For the royal family see below, p. 59, n. 4.

principle in the Visigothic period:[1] indeed, Isidore viewed the evil king in precisely the same way as had St Augustine and Gregory the Great – as God's punishment for a wicked people.[2] The episcopal attitude is encapsulated in the pronouncement of the bishops at the Sixth Council of Toledo:

Nefas est enim in dubium inducere ejus potestatem, cui omnium gubernatio superno constat delegata judicio.[3]

The fiction of abdication was that adopted when Svintila was in fact toppled by armed revolt:

Scelera propria metuens *se ipsum regno privavit* et potestatis fascibus exuit.[4]

The introduction of royal unction, perhaps on the accession of Sisenand which followed Svintila's fall, served only to raise the king even higher above his people and thus to protect him even more securely against any lingering populist notions:[5] certainly it

[1] Despite d'Abadal, *Visigots...catalans*, p. 74, who holds that it found application at IV Tol. But see below, in text, for Svintila's deposition. In fact, c. 75 of the council reads easily as a clever condemnation of the new king, Sisenand: but for a convincing explanation of the language used in terms of a recently suppressed revolt by Iudila, see Thompson, *Goths*, pp. 173–7. On the sources of *Etym.* IX. 3. 4 and the related Isidorian texts, see Anton, pp. 57, n. 58, 388, n. 144.

[2] Cf. *Sent.* III. 48. 7, 11, and on the texts M. Reydellet, 'La conception du souverain chez Isidore de Séville', *Isidoriana*, pp. 460–1.

[3] VI Tol. 14.

[4] IV Tol. 75: cf. Orlandis, *Poder real*, pp. 18–21. There is no more basis here than there is elsewhere for the assertion of Valdeavellano, *Curso*, p. 195, that 'el Rey visigodo podía ser depuesto si no gobernaba rectamente'. Whatever view is taken of Wamba's loss of the throne, there can be no question of justified deposition.

[5] The *terminus ante quem* for the introduction of royal unction is 672, for the texts referring to Wamba's anointing in that year (*HW* 2–4: cf. also *Chron. Reg. Visig.* 44) give us clearly to understand that the rite was not new, as J. de Pange, *Le roi très chrétien* (Paris, 1949), pp. 121–2, observes. The view that already Reccared was anointed (thus, e.g., Sánchez-Albornoz, 'Ordinatio principis', pp. 14–15) has no evidence in its favour, for *HF* IX. 15 is not to the point, and *DEO* II. 26. 2 (adduced by Sánchez-Albornoz) simply contrasts the O.T. unction of kings and priests with the contemporary reception of the chrism by all Christians (see *DEO* II. 26. 1 and R. Kottje, *Studien zum Einfluß des Alten Testamentes auf Recht und Liturgie des frühen MAs* (Bonn, 1964), p. 96, n. 17). A clear *terminus post quem* is on the other hand provided by *Etym.* VII. 2. 2: 'Sicut nunc regibus indumentum purpurae insigne est regiae dignitatis, sic illis [sc. Iudaeis] unctio sacri unguenti nomen ac potestatem

implied for the ministering *sacerdos* no later right of lawful authority over the king.[1] What capital the bishops would eventually have made out of the constitutive unction witnessed at the elevation of Wamba and of Ervig must remain, given the fall of the kingdom only a generation later, simple conjecture.[2] If

regiam conferebat', where the contrast with O.T. times would have been ineffective and absurd if royal unction was practised when Isidore wrote. Cf. also *Etym.* VI. 19. 51 and Reydellet, p. 466, n. 36. Parts of the *Etym.* were first published in 620 (see J. A. de Aldama in *Miscellanea isidoriana* (Rome, 1936), pp. 62–4, and Lynch, pp. 34–51, esp. 43), but if the accession of either Reccared II or Svintila in 621 had witnessed the introduction of anointing, Isidore would surely have mentioned it in the *HG*: the *arg. ex silentio* is here wholly in order. VI Tol. has nothing to offer, despite E. Eichmann, 'Die rechtliche und kirchenpolitische Bedeutung der Kaisersalbung im MA', *Festschrift Georg von Hertling* (Kempten–Munich, 1913), p. 263, n. 7, but there are some grounds for thinking that Chindasvind may have been anointed in 642: see Zeumer, *LV*, p. 460, n. 4, and Sánchez-Albornoz, 'Ordinatio principis', p. 13, n. 43. The most likely date between 621 and 642 is undoubtedly 631, when unction would have provided protection through sanctification for Sisenand, who had seized the throne: the parallel with Pepin is not difficult to draw. Quite in keeping with 631 are the references in IV Tol. 75 to the king as the Lord's Anointed (both Ps. 105. 15 and I Sam. 26. 9 were cited, as also at XVI Tol. 9, when unction was certainly practised). So is the designation of the king as the *minister Dei*: generally on the connection of the royal *ministerium Dei* and unction, see Eichmann, p. 263. That the association of the *sacerdotes* in the appointment of a new ruler is witnessed for the first time in IV Tol. 75 may also reflect the recent introduction of anointing. I do not know what 'legal texts' with 'direct testimony' J. M. Lacarra had in mind when he remarked at Spoleto in 1959 that it was 'clear' that the Visigothic kings were anointed in the first third of the seventh century (*Sett.*, VII (1960), 398).

[1] Aubin, pp. 84–5, exaggerates the control exercisable by the *sacerdotium* at a stage when the stupendous potential of unction could scarcely have been glimpsed. Certainly its significance as an instrument of legitimisation for the king was well grasped: note that the rebellious Paul made a point of declaring that he had been anointed in his *Epistola ad Wambam*: 'In nomine Domini Flavius Paulus *unctus* rex'. But it is highly pertinent to the matter of sacerdotal control to note that Wamba (allegedly) *instructed* that his successor be anointed: see XII Tol. 1: 'Wamba... Ervigium post se *praeelegit* regnaturum et sacerdotali benedictione *ungendum*... Speravit pariter et *instruxit*, ut...Ervigium in regno *ungere* deberet [Julianus]'.

[2] For Wamba see *HW* 3: 'Sacraretur in principe' (the earlier 'regnum...suscipiens' referring, clearly enough, simply to Wamba's acceptance of the throne) and for Ervig XII Tol. *Tomus*: 'Et regnandi conscenderim sedem et sacrosanctam regni perceperim unctionem' and c. 1: 'Ervigius...regni conscenderit culmen, regnandique *per* sacrosanctam *unctionem susceperit potestatem*'. Note also 'in regno ungere' (last note) and *CH* 49: 'Consecratur in regno'. See Orlandis, *Poder real*, pp. 54–5, and Ullmann, *Carolingian Renaissance*, p. 82: E. Müller, 'Die Anfänge der Königssalbung im MA und ihre hist.-politischen Auswirkungen', *HJ*, LVIII (1938), 337–8, is unconvincing.

any bishop claimed more than the right of participation in the appointment of the monarch – a right which was in any case less valuable than is usually thought[1] – no trace of his activity or ideas has survived.[2]

Theory was a long way from practice, however, and the great men of the kingdom needed no elaborate doctrine of justified tyrannicide or deposition as an excuse to rise in arms. No Visigothic king could have been unaware of the distressing readiness of his people – the 'Gothic disease', Fredegar called it[3] – to act *in necem vel abiectionem* of the monarch. It was this factor which doubtless constituted the really effective check on royal arbitrariness, although the check

1 See above, p. 24, n. 3. The Church itself was not, as is often said, staunchly in favour of elective monarchy: see H. da Gama Barros, *Hist. da administração publica em Portugal nos séculos XII a XV*, 2nd edn by T. de Sousa Soares (11 vols, Lisbon, 1945–54?), III, 294–6, E. de Hinojosa, *Obras* (2 vols, Madrid, 1948–55), I, 46–7, and Orlandis, 'La iglesia visigoda y los problemas de la sucesión al trono en el siglo VII', *Poder real*, pp. 43–55 (previously in *Sett.*, VII (1960), 333–51). For Isidore, see *HG* 65, expressing the hope that Ricimer would be 'regni successione dignissimus' and note also the saint's acceptance of the normality of hereditary succession in the earlier period when he wrote of the death of Theodosius, son of Athaulf: 'Nec stabit semen eius...qui patris in regnum succederet' (*HG* 19). It was Braulio and others who, with a reference to David and Solomon, asked Chindasvind to associate Reccesvind in the throne (*Ep.* 37). For the view that heirs-apparent figure on some Visigothic coins, see Mateu y Llopis, 'Arte monetario', pp. 36–7, 54–5: but cf. Miles, p. 46.

2 Isidore's declaration that the monarch was subject to the 'religionis disciplina' and bound to preach the faith by his laws (*Sent.* III. 51. 3) does not detract from the king's stature: what Christian king would have denied this? Nor is an auxiliary function in my opinion indicated by Isidore's remark (*Sent.* III. 51. 4) that the royal task was to compel to righteousness by terror those not persuaded by priestly admonitions. (Note the echo of this in IV Tol. 32.) For the priests were the king's servants in the protection of the *ecclesia* divinely entrusted to the royal protection, and that this protection involved the action of the guardian rather than the police-man (I employ the useful distinction of W. Ullmann, *A hist. of political thought: the MA*, 2nd edn (London, 1970), p. 64, n. †) is shown by the royal accountability: 'Cognoscant principes saeculi Deo debere se rationem reddere propter Ecclesiam, quam a Christo tuendam suscipiunt. Nam sive augeatur pax et disciplina Ecclesiae per fideles principes, sive solvatur, ille ab eis rationem exiget, qui eorum potestati suam Ecclesiam credidit' (*Sent.* III. 51. 6). Cf. also *Sent.* III. 49. 3, and generally Romero, p. 63. To speak of Isidore's 'subservience to the secular power' (thus P. J. Mullins, *The spiritual life according to Saint Isidore of Seville* (Washington D.C., 1940), p. 40) misses the point, however, for it was of the essence of the king's position that he was not a purely secular figure. See also below, pp. 124ff.

3 Fredegar, IV. 82: cf. *HF* III. 30. Nevertheless, only Liuva II and Witteric are known to have been murdered in the Catholic period.

would only have applied, of course, when the law was bent or ignored to the detriment of the optimates. The power and greed for further power of the *maiores* was the constant political reality with which, for all his theocratic status, the king had always to reckon and the rock on which policies based upon nothing more substantial than theoretical royal supremacy were bound sadly to founder.

## Chapter 3

# ROYAL GOVERNMENT, 1

The recognition of the behavioural norms most conducive to the welfare of society and the subsequent translation of these into the form of promulgated written law was, it has been said above, the prime task of the Visigothic monarch. In no other aspect of government, indeed, did he so faithfully and directly fulfil his unique theocratic role as here, in the provision of law, for law was the product of his will and of that alone: the king enjoyed what may be termed a true legislative absolutism in that no need for the participation of others existed and in that he bore immediate, personal and total responsibility for his creation. But the *salus* of the king's subjects could not be assured by the simple existence of law: the provision of means for its application and enforcement was an essential corollary. And however developed the legal and judicial system, it was of no avail if the king had not the financial and military power with which to preserve the tranquillity of the realm against internal dissidents and external foes. The king's role as the divinely sanctioned custodian of the kingdom and its inhabitants could not be fulfilled unless to the ideational activity which produced legislation were added the executive activities of judgement, defence and revenue-raising. In the nature of things, however, it was not possible for him to act the monocrat in these fields as it was in that of legislation. His own control of, and participation in, all aspects of government always remained as a necessary consequence of his supreme accountability to God, but he had no choice but to rely upon others to carry out the bulk of the work. A variety of functionaries operated therefore in the royal service, from the great dignitaries in the royal entourage down to the *servi fiscales* who administered the crown estates, but at the level of local government the chief and constant burden fell upon those officers who combined judicial, administrative and financial functions in their persons – the dukes in the half-dozen provinces of the kingdom, the counts in the cities and the *tiuphadi*, or thousand-men, in the country areas.

That delegation inevitably involved a severe restriction in practice on the theoretical supremacy of the monarch is obvious. The Visigothic king was no more capable of providing effective government at the local level while at the same time ensuring that local officers did not act in disregard of the central authority than was any other ruler until very modern times. He was obliged either to take the strong men of the kingdom into governmental partnership or to make strong those lesser men whom he raised to office: in either event the officers were in the most favourable position to follow an independent and selfish line of their own. Office admittedly involved responsibility and accountability to the king as well as privilege and power. But the constant harping of the laws on some or other form of corruption, negligence or disobedience by the royal officers, while it demonstrates the earnestness with which the king viewed his paternalist function as defender of the people, reveals the rifeness of the offences themselves. For all the high principles of the theocratic monarchy, for all the exalted status of the king, government was carried on in accordance with the royal wishes only to the extent that the king's officers determined, and it is all too plain that governmental disintegration was already far advanced before the Arabs landed at Gibraltar.

The central organ of government was the royal court. We know very little of the court and its functionaries, but the titles borne by the *viri illustres* appearing in the lists of those present at various of the Toledan councils point clearly enough to the spheres of activity, sometimes household, sometimes public, of their holders.[1] In charge of the royal treasuries was the *comes thesaurorum*,[2] while distinct dignitaries, the *comites patrimoniorum*, supervised the administration of the crown lands and the collection of taxes.[3] The chancellery was

---

[1] On the following see Stroheker, *Germanentum*, pp. 230–2, drawing attention to the late-Roman and Byzantine influences, and Valdeavellano, *Curso*, pp. 201–2. The names and titles of the laymen attending the councils are conveniently collected in Zeumer, *LV*, pp. 485–6.

[2] Appearing only at XIII Tol. For theft 'de tesauris publicis', see VII. 2. 10.

[3] The lists of IX, XIII and XVI Tol. each show one *c. patrimonii* (*-iorum*) present, but VIII Tol. was attended by two. A *c. patrimonii* appears also in XII. 1. 2 and the *actor rerum fiscalium* of II Sev. 1 (where the *rector rerum publicarum* is perhaps, as Thompson, *Goths*, p. 294, suggests, *dux* of Baetica: for the same title, see Ildefonsus, *DVI* 7) is probably identical.

presided over by the *comes notariorum*,[1] the chamber by the *comites cubiculariorum*.[2] The *comes spatariorum* controlled the personal body-guard of the king – some at least of whose members were themselves *comites*[3] – while provisions and stables were the respective provinces of the *comites scanciarum* and the *comes stabuli*.[4] Of these dignitaries only the *comes patrimoniorum* will require further mention, for there are no significant references to the others outside the conciliar lists. Royal and public notaries and their *pueri* appear in one law and the names of a few slave functionaries in another,[5] but otherwise we know nothing even of the staffs which most of them must have controlled.

The title of count held by all these high officers was not unique to them. Throughout the kingdom there were to be found the *comites civitatum*, upon whom the civil, particularly judicial, administration essentially depended, and the *comites exercituum*, who were the divisional commanders of the provincial armies. But the title was bestowed also upon other men who were sometimes present at the proceedings of the councils, but who held no specified office,[6] and it seems clear from this that it was a personal title which did not involve any necessary and defined administrative function, even though it was invariably borne by the individual who played a particular governmental role. Even the great office-holders were content to subscribe simply as *comites* on some occasions.[7] The title of *dux* which was

---

[1] The *notarii* of the Visigothic sources were not notaries in the modern sense but secretaries, scribes (particularly clear in iv Tol. 4): see H. García, 'Notas para unos prolegómenos a la hist. del notariado esp.', *Estudios hist. y documentos de los archivos de protocolos*, ii (Barcelona, 1950), 132ff.

[2] Two of whom – both also *duces* – appear at the head of the viii Tol. list. One was present at ix Tol. and two, one as a *c. cubiculi*, at xiii Tol. Note also John of Biclar, 590. 3: 'Quidam ex cubiculo eius, etiam provinciae dux'.

[3] See the list of subscribers to xiii Tol. and on the *spatarii* C. Sánchez-Albornoz, 'El aula regia y las asambleas políticas de los godos', *CHE*, v (1946), 68–70. A *spatarius* appears also in the final edict of xvi Tol.

[4] No less than seven *cc. scanciarum*, five of them dukes, subscribed at xiii Tol. At viii Tol. there were three dukes among the five *cc. scanciarum*. On the title, which must surely sometimes have been honorary, see Stroheker, *Germanentum*, p. 231 with n. 3. The *c. stabuli* appeared only at xiii Tol.

[5] See vii. 5. 9 (an unattributed Novel) for the *notarii* and ii. 4. 4 for the 'stabulariorum, gillonariorum, argentariorum coquorumque prepositi'.

[6] Of the seventeen laymen at viii Tol. one appeared simply as 'comes', another as 'comes et dux', four as 'comes et procer'.

[7] At xv Tol., e.g.: compare the subscribers with those at xiii Tol.

additionally held by some of these important men was similarly personal.[1] But it too was the title regularly conferred upon particular royal officers – the governors of the provinces and the generals commanding the provincial armies.[2]

The *comes* was what he was, in fact, because of his personal relationship with the king: he was, in this respect, the lineal descendant of the member of the *Gefolgschaft* which surrounded the Germanic leader of Tacitus's time and which a variety of sources and terms indicate had continued to surround the early Visigothic king.[3] It was simply that under the pressure of new circumstances, particularly the governmental demands now burdening the king, and no doubt under the influence of the Roman *comitatus*, the essentially military *Gefolgschaft* had metamorphosed into a far more flexible institution. In just the same way, but at a lower level, the *saiones* in the service of individuals throughout the kingdom had taken on other than military functions.[4] As 'companions' of the king, the counts were the men whom he now naturally chose to assist him both privately and in the sphere of government, using them sometimes to fill posts of specified responsibility at court, sometimes to fulfil regular military, administrative and judicial functions in the kingdom at large and sometimes to undertake particular tasks as particular problems arose.[5] The important point is that counts and dukes – for it is convenient to distinguish them, although every duke was also a 'companion' – were such by virtue of their personal relationship

[1] Gibert, 'Particularismo', p. 43. In the conciliar lists *dux* always stands unqualified by indication of function – though the *dux* is always also a *comes*.

[2] Generally on the dukes (though with confusion of military dukes and others), see F. Dahn, *Die Könige der Germanen*, 2nd edn, VI (Leipzig, 1885), 323–7, and Gama Barros, VII, 393–4: further comments throughout this chapter. The *d. provinciae* appears in II. 1. 18, 19, *HW* 7 etc.: note also that Gallia is a *ducatus* in XVII Tol. *Tomus* (553d). We never meet a *comes provinciae* (who is not evidenced by 'provinciarum comites' in VIII. 1. 9 or 'seu a provincie sue duce vel comite' in II. 1. 19: see also Gama Barros, VII, 395–7) or a *d. civitatis* (except in *VPE* V. 10. 6, where the probable explanation of 'ducem Emeritensis civitatis' is that Duke Claudius of Lusitania (see John of Biclar, 589. 2) was also *c. civitatis* of Merida, the capital).

[3] Tacitus, *Germania* 13–15: the texts mentioned are collected and discussed in Sánchez-Albornoz, *Orígenes del feudalismo*, pp. 19–30. The reception of offenders back into royal favour by accepting them as 'participes mensae suae' (XII Tol. 3) certainly recalls Germanic practice.

[4] Below, p. 188.

[5] Below, p. 227, n. 3, for an example.

with the king. There is no indication of a hereditary comital and ducal nobility.[1]

It is both natural and correct to identify with these men the *maiores palatii – seniores, optimates, primi* and *primates palatii* are variant phrases of an equivalent meaning[2] – who appear in the laws and other sources. Of frequent occurrence in the texts is the term *palatinum officium*,[3] which is occasionally used, quite correctly, to designate the whole body of men in the direct service of the king, including even the lesser slaves of the household,[4] but which is usually employed in a less comprehensive sense to indicate merely the higher echelons of that large group. This restricted meaning appears clearly in Ervig's army law, IX. 2. 9, where laymen are divided into those of higher military standing – 'id est dux, comes seu etiam gardingus' – and lesser individuals – 'inferiores sane vilioresque persone' – but where later the distinction is rather between those 'ex palatino officio' on the one hand and the soldiers required to follow their 'ducem aut comitem aut etiam patronum' on the other. The context makes it clear that the changes of terminology are not changes of meaning, and that the *palatinum officium* thus comprised dukes, counts and *gardingi*.[5] But elsewhere the *palatinum officium* is shown to have been composed of the *optimates palatii* and the *gardingi*.[6] It follows that dukes and counts were meant

[1] But see below, p. 184.

[2] But note v Tol. *Praef.* (389b): 'Cum optimatibus et senioribus palatii', where the two groups appear distinct. The *seniores palatii* may at this time (636) have been the counts as a class, with the *optimates pal.* the chief dignitaries in the immediate entourage of the king, for later in the records of the council is found 'tam optimatum quam comitum...sollicitudo' (col. 394a/b). But certainly the terms were later equivalent: see, e.g., XIII Tol. 2.

[3] Of which *aulae regalis officium* is an equivalent. The *pal. off.* is first mentioned in XII. 2. 14 (of 612), but the chamber (John of Biclar, 590. 3) and *c. patrimonii* (XII. 1. 2) are found already under Reccared. That Leovigild organised the *pal. off.* seems likely, especially in view of his other Byzantine-inspired activities: thus, but with sensible caution, Sánchez-Albornoz, 'Aula', pp. 22–7, Stroheker, *Germanentum*, pp. 230–1.

[4] See II. 4. 4, *Iudicium* 5 and XIII Tol. *Tomus* (488c), 6 and *Lex edita*.

[5] Differently Thompson, *Goths*, p. 254, denying that the *gardingi* belonged to the *pal. off.* But see next note.

[6] XIII Tol. 2: 'De accusatis sacerdotibus seu etiam optimatibus palatii atque gardingis ...decrevimus, ut nullus deinceps ex palatini ordinis gradu, vel religionis sanctae conventu...ab honore sui ordinis vel servitio domus regiae arceatur...sed is qui accusatur...in publica sacerdotum, seniorum atque etiam gardingorum discussione

by the various expressions used to indicate 'the greater men of the palace':[1] it further follows that the *gardingi*, although *palatini*, were of lowlier status.[2]

The role of the dukes and counts will be elaborated upon below. To the king they were – to use the happy phrases which Reccesvind applied to the *illustres viri ex officio palatino* in his *Tomus* to the Eighth Council of Toledo – 'in regimine socios, in adversitate fidos'. As a collective body, the *maiores palatii* had little constitutional power as against the king – all that is witnessed is a certain right, mentioned earlier, in the case of the reprieve of some traitors – but in fact it was upon them that the king wholly relied for the day-to-day governance of the kingdom. But what was the role of the *gardingus*?[3] He was clearly a man of importance, who had the ear of the king,[4] and we find *gardingi*, like the *optimates palatii* and the bishops, entitled after 683 to trial before their peers and perhaps present at the promulgation of Ervig's code.[5] The *gardingus* Hildigisus was a significant enough figure to be singled out for mention by Julian of Toledo for his part in the rebellion of Paul against Wamba. Although inferior in title to the *comites*, the *gardingi* could perhaps expect to be elevated

deductus...legum poenas excipiat...Nam et de caeterorum ingenuorum personis, qui palatinis officiis non haeserunt...'. The *seniores pal.* and *gardingi* are distinguished also in some MSS of II. I. I and in *Iudicium* 5.

At the end of IX. 2. 9 a distinction is drawn only between the *primates pal.* and the *minores personae*. But this section concerns corruption among army officers and their subordinates, and the *gardingi* belong to neither category.

[1] But at XIII Tol. four of the 'viri illustres officii palatini' subscribed simply as *proceres*. I think it likely that these men were also *comites*: one of them, Audemundus, later subscribed at XV Tol. as 'comes' and later again, at XVI Tol., as 'comes procer', and another, Teudila, appeared as a *comes* at XV Tol. Teudila also subscribed the acts of XII Tol. but, exasperatingly, no subscribers there indicated their rank. At VIII Tol. four men were described as *comes procer* but there was no simple *procer*. If the *proceres* were not also *comites* their absence from IX. 2. 9 could in any case be explained in terms of their possible character, suggested below, as legal advisers at the court, unconcerned with military affairs.

[2] *Gardingi* no doubt figured among the *mediocres palatii* contrasted with the *primi pal.* in Reccesvind's XII. 2. 15. Note also the distinction between *juniores/minores* and *seniores/primates* of the palace in VI Tol. 13. But there is no reference to the palace in Fredegar, IV. 82, and hence no basis for the identification of the *mediogres* there with the *gardingi* by R. d'Abadal, 'La monarquia en el regne de Toledo', *Homenaje a Jaime Vicens Vives*, I (Barcelona, 1965), 196.

[3] Exhaustive but exhausting on the *gardingus* is Sánchez-Albornoz, *Orígenes del feudalismo*, passim.    [4] See below, p. 227, n. 3.

[5] XIII Tol. 2; II. I. I (in some MSS).

to the higher status.[1] But there is no hint of an administrative province which was peculiarly that of the *gardingus* or of his exercise in the king's name of authority, civil or military, over any section of the population at large.[2]

The character of the *gardingus* is best accounted for in terms of personal loyalty and special military service.[3] We noted above that all the king's subjects were obliged to take an oath of allegiance: but the members of the *officium palatinum* – including, that is to say, the *gardingi* – would present themselves in person before a king newly ascended to the throne in order to swear their loyalty.[4] If this was the oath taken and broken by the rebel duke Paul, it was in written form.[5] It seems certain that it is with these *palatini* that we should identify the *fideles regis*, individuals who owed *promptum ac fidele obsequium, sincerum servitium*, to the king and whose duty was obedience and *salutis ejus custodia vel vigilantia*,[6] but who were certainly not military figures alone.[7] Since the *gardingus* had no govern-

[1] Cf. *HW* 7, describing Hildigisus as 'sub gardingatus *adhuc* officio consistentem'. Did Hildigisus perhaps rebel because he felt slighted at lack of promotion? The appearance of an Ildigisus among the *viri illustres* at XII Tol. in 681 gives particular point to c. 3, dealing with the reception back into communion of traitors again enjoying royal favour.

[2] See, convincingly, Sánchez-Albornoz, *Orígenes del feudalismo*, pp. 77–106.

[3] Thus, wholly acceptably, ib., pp. 107–33. But the discovery of separate origins for *gardingi* and *comites* in, respectively, the *Gefolgschaft* and the Roman *comitatus* is unconvincing and artificial. The king rather used the men pledged to his service according to their trustworthiness and proven capabilities: those of especial value were designated 'companions' and those who had not reached this high status and were restricted to personal military service, *gardingi*. Note that the *comites* known by name were overwhelmingly Gothic in race. The much-discussed *leudes* of IV. 5. 5 were in my opinion not the king's retainers but soldiers in general. See A. d'Ors, 'Dudas sobre *leudes*', *AHDE*, XXX (1960), 643–7: *contra*, Sánchez-Albornoz, *Orígenes*..., pp. 30–8 (where also earlier literature), and 'Aula', p. 24, n. 44, P. Merêa, 'A lei IV. 5. 5 da *Lex Visigothorum* e o poder paternal do direito visigótico', *BFD*, XLI (1965), 67, n. 12. But Sánchez-Albornoz, '"La pérdida de España." El ejército visigodo: su protofeudalización', *CHE*, XLIII–XLIV (1967), 27, n. 122, reports d'Ors now to have changed his mind.

[4] II. 1. 7 (Egica): 'Ut moris est'.

[5] *Iudicium* 6. Paul's *socii* had themselves sworn 'ut et fideles illi essent' even to the death: ib.

[6] Phrases from V Tol. 6, VI Tol. 14.

[7] VI. 1. 6 (below, p. 94) argues against a purely military character, as does 'inutilis in rebus commissis' in VI Tol. 14 where military *res* alone are surely not meant. The *viri illustres* were *in adversitate fidi* (above, in text). Generally on the *ff. regis* (further mentioned in IX. 2. 8, where also *nostri homines*) see Sánchez-Albornoz, *Orígenes del*

mental role, however, the suggestion that the obligations of his *fidelitas* took a personal military form is peculiarly convincing: we know, in fact, that his participation in campaigns was a matter of great significance to the king.[1] And since army service was a general duty, it is necessary to think in terms of a special form of military contribution. This could hardly have been simple cavalry-service,[2] for all important men would in any case have fought on horseback, mounted warfare being, as will appear, the particular strength of the Goths. One might speculate that the obligation of the *gardingus* was rather to provide a band of mounted, or at least highly trained, soldiers on the royal demand. In Ervig's army law the *gardingi* do in fact appear as *patroni*, leading their own men on campaign and distinguished from the military dukes and counts who were the chief officers of the regular units.[3]

But service was not to be had for nothing. Loyalty had to be made worthwhile: royal munificence was a political necessity, for only by gifts and grants to those in his service could the king hope to keep them faithful to himself and – particularly important, given the absence of a constitutionally recognised hereditary monarchy – perhaps to provide some protection for his family when he died.[4] It was simple self-interest and concern for dynastic advantage which led kings like Chintila and Reccesvind to try to guarantee the position of their supporters for the future.[5] Service was bought and rewarded by the monarch, as it was by the great men of the kingdom, in two

*feudalismo*, pp. 41–76. To Thompson, *Goths*, pp. 252–3, they were identical with the *gardingi*. But I can see no contrast between the *optimates/seniores palatii* and the royal *fideles* in v Tol. *Praef.*, while in Mer. 3, ordering daily masses for the safety of the king, his *fideles* and the army, *fideles* surely includes the dukes and counts who were the commanders and the king's right-hand men?

[1] IX. 2. 9.
[2] Thus, Sánchez-Albornoz, *Orígenes del feudalismo*, pp. 145–50, accepted by d'Abadal, 'Monarquia', pp. 197–8.
[3] IX. 2. 9: see below, p. 75.
[4] Canons concerned with the protection of the royal children and their property are v Tol. 2, vi Tol. 16, xiii Tol. 4, iii Sar. 5, xvi Tol. 8, xvii Tol. 7. See also xv Tol. (520a–524b), with the contrary purpose. The person of a widowed queen was of especial significance, since she was bound to have influential support: see on the matter J. Orlandis, 'La reina en la monarquía visigoda', *Poder real*, pp. 102–23 (also in *AHDE*, xxvii/xxviii (1957/8), 109–35) and xiii Tol. 5, xvii Tol. 7. iii Sar. 5, ordering the widowed queen to enter a nunnery, was circumstantial, since aimed at Egica's mother-in-law: see Dahn, *Könige*, p. 480, Thompson, *Goths*, p. 243.
[5] See below in text for Chintila and above, p. 45, below, p. 63, for Reccesvind.

principal fashions. Outright gift was one method. Royal donations were, juridically speaking, in no way different from any others: they were held in full ownership by their recipient and irrevocable except in the event of his or her 'culpa' – which is doubtless to say, *ingratia*.[1] Such gifts, as a rule richer than those to be had elsewhere, would always have been eagerly sought after, but their value could only have been enormously enhanced – and the king's own political position correspondingly strengthened – once Chindasvind had introduced restrictions on the disposal of goods by those with direct descendants, for property received by donation was exempt from these.[2]

Alongside gifts proper, kings also made use of grants *in stipendio*.[3] These were remuneratory concessions of land, made also by patrons to their private soldiery and by the Church to its servants, clerical or lay, and held conditionally upon the obedience and service of the grantee.[4] In that they were of indefinite duration and economically gratuitous,[5] they corresponded in character to those concessions made *iure precario* in classical times,[6] but they differed from these in that they might not be revoked at will but only when the stipendiary was in breach of his obligations.[7] For a *fidelis regis* such a breach was

[1] See II. 1. 8, IV. 2. 16, 5. 5, and especially v. 2. 2, 3. For gifts to the king, on the other hand, see II. 1. 6.

[2] See below, p. 237, with n. 6.

[3] See XIII Tol. 1, showing treatment of traitors' forfeited property in three distinct ways – (i) 'fisci...juribus applicata', (ii) 'largitione principali...donata' and (iii) 'in stipendio data': cf. the 'concedere vel donare' of some MSS of IX. 2. 9 and the *conpendia* received from the king by judges in XII. 1. 2. On the whole matter of grants *in stipendio* see Sánchez-Albornoz, *Orígenes del feudalismo*, pp. 157–90, and idem, *El 'stipendium' hispano-godo y los orígenes del beneficio prefeudal* (Buenos Aires, 1947), passim. A useful review of the latter is that by Merêa, *Estudos*, pp. 299–312.

[4] Patronal grants (nowhere in fact called *stipendia*): below, p. 187. Church *stipendia*: IV. 5. 6, v. 1. 4, 1 Sev. 2, Narb. 10–13, IV Tol. 33, VI Tol. 5, Mer. 12, 13, XVI Tol. *Tomus, 5*.

[5] See the arguments of Sánchez-Albornoz, *Stipendium*, pp. 28–40.

[6] Sánchez-Albornoz, *Stipendium*, passim, argues that the Visigothic *stipendium* was directly derived from the Roman *precarium*: see further idem, *Estudios sobre las instituciones medievales esp.* (Mexico City, 1965), pp. 521–46, against the opposing view of E. Levy, 'Vom römischen Precarium zur germanischen Landleihe', *ZRG.RA*, LXVI (1948), 1–30, echoed in idem, *Weströmisches Vulgarrecht. Das Obligationenrecht* (Weimar, 1956), pp. 251ff. But see next note.

[7] Differently Sánchez-Albornoz, *Stipendium*, pp. 39, 85, 89 *et saepe* (but cf. p. 96: 'Concesiones vinculadas a la prestación misma de tales servicios y a la duración de

represented either by his *infidelitas* or by his *inutilitas in rebus com-missis.*[1] In the case of patronal *stipendia*, the death of a particular benefactor or beneficiary presented no problems: the lands continued to be held by the stipendiary or by his children as long as the services required were rendered, either to the original patron or to his heirs. And the same applied in the case of ecclesiastical *stipendia*, where, indeed, the patron could never die.[2] But the loyalty of a *fidelis regis* was to a particular king, whose successor might well not be his son, and the question of the fate of *stipendia* held by the *fidelis* in return for service was therefore a tricky one. If right to these *stipendia* legally ceased at the death of the royal grantor, it was nevertheless no doubt the practice that many *fideles* were taken into the service of the new ruler and allowed to retain their holdings.[3] No law reflects the canon which decreed that future kings should not dispossess Chintila's *fideles* of the positions and property they had acquired but rather treat this property as theirs in full gift, disposable at will and revocable only on the grounds of proven *infidelitas* – that is to say, *culpa* or *ingratia* – towards the dead king,[4] and the provision is best seen as Chintila's circumstantial device to bind his *fideles* the closer to him and perhaps to win their support for the succession of his son, Tulga, who would be most likely to adhere to the terms of the canon.

los mismos'). But in IV. 5. 6, ordering the return of goods usurped by bishops and distributed by them *in stipendio*, neither bishops nor stipendiaries had lawful title: in any case, statute is statute. And in VI Tol. 5 revocation was on the grounds of disobedience: cf. Mer. 13.

[1] VI Tol. 14. I have followed Sánchez-Albornoz in treating this canon as concerned with grants *in stipendio*, but have my doubts. The text is not explicit and the next canon, concerning donations to the Church (differently Sánchez-Albornoz, *Orígenes del feudalismo*, p. 163, n. 16, seeing conditional grants) refers back to VI Tol. 14 in terms suggesting that donations were dealt with there also. Only revocation *causa inutilitatis* argues against donations as the subject-matter. See also XIII Tol. 2, *in fine*, denying the king's right to dispossess his servants 'aut servitii sui officio torpentes aut in commissis sibi actibus...mordaces vel potius negligentes' of *res propriae*, where the right to dispossess of royal grants is perhaps implied.

[2] When a cleric's widow was permitted 'sola miseratione' to retain land held by her husband if she commended her children to Church service, 'mercifulness' was involved because, we should believe, the children were not of the age to perform the services required (V. 1. 4).

[3] The personal appearance of palatine officers before a new king is relevant here.

[4] VI Tol. 14. If revoked the property was 'fidelibus largiendum'! Cf. V Tol. 6 for an earlier attempt similarly to protect the *ff. regis*.

The significance of these grants of land *in stipendio* for the question of the origins of feudalism will not have been missed. It was, in fact, precisely the concession of land in return for military service in the future which was the hope of St Fructuosus' brother-in-law when he approached the king with the request that he be granted monastic estates 'quasi pro exercenda publica expeditione'.[1] Since service in the army was the duty of all, some special military obligation must have been envisaged here, and it is tempting to believe that this was precisely that suggested above, the provision of a band of able, professional soldiers, perhaps mounted. Such an obligation would have been expensive to fulfil and would fully have justified the grant of lands. It may be, therefore, that we have here the case of a would-be *gardingus*, especially since the applicant, to judge by his marriage to the daughter of a duke, was of high birth. However that may be, it would be unduly cautious not to conclude that the basic feature of feudalism in its narrower, military sense existed already in the seventh-century Visigothic kingdom: if we cannot call the Visigothic state feudal we can at least talk with justification of Visigothic feudalism.

Grants of lands to his supporters were probably the most considerable outgoing which the king had to face, but the expenses of the upkeep of the court and the army, together with extraordinary expenditure in the form of the endowment of churches, the rewarding of informers and other items of a greater or lesser nature all added to the bill.[2] The land and money needed to defray these various expenses were provided in the main by the crown estates and those belonging personally to the king, their revenues and the proceeds of taxation. It is clear that from the earliest times the Visigoths rejected the view of a patrimonial kingdom and drew a distinction between the king's personal possessions and the lands of the fisc – presumably originally comprising the old Imperial estates.[3] In the code the

---

[1] *VSF* 3, on which see Sánchez-Albornoz, *Orígenes del feudalismo*, pp. 168–73, and idem, *Stipendium*, pp. 123–9, who yet does not think of the applicant as an intending *gardingus*. Merêa, *Estudos*, pp. 261–2, 310, is critical.

[2] For royal foundations see John of Biclar, 587. 7, Isidore, *Chronica* 416a, *FV* 9 etc. The church of St Juan de Baños still bears Reccesvind's dedicatory inscription (reproduced in R. Menéndez Pidal (ed.), *Hist. de Esp.*, III: *Esp. visigoda* (Madrid, 1940), p. 510). For informers see VII. 6. 1, XII. 2. 14.

[3] See Dahn, *Könige*, pp. 249, 252–3.

distinction was explicit.[1] A notable Reccesvindian law, II. I. 6, provided that property which the king gained from his relations by right of inheritance or by some or other transaction, or which he acquired in any manner before becoming king, was subject to the normal laws of inheritance. But property acquired by the king while he held office and in his royal capacity – 'pro regni apice' – was to pass on his death into the control of his successor in the kingdom, given always – and the proviso was of the utmost significance – that he had not disposed of it in some way, as was his right: it was then in turn open to his successor to dispose of it as he wished. Despite appearances, the law was *législation de circonstance*: it seems clear that Reccesvind made the measure retroactive to the time of Svintila, thirty years before, precisely because the personal heirs of past rulers had successfully asserted rights of intestate inheritance over property which these monarchs had acquired 'pro regni apice' and it was his purpose both to reclaim this and to dispose of it freely himself.[2] Unfortunately, neither II. I. 6 nor the *Decretum* of the Eighth Council of Toledo with which it is closely connected speaks directly of the king's rights over long-standing crown possessions. But that a distinction was recognised between these and acquired property is not only apparent from the law – for established crown lands had clearly not passed to private heirs by way of intestate succession as had acquisitions – but an essential postulate, given the absence of accepted hereditary monarchy. If all crown property had been at the free testamentary disposal of the kings, as acquisitions were both before and after Reccesvind's day,[3] they would not have neglected to avail themselves of the opportunity of so enriching their friends and relatives that a successor, if chosen from outside this circle, would have been left virtually destitute. Long-established crown property,

[1] Further to the following, note IX. I. 21 (Egica): 'Fisci vel proprietatis nostre' and XIII Tol. 6: 'Locorum fiscalium atque etiam proprietatis regiae'. For the distinction of royal from public *utilitas*, see M. Torres, 'El estado visigótico', *AHDE*, III (1926), 375–6, 425–6, 474–5: note that a fiscal suit is *utilitatis publice actio* in II. 3. 10.

[2] See the excellent exposition of Zeumer, XXIV, 45–57, who investigates the relationship between II. I. 6 and VIII Tol. *Decretum judicii*, in which the bishops and palatine officers had put forward distinct proposals favourable to themselves. But they confirmed the king's law in c. 10. A useful account also in Ziegler, pp. 107–12.

[3] In II. I. 6 Reccesvind disclaimed any right to repossession of acquisitions earlier disposed of by will.

with some possible minor exceptions,[1] must be thought to have been inalienable.[2]

It seems likely that the *villici* whom we occasionally meet in the laws were functionaries acting, rather like the Frankish *domestici*, as the overseers of groups of these crown estates.[3] Certainly they were important men, judges and revenue-collectors, whose possible abuse of power was a matter of serious concern to the king.[4] No doubt the *actores* and *procuratores* who administered the particular estates were frequently slaves, *servi fiscales*,[5] but they possessed nevertheless considerable power, for the law had to insist that they did not proceed extrajudicially against a freeman in dispute with a lesser slave of the estate but represented this latter in court.[6] It was even necessary for the king to instruct the *servi fiscales* that they might not alienate lands or slaves from crown ownership or manumit the *mancipia*: the emancipation of crown slaves might occur only by written disposition of the king. But they were permitted to sell lands or slaves to their *conservi* and to use the proceeds for their own pious purposes.[7] The *servi fiscales* who bought from them clearly had money to spare and could recognise the possibility of profit in administering more land: it seems probable therefore that they were allowed to keep a proportion of the income their estate yielded.

The tax system of the Visigothic kingdom is profoundly obscure. But it is at least apparent that the basic taxes fell on lands, houses and slaves, for it was the reception of precisely these objects of property from a *curialis* or *privatus* liable to provide horses for the *cursus*

---

[1] The manumission of crown slaves is mentioned in v. 7. 15, 16, and alienation in XII. 2. 14, and there is no mention of compensatory provision from the king's private resources. But a slave should perhaps be classed as an acquisition.

[2] A conclusion wholly in harmony with the view of the tutelary role of the king which has been set out above. The essential question of alienability is not dealt with in the unfruitful and sometimes inaccurate article of L. López Rodó, 'Distinción entre los patrimonios de la corona y del rey en la monarquía visigótica', *Colección de estudios en homenaje al profesor Camilo Barcia Trelles* (Santiago, 1945), pp. 345–67. Idem, *El patrimonio nacional* (Madrid, 1954), has not been available to me.

[3] See Sánchez-Albornoz, *Orígenes del feudalismo*, pp. 98–101, though with confusion of royal and other *villici*.

[4] See VIII. 1. 5, XI. 1. 2, XII. 1. 2: for the earlier period Cassiodorus, *Variae* v. 39.

[5] See XIII Tol. 6.

[6] XII. 1. 2: cf. VIII. 1. 5.

[7] v. 7. 15, 16: cf. v. 7. 19 (Egica) and III Tol. 15, requiring bishops to seek royal confirmation of endowments by *servi fiscales*.

*publicus* and (*vel*) to pay taxes which obliged the new owner, by order of v. 4. 19, to assume the liabilities of the alienator.[1] Registration was no doubt in those same polyptychs in which, in Sisebut's time, had been inscribed the names of enfranchised slaves of the Jews.[2] It appears from a sixth-century conciliar text that the assessment of tax was made on the basis of a unit known as a *modius canonicus*, but the extent of this, though it was certainly not less than a *iugerum* in the case of arable land, is unknown.[3] Crown slaves also paid taxes, for when in 683 Ervig wrote off the arrears of *tributum* outstanding from the years before his accession, the remission was in favour of both the *privati* and the *servi fiscales*.[4] Indeed, the payment of *tributum* was, with the alternative of direct service, a prime indication of their servile status,[5] and was demanded, clearly to ensure that crown rights of ownership were maintained, even when the slave had severed his immediate connection with the fisc.[6]

It is usually asserted that the Goths as a whole were exempt from taxation, at least in the early years, either on all the property which they held and acquired or at any rate on the portion they received in the original division of lands.[7] This may be so, but it is not shown

[1] The early statement that *curiales* and *privati* ought not to alienate their property is explicable in terms of a characteristically Chindasvindian concern for the fate of their children. Further on v. 4. 19, below, in text.

[2] XII. 2. 13: 'Et prenotati in polipticis publicis adque secundum eorum peculium iustissima aderatione censiti'.          [3] Below, p. 70, n. 1.

[4] XIII Tol. *Tomus*, 3 and final edict (cols 502–3), XII. 1. 3. I cannot see the grounds for holding that only the tax on slaves was remitted (thus Thompson, *Goths*, pp. 215, 233). *Tributum* certainly did not indicate a tax on slaves alone, and tax-payers would hardly have surrendered arable land and vineyards (thus the edict) to pay such a levy. Egica too remitted *tributum*: III Sar. *Epil.* (322b), XVI Tol. 8. For remission or tax-lightening by Reccared see *HG* 55 (where also 'tributa').

[5] See X. 2. 4, declaring the general fifty-year limitation period (X. 2. 2) inapplicable in the case of fugitive crown slaves 'quamvis nihil in pensione tributi persolverint'. X. 2. 5 (Egica) revoked this privilege (and that exempting cases concerning crown slaves *in contentione* from the thirty-year rule) on condition that the fifty years had passed 'sine aliqua tributi vel servitii inpensione'. See also XVI Tol. *Tomus*: 'Ab omni palatino expulsa officio sub tributali impensione fisco debeant perpetim inservire'.          [6] Below, p. 68, n. 3.

[7] Thus, e.g., E. Pérez Pujol, *Hist. de las instituciones sociales de la Esp. goda* (4 vols, Valencia, 1896), II, 184, F. Thibault, 'L'impôt direct dans les royaumes des ostrogoths, des wisigoths et des burgundes', *Nouvelle revue hist. de droit français et étranger*, XXVI (1902), 34–8, and, particularly, C. Sánchez-Albornoz, *Ruina y extinción del municipio romano en Esp. e instituciones que le reemplazan* (Buenos Aires, 1943), pp. 133–9. But doubtful is d'Ors, *Código*, pp. 176, 179–80.

by the sources. The text normally adduced in support, x. 1. 16, provided that a Roman 'third' usurped by a Goth be restored to the rightful owner 'sine aliqua dilatione...ut nihil fisco debeat deperire' and appears thus to point to Gothic exemption. But if the law is read in conjunction with its immediate predecessor – which, indeed, if read in isolation makes little sense – a different interpretation presents itself. The probable meaning of this first law is that a landlord and his tenant-farmer (*accola*) should share the tax due on a 'third' illegally held and then restored, the sum required from each being determined by the proportion of the usurped land held.[1] It was surely because the Roman who had lost his *tertia* was for that very reason in no position to pay the tax due upon it, and because the Gothic usurper was also paying nothing – for legal liability would still have been the owner's – that x. 1. 16 urged the authorities to restore an appropriated 'third' without delay, so that the fisc, being then able to claim its allotment from the proven usurper, might lose nothing. Nor does v. 4. 19, referred to above, evidence Gothic exemption. Chindasvind's purpose, it seems clear, was to call a halt to the loss of revenue occasioned by the alienation of taxable property to immunity-holders: the requirement of a declaration of tax-liability when the new owner was not already a tax-paying *curialis* or *privatus* was doubtless to ensure that his name would appear in the tax-registers from which it had previously been absent.[2] But there is no

[1] The title of x. 1. 15 is 'Ut, qui ad excolendum terram accipit, sicut ille, qui terram dedit, ita et iste *censum* exolvat'. The text reads: 'Qui accolam in terra sua susceperit, et postmodum contingat, ut ille, qui susceperat, cuicumque tertiam reddat, similiter *sentiant* et illi, qui suscepti sunt, sicut et patroni eorum, qualiter unumquemque contigerit'. The sense of *sentire* here is perhaps 'to suffer the ill-effects of'. For other interpretations of the law see d'Ors, *Código*, pp. 183–4.

[2] Since *privati* and *curiales* are treated identically throughout the law I cannot believe that it had anything to do with the release of the curials from the bonds of their office, as Thompson, *Goths*, pp. 211–12, holds. Rather, I follow the thesis of Sánchez-Albornoz, *Ruina*, passim, but especially pp. 50ff. (echoed in idem, 'El gobierno de las ciudades en Esp. del siglo V al X', *Sett.*, VI (1959), 359–87), that the *curiales* were no longer possessed of any significant governmental role. But some minor functions were perhaps still exercised in the early seventh century: see *FV* 21 and 25 (the only other seventh-century allusions to the *curia*, apart from the worthless *Etym.* IX. 4. 23ff. and IV Tol. 19, which elsewhere does not reflect contemporary reality), referring to registration in the *gesta publica*, where the suggestion of Sánchez-Albornoz, *Ruina*, pp. 101–2, that these *formulae* date in content from the fifth century is not easy to reconcile with the absence of *institutio heredis* in the first and the dating by regnal years in the second.

more evidence that these immunity-holders were the Goths as a whole than there is that the tax-paying curials and *privati* were exclusively Roman.[1] Favoured individuals may have been exempt, or immunity may have been enjoyed by the palatine officers. We cannot know.[2]

Some sort of a case, on the other hand, can be made out for the exemption of the Church from tax liability,[3] a case undisturbed by v. 4. 19, since this dealt only with the reception of taxable property by individuals. The scanty evidence consists chiefly in a law of Wamba issued in December 675.[4] Since the Church never died, it was a general canonical rule that ecclesiastical freedmen and freedwomen remained, with their children, *in obsequio ecclesiae* and that even the children of unions with persons of free birth did not escape this obligation.[5] Property inherited from a free parent thus passed into the control of the Church. Wamba recognised the profitable convenience to the Church of this regime and drastically altered it. Children born of such mixed unions within the thirty years preceding 675 were now to have the status of free persons and to inherit all the property stemming from their freeborn parent. As for the future, Wamba decreed that the judges were to proceed against mixed unions: they were to flog the marriage-partners and to separate them, and this, if necessary, three times. But if the couple persisted in their

---

[1] Differently, Sánchez-Albornoz, *Ruina*, pp. 64, 136.

[2] It may be noted that the Ostrogoths were not exempt from the land-tax: Jones, *Empire*, I, 251.

[3] A view not found in the literature, however: see, e.g., Dahn, *Könige*, pp. 256–7, Pérez Pujol, II, 185, and III, 264–8, G. Martínez Díez, *El patrimonio eclesiástico en la Esp. visigoda* (Comillas, 1959), pp. 174–83.

[4] IV. 5. 7, which, remarkably, T. Melicher, *Der Kampf zwischen Gesetzes- und Gewohnheitsrecht im Westgotenreiche* (Weimar, 1930), p. 134, saw as a *concession* to the Church. In fact, the bishops must have regretted their complimentary remarks about Wamba at XI Tol. (*Praef.* and c. 16) a few weeks earlier.

[5] See III Tol. 6, I Sev. 1, IV Tol. 69, 70 ('quia nunquam moritur eorum patrona'), IX Tol. 15: IX Tol. 13, 14, and Mer. 20 refer to free–freed unions. Rejection of ecclesiastical *patrocinium* by freed persons or their descendants brought enslavement *ingrati actione* (IV Tol. 71, VI Tol. 10, Mer. 20: cf. II Sev. 8 for a case) as did failure to profess their status within a year of the induction of a new bishop (IV Tol. 70, VI Tol. 9: but cf. the later more sympathetic III Sar. 4). Freedmen and their descendants might not dispose of their *peculia* to outsiders, and if they lacked direct heirs the property passed to the Church: I Sev. 1, IV Tol. 74, IX Tol. 16. For valid manumission and freedom from *obsequium* see below, p. 179, n. 6. See further Martínez Díez, *Patrimonio*, pp. 136ff.

relationship, they suffered no further direct punishment. The king simply ordered that any children of the union should be enslaved to him and that the free parent's property, as well as any goods acquired by the children, should pass to the parent's free heirs. The reason for Wamba's action is expressed early in the law: he legislated because:

Quod in augmentum publice utilitatis debuit crescere, hoc in manifestam inligationem persone vel rerum cognoscitur devenire, dum his, qui de tam infami coniugio nascitur...una cum rebus suis omnibus ecclesiasticae servituti addicitur.

But how was the existing practice contrary to the *publica utilitas*? It left no-one destitute,[1] and Wamba obviously had no humanitarian concern for the welfare of the children. *Publica utilitas* can bear no military significance here, for the Church and its servants were not exempt from military obligations. But *publica utilitas* is used elsewhere in connection with taxation,[2] and it may be suggested that it was precisely because the Church enjoyed immunity from taxation that Wamba considered its acquisition of property detrimental to the public interest.

Support for the view that the Church was exempt is furnished by a canon of the Third Council of Toledo which provided for the repayment to the Church of the *tributum* rendered on a slave cleric *ex familia fisci* in recognition of crown ownership.[3] Moreover, the free clergy were exempt from taxation on their own lands,[4] and the

[1] Destitution was the apparent concern in IV. 5. 1, where Chindasvind condemned the disposal of property to the detriment of children 'ut utilitatibus publicis nihil possint omnino prodesse' and took action to restrict parental freedom: 'Sed ne ...utilitati publice quandoque depereat, quod perire non debet...'. But it is not impossible that despite references to transfer 'causa luxurie...in personas extraneas' etc., Chindasvind had the Church in mind: certainly his new law must seriously have affected its accumulation of property.

[2] E.g., II. 1. 22 (?), v. 4. 19, XII. 2. 18 (Egica), XVI Tol. *Tomus* (530a).

[3] III Tol. 8: 'Clericos ex familia fisci nullus audeat a principe donatos expetere, sed reddito capitis sui tributo Ecclesiae Dei cui sunt alligati, usque dum vivent regulariter administrent'. The last part of this cannot mean: 'Let them serve the church...' (thus J. Vives, *Concilios visigóticos e hispano-romanos* (Barcelona–Madrid, 1963), p. 127) for *administrare* takes the accusative. Rather, 'Ecclesiae' is dative: the tax is to be restored to the church. Restored by whom, if not the king, to whom it had been paid in recognition of crown ownership? For different views of the canon, see Pérez Pujol, III, 264, n. 2.

[4] IV Tol. 47: but a different view of the text in Martínez Díez, *Patrimonio*, pp. 180–1.

68

reason given – that they might be at liberty to devote themselves to God's service – would justify *a fortiori* the exemption of Church lands in general. Lastly, there is a negative argument from the almost total absence in the sources of the period of any reference to ecclesiastical payments to the crown. The only texts which might be adduced as positive evidence that the Church was taxed are the *Tomus* and fifth canon of the Sixteenth Council, where bishops were forbidden to use the resources of the parish churches 'pro regiis inquisitionibus' but exhorted to pay the 'solita perquisitionum obsequia' from the estates of the cathedral church. None of the terms used here appears elsewhere in connection with the payment of taxes. It is unclear what the texts mean, but we should perhaps understand them to be concerned with voluntary but customary (*solita*) aids or with hospitality and gifts offered to the king when he was on progress around the country (*regiae inquisitiones?*).[1]

The *curiales* no longer played any part in the collection of taxes,[2] but they had not been replaced by special revenue-officers. The major functionaries charged with the duty of tax-collection in Ervig's day were rather the duke, count, *tiuphadus*, *numerarius* and *villicus*, together with their deputies.[3] Of these officers, the first three were the regular civil servants of the king and the last probably the overseer of a group of crown estates: all these men had clearly defined areas over which they exercised authority in the king's name and within which, we can reasonably assume, they were responsible for the gathering of the revenue. The position of the *numerarius* can be clarified by reference to the precious evidence of a document of 592.[4] From this it would seem that certain cities within each province were the centres of large financial districts, for Barcelona appears as the centre to which were paid the taxes from an area containing other cities of the size and importance of Tarragona, Egara, Gerona and Ampurias. Perhaps these central cities were those in which royal treasuries were built. The two *numerarii* of Barcelona, appointed by the *comes patrimonii*, had fixed the rate at which tax was to be paid, and this rate was confirmed by the bishops of the tax-paying terri-

---

[1] *Inquisitio* in the code means '(judicial) inquiry', *obsequium* 'formal obedience'.
[2] Sánchez-Albornoz, *Ruina*, pp. 54–68.
[3] All in the edict of remission of xiii Tol.
[4] The *De fisco Barcinonensi*, found at the end of the canons of i Barc.

tories at fourteen *siliquae* for each fiscal unit. Those who wished to pay in kind were to arrange this with the *numerarii*.[1]

On the – admittedly dangerous – assumption that a similar regime continued to operate until Ervig's reign, and bearing in mind other texts which refer now to the election of a *numerarius* by the bishop and people, now to his appointment by the king, one might hazard the hypotheses that while the *villici* were responsible for the collection of taxes from crown estates, the *tiuphadi* and the *comites civitatum* (or, in provincial capitals, the *duces*) were entrusted with the task of gathering the taxes due from the territories under their respective jurisdictions; that a local *numerarius*, chosen by the bishop and people in each city,[2] was responsible for supervising the tax-lists and checking the accounts; and that the goods or monies – with the exception of some which were doubtless diverted at local level for the provisioning of the army – were then passed on to the central financial cities where they were received, just as they had originally been demanded, by *numerarii* appointed by the king or by the *comes patrimonii*.[3]

[1] 'Pro uno modio canonico…exigere debeatis…siliquas octo, et pro laboribus vestris siliquam unam, et pro inevitabilibus damnis vel inter pretia specierum siliquas quatuor quae faciunt in uno siliquas quatuordecim'. (There were clearly two *numerarii*, each taking a fee of one *siliqua*.) It is out of the question that this establishes the commutation rate for payments in grain (for any other commodity would surely have been specified). Fourteen *siliquae* (seven-twelfths of a *solidus*) for a *modius* would give a price nearly double the one *tremis* paid in Gaul in time of famine (*HF* VII. 45: see D. Claude, 'Zu Fragen der merowingischen Geldgesch.', *Vierteljahrschrift für Sozial- und Wirtschaftsgesch.*, XLVIII (1961), 238) which was itself unheard-of and far in excess of anything known elsewhere (see the statistics gathered in Jones, *Empire*, I, 445–6). Nor can *modius* have its occasional meaning of a third of a *iugerum*, for the rate would still then have approached three times the highest known elsewhere for arable land, that in southern Italy under Valentinian III, where, it has been estimated, more than two-thirds of the crop would have gone in taxes even if the yield had been as high as in Egypt: see Jones, *Empire*, III, 129, n. 128, and idem, *The decline of the ancient world* (London, 1966), pp. 179–80. *Modius canonicus* should therefore in my view be identified as the technical term for a fiscal unit. No doubt the extent of the lands comprising this varied according to produce, but anything less than a *iugerum* of arable land is unthinkable. When the text later declares: 'Si quis sane secundum consensum nostrum acquiescere noluerit vel tibi inferre minime procuraverit in specie, quod tibi convenerit, fiscum suum inferre procuret', a comma is needed after *procuraverit*.

[2] Cf. XII. 1. 2.

[3] For appointment by the *c. patrimonii*, see the cited document of 592, and for that by the king the final edict of XVI Tol. (549b/c), where the city concerned was Merida, likely to have been one of the financial centres.

Regular taxes apart, customs dues were no doubt still levied,[1] and a special tax paid by the Jews is witnessed for Egica's reign.[2] Services were also exacted:[3] the obligation to provide horses for the *cursus publicus* has already been mentioned, and other services – from which the free clergy and, perhaps, Church slaves were exempt[4] – perhaps corresponded to the old *munera sordida* of the Romans – the maintenance of bridges, the repair of roads and so on. The tendency of royal officials to extort unlawful services, as well as to levy taxes, for their own ends was recognised and forbidden.[5] The fisc profited also from other sources whose importance must not be underestimated. The action of the law often brought confiscated land or money exacted in fines,[6] while several offences involved enslavement to the fisc or – which might amount to the same thing – to a person of the king's choosing.[7] Inheritance to *bona vacantia* was a further occasional source of gain.[8] But the pressures on the king were doubtless heavy enough to ensure that much of what accrued to the fisc was swiftly given or granted away to the *fideles regis*.

The effectiveness of such donations or concessions would most clearly have been displayed in times of war and insurrection. That control of the armed forces was a necessary royal prerogative if the king was to be able to fulfil his divinely imposed task of protection is self-evident, but the monarch's supreme military role was by no means a consequence of his apotheosis. Visigothic kingship had emerged from war-leadership, and its military character would have remained substantially the same whether the kings had discovered

[1] See Cassiodorus, *Variae* v. 39. 7, and below, p. 198.
[2] xii. 2. 18 (Egica), xvi Tol. *Tomus* and c. 1. Those Jews truly converted were exempted (the non-converted taking over their contributions) but required to pay 'ut caeteri ingenui...quidquid pro publicis indictionibus a principe eis fuerit imperatum ut veri Christicolae' by xvi Tol. 1. The Jewish tax was taken over at the time of the general enslavement of 694 by freed and endowed Christian slaves: xvii Tol. 8.
[3] See Gama Barros, vii, 183–5.
[4] iv Tol. 47 (clergy); iii Tol. 21 (slaves).
[5] xii. 1. 2 and iii Tol. 18, 21: see also below, p. 119. For corruption in tax-gathering, see *De fisco Barc.* and the remissory edict of xiii Tol.
[6] See ii. 1. 6, 8, 9, 11, 33, iii. 4. 18, 5. 2, vi. 2. 1, 5. 12, vii. 5. 1, 2, 6. 2, viii. 4. 24, 25, ix. 2. 9 and many others, particularly the anti-Jewish laws.
[7] ii. 1. 8, iv. 5. 7, ix. 2. 9 and the texts cit. below, p. 78, n. 9, may serve as examples. All the Jews enslaved in 694 were at the disposal of the fisc: xvii Tol. 8.
[8] See below, p. 249.

the benefits of the theocratic programme or not. The king summoned and dissolved the host[1] – although his officers undoubtedly had the authority to call men to arms in the event of sudden attack or rebellion[2] – and either commanded it in person or delegated the command to others:[3] his council-of-war was formed, as we should expect, by the *primates palatii*.[4] Liability to military service fell upon all the freemen and freedmen of the kingdom, Roman and Goth, ecclesiastical and lay, with the sole known exceptions of the monks and the royal freedmen, and upon the *servi fiscales*:[5] those required to serve had also to bring with them, as we shall see, a proportion of their slaves. The age limits for service are not expressly stated, but the indications are that they were twenty and fifty.[6]

The standing army consisted of the garrison troops whose existence in the cities and *castella* is shown by the commissariat law, IX. 2. 6. How widely these troops were dispersed throughout the kingdom is unknown, but it is inconceivable that every city possessed a garrison: the cost of provisioning would have been prohibitive, and the value of the troops, necessarily few in numbers, trifling. That the city count was to be appealed to for assistance by a lesser judge unable to arrest a wrong-doer[7] does not argue that garrison troops were available for the count's use or, indeed, at his command if they were available: his own *saiones* or other retainers would doubtless usually have sufficed. The danger of rebellion would have been best met by

[1] IX. 2. 9; *HW* 29.
[2] *Arg. ex* IX. 2. 8, 9.
[3] Cf. IX. 2. 9 and for a full account of the only campaign reported at length, that of Wamba in 673, Thompson, *Goths*, pp. 219–26 (based essentially on *HW* and *Iudicium*). For an early example of delegation resulting in an overwhelming defeat of the Franks, see John of Biclar, 589. 2: other references to the defeat in *HF* IX. 31, *VPE* V. 12. 5 and *HG* 54.
[4] At least, Wamba's was: *HW* 9.
[5] IX. 2. 8, 9. That clergy had not earlier been forbidden to take up arms *pro patria* is the clear message of IV Tol. 45. For the exemption of monks cf. *VSF* 14: the number of applicants seeking admission to Fructuosus' foundation was thought likely to threaten the military strength of the province. Royal freedmen were required to serve by V. 7. 19 (Egica). It seems likely that the duty of military service had been imposed upon the Romans after the religious unification, but when is unknown: see Sánchez-Albornoz, 'Pérdida de Esp.', pp. 8–12.
[6] Only slaves between these ages were liable according to two MSS of IX. 2. 9, where exemption for all on the grounds of youth or old age is admitted in all versions. Note also the significance of the same age-group in the earlier version of VIII. 4. 16.
[7] VII. 4. 2.

large garrisons in the principal cities. But the majority of the permanent troops were no doubt to be found stationed in the northern complex of *castra* and fortresses which formed the first line of defence against the incursions of Franks, Basques and Cantabrians, and in the cities which constituted the second line.[1]

Of the composition of the field army, called out when required, we know a fair deal and can infer more. The largest unit within any *exercitus* was the *tiupha*, commanded by a *tiuphadus* and almost certainly consisting in theory of a thousand men.[2] The *centena* – apparently the basic unit[3] – and the *decania* figured as subdivisions of this sizeable force and the *quingentenarius*, the *centenarius* and the *decanus* as subordinate officers to the *tiuphadus*.[4] It is a common but probably incorrect notion that the army was organised into units based on the territorial areas of the *civitas* and the province under the command of the city counts and the provincial dukes, who would thus have combined the military with the civil leadership of the territories they controlled. In fact, there is no evidence that the city count held any position in the military chain of command: the only functions which we know him to have fulfilled in connection with military matters were the supply of rations and the imposition of punishment on those guilty of failure to enlist, desertion, or the abetting of these offences,[5] and neither activity argues for his exercise of command. Remarkably enough, if the city count was the local commander, he was not even to be found with the units of the field army when they assembled, for notification of absentees or deserters had to be sent to him by the *tiuphadus* by letter.[6] But notification was also made 'preposito comitis', to the count's officer, who, since there

---

[1] For the military organisation in the north, modelled upon the Byzantine defence system, see *HW* 9–11 and the convincing account of Vigil and Barbero, pp. 314–28, with a map on p. 339.

[2] Cf., e.g., IX. 2. 1 and see Pérez Pujol, I, 506–7. In the Fuero Juzgo the *tiuphadus* of IX. 2. 1 is replaced by 'el que ha en guarda mil caballeros en la hueste' (cit. by Gama Barros, VII, 405). On the thousand as an institution see R. Wenskus, *Stammesbildung und Verfassung. Das Werden der frühmittelalterlichen gentes* (Cologne–Graz, 1961), pp. 443–4.

[3] Dahn, *Könige*, p. 209.

[4] IX. 2. 1, 3, 4.

[5] IX. 2. 6 (rations), IX. 2. 1, 3–5. The penalties of these last three laws were actually replaced by those of IX. 2. 9, but it is reasonable to assume the continuing jurisdictional responsibility of the *c. civitatis*.

[6] IX. 2. 5.

is no hint of written communication, was probably to be found with the assembled troops.[1] It is unlikely that the count served by this man was the city count, for communications to the last-named would surely then have come from the *prepositus*, not the *tiuphadus*. The *prepositus* in question was rather the subordinate of the military count.

This dignitary, the *prepositus hostis*, appears in two laws. In one he is found with the army in the field: only with his permission or with that of the *tiuphadus* might a junior officer allow one of his men to return home.[2] In the other he appears as a functionary quite distinct from the city count. In the cities and fortresses either this latter or an official known as the *annonarius* was responsible for the distribution of rations to the garrison troops and for supplying the needs of the forces called up into their units:[3] presumably he maintained stockpiles of provisions in readiness for mobilisation.[4] If the troops, garrison or otherwise, found themselves defrauded of their supplies by the peculation of the city count or *annonarius*, it was the *comes exercitus sui*, the count of their army, whom they approached and who in turn approached the king for satisfaction.[5] It is significant that the military count possessed no civil authority which might allow him to compel the city count to provide the supplies without royal intervention. The law shows that the troops of the kingdom were grouped into separate armies, each under the command of a *comes*,[6] and another text demonstrates the existence of a larger unit still, the army of the province. Although manuscript variations leave room for doubt, it is most probable that the commanding officer of this force was known specifically as the 'dux exercitus provinciae', an appellation which distinguishes him from the civil *dux provinciae*.[7]

---

[1] Ib. If the text is actually a corruption of *preposito hostis* or *comiti exercitus*, as Zeumer's note to the law suggests, what I go on to say has the greater force.

[2] IX. 2. 3.

[3] IX. 2. 6, where, pace Thompson, *Goths*, p. 146, I consider the *erogator annone* identical with the *comes civitatis vel annonarius*. But the point is not essential to my argument.

[4] Living off the land was sternly forbidden: VIII. 1. 9. Discipline was severe in the Visigothic army, to judge from *HW* 10.

[5] IX. 2. 6, where the *comes* in question is described also as *prepositus hostis*.

[6] Or perhaps more than one count, for complaint to *a* count of their army might be meant. If so, the army was no doubt the provincial one.

[7] The text is *VSF* 14, where neither *ducis* (Nock's reading) or *duces* (also in the MSS) is suitable.

The most important military officer of whom we have mention was, finally, the *dux exercitus Hispaniae* who was St Fructuosus' father and whom we may surmise to have been, under the king, the commander-in-chief.[1]

Military leadership at the higher levels was apparently kept separate from civil, then. But this does not mean to say that particular dignitaries did not sometimes hold both military and civil office at the king's convenience – thus Claudius in the late sixth century[2] – or, even less, that provincial dukes and city counts had no duty to serve: indeed, breach of their military obligations was particularly severely punished. Certainly, however, such influential men as these – *fideles regis* and often in control of sizeable private armies – were not to be found as members of *tiuphae* under the command of *tiuphadi* regarded, militarily speaking, as 'inferiores...vilioresque persone':[3] nor were the *gardingi*. It was undoubtedly these men who constituted those palatine officers who as *patroni* themselves led their retainers on campaign.[4] Whether the *buccellarii* and *saiones* of a non-palatine lord were incorporated with the regular *tiuphae* or whether they formed separate units under their patron's immediate command, we do not know. But such men were certainly required to serve, even if their patron was too ill to accompany them.[5]

The number of troops was further swelled by soldiers drawn from the ranks of the slaves.[6] All those obliged to serve, including the *servi fiscales*, were required to bring with them one-tenth of their total force of slaves: failure to produce the correct proportion resulted in the confiscation of those left behind. These men did not act as camp-followers but as fighting troops,[7] and their masters were compelled to have them armed as such: some were to have breastplates, others to be equipped as slingers, most to have shields, swords, lances

---

[1] *VSF* 2.

[2] See John of Biclar, 589. 2. Claudius is the only example that I know of, but cf. the scholion referred to below, p. 138, n. 1, where Froga appears as *comes et praefectus Toleti*.

[3] Thus IX. 2. 9.   [4] Ib.

[5] Ib.

[6] For the following see IX. 2. 9.

[7] I see no reason to think, with Melicher, *Kampf*, p. 104, that they did not serve as soldiers already well before Ervig's reign: cf. *CE* 323 and the *Antiquae* IV. 2. 15, VIII. 1. 9, the first two of which texts show them gaining booty for their masters: further, II. 5. 13.

or bows and arrows.[1] The slaves would naturally have served as infantry, like the humble freemen, with the units of mounted lancers and javelin-throwers – in whom, according to Isidore, the Goths particularly trusted[2] – formed by the richer men and especially, perhaps, the *gardingi* and their bands. Of the proportion of horse to foot and of the tactics used in battle we know nothing, but there are interesting indications of the employment of siege-artillery in the investment of walled cities and of the use of the fleet in combined land–sea operations.[3] The only contemporary figure relevant to the numbers of troops involved in military ventures appears in Julian's account of Wamba's campaign against Paul, where 10000 chosen men are reported to have been sent forward to assist a small besieging force at Nîmes.[4] If the figure is reliable – and Julian had better reason to understate than to exaggerate – a very large number of men was mobilised for the original campaign against the Basques, for Paul must have taken a considerable detachment of the army with him when he was dispatched to quell the rising of which he in fact assumed the leadership, and Wamba would clearly have kept a force with him when he sent the 10000 forward. Whatever the original number, the mobilisation had not been general, for the king had considered but decided against postponement of hostilities while reinforcements were called up,[5] and Paul had himself enlisted further troops.[6]

Despite this, it is quite clear that the unwillingness of men to fulfil their military obligations was a matter of grave concern in the reign of Ervig, and Egica's later extension of the duty of service to royal freedmen suggests that the problems posed by such recalcitrance were becoming even more acute.[7] A law of Wamba, issued after the suppression of Paul's rebellion, had provided loss of the right of

[1] On these and earlier Visigothic weapons see E. A. Thompson, *The early Germans* (Oxford, 1965), pp. 116–18 (laying the myth of Adrianople as a cavalry victory), 125–7.

[2] *HG* 69, 70. See generally C. Sánchez-Albornoz, 'La caballería visigoda', *Wirtschaft und Kultur. Festschrift zum 70. Geburtstag von Alfons Dopsch* (Baden bei Wien–Leipzig, 1938), pp. 92–108 (with reference also to the Arab sources), and idem, 'Pérdida de Esp.', pp. 19–25 (with reference also to relevant grave-finds). The horse appears as the most highly prized animal in the laws: see below, p. 215.

[3] For artillery see, convincingly, Thompson, *Goths*, pp. 266–7, and for combined operations *HW* 12, 13. Further on the fleet below, p. 198.

[4] *HW* 15.     [5] *HW* 9.     [6] *HW* 7.

[7] v. 7. 19. But Egica in fact speaks of the existing 'copia bellatorum'.

testimony as one of the regular penalties for those who shirked their duty,[1] but only eight years later Ervig was forced to restore the right to those who had forfeited it – and even to permit the re-opening of cases where the evidence of such individuals had not been admitted – because, as he no doubt exaggeratedly put it, well-nigh half the inhabitants of the kingdom were unable to testify, to the obvious detriment of law and order.[2] His own army law of 681, IX. 2. 9, in fact replaced Wamba's, although this remained in the code. All those summoned to arms by duke, count, *tiuphadus*, vicar or whomever – he was thinking, no doubt, of the *servi dominici*, who elsewhere are referred to as the bearers of the summons[3] – were obliged to present themselves at the time and place specified, as were those who had received no summons but knew of the situation. No restriction of the obligation to those living within a particular area was provided as it had been in Wamba's law. Penalties for dis-obedience were harsh: loss of property and banishment for a duke, count or *gardingus* and two hundred lashes, *decalvatio* and a fine of one pound of gold for others, with enslavement the alternative if they could not pay. The same punishments were inflicted on deserters and on those who failed to acquit themselves honourably. There were reasonable exceptions from service: those with royal permission and those too young or too old were exempt, as were those who could prove that they had been too ill to travel. Corruption by the military authorities in the form of the release of a man from service, whether on receipt of a bribe or for some other unlawful reason, involved one of the *primates palatii* – the king was thinking of the military dukes and counts – in a fine of a pound of gold and, strangely, fourfold restitution to the briber, while a lesser person lost his property and office and was placed at the mercy of the king. Both desertion and corruption had been the subjects of earlier *Antiquae*, the penalties of which were now rendered inapplicable by this sweeping new law.[4]

If sparseness of information prevents a fuller account either of the military system or of the financial organisation, evidence concerning

[1] IX. 2. 8.
[2] XII Tol. *Tomus* (469a/b), 7. During which campaigns, one wonders, had the offences taken place? Had Wamba's law not in fact been applied retrospectively?
[3] IX. 2. 2, 5.          [4] IX. 2. 1, 3–5.

the governmental activity which presented the most constant demands upon the king and his officers, the administration of justice, is relatively abundant, although important gaps in our knowledge remain and much is controversial. It has been suggested that the *proceres* whose subscriptions to the acts of the Eighth, Thirteenth and Sixteenth Councils of Toledo have survived were, below the king himself, at the summit of the judicial hierarchy.[1] Certainly the king must have had in his entourage a group of men versed in the law who could deal on his behalf with the legal matters referred to him, for the burden of these could only have been heavy. Wholly in accordance with theocratic premises, the king was regarded as the supreme judge, to whom lay ultimate appeal for both laymen and clerics and to whom were submitted cases not dealt with in the code for resolution by his discretionary judgement, which might then form the basis of a new statutory provision.[2] That the king acted also as a judge of first instance is beyond doubt.[3] The bishops were required to notify him of oppression by his officers;[4] charges might be laid before him in person;[5] capital crimes alleged against those of high standing by one of equivalent rank were certainly dealt with by him or by his appointed delegates.[6] Almost casually the king was mentioned in the code as involved in cases concerning the falsification of documents and the invalid disposal of taxable property.[7] In one case – that of a slave offending for the second time against the coinage laws – sentence was expressly reserved to the king:[8] in many other laws we find him deciding who should benefit from an offender's enslavement,[9] who should receive a sum of money exacted in penalty,[10] or, indeed, what should become of a criminal's person and goods.[11] Fugitive slaves who refused information as to their owners were

[1] Thus Sánchez-Albornoz, 'Aula', pp. 48–57.
[2] For appeals see below, pp. 119–21, and XIII Tol. 12 (clerics), and for discretion and new laws II. 1. 13 (put against its Roman background by Zeumer, XXIV, 70–2), II. 1. 14. For II. 1. 13 see also E. Kaufmann, *Aequitatis iudicium* (Frankfurt am Main, 1959), pp. 56–8.
[3] Cf., e.g., II. 2. 6, 7, 10 (Egica), VI. 1. 2 etc.
[4] Below, p. 119.
[5] VI. 1. 6: cf. II. 2. 10 (Egica), III. 4. 13, V. 4. 19, VI. 5. 14, and for usurpation by metropolitans IX Tol. 1.     [6] VI. 1. 2.
[7] VII. 5. 2; V. 4. 19.     [8] VII. 6. 2.
[9] III. 2. 2, 4. 17, 6. 2, VI. 2. 1, 3. 1, VII. 6. 2 etc.
[10] III. 1. 2, 4. 17, X. 2. 3 etc.     [11] II. 1. 9, VI. 2. 4 etc.

sent to the court for further investigation.[1] The king himself sometimes examined the child of a baptised Jew to discover whether the
right of testimony should be granted it,[2] while royal confirmation
of the episcopal–judicial decision in certain testamentary matters was
required.[3] Given also the duty of the king as supreme custodian of
justice to ensure that wrong-doers were brought to court and his
responsibilities, already noted, in the exercise of clemency,[4] the com-
pelling need for a body of expert legal advisers can easily be seen.
That the *proceres* formed this body is unverified but well possible.
Would it not have been from their ranks also that were drawn the
*pacis adsertores*, judges holding a special royal commission to preside
in specified cases?[5]

Below the king and his tribunal the *dux* stood at the summit of the
judicial hierarchy of the province which he governed.[6] It was to him
that appeals against the decisions of lower courts might be directed
and to him that it fell to take action against the illegal exercise of
judicial or executive authority.[7] Understandably, lesser judges had
recourse to him when unable themselves to bring powerful offenders
to book.[8] It is clear that the duke acted also as a judge of first instance,[9]
but further detail is lacking.

Clearly inferior to the duke was the city count, the most important
single governmental dignitary of the Visigothic kingdom. The
count's jurisdictional sphere embraced the *civitas* and its surrounding
countryside, but in both areas other judges were also to be found.
The relationship of these other functionaries with the *comes civitatis* is
closely bound up with the question of the meaning to be attributed
to the term *iudex* in the laws.[10] That the word was at times used to

---

[1] IX. I. 9.    [2] XII. 2. 10.

[3] II. 5. 13. At an earlier stage notification had also to be made to the king of fines
imposed for military offences: IX. 2. 3–5.

[4] For recourse to the king by judges unable to act, see III. 4. 18, 5. 2, 6. 1, IV. 5. 6,
VII. 1. 1, XII. 3. 26.

[5] II. 1. 17: cf. II. 1. 27 and the reference to special royal judges in II. 1. 31. For a case
of special appointment see below, p. 227, n. 3, where the judge is a *comes* (which is
not to say that he is not also a *procer*).

[6] Note his appearance at the head of the list of judges given in II. 1. 27.

[7] Below, p. 120 (appeals); II. 1. 18.

[8] Cf. II. 1. 19, VII. 1. 1 (where *duci* is to be preferred to *iudici* in line 20).

[9] Cf. II. 2. 7, III. 4. 17, IV. 5. 6, VI. 5. 12 (in Chindasvind's version).

[10] A matter examined in detail in Sánchez-Albornoz, *Ruina*, pp. 74–83, whom
I largely follow.

designate an official quite distinct from the city count is clear. Cases against the *iudex* might be heard by the count or his delegates; the *iudex* was enjoined to call upon the count for assistance in the constraint of criminals; the *iudex* was obliged to declare the property found on a criminal or fugitive to the count; the *iudex* might be punished by the count for dereliction of duty.[1] Nevertheless, *iudex* was not the particular title of an official of a certain rank,[2] for it is inconceivable, if it had been so, that he would have been omitted from the lengthy list of those holding judicial authority – the 'dux, comes, vicarius, pacis adsertor, thiuphadus, millenari quingentenarius, centenarius, defensor, numerarius' – which Reccesvind provided in II. I. 27.[3]

In fact, *iudex* meant neither more nor less than 'judge', and as such was employed with different connotations in different places. Sometimes it was used to indicate anyone with judicial authority – including, that is to say, the provincial duke and the city count.[4] On other occasions it was used to refer to a particular judge: we hear, for example, of the 'provincie iudex', who was evidently the duke.[5] But at other times again it was used in contrast with *comes* to designate any judge whose jurisdiction was subordinate to that of the count:[6] it is understandable that having expressly mentioned the city count the legislator should have made use of the convenient general term

---

[1] II. I. 31; VII. 4. 2; IX. I. 20; III. 4. 17.

[2] Differently, Merêa, *Estudos*, pp. 286–93: see also Thompson, *Goths*, pp. 139ff., 213.

[3] Merêa, *Estudos*, pp. 290–2, is unconvincing. Of the certain judges of the kingdom only the *villicus* is omitted from this list.

[4] Cf. XII. 3. 2: 'Iudicis, in cuius civitate, castra vel territorio', XII. 3. 26: 'Iudices universi per diversa loca vel territoria constituti', II. I. 19–21, III. 2. 2 etc. *Iudex loci* in, e.g., VIII. 4. 29, XII. 3. 20, means nothing but 'the local judge': thus already, clearly, in III Tol. 18. Since the area entrusted to a judge is described as a *territorium* (cf. II. I. 18, 2. 7, 4. 5, VII. I. 5 etc.), *iudex territorii* in III. 6. 1, IV. 4. 1, VI. 4. 4, XII. 3. 25 etc. similarly means nothing but 'the judge of the jurisdictional area concerned'. But *territorium* is, like *terra*, an elastic term, and is also used to indicate a much larger area: thus we find *comites territorii* and *episcopi territorii* in IX. I. 21 (of Egica).

[5] VI. 3. 7: 'Provincie iudex aut territorii': but 'judices provinciarum' in IV Tol. 65 does not necessarily mean the dukes. Cf. also IX. I. 6: 'Iudici vel vicario proxime civitatis aut territorii', X. I. 16: 'Iudices singularum civitatum'.

[6] E.g., IV. 2. 14, VI. I. I, VII. I. 5 *et saepe*. In II. I. 13 we find *iudex* used both in its widest and in this less general sense: 'Nullus *iudex* causam audire presumat, que in legibus non continetur; sed *comes civitatis vel iudex*...conspectui principis utrasque partes presentare procuret'.

*iudex* rather than have tediously catalogued the various functionaries he had in mind. *Iudex*, in other words, was an elastic term, now comprehensive in its scope, now more particular.

The jurisdictional spheres of the different judges can perhaps be established. The *comes civitatis* himself operated, of course, within the city proper, assisted by a deputy, *vicarius*, and with some of the judicial burden taken from his shoulders by the *numerarius* and the *defensor*. But outside the immediate area of the city other judges, although subject to the count, held sway. Thus, it was the count who was envisaged as taking action against a prostitute active 'in civitate', but a *iudex*, simply, who was the competent authority when she marketed her charms 'per vicos et villas' and who, if negligent, was proceeded against by the count.[1] If we omit the *pacis adsertor* and those other personages already mentioned from the list of judges in II. 1. 27 we are left with four dignitaries – the *tiuphadus, millenarius, quingentenarius* and *centenarius* – with one or more of whom this 'country' judge may be identified.[2]

Elsewhere in the code the last two functionaries are mentioned – and then briefly – only as military officers subordinate to the *tiuphadus*, while the *millenarius* is not alluded to at all, although already in the *Codex Euricianus* he had appeared as a judge.[3] The identification of the *millenarius* with the *tiuphadus*, who, as we have seen, was almost certainly the commander of a thousand men, makes etymological sense:[4] moreover, it would satisfactorily explain the absence of further reference to the former in the code. But although the Visigothic laws are not free of tautology, it is perhaps unlikely that two distinct terms would be used in immediate juxtaposition in a single law to denote the same individual.[5] The explanation may be that at an early stage civil and military jurisdictions were separate also at the lower governmental level, the *millenarius* being the judge and the *tiuphadus* the military officer, but that the latter took over the form-

---

[1] III. 4. 17. Note that, quite in accordance with what has been said above, the *comes* himself is in one place here referred to simply as *iudex*.

[2] Some MSS also mention the *decanus* – a military officer, like the others.

[3] *CE* 322.

[4] See Zeumer's note to II. 1. 16. Note further *Etym.* IX. 3. 30: 'Chiliarchae sunt qui mille praesunt, quos nos millenarios nuncupamus'.

[5] The identification is therefore denied by, e.g., Gama Barros, VII, 403ff., Thompson, *Goths*, p. 145, n. 2.

er's judicial functions and that II. I. 27 reflects the still incomplete changeover. Certainly there is no text referring to the judicial activity of the *tiuphadus* which predates Chindasvind, although his military role is witnessed already in several *Antiquae*.[1] But in and after Chindasvind's time he figures prominently in several laws as a judge to whom Reccesvind conceded the right of hearing all cases, criminal or not.[2] The *tiuphadus* also played a part in the financial administration, as we have seen. It is justifiable to suppose, then, in the admitted absence of precise information, that the *tiuphadus* was the chief judge in the country districts, possessing jurisdictional authority, perhaps, over those families whence the *tiupha* which he commanded in war was drawn.[3] Lesser jurisdictions may be assumed to have been exercised by his subordinate military officers, the *quingentenarius* and the *centenarius*.

Certain judicial personages remain to be dealt with.[4] The *villicus*, occasionally mentioned as possessing judicial powers although not listed in II. I. 27, no doubt had as his sphere of operation the crown estates of which he would seem to have been the overseer.[5] Both the *defensor* and the *numerarius* were based in the towns,[6] but it is difficult to know what particular judicial functions they exercised there. The *defensor* appeared in the Breviary as entrusted with the hearing of minor criminal cases,[7] and some such jurisdiction perhaps remained his preserve during the later period. But the *numerarius* was certainly a tax-official, and the implication of a law of Reccared, which forbade the practice whereby *defensor* and *numerarius* exchanged functions after a year of office,[8] to the detriment of the people, is that the

---

[1] IX. 2. I, 3–5.
[2] II. I. 16: cf. II. I. 24, IV. 5. 6, IX. I. 21 (Egica).
[3] See also Gama Barros, VII, 407.
[4] Who the *tribuni* mentioned solely in XI. I. 2 but alongside *comites* and *villici* were, I do not know. That they were dukes is unlikely, since the *tribuni* appear in the law after the counts. Were *tribuni* perhaps *vicarii*, as O. M. Dalton, *The 'Hist. of the Franks' by Gregory of Tours*, II (Oxford, 1927), 598, suggests for sixth-century Gaul?
[5] Gama Barros, VII, 432ff., and Sánchez-Albornoz, *Ruina*, pp. 80–1, deny his judicial status. But the texts – VIII. I. 9, IX. I. 8 (not in the code), IX. I. 9, X. I. 16, XII. I. 2 – tell in my view a different story.
[6] *Arg. ex* XII. I. 2.         [7] *LRV.CT* II. I. 8, *Interpretatio*.
[8] XII. I. 2: 'Numerarii vel defensores annua vice mutentur'. But Thompson, *Goths*, p. 126, takes this to mean that the officials laid down their offices at the end of a year.

*defensor* was intended to act as a restraining influence upon the *numerarius*.[1] Perhaps the *defensor*, alone or together with the *numerarius*, heard appeals against tax-assessments: collusion between them certainly appears to have been the target of Reccared's law – which went on to impose one of the largest fixed fines of the whole code, ten pounds of gold, upon a judge who allowed himself to be bribed by either. There is clear evidence against the view, sometimes maintained, that the *numerarius* was the exclusive judge in matters pertaining to fiscal possessions.[2] Every judge was entitled to appoint a deputy who might hear cases in his absence: the same right was possessed by the deputies themselves.[3] The vicar of the city count was mentioned by name,[4] and the *tiuphadi* were expressly exhorted to hear cases in the presence of other persons who might then assume the judicial role when the *tiuphadi* were away.[5] It is difficult to believe that the interests of justice were served by a system which so patently invited judicial negligence. Only when the deputy was a slave did the law insist that the appointing judge be held responsible for what judicial misdeeds might ensue from delegation.[6]

It was to these various personages that jurisdictional authority within defined areas was entrusted by the king or by those whom he had appointed: the illegal exercise of such authority, either by judges who overstepped the boundaries allotted to them or by men who had been conceded no right of jurisdiction, was a serious offence.[7] Two exceptions may be noted here.[8] First, the slave-owner judged his own slaves when no outside party was involved.[9] And second, there were judges not appointed by the king or another judge but agreed upon by the litigants in a particular case.[10] The importance of these figures must not, however, be exaggerated. Their right to judge and authority to execute their judgements

---

[1] Note *Etym.* IX. 4. 18: 'Defensores dicti, eo quod plebem sibi commissam contra insolentiam inproborum defendant. At contra nunc quidam eversores, non defensores existunt'.

[2] Cf. II. 3. 10.    [3] II. 1. 15.

[4] II. 1. 24. There are general references to *vicarii*, probably usually comital, in III. 6. 1, IV. 5. 6, VIII. 1. 5, IX. 1. 6, 21 (Egica), etc.

[5] See below, p. 99, n. 6. For delegation see also II. 1. 31, 4. 5.

[6] II. 1. 18.    [7] II. 1. 15, 18.

[8] For clerical jurisdiction see below, pp. 151–2, and for jurisdiction over foreign merchants, p. 198.

[9] Below, p. 177.    [10] Cf. II. 1. 15, 18, 27.

sprang from the royal will, even if their appointment did not, and they too were subject to the duties imposed upon all judges, including that of using only the one territorial code which held the royal laws. Moreover, there is no indication that their decisions might not be appealed against, like those of the regular judges. These 'popular' judges – often, we may think, ecclesiastics – existed on sufferance, in other words, and only within the framework of an otherwise wholly royal system: there is no possibility of their being used to support any thesis of a powerful 'popular' jurisdictional organisation alongside the royal. It was the royal judges, possessed of general competence to deal with all cases handled in the code, criminal and 'other'[1] – what we may best, though not altogether satisfactorily, term 'civil' – who unquestionably dominated the scene. To the question of their administration of justice we now turn.

[1] II. I. 17: cf. for the distinction II. I. 12, 16, X. 2. 3.

*Chapter 4*

# ROYAL GOVERNMENT, 2

It is wholly in keeping both with the character attributed above to the Visigothic king and with the willingness of the barbarian Goths to adopt the superior juridical notions offered by *Romanitas* that the law of the code was built upon the principle that remedy for wrongs should be sought in the courts at the hands of the authorised judges. It would be naïve, no doubt, to believe that feud was unknown to the Visigothic kingdom: perhaps, indeed, it was feud with which the *pacis adsertores*, dispatched by the king 'sola faciende pacis intentione',[1] had most often to deal. And simple justice, then as now, demanded that a man be permitted a measure of self-help: as Chindasvind pompously remarked: 'Commodius erit irato vivens resistere, quam sese post obitum ulciscendum relinquere'.[2] Killing in self-defence, even to forestall attack, was no offence:[3] nor was it a culpable act to kill in defence of a woman's virtue.[4] Both the daytime thief who tried to defend himself with a weapon and the nocturnal one who was caught in the act of stealing might be killed with impunity:[5] so too might the *pervasor*.[6] The law even went beyond the admission of the propriety of killing in defence of person or property to allow, in certain circumstances, the summary dispatch of a woman guilty of sexual misbehaviour, together with her lover.[7] Private arrest of criminals and even debtors was permitted, as we shall see, and in certain special eventualities property might lawfully be seized by private individuals.[8]

---

[1] II. 1. 17.      [2] VI. 4. 6.

[3] Ib.: cf. VI. 4. 2, 5. 12 (Chindasvind), 5. 19 and the special case of IX. 3. 2. Ten *solidi* were payable by the man who first drew his sword, even though it was not used: VI. 4. 6.

[4] III. 3. 6: cf. III. 3. 2 for the justified recovery by force of an abducted woman.

[5] VII. 2. 15, 16. Both laws echo provisions of the Twelve Tables, but I am more willing than is L. G. de Valdeavellano, 'El apellido. Notas sobre el procedimiento *in fragranti* en el derecho esp. medieval', *CHE*, VII (1947), 72–3, to see Germanic influence: see Brunner, *Rechtsgesch.*, II, 631.

[6] VIII. 1. 13.      [7] Below, pp. 234, 240.      [8] Below, p. 219.

But these were exceptional cases. Neither feud nor self-help – the two inextricably connected in Germanic practice – was accorded a regular and legitimate place in the legal scheme of things. Indeed, their maintenance would have been grotesquely out of place in view of the sophistication of the criminal law of the code. It was not that this law rejected the primitive principle of talion, retaliation in kind, but rather that it took into important account – what feud in its brute simplicity could not do – the extent to which an injurious act was the result of premeditated intent, culpable negligence or pure accident, and made the consequences to the actor dependent upon this. The principle that no crime existed when an act was not voluntarily committed was explicitly stated,[1] and although a man was also held responsible for wrongs resulting from his negligence, it is clear that the wholly accidental infliction of some or other sort of injury involved no legal liability. The laws on killing, in particular, go into casuistic detail on this matter.[2]

In any case, feud – or rather, what enabled feud to flourish, the collective responsibility of the kin – was expressly rejected.[3] 'Omnia crimina suos sequantur auctores', declared an *Antiqua*: a crime was the responsibility of the perpetrator alone and died with him, to the exclusion of liability on the part of relatives or neighbours[4] – although his heirs were no more exempt from the obligation to pay from his estate, as far as was possible, the financial consequences of his offence than were the heirs of a debtor.[5] Not only was the Germanic custom of visiting the crimes of the individual upon his family in profound opposition to the Roman principle of exclusive personal liability and intransmissibility,[6] but the very notion of self-help, with all its

[1] Below, p. 87, n. 1.    [2] See below, App. II.
[3] Quite unjustified is the reference of B. S. Phillpotts, *Kindred and clan in the MA and after* (Cambridge, 1913), p. 264, to 'West Gothic custumals' as showing 'division of wergild between kinsmen, definitely organised blood-feuds between kindreds, and oath-helpers of the kindred', if she alludes, as she apparently does, to the Visigothic period.
[4] VI. I. 8: 'Ille solus iudicetur culpabilis, qui culpanda conmittit, et crimen cum illo, qui fecit, moriatur': cf. VII. 2. 19. But note Chindasvind's treatment of his opponents' womenfolk (below, p. 232, n. 2), the inclusion of children in the enslavement ordered by XVI Tol. 10, that of wives and children in the Jewish enslavement of 694 (XVII Tol. 8), *VPE* v. 11. 19 etc.
[5] v. 6. 6, VII. 2. 19, 5. 8: cf. II. 4. 7, *in fine*, for charges against a dead man.
[6] But see *LRV.CT* IX. 30. 4 (of 399), with *Interpretatio*. Was this inspired by the need to counteract Germanic influence?

implications of independent judgement as to when and how severely subjective rights had been violated, stood in stark contrast with the concept of government from above by means of the king and his law. The king's position as the supreme custodian of the kingdom, with personal responsibility for justice and tranquillity, to which ends his laws were designed, made such crude ideas impossible to maintain. It might indeed be thought that the logic of the king's status demanded that the pursuit of all criminals be a royal responsibility, to be delegated as a duty to the judges or to the members of the community at large. This was not the case: prosecution was, in the case of many crimes, a right possessed only by certain interested parties, whose failure to take action in fact allowed the malefactors to escape scot-free. But this was not because the king retreated from the implications of his position and left to the whim of the individual the bringing to book of an offender against the public well-being. Rather, it was because the Visigoths gathered together under the one heading of *crimina* not only offences against the king or the community as a whole but also those against an individual where no monarchical or public interest was considered to be involved. There existed, in other words, no terminological distinction between public and private offences on the lines of that of the Romans between *crimina* and *delicta* or that of modern English law between crimes and torts. The conceptual distinction, on the other hand, found expression in both the procedural and the penal spheres. It was not logic which was lacking but an appropriate terminology and, we might think, a proper awareness of the extent to which society in general had an interest in the pursuit and punishment of certain wrong-doers.[1]

[1] Yet the king declared (VI. 5. 12, 15) that a criminal ought always to receive his deserved punishment. I have avoided here, as a task beyond my powers, any attempt to define the Visigothic *crimen*. The characteristic feature of those acts described as *crimina* or *scelera* (synonyms: see V. 4. 18, VI. 2. 1, VII. 4. 2 etc.) is a punitive consequence. But damage to clothing was a *crimen*, and the consequences yet rather compensatory: VIII. 4. 21. The freeman paid simple compensation for his destruction of a kitchen-garden (not in fact called a *crimen*), but the slave was also punished, by lashing: VIII. 3. 2. Conversely, a punitive consequence does not argue for the necessary existence of a crime: 'crimen videri non potest, quod non est ex volumtate conmissum' (VIII. 3. 6), but types of *casus* were certainly punished (below, pp. 260–3). A doctor who bled and (negligently) killed a free patient was placed at the mercy of the bereaved family, but had merely to replace a slave victim: XI. 1. 6. The problems are not made the easier of solution by the use of *damnum*, *compositio* and *satisfactio* to indicate both compensation and financial punishment.

That the *accusationis licentia* was normally restricted to the victim of a crime or to an individual closely connected with this person may be inferred *e contrario* from the specific concession of a general right of accusation in certain exceptional cases. Thus, the accusation of an adulteress was in the first instance the right of the injured husband: only if he, and after him his children and other relatives, declined or were unable to instigate proceedings, was the king prepared to act.[1] Similarly, in the case of killing the right of accusation lay first with the *proximi* of the dead person and only if they took no action with the other relatives or the public at large.[2] Particular extensions in these two cases argue powerfully for general restriction. Precisely because private accusation was the norm it received little direct attention in the code. But it can be assumed as beyond reasonable doubt that where an offence was perpetrated against the interests of an individual – wounding, theft, housebreaking, kidnapping and so forth – and where the law made no express exception, a criminal would be brought to trial only if a party directly involved chose to take action against him. True, it was considered the duty of children and other relatives who inherited the property of a *de cuius* to prosecute those guilty of crimes against him, but there is no evidence of the regular use of sanctions against them if they neglected to do so.[3]

Sanctions for non-prosecution were, however, imposed when adultery or murder had been committed: at the same time the kings extended an eventual right of accusation to all and provided for *de officio* action by the judge – in the case of murder, at least – if no-one should accuse. In other words, account was taken of the public aspect of the crimes: an option to accuse limited to certain individuals did not constitute an adequate safeguard for the moral welfare and physical security of the king's subjects. General accusation was specifically referred to in only one other law.[4] But it was presupposed when VI. 1. 6 dealt with accusations of treason, interference with royal or judicial documents, falsification, counterfeiting, poisoning, sorcery and adultery made direct to the king, and must have been the rule in many other cases also – like the offence of immoral behaviour

---

[1] III. 4. 13: cf. VI. 1. 6.      [2] VI. 5. 14, 15.
[3] VI. 5. 14 only moralises. Differently, Roman law: see M. Lauria, 'Accusatio-inquisitio', *Atti della Reale Accademia di Scienze Morali e Politiche*, LVI (1934), 348–9. For children as plaintiffs, see also III. 6. 2.
[4] IV. 5. 6.

by those under religious vows, where the judges were exhorted to proceed against the transgressors 'etiam si nullus accuset'.[1] *De officio* judicial action was envisaged here, as it was in those other cases where the judge was required to take action as soon as knowledge of an offence came to him or where penalty was clearly non-private in form. On every occasion the laws concerned dealt with crimes committed against the material interests of the king or of the community – like counterfeiting or riotous assembly[2] – or against the *mores* of society – like prostitution or the exposure of children.[3] In every case, also, a general right of accusation open to the free public at large can confidently be assumed.[4]

The distinction drawn between the private and the public crime was reflected in the penal regime. Although most major criminals suffered a public penalty in the form of *infamia*,[5] which deprived them of their right of testimony,[6] a private crime regularly had as its consequence a penalty imposed wholly or primarily to the advantage or satisfaction of the wronged party, and a public crime one to the benefit of the king or with a solely punitive purpose. As punishments for public crimes appear, for example, execution,[7] blinding,[8] castration,[9]

---

[1] III. 5. 2.         [2] VII. 6. 2; VIII. 1. 3.

[3] III. 4. 17; IV. 4. 1 ('iudicibus et accusare liceat et damnare'). It is difficult to establish the regime in the case of a freewoman's fornication with her own slave or freedman or with another's slave, handled in III. 2. 2, 3, 3. 1, 2, 4. 14: de *officio* action, prosecution by the family and an array of penalties (death, lashing, enslavement to a person of the king's choice, to the family or to the slave's master) all appear. Perhaps the matter was treated like killing and adultery?

[4] Slaves were probably excluded. There are references only to slave informers: cf. also VI Tol. 11.

[5] Killers, sorcerers, thieves, poisoners, *raptores*, perjurers and those who consulted diviners were branded with *infamia* in II. 4. 1, where the vague *criminosi* perhaps indicates those infamised for other, particular, offences: on these, see Melicher, *Kampf*, pp. 175–6.

[6] II. 1. 19, 4. 7, 11, VI. 5. 12 etc.: the rights of accusation (in public crimes only?) and of court representation of others were probably also forbidden (III. 5. 3 and Melicher, *Kampf*, p. 173). L. Pommeray, *Études sur l'infamie en droit romain* (Paris, 1937), pp. 258–65, connects *infamia* with flogging (see II. 1. 19, 33, 4. 11 etc.) and *decalvatio* (VI. 4. 5: 'Ad...infamiam...decalvetur') and regards it (*contra*, Melicher, *Kampf*, pp. 172–7) as the direct descendant of Roman *infamia*. Rather, it represents an understandable amalgam of Roman and Germanic traditions, with the latter predominant, while flogging is both too frequent for an absolute connection to be asserted and in fact clearly a distinct penalty in II. 4. 2.

[7] II. 1. 8, VI. 3. 1, 7 etc.         [8] The reprieve penalty in II. 1. 8, VI. 3. 7.

[9] III. 5. 4, XII. 3. 4: cf. *HW* 10.

amputation of the nose or hand,[1] enslavement to the fisc or to a person of the king's choosing,[2] exile – which meant banishment to another region of the kingdom and sometimes involved confinement as a penitent in a monastery[3] – excommunication and deposition from office:[4] most common, however, were confiscations and fines to the benefit of the fisc, flogging and scalping (*decalvatio*).[5] Many of these sanctions were also appropriate for use in private crimes. The abduction of a woman, *raptus*, was certainly a private crime, for example,[6] but the rape which might follow it was nevertheless in certain circumstances punishable capitally.[7] Death threatened the criminal who suffered the – obviously private – penalty of delivery into the arbitrary power of his accuser.[8] Blinding appeared

[1] Nose: xii. 3. 4. Hand: vii. 5. 1 (falsification of royal documents or seal), vii. 6. 2 (coinage offences, but only for slaves): cf. vii. 5. 9 (unattributed and late) ordering amputation of the right thumb for unauthorised copying of royal laws, decrees etc. R. S. Lopez, 'Byzantine law in the seventh century and its reception by the Germans and the Arabs', *Byzantion*, xvi (1942–3), 445–61, would attribute manual amputation to Heraclius's influence. But Lopez does not show that vii. 5. 1. is not an *Antiqua* (as is indicated by the oldest MS), and the penalty was in fact well-known in the West for traitors already in the sixth century: see John of Biclar, 588. 1, 590. 3, and cf. *HG* 57. For Gaul, see *HF* v. 25, vii. 20, 47.     [2] See p. 71.

[3] xii. 3. 27 shows that exiles did not leave the country: cf. *VPE* v. 6. 23–8 (where a monastery is the location). Many of the anti-Jewish laws included the penalty: see also iii. 6. 2, iv. 4. 1, x. 2. 7 etc. For the connection with monastic confinement and penitence, compare the texts of iii. 5. 1, 2 and 5. But xii. 3. 27 (judicial supervision) shows the connection was not necessary.

[4] Excommunication: below, pp. 127–8. Deposition: ii. 1. 6, 8, vii. 4. 5, xii. 2. 2 etc. Penal (and preventive) imprisonment (*retrusio*) appears only for sorcerers (vi. 2. 4): but cf. x. 2. 7. Penal torture appears in vi. 2. 1 (slaves): but cf. vi. 2. 3.

[5] Confiscations and fines: above, p. 71. For flogging, see ii. 1. 8, 9, iii. 4. 17, vi. 2. 1, 4, *et saepe*: the Visigoths were exceptional among the barbarians in their willingness to lash freemen, as H. Conrad, *Deutsche Rechtsgesch.*, i (Carlsruhe, 1954), 230, observes. *Decalvatio* is frequently linked with flogging (e.g., xii. 3. 2–9). Scalping rather than simple shaving of the head is in my view conclusively indicated by Mer. 15: 'Quia omnino justum est ut pontifex saevissimam non impendat vindictam, quidquid coram judice verius patuerit per disciplinae severitatem absque turpi decalvatione maneat emendatum'. For earlier literature on this vexed question see Lear, 'Public law', pp. 15–16.     [6] Cf. iii. 3. 7.

[7] iii. 3. 5: cf. iii. 3. 4. The slave rapist of a freewoman was burned regardless of whether abduction had also occurred: iii. 3. 8, 4. 14. But one wonders if death sentences in 'private' cases could not always be avoided on the payment of composition: see below, p. 203, n. 2, and pp. 259–60.

[8] See vii. 3. 3: further, iii. 3. 11, vi. 1. 2 (*in fine*) and xi. 1. 6. But in iii. 3. 2 slavery seems to be meant (doubtless also in vi. 2. 3) and execution is sometimes expressly excluded: see text and iii. 4. 13, 6. 2 etc.

in a Chindasvindian law as the punishment for a killer who had sought sanctuary, though Ervig substituted the fate of delivery into the *potestas* of the victim's family, to suffer as they chose *excepto mortis periculo*.[1] Amputation must frequently have been the consequence of wounding, for the principle of talion was applied.[2] Flogging was commonly ordered for the perpetrators of private offences, sometimes alongside other punishments,[3] sometimes in lieu of financial payments,[4] sometimes – but rarely for freemen – on its own.[5] Enslavement to the victim of a crime was a usual form of private penalty, either as a direct statutory punishment or as a substitute when the criminal was unable to pay composition.[6] Composition, in money or kind and either laid down as a fixed amount or arrived at by using the injured interest as a multiplicand, with the multiplier varying according to the offence, itself constituted the characteristic form of private penalty.[7]

What sort of reward accusers in public crimes normally stood to gain we do not know,[8] but it is difficult to believe that anyone not motivated by a consuming hostility or by a remarkably selfless public-spiritedness would have exposed himself to the penalties incurred by the failure of a charge unless there was profit to be had from success. Occasional references show that rewards were certainly paid to informers, free or slave, in public cases.[9] So they were too in private cases: the informant in a successful prosecution for theft received the value of the object stolen or, if the offender was unable to pay the composition required, one-third of its value, while the

---

[1] VI. 5. 16: cf. VI. 5. 18, where the sentence was originally exile.
[2] Below, p. 263.
[3] III. 3. 1, 12, 4. 14, VI. 4. 2, VII. 3. 2, VIII. 4. 30 etc.
[4] Below, p. 162.
[5] E.g., VI. 4. 3, IX. 1. 19: for slaves see below, p. 174.
[6] Examples of both in the texts cit. p. 162, nn. 6, 8.
[7] Examples are too abundant to require citation. Multiple payments and those in kind were typical of the vulgar law (Levy, *Obligationenrecht*, pp. 127–8), while fixed sums payable on each injured object etc. were Germanic (idem, *Schriften*, p. 142), although there were Roman precedents.
[8] No doubt they frequently benefited from sentences of enslavement to a person of the king's choice. Cf. also III. 4. 13, VI. 5. 15.
[9] VII. 6. 1, XII. 2. 14: cf. XII. 3. 16, with payment by the transgressor. The laying of information might also be necessary to avoid the imputation of guilt: see III. 5. 4, *re* homosexual assault. VII. 1. 5 is not concerned with informers, despite the title (but note the early MS R1) and chapter-heading.

thief who informed on his accomplices went unpunished on repayment of his share of the loot.[1] An informer had to be very sure of his facts, however, for if an accused was found innocent under torture and the *index* could not prove the information he had laid, he was liable to suffer the consequences which would have faced the accused if found guilty and was enslaved into the joint power of the innocent accused and the deceived accuser if he could not pay the composition demanded.[2] The law protected slave-owners against the loss which would be occasioned them, in consequence of this ruling, if their *mancipia* laid false information by the simple device of denying trustworthiness to slave informers not vouched for by their masters.[3]

Private or public, all crimes had one common factor in their legal treatment, and it is upon this, the jurisdictional role of the public authority, that the emphasis deserves to be placed. From the moment of accusation, the whole procedure which led to the imposition of punishment – indeed, the very decision as to whether punishment should be imposed – was in the hands of the king's judges: the penalty itself was that established by the king's law. If it was still often up to an interested party to prosecute a wrong-doer, in other words, and if punishment still often took a private form, freedom of action and method in proceeding against the criminal was nevertheless now circumscribed by the obligation to act only within the framework prescribed by the king through the law.

Although there existed certain far from insignificant differences between the rules of procedure and evidence in criminal cases and those in civil, it would be incorrect to think in terms of two quite distinct regimes. That the proceedings were basically identical whatever the object of the suit is to a large extent implicit in the very absence of a specific technical terminology which would indicate the nature of the plaint. *Accusare* or one of its derivatives came nearest to possessing such a technical sense, for the laws spoke regularly of accusation in connection with the laying of criminal charges. But accusations for debt also appeared,[4] and in any case the *accusator* was also described as the *petitor*,[5] the general term for plaintiff, just as the defendant in both criminal and other cases was *is qui pulsatus est*.[6]

---

[1] VII. I. 4; VII. I. 3. Cf. also VII. 5. 2 (in two MSS), *re* falsification.
[2] VII. I. I.      [3] VII. I. 2.      [4] II. 4. 7: cf. v. 6. 6.
[5] V. 6. 6, VI. I. 2, 5 etc.      [6] II. 2. 5, VI. I. 2.

Similarly, the initial approach to a judge was termed *interpellatio* whether a criminal or a civil suit was in question.[1] But there is no need to rely upon the negative evidence of the language. A careful reading of those many laws of the second book of the code which provide particulars of matters concerning procedure and the law of evidence shows quite clearly that they had criminal just as much as civil proceedings in mind.[2] These laws, taken in conjunction with others which establish special rules for criminal cases, allow the construction of a reasonably detailed account of how a case involving freemen was initiated, brought to court and heard, and of how judgement was made and executed.

Although the private summons was perhaps not unknown to Visigothic law,[3] and although parties in dispute may well have concluded voluntary stipulatory agreements to have their conflicts resolved by a judge,[4] the compulsive judicial summons was the normal preliminary to a hearing. When complaint was lodged with a judge, it was his duty, given the adequacy of the plaint, to summon the defendant to appear: corrupt rejection or procrastination on the part of the judge involved him in punishment, while the case remained open.[5] In the event that plaintiff and defendant lived in different jurisdictional areas, however, the judge approached was required to write to the competent authority, enjoining him to take action: refusal or delay by this second judge led to the temporary sequestration of his property, for the benefit of the *petitor*.[6] The rule was, therefore, that cases followed the defendant's forum. No doubt it was at the time of complaint that the victim of theft secretly informed the judge of what had been stolen.[7] Once a criminal charge had been lodged, the accuser was forbidden to come to a private

---

[1] Compare II. 1. 19 (where *interpellator* also = *petitor*) with VI. 4. 3, *in fine* (wounding), and VII. 4. 1 ('pro crimine interpellatus').

[2] E.g., II. 2. 5, 9 etc.

[3] See X. 2. 6: 'Possessor...sive a iudice seu a repetente conmonitus', where a formal approach of legal consequence is involved. But the plaintiff may have simply delivered the judicial summons: cf. also II. 1. 12, *in fine*, and p. 94, n. 4, below.

[4] It should be remembered that judges were sometimes appointed by the parties.

[5] II. 1. 20: see below, p. 118. The power of lawful refusal (on grounds of prescription, e.g.) is clear from the punishment for corruption.

[6] On the complicated II. 2. 7, providing even for distraint upon the property of someone unconnected with the case, see Dahn, *Studien*, pp. 252–4.

[7] Required by VII. 2. 1. Judicial search was clearly envisaged.

agreement for the payment of composition by the defendant, on pain of a fine of five *solidi*, paid to the judge: it was not so much the public interest as a notion of contempt of court which underlay this provision.[1] Accusation could also be made direct to the king in public cases, if not in person either through one of the king's *fideles* or through a representative armed with a formal letter giving details of the charge. But the penalty for false accusation to the king was harsher than that normally inflicted.[2]

The summons itself took the form of a letter impressed with the judicial seal,[3] and had to be delivered to the defendant in the presence of freeborn witnesses.[4] The failure of the defendant to appear within a given period of grace after the date stipulated resulted in transfer to the plaintiff of the property which was the object of the litigation 'reservato negotio dilatoris' and in the liability of the defaulter to pay compositions, both to the complainant *pro dilatione* and to the judge *pro contemtu* – given always that the delay was not due to illness or to some other unavoidable hazard, like snow in the mountain passes, or floods.[5] There is no indication that either party was required

---

[1] VII. 4. I (where the title has 'pro crimine interpellatus', but the text in most MSS refers only to theft): 'Si iudex...contemnatur. Si quis...iudicem...contemnens ...'. It is not clear whether the case remained open. For a later generalisation of the prohibition, see II. 2. 10 (Egica), with harsher penalties.    [2] VI. 1. 6.

[3] II. 1. 19: 'Admonitione unius epistule vel sigilli'. Zeumer, XXIII, 85–7, considered a (sealed) *epistola* to have been delivered when the complaint was oral, and *sigillum* to indicate the judicial seal affixed to a written complaint. But 'unius' rather suggests that letter and seal belonged together, and the lack of variation in the phrase *epistola vel sigillum*, which occurs four times in the law, in turn suggests that it was a technical phrase equivalent to *epistola sigillata*. Note also *sigillum negare* in II. 1. 20. How would the date and place of the hearing have been formally communicated to the defendant if the plaintiff's written complaint alone was delivered? The law allows, in my view, no conclusion as to the form of complaint required or the forms permitted. For an earlier written accusation of *invasio*, see *FV* 35.

[4] II. 1. 19, where 'Qui a iudice missus extiterit' delivered the summons: doubtless the judicial *saio* was the regular messenger, but sometimes, perhaps, the plaintiff acted.

[5] Ib. The law is detailed but as obscure as is much Chindasvindian legislation. For its special treatment of contumacious clerics, see below, pp. 152, 157. Interesting is the provision that corporal punishments in place of compositions be mitigated for reasons of age or health. Naïve, however, is the ruling that a defendant travelling more than 200 miles to court and allowed, therefore, a longer period of grace should be fined more heavily if late than another, having a shorter journey and period of grace. See also VIII. 1. 7, and for a temporary possessory order, below, p. 101, n. 4, where there is, however, some problem of reconciliation with II. 1. 19.

at the summons stage to furnish any written guarantee that he would attend the hearing: the device of the *placitum*, which included an agreed penalty-clause, was rather used when the summons had been answered but the case then adjourned, in lieu of a second summons.[1] But a man who had wilfully evaded the service of a summons might also be forced, during a legal holiday, to pledge his later appearance in this way: if his word was suspect, he might even be imprisoned if nobody would stand as his guarantor.[2] It was the judge's responsibility to see that both parties were bound by any *placitum*, and he was himself liable for payment of the sum in which he had bound one party to appear if the other, not bound, failed to turn up.[3]

Although the judicial summons can be taken as the regular procedural introduction to a case, there is plenty of evidence bearing on the use of arrest and pre-trial imprisonment. A case where imprisonment was provided for has just been mentioned, and there is no reason to think that a criminal action alone was in the legislator's mind: it is clear from other laws that arrest and imprisonment for debtors was not unusual.[4] A defaulting defendant must have been arrested, for how else could the punishment for his offence have been imposed? And in those cases where a possessory order did not satisfy the plaintiff's claim, arrest of a defaulter must have been necessary in order that the case be heard and judgement executed. Unquestionably, however, arrest would normally have been appropriate in criminal rather than civil cases. Several laws did in fact provide for the immediate arrest of a suspected criminal, and others dealt with matters connected with his custody.[5] It may well be that *de officio* action was regularly accompanied by arrest, and it is difficult to

---

[1] See II. 1. 22, where *definitio* is the term, and below, in text. Adjournment was no doubt often necessary when a third party had to be summoned, as in the *Anefangsverfahren*: see II. 2. 1 and below, p. 254, n. 2.

[2] II. 1. 12: 'Qui necdum ad iudicium ante conpulsus, et tamen, sciens esse se quandoquidem conpellendo, reliquis se temporibus dilatans...illi, a quo pulsandus est, se...ostendit'. Delay in answering an accepted summons may rather have been in mind here, for *conpellere* is used to mean both 'to summons' and 'to force'. But my interpretation seems preferable, for a defaulter would surely have been arrested and punished for his criminal contumacy. *Se dilatans* perhaps stems from confusion with *se latitans*.                 [3] II. 2. 4.

[4] See XI. 1. 8 and below, in text.

[5] Arrest: III. 2. 3, 4. 17, V. 4. 11, VI. 5. 17, VII. 6. 2, VIII. 1. 3 etc. Custody: XI. 1. 8 and below, in text. For the *saio* as the arresting officer, see II. 1. 18. A slave-owner failing to present his accused slave was arrested: VI. 1. 1.

believe that defendants charged with serious crimes were permitted their freedom until the hearings and thus allowed the opportunity to make good their escape.[1] The matter was probably one of judicial discretion, with decision based upon such criteria as a defendant's status, possessions, record and so on. Certainly it is not to be thought that all alleged criminals were arrested.[2]

Arrest might prove a problem, however, if the accused had fled to sanctuary. Asylum might be sought in any church or with the bishop,[3] and was taken advantage of not only by criminals but also by debtors and runaway slaves. The fugitive was required to lay down his arms before he took refuge and might be lawfully removed by force if he did not do so, even killed if he resisted.[4] Remarkably enough, the law prescribed no penalty for the unauthorised removal of a criminal,[5] but it did provide for the case of slaves and debtors: the offending lord or creditor forfeited his punitive or legal rights with regard to the victim of the outrage and was required to pay a composition of one hundred or thirty *solidi*, depending upon his status, to the church.[6] The correct procedure was for the pursuer to contact the relevant ecclesiastical authority who would yield up the fugitive after having arranged that the slave should not be punished or that the debtor should have a further period of grace for repay-

---

[1] See II. 1. 12 (arrest of capital offenders at any time) and VI. 4. 8 (possible imprisonment of assailant when victim might die). Note also IX. 1. 21 (Egica), *in fine*.

[2] II. 2. 6, 9, VI. 1. 2, witness the summons procedure in criminal cases, while VII. 4. 1 presupposes it. Both VII. 1. 5 and VII. 4. 2 appear to provide for arrest in all criminal cases. But in VII. 1. 5 the words: 'Et cum agnoverint crimen admissum, reum comes aut iudex conprehendat' can be taken to refer to the seizure of a convicted criminal for punishment, dealt with in the immediate continuation of the text (note also the later balancing sentence: 'Si vero innocens adprobatur, de iudicio securus abscedat') and in VII. 4. 2: 'Quotiens...quilibet in crimine...accusatur, ad corripiendum eum iudex insequatur. Quod si forte ipse iudex solus eum conprehendere vel distringere non potest, a comite civitatis querat auxilium', *corripere* means nothing but 'to bring to trial' and the second sentence provides for the case when arrest (either following contumacy or not) has been impossible. In 683, XIII Tol. 2 forbade the pre-trial imprisonment of the *seniores palatii*, *gardingi* and bishops except in certain cases where 'libera custodia' was permitted. The ruling appears to have applied also to ordinary freemen, but that is difficult to believe.

[3] But only III. 3. 2 and IX. 2. 3 referred to the bishop. Sanctuary began at the church porch (IX. 3. 4), but XII Tol. 10 declared the fugitive protected within thirty *passus* of the doors.                    [4] IX. 3. 1, 2: cf. *HW* 12.

[5] But XII Tol. 10 threatened all sanctuary-breakers with excommunication and *regia severitas*.                    [6] IX. 3. 3.

ment.[1] It is not clear what happened in the case of criminals. We are told only that if the *reus* did not merit the death penalty the cleric should intercede with the pursuer on the fugitive's behalf 'ut ei veniam det, et exoratus indulgeat'.[2] No doubt this meant simply that the pursuer should agree on oath not to administer or insist upon corporal punishment.[3] But what happened if he would not agree we do not know. Although the law just cited makes an express exception of the criminal guilty of a capital offence, all those laws which mention sanctuary in connection with particular crimes in fact deal with criminals facing the death penalty and provide for its commutation.[4]

If arrest might be complicated by flight to sanctuary, it might also be made difficult by the brute fact that its intended subject was prepared to resist and had more effective force at his command than did the judge. If an individual's power was not such a significant factor in allowing him to snap his fingers at the law as it would have been if summons or arrest had been the sole responsibility of the plaintiff, it could still matter, and there are revealing references to judges unable to take action against offenders and obliged to have recourse to higher authority.[5] The judge's first step if he was unable himself to force an accused to court was in fact to approach the city count, whose duty it was to help him.[6] But judicial arrest was not always necessary, for sometimes the accused would have been seized by the victim of the crime or by someone else:[7] even debtors attempting flight might be apprehended by their creditors and then presented to the judge.[8] It was assuredly fear of the infliction of private justice which inspired the provision that a captured criminal might not be held for longer than a day and a night before presen-

---

[1] V. 4. 17 (slaves), IX. 3. 4.  [2] IX. 3. 4.

[3] For the oath, see VI. 5. 16 (though a capital case) and XII Tol. 10 (with penalties for clerics who failed to yield up fugitives). For the famous case of breach of oath by Leovigild, see *HF* v. 38.

[4] III. 2. 2, 3. 2, VI. 5. 16, 18, IX. 2. 3 (though cf. IX. 2. 9). For sanctuary affecting excommunication, see VI Tol. 12, and for commutation of exile to slavery as its result, *VPE* v. 11. 17–19.

[5] Above, p. 79, n. 4, for references.

[6] VII. 4. 2.

[7] See VII. 2. 20 for an outsider's reward for capture of an escaped criminal and VIII. 4. 19 for non-liability for injury caused by a dog during attempted arrest.

[8] VI. 4. 4: see also the account of sanctuary above.

tation, on pain of a mulct of five or ten *solidi*.[1] Unlawful seizure and detention were, of course, punishable offences.[2] Those imprisoned and found guilty were required to pay one *tremis* to cover the expenses of their custody: remarkably, the law had to insist that an innocent man who had been imprisoned had nothing to pay.[3] Breaking a man out of prison or connivance at his escape by the *carcerarius* was itself a serious crime, involving the offender in the penalty which the escaped prisoner would have suffered.[4] Freeing a captive held privately had the same consequences unless the man responsible could present him before the court: in any case, he suffered one hundred lashes 'pro sola presumtione'.[5]

The arrest and imprisonment for later execution of criminals guilty of capital offences was a matter of such importance that it was permitted even during the religious and other legal vacations. Religious respect dictated that no-one otherwise should be placed or remain under any sort of judicial compulsion on the particular feasts of Christmas, Circumcision, Epiphany and Ascension, on any Sunday or during the week before and the week after Easter, unless the case had already begun, in which event it was adjourned, with the defendant bound by *placitum* or on the security of a guarantor to appear on its resumption,[6] or unless a defendant had avoided the service of a summons.[7] The same exceptions were admitted during the periods of the harvest and the vintage when economic exigencies otherwise made it desirable to prohibit judicial activity in civil, though not in criminal, matters.[8] The duration of these religious and other holidays was in total quite extensive, amounting to something like one-third of the year where non-criminal cases were concerned. But corrupt judicial procrastination was not tolerated once a case had opened: the judge had a maximum of eight days in which to bring

---

[1] VII. 2. 22: cf. VII. 2. 14.
[2] VI. 4. 3 and 4, though the two conflict.  [3] VII. 4. 4.
[4] VII. 4. 3.  [5] VII. 2. 20.
[6] II. 1. 12. This is the best that I can make of: 'Per hec tempora nullus ad causam dicendam venire cogatur vel sub executione aliqua deputetur; nisi forte causa, pro qua conpellitur, cepta iam aput iudicem fuisse videatur. Nam...si inquoata fuisse hactio repperitur, ad peragendum negotium absque ulla feriatorum dierum obiectione cogendus est qui pulsatur; ita ut...placito districtus abscedat...[aut] pro se fideiussorem adhibeat, quatenus peractis temporibus supradictis ad finiendam ...causam...remota dilatione occurrat'.  [7] Ib.
[8] Ib. For the dates, below, pp. 211, 212.

it to a close and had himself to pay the expenses incurred by the parties during the extra days if it ran on.[1] No doubt the two rest-days a week which the magistrate was permitted were not included in this eight-day period: on the other hand, the period in fact allowed less time for the hearing than might be thought, for no judicial business was carried on in the afternoons.[2] Adjournment was provided for in the event of the judge's illness or involvement in other affairs of government.[3]

We know nothing of the construction or site of the court itself, and the evidence concerning publicity in the proceedings is difficult to interpret.[4] The basic rule was stated by an obscurely worded law – of Chindasvind, not surprisingly[5] – which appears to have provided that those who had no business before the magistrate should be barred from the courtroom, entry to which should be open only to those who 'ought to be present'. The vague phrase 'quos constat interesse debere' was presumably used to indicate the principals or their representatives, the witnesses, the judge himself and those who might join him in hearing the case,[6] what court officers there were,[7] and at times, as we shall see, members of the public required to be present. The judge had the right, however, to select other *auditores* with whom he might, if he wished, confer about the case. The express motive of the law was to ensure the maintenance of a calm and seemly atmosphere during judicial hearings,[8] and it is probably

---

[1] II. I. 22. No doubt the presumption was of *dolus* or *calliditas* once the period had elapsed.  [2] II. I. 20.

[3] II. I. 22, where 'publice utilitatis indictio' perhaps refers specifically to tax matters.

[4] Although dogmatism is quite out of place here, I should say that I find the arguments of Sánchez-Albornoz, *Ruina*, pp. 86–92, 139–42, in favour of jury-courts, totally unconvincing. Against his interpretation, see Merêa, *Estudos*, pp. 283–5. The laws of the code consistently treat the judge as responsible for investigation, decision and sentence alike.

[5] II. 2. 2: 'Audientia non tumultu aut clamore turbetur, sed in parte positis, qui causam non habent, illi soli in iudicio ingrediantur, quos constat interesse debere. Iudex autem si elegerit auditores alios secum esse presentes aut forte causam . . . cum eis conferre voluerit, sue sit potestatis. Si certe noluerit, nullus se in audientiam ingerat, partem alterius . . . inpugnaturus, qualiter uni parti nutriri possit inpedimentum'.

[6] Cf. II. I. 16: 'Thiufadi tales eligant, quibus vicissitudines suas audiendas iniungant, ut ipsis absentibus illi causas et temperanter discutiant et iuste decernant'. Such men may have been the *auditores* of VII. 5. I.

[7] Bailiffs to expel the unruly, e.g. One might assume also the presence of a secretary: but note II. I. 25: 'Iudex . . . iudicia . . . conscribat'.

[8] Cf. XI Tol. I for conciliar hearings.

correct to see in it a deliberate attempt to avoid the pressures which had been imposed upon the Roman judge by the shouted opinions of the near-by public at large and by the efforts of those important men who had enjoyed the right to sit with him as *residentes*, and to have their views heard by him, to exercise influence on their clients' behalf.[1] Refusal to keep silence at the judicial command was punished in a Visigothic court by a fine of ten *solidi* and expulsion, but a *potens* who was so determined to act the patron that he defied the order to leave had to pay the very heavy fine of two pounds of gold and was forcibly thrown out. Ordinary freemen and slaves who similarly stood their ground suffered fifty lashes.[2]

That Chindasvind's law laid down the general rule that the publicity of the proceedings was a matter of judicial discretion seems probable.[3] It is likely, in fact, that the rule had been in force already at an earlier stage, for an *Antiqua* had permitted the judge to insist, in the interests of good order, that several individuals involved in a joint action should not all enter the court but should rather choose one of their number to conduct the case on behalf of all,[4] and if principals might thus be excluded it would be strange if the public at large had right of admittance. But the exercise of judicial discretion was subject to one important condition. In criminal cases the judge was forbidden to examine an accused in the absence of other persons lest collusion should occur and torments be inflicted on an innocent man.[5] It is this provision which in part explains the references in the criminal laws to public accusations, public examinations and public convictions.[6] No doubt judges often allowed a large number of the public to attend criminal trials as *auditores*: it

---

1 See on these A. Checchini, *Scritti giuridici e storico-giuridici*, II (Padua, 1958), 159–97.
2 II. 2. 2, 8. Differently, Zeumer, XXIV, 91–2.
3 Thus, strongly, M. A. von Bethmann-Hollweg, *Der Civilprozeß des gemeinen Rechts in geschichtlicher Entwicklung*, IV, part I: *Der germanisch-romanische Civilprozeß im MA. Vom fünften bis achten Jahrhundert* (Bonn, 1868), p. 222.
4 II. 2. 3. For joinder, see also X. 1. 4.
5 VII. 1. 5: 'Comes tamen aut iudex nullum discutere solus presumat'. Many other laws show that it was not the presence of two judges which was required: an apparent reference to this in the last sentence of VII. 1. 5 is imputable to inadequate drafting.
6 II. 5. 19 (Egica), III. 4. 13, 17, 6. 2, IV. 5. 1, VI. 5. 12, VII. 5. 2, VIII. 1. 11, XII. 1. 3 (Ervig, A.D. 683): cf. 'coram multis' (VI. 2. 2). But *publice* may sometimes mean 'before the public authorities'. In II. 5. 19 and XII. 1. 3, the references are to XIII Tol. 2, for which see above, p. 45, n. 3.

would have been from these persons that the 'honest men' whose presence was required during inquisition by torture would have been chosen.[1] But two or three witnesses probably sufficed, as they did when a bishop elected to investigate the criminality of one of his *subditi* himself rather than to hand the case over to the public authorities.[2] Criminal cases apart, the presence of outsiders, in the form of *sacerdotes* or other 'suitable' men, was only required when a bishop reheard a case together with an allegedly unjust judge.[3]

Certain general rules governed the proceedings. Cases might not be heard if their origins lay in events occurring more than thirty years, or, exceptionally, fifty years previously.[4] The magistrate was obliged to use only the laws of Ervig's code: anyone who offered him some other law book, and the judge himself if he then neglected to destroy it, was punished with far and away the largest fine of the code, thirty pounds of gold, unless the older laws were brought forward 'ad conprobationem preteritarum causarum'.[5] Cases completed before 21 October 681 were not to be revived in the light of changed provisions, but those begun but not finished were to be judged in accordance with the new *corpus*.[6] Neither ignorance of the law nor the claim that an alleged crime did not figure as the object of a particular ruling constituted a defence,[7] but matters outside the scope of the code were referred to the king.[8] Either principal might choose not to appear in person but to avail himself of the services of a *mandatarius* in a civil case: so too might the accuser in a criminal action, though the accused had no doubt to present himself personally, at least in major cases, where the possibility of recourse to

[1] VI. I. 2: cf. VI. I. 5.
[2] XI Tol. 7.
[3] II. I. 30. A court appearance of the *boni homines* of IX. I. 21 (Egica) and X. I. 17 is not in question, while a court dispute is not involved in V. 6. 3.
[4] For thirty years see X. 2. 3 (with a penalty of a pound of gold for a litigant in breach), X. 2. 4 (where Reccesvind declared that the period seemed 'non iam quasi ex institutione humana, sed veluti ex ipsarum rerum...processisse natura'), *et saepe* in laws and canons. X. 2. 6 provided for judicial action when the limit was approaching, so that the suit might not die: the *saio* was ordered (in an Exemplar, printed at the end of the law) to put the *petitor* in temporary possession of what he claimed. For fifty years, see IV. 3. 2, X. I. 16, 19, 2. 1, 2, 3. 4, and for no limitation period IV. 5. 6, X. 2. 4 (but revoked by Egica's X. 2. 5). Cf. further X. 2. 7, declaring those years spent in prison or exile not to be included in the thirty or fifty years.
[5] II. I. 11: cf. II. I. 10.　　　　　[6] II. I. 14: for the date, II. I. I.
[7] II. I. 3, VI. 4. 5.　　　　　[8] Above, p. 78.

torture existed.[1] Choice of an *adsertor* was, however, limited, except for those acting on behalf of the fisc.[2] No-one otherwise might appoint an attorney of more powerful standing than his opponent, 'ut non equalis sibi eius possit potentia opprimi vel terreri'.[3] Slaves might be employed as *mandatarii* only by their owners, by freemen of humble estate or by the Church,[4] and a woman might not accept a mandate at all, although she was perfectly entitled to conduct her own case.[5] Appointment was by means of a witnessed document:[6] a copy of this was retained by the judge and the name of the *mandatarius* included in the written judgement at the end of the case.[7] An *adsertor* might be removed from his position for fraud or negligence,[8] while collusion obliged him to pay his *mandator* whatever the latter had lost or failed to win as a result.[9] Reward for the mandatory was fixed beforehand and paid regardless of the outcome of the case, but if he failed to hand over within three months what had been awarded to his principal, he forfeited all claim to payment.[10] The death of principal or representative before a case was heard annulled the mandate: once decision had been given, however, the heirs of an *adsertor* who later died were entitled to his agreed emolument.[11]

The status of the participants once established, the hearing began. The burden of proof rested upon the plaintiff,[12] but evidence was heard from both sides.[13] Witnesses and documents were the prime sources of this, with precedence in the hearing given to the former but evidentiary priority to the latter if the verbal account of a witness was in conflict with the terms of a document which he had sub-

---

[1] II. 2. 4, 3. 4. Roman law (reflected still in VI Tol. 11) had not permitted the use of *mandatarii* in criminal cases. On the following laws, see Zeumer, XXIV, 94–8, and on the vulgar law background Levy, *Obligationenrecht*, pp. 287ff.

[2] II. 3. 10: cf. II. 3. 3. See above, p. 89, n. 6, for the probable exclusion of *infamati*.

[3] II. 3. 9.    [4] II. 3. 3. Church *mandatarii* are perhaps in mind in Mer. 21.

[5] II. 3. 6. A husband might represent his wife without a mandate only when he gave security that she would not reject the decision. She was free to do this, but subject to penalty if she too was then defeated.

[6] II. 3. 3: but cf. below, p. 173. See *FV* 41 for an example, and cf. *FV* 42, 43.

[7] II. 3. 2.    [8] II. 3. 5, 7.

[9] II. 3. 3. Was the case reheard?

[10] II. 3. 7.    [11] II. 3. 8.

[12] Particularly clear from II. 1. 25: cf. also VI. 1. 2: 'Habeat prius fiduciam conprobandi quod obicit...quod si probare non potuerit...per probationem convictus...aut si convinci non potuerit', *FV* 40 etc.

[13] II. 2. 5: cf. II. 4. 2, V. 7. 8, *FV* 40 etc.

scribed.[1] Information concerning witnesses is relatively detailed. Testimony could be given by any free person over the age of fourteen and of rational mind,[2] unless he or she was a Jew, when restrictions were imposed,[3] or was branded with *infamia*. The evidence of a litigant's relatives, however, was admissible only when the case solely concerned members of the family or when no other witnesses were available.[4] At least two 'suitable' witnesses were required before a judge might base a decision upon their evidence,[5] and 'suitable' here meant not only freeborn but honest-minded and well-off.[6] Witnesses had to present themselves in person – unless prevented by age, illness or distance, when affidavits sworn before a judge or his delegate might be produced before the court by mandatories[7] – and were questioned by the judge, who then made the decision as to who were the more credible.[8] It was these witnesses alone who at the end of the case made sworn written depositions of what they knew, for evidence was not given on oath.[9] A man could not be forced to give evidence, but if he declined to say what he knew of a matter or said that he knew nothing, but refused to swear to that, he lost his right of testimony and, if an ordinary freeman, was lashed, 'quia non minor reatus est vera subprimere quam falsa confingere'.[10] In fact,

---

[1] II. 1. 23; II. 4. 3, also providing for calligraphic examination when a witness denied that an adduced document bore his subscription. Cf. also II. 5. 18 (Egica) and II. 5. 3 (Egica), insisting that a witness read a document, or have it read to him, before subscription.　　　[2] II. 4. 12, 5. 11.

[3] Below, p. 136.

[4] II. 4. 13: see Zeumer, XXIV, 105–8, d'Ors, *Código*, pp. 64–6, and note the contrast with Germanic practice.

[5] II. 1. 25, 4. 3: cf. VI. 5. 5. Biblical influence (Deut. 17. 6, 19. 15 etc.) can hardly be doubted, despite *LRV.CT* XI. 14. 2 (itself also influenced?).

[6] II. 4. 3. But the evidence of slaves was occasionally admissible: below, p. 173.

[7] II. 4. 5.　　　　　　　　　　　　[8] II. 4. 2.

[9] I say this without much conviction. The text is II. 4. 2: 'Iudex, causa finita et sacramentum secundum leges, sicut ipse ordinaverit, a testibus dato, iudicium emittat; quia testes sine sacramento testimonium peribere non possunt'. I incline to the view in the text because: (i) the existence of written depositions made after the hearing is assured, (ii) VIII Tol. 2 offers slight support: 'Omne etiam quod testis astipulat, tunc verius constat, cum id adjectio jurationis affirmat' and (iii) an oath after testimony is implied by the later words of the law: 'Si...quisquam... testimonium peribere noluerit, aut si nescire se dixerit [that is, during his evidence], id ipsum etiam iurare distulerit'. See also Zeumer, XXIV, 99–100, and H. Brunner, *Forschungen zur Gesch. des deutschen und französischen Rechtes* (Stuttgart, 1894), pp. 117–20 (for a later time): *contra*, d'Ors, *Código*, p. 64.

[10] II. 4. 2.

however, both false testimony and the persuasion of someone to offer it were punished more severely than suppression of the truth: the culprit was declared infamous and required to pay composition to the value of whatever it was that the victim of the perjury had lost, or stood to lose.[1] Even the intent to commit perjury was a criminal offence: *placita* whereby men undertook to give witness in support of each other regardless of the truth were naturally invalid, like any agreements 'de turpibus et inlicitis rebus',[2] but they also brought those who made them one hundred lashes each.[3] Proof of perjury or of prior incapacity to testify might lead to the reopening of a case or the reversal of a decision, but the rules were both complex and obscure.[4] The most important points were, first, that a confession of perjury was not regarded as in itself sufficient foundation for the revival of a case – for the self-alleged perjurer might have been bribed or threatened into his declaration by the vanquished litigant[5] – and, second, that the evidence of a dead man might be impugned only when there could be produced either a written confession – in which, men must piously have thought, corruption would play no part–or a written judicial declaration of his criminality.[6]

While, in the nature of things, the oral testimony of witnesses would have provided the bulk of the evidence in criminal cases, in civil matters documentary evidence would frequently have been available. Our knowledge of the extent of lay education in the Visigothic kingdom is scanty, but the frequency of reference in the laws to *scripturae* of one sort or another and to witnesses who subscribed these rather than made their marks upon them perhaps indicates that elementary instruction in reading and writing was not so very rare.[7] Although a form of document was not a constitutive requirement for

---

[1] II. 4. 6, 9: but distinct penalties for a particular case in II. 4. 3.
[2] II. 5. 7.        [3] II. 4. 11.
[4] Cf. II. I. 25, 4. 6, 7, 8 (Egica), and Zeumer, XXIV, 103–4.
[5] II. 4. 6, 7.        [6] II. 4. 7.
[7] For laymen, see P. Riché, *Éducation et culture dans l'occident barbare*, *VI*ᵉ*–VIII*ᵉ *siècles* (Paris, 1962), pp. 294–310. See also, on Gothic rather than Roman *subscriptores* to the slate documents, M. C. Diaz y Diaz, 'La cultura de la Esp. visigótica del siglo VII', *Sett.*, V (1958), 817. On *subscriptio* and *signum*, see Zeumer, XXIV, 15–29: the first was a short statement in the first person and the second a mark, usually a cross, but probably embellished with flourishes ('evidentibus signis': VI. I. 6) and therefore identifiable (cf. II. 5. 15). The *signa* of witnesses figure in later Visigothic law as they did not in Roman.

the valid and irrevocable performance of any one of the three major transactions, sale, exchange and donation,[1] it is abundantly clear from the laws and *Formulae* that it was a regular concomitant, with its significance essentially probative,[2] occasionally dispositive. A brief digression to glance at sale and donation – for barter received no independent treatment but was regulated by the rules on sale[3] – will help to make this apparent and, with the addition of some comments on the institution of the testament, be of intrinsic interest, since it was with precisely these civil matters that the judges would have had most often to deal.

The fundamental concept which underlay the various provisions on sale was common to both Roman vulgar law and Germanic practice: it was the identification of *venditio* not, as in classical law, with a transaction generative of an obligation to convey in return for payment, but with the transfer of title as the instantaneous consequence of payment.[4] It was only as an evidential device by which payment could be proved that a document played a part in the law of sale: equally adequate, however, was the testimony of witnesses.[5] Once payment was established, the sale was good: even if payment was not total, the failure of the buyer to pay what remained at the appointed time did not void it, though interest had to be paid and there might, of course, be an agreement to rescind.[6] Payment once made, the validity of the sale could not later be attacked on the grounds that the price was too low:[7] if, on the other hand, no pay-

---

[1] With the single exception of a conjugal donation.

[2] Particularly clear from *FV* 12, 13, 27, 28: see A. Ehrhardt in *ZRG.RA*, lI (1931), 178.

[3] v. 4. 1: cf. *FV* 27. The document discussed by Diaz y Diaz, 'Un document privé', concerned an exchange.

[4] See Levy, *Law of property*, pp. 156–61, and *Schriften*, pp. 205–6, 213–14, whose comments on the *CE* apply equally to the later regime. Differently on payment as the *essentiale negotii*, d'Ors, *Código*, pp. 211–20, and differently again Merêa, *Estudos*, pp. 83–104. Further on Visigothic sale see R. Fernández Espinar in *AHDE*, xxv (1955), 337–72.

[5] v. 4. 3: see Levy, *Law of property*, pp. 156–9. Payment was presupposed by the existence of the *scriptura* which regularly included receipt of the price: cf. *FV* 11. Differently, H. García, p. 136, holding the *scriptura* a substitute for the price.

[6] v. 4. 5: see Merêa, *Estudos*, pp. 92–4. Penalty threatened the fraudulent buyer who gave less than was declared (one thinks, e.g., of adulterated coin), but there is no indication of voidance: v. 4. 6.

[7] v. 4. 7: see Levy, *Obligationenrecht*, p. 211, though I cannot recognise the contrast with v. 4. 6 (last note).

ment had been received, although the 'vendor' thought it had, there was no sale.[1] Similarly, the mere delivery of an earnest of the intention to buy, in the form of *arrae*, did not constitute a sale: the intending vendor was bound to a future *venditio*, but his obligation ceased if payment was not presented at the time agreed, and the potential buyer might recover his earnest and withdraw without penalty.[2] Transfer, as opposed to payment, was not taken into special account by the laws – which, however, regularly assumed it to have occurred.[3]

The valid performance of sale rested, then, upon payment. But other factors might void a sale in this aspect correctly performed. On the one hand, the transaction had to be consensual: a sale made under duress was void, in the same way that a forced donation or exchange was void.[4] On the other, there had to be certain and genuine title vested in the vendor (or donor): a man might not lawfully alienate property which was the subject of legal proceedings, which belonged to someone else or which was physically possessed by another, who

[1] v. 4. 16.
[2] v. 4. 4: see Levy, *Law of property*, pp. 159–60, *Obligationenrecht*, pp. 234–5. Although v. 4. 4's forerunner, *CE* 297, cannot be examined in detail here, I must, with the utmost respect for that eminent Romanist, Professor d'Ors, express misgivings as to the correctness of his reading (*Código*, p. 29) of *dederit* for Zeumer's *acceperit* (not marked as doubtful) in the first sentence: 'Qui arras pro quacumque acceperit re, praetium cogatur implere quod placuit' (where *praetium* is not definite: *negotium* is suggested by von Schwerin, p. 53). The difficulty of establishing certain readings of the Eurician texts is illustrated by, e.g., the same author's variant versions of *CE* 327 in *EV*, I (Rome–Madrid, 1956), 131, and *Código*, p. 41. Against *dederit* is not only the continuation of the text: 'Emptor vero' – for *vero* regularly implies a contrast of subject with what has preceded – but also the strangeness of a provision which would first state in unqualified fashion the obligation of the intending purchaser ('cogatur implere') but then continue by declaring that he is to receive back the *arrae* if he does not pay at the appointed time! Moreover, 'arras *tantummodo* recipiat' signifies 'let him receive *only* the earnest' – where 'only' makes little sense if it was the purchaser who was earlier bound by the law to payment, rather than the seller who was bound to convey on payment. In v. 4. 4 the text begins: 'Qui arras...acceperit, id cogatur inplere quod placuit', continues (with a real contrast): 'Emptor vero...' and ends: 'Arras tantummodo recipiat, quas dedit, et res definita non valeat'. Certainly here there is no obligation on the part of the intending purchaser. Note also 'res definita', not *venditio facta*: no sale had taken place. For reservations, see also Levy, *Schriften*, pp. 307–9.
[3] Not, of course, in v. 4. 4 (last note). See v. 4. 2 and Levy, *Law of property*, pp. 160–1, d'Ors, *Código*, pp. 211–12, for the irrelevance of *traditio* to *venditio*.
[4] v. 4. 3; v. 2. 1 (cf. v. 2. 7); v. 4. 1.

claimed it as his own.[1] Particular rules provided for voidance or voidability in other cases,[2] but in its main features the unimpeachable *venditio* was characterised by, first, the agreement of the parties about the transfer of a true title and, second, the payment of the agreed price or a considerable part of it.

Basically also in accordance with vulgar law developments was the law of donations,[3] where the gratuitous character of the transaction was fully accepted and there was no trace of the Germanic requirement of counter-performance, *launegild*. The essential feature of the performance of *donatio inter vivos* was the transfer and acceptance of the thing donated. This might be validly and – subject to reversal *causa ingratiae* – irrevocably effected in no more elaborate manner than by the corporal delivery by the donor and reception by the donee of the property concerned – expressed, no doubt, in the case of immovables by their respective quittance and entry.[4] Only in the particular case of donations between husband and wife, where the legislator was perhaps concerned to protect a spouse against the consequences of acts of spontaneous but undue generosity, was a written deed of gift insisted upon.[5] But donations might also come about *per scripturam*, with subsequent physical possession by the donee. There was no need here for a formal *traditio cartae*: once the deed of gift was, with the donor's consent, in the hands of the donee, *vera traditio* was held to have occurred.[6] From the donor's point of

---

[1] See v. 4. 8, 9, 20 (commented on below, pp. 254–5), though note x. 1. 6 (below, p. 209). See further v. 1. 2, 3 (uncanonical sales), 4. 13 (unlawful sales by slaves), *FV* 11, with a declaration of title, and for purchases of stolen goods, below, p. 194, with n. 6, pp. 251ff.

[2] E.g., v. 4. 2, 12, 14, IX. 1. 10.

[3] Generally on vulgar law and Visigothic donations, see Levy, *Law of property*, pp. 138ff., 164–6, whom I do not, however, entirely follow.

[4] v. 2. 6: cf. II. 1. 6, involving immovables, where *definitio* is 'sine scripture textum tantumodo coram testibus', and IV. 5. 3. On revocation for ingratitude in the vulgar law, see Levy, *Obligationenrecht*, pp. 245–7. Visigothic donations are not explicitly declared subject to it (but see *CE* 308 and d'Ors, *Código*, pp. 235–6), but its rule is assumed: see *FV* 29, with a disclaimer, and note the provision for cancellation of a *donatio reservato usufructu* in v. 2. 6 'etiam si in nullo lesum fuisse se dixerit'. See further above, p. 60, and below, p. 156, with n. 3.

[5] v. 2. 7: see below, p. 236. I can agree neither with Merêa, *Estudos*, p. 73, that *CE* 307, the forerunner of v. 2. 7, established a general regime for all gifts, nor with d'Ors, *Código*, pp. 236–8, that it gave the form only of donations *mortis causa*. See Levy, *Law of property*, p. 164, King, pp. 184–9.

[6] v. 2. 6: see Merêa, *Estudos*, pp. 76–7, Levy, *Law of property*, p. 166.

view, alienation had then taken place and the gift was irrevocable: nevertheless, the donation was not perfect until the donee had physically taken possession of, or entered upon, the property donated, for if he were to die before that moment, ownership reverted to the donor or to his heirs.[1] While delivery might take either a corporal or a written form, in other words, acceptance had always to be corporal in order that perfect performance be achieved.

This rule applied no less when the donation was *mortis causa*. But in the case of such a gift, the transfer of the *scriptura* by no means signified the extinction of the donor's rights: although the legislator spoke of a donation *retento usufructu*, the notion did not have its old technical sense, for the donor's rights in the property did not constitute a *ius in re aliena* but were those of an owner.[2] The donation which took effect only upon the donor's death was revocable at his pleasure – although he might have to reimburse the deprived donee for expenses undergone in anticipation of the gift – and this, precisely, 'quia similitudo est testamenti'.[3] The testament was a device which the Goths had early taken over from Roman law.[4] Reservations in favour of direct descendants apart, any free and sane person over the age of fourteen was at liberty to dispose of his property as he wished.[5] Like all written documents, a testament was invalid if it did

---

[1] v. 2. 6: 'Quod si ipsum, cui res donate fuerant, fatalis casus ab hac vita subduxerit, antequam rem sibi donatam caperet, ad donatorem vel ad heredes donatoris res ipsa pertineat'. This part of the law appears shortly after that requiring a deed of gift found among a deceased's possessions to be handed over to the named donee, but does not, in my view, mean simply to say that the death of a donee before he had received the *scriptura* invalidated the donation, since: (i) the goods had already been given ('donate fuerant'), (ii) there is reference to reversion 'ad donatorem', and (iii) the text has 'rem...caperet', not 'scripturam...caperet'. The provision is rather of general scope, and applies equally to donations *inter vivos* and *mortis causa*. See H. Steinacker, 'Der Ursprung der *traditio*', *Festschrift des akademischen Vereines deutscher Historiker in Wien* (Vienna, 1914), p. 16: the work has not been available to me, but is cited in Merêa, *Estudos*, p. 78, n. 53 – who himself takes a different view.

[2] For the confusion of *donatio post obitum* and *don. res. usufructu*, see J. A. Rubio in *AHDE*, IX (1932), 8–14 – an essential account.

[3] v. 2. 6: for the confluence of the institutions of *d. mortis causa* and *testamentum*, see also IV. 2. 4, 19 etc., and on the confusion of notions in *FV* 21, Merêa, *Estudos*, pp. 110–11.      [4] *CE* 308, 320.

[5] See IV. 2. 20 and below, pp. 244, 246–8, for capacity and reservations. But a will was not totally invalid if the restrictions were ignored: II. 5. 10. A lunatic might make his will during a period of temporary sanity: II. 5. 11.

not bear the exact date of its production or if it was extorted by force.[1] But no requirements as to the internal form of the document appeared in the laws of the code,[2] where the concern of the legislators was exclusively with the problem of establishing the authenticity of the *scriptura* as a genuine expression of the will of the deceased. To judge by the *Formulae* of the early seventh century, practically anything went:[3] certainly the basic Roman feature of *institutio heredis* was entirely lacking, even though it still appeared in an episcopal testament of 576.[4]

The legislators took into account four types of written testament, each distinguishable from its fellows by virtue of the device it employed to demonstrate its authenticity and each requiring correspondingly distinct legal treatment for the purposes of probate.[5] The testament which bore the *subscriptio* of the testator and either the subscriptions or the marks of the witnesses was, it seems, accepted without further ado.[6] But such a variety could not have been the most common, and the second probably represented the norm. This was the testament which the testator had been able to confirm only with his mark: in such a case a witness would guarantee the genuineness of this *signum* by his own subscription, but this individual was required later also to swear to the mark's authenticity.[7] A third testament was that to which the testator had been unable to add either his *subscriptio* or his *signum*, but which a representative had confirmed for him. The validity of such a document – rejected out of hand if the testator recovered from the severe affliction which had made it necessary, but then failed to confirm it by his own hand – was assured only when the representative and the other witnesses swore

[1] II. 5. 1, 2, 16 (date); II. 5. 5, 9 (extortion, for which see also p. 106, n. 4, above, and p. 235, below).
[2] Note the casualness of II. 5. 16, concerning the holograph will: 'Scribat ea, que hordinare desiderat; ita ut specialiter adnotetur, quecumque iudicare voluerint, vel que de rebus suis habere quemquam elegerint'.
[3] On *FV* 21–6, see Merêa, *Estudos*, pp. 109–13.
[4] *Testamentum Vicentii episcopi*, ed. F. Fita in *BRAH*, XLIX (1906), 155–7. Cf. also *VPE* IV. 4. 4.
[5] Basic on the following is Zeumer, XXIV, 26–9.
[6] II. 5. 12. How many witnesses were required? In v. 7. 1, dealing with testamentary manumission 'per scripturam aut presentibus testibus', the number appeared as three or five: but note that for donations *inter coniuges* (where those *mortis causa* were doubtless included), two or three were needed: v. 2. 7.
[7] II. 5. 12.

before a judge that the will was written according to the wishes of the testator and that they had been requested by him to act in their respective functions.[1] The fourth type, the holograph testament, written and subscribed by the testator in the absence of witnesses – most often, no doubt, a soldier's will[2] – presented most problems. Probate here was dependent upon the satisfactory comparison of the handwriting of the document with that of three specimens of the alleged testator's script, and was signified by episcopal and judicial subscription of the document.[3] Calligraphic comparison of subscriptions or marks was in fact the central feature of the procedure when the authenticity of any document was called in question.[4]

Alongside the written stood the oral will. The requirement here was that the witnesses swear to its terms before a judge and confirm their oath by *subscriptio* or *signum*, which had itself to be witnessed: they stood to gain as reward one-thirtieth of the cash left by the deceased.[5] When the witnesses were slaves – as must frequently have been the case if, for example, a man died on the battlefield – the validity of an oral will depended upon the preliminary establishment of their trustworthiness, the subsequent confirmation of their oath by the presiding bishop and judge, and finally royal approval.[6] In all cases, a written or oral will had to be presented publicly to a bishop within six months:[7] fraudulent suppression was punished as falsification.[8] An exception had to be made in the case of the holograph will, however, the nature of which was such that it might well not be presented within this period, since knowledge even of its existence might be lacking: thirty years were therefore allowed in which the beneficiary or his successors might present it, although no more than six months might elapse between reception and presentation.[9]

Given the important role of documents in these and other fields, it is understandable that forgery should have been harshly dealt with. The particular offence of forgery was in fact subsumed within the

---

[1] II. 5. 1, 12.   [2] Cf. II. 5. 13.
[3] II. 5. 16.
[4] Details in II. 5. 17: see also II. 4. 3, 5. 15, and generally Zeumer, XXIV, 30–8. The term employed, *contropatio* (used in a more general sense in III. 1. 5, IV. 5. 3, VI. 1. 5, X. 1. 17), is unique to the Visigoths. For lost documents, see VII. 5. 2.
[5] II. 5. 12.   [6] II. 5. 13.
[7] II. 5. 1, 12, 14: cf. V. 5. 10, 7. 1. But II. 5. 16 refers to presentation to bishop and judge, and several texts show the judge involved in probate.
[8] Below, p. 111, n. 4.   [9] II. 5. 16.

general crime of falsification, which was widely enough construed to embrace virtually any form of fraudulent dealing, including verbal deception.[1] To produce a false document or knowingly to use one,[2] to tamper with a genuine document, to suppress, to steal or to destroy it, to forge a seal, to deceive someone into written abandonment of his rights, to enter into a fraudulent agreement, to assume a false name, to lie about one's birth or parents or to commit some other imposture, even to open a will before the death of the testator – all these were actions of the falsifier.[3] The penalties were *infamia*, flogging and composition in the form of whatever sum had been involved in the fraud or of one-quarter of the property of a *potentior*, when this represented a greater amount: enslavement was the fate of those unable to pay.[4] That falsification was to some extent recognised as a 'public' crime, at least when committed by a *potentior*, is shown by the appropriation of one-quarter of this proportion by the king.[5] Wholly public, on the other hand, and with distinct penalties, were the offences of tampering with a royal document, forging the royal seal and so on: here, the ordinary freeman forfeited not property or liberty but the offending hand, while the *honestior* had to yield up to the fisc no less than one-half of his possessions.[6]

In some criminal cases the failure of the accuser to prove his case by direct evidence might be followed by the use of torture against the accused.[7] The employment of torture against freemen was not in

[1] VII. 5. 7.
[2] Unwitting use: VII. 5. 3.
[3] See VII. 5. 2–4, 6–8.
[4] The best I can make of VII. 5. 2, the basic law on falsification, which is characteristically Chindasvindian in its obscurity: *infamia* does not appear there, but can confidently be assumed, both on *a priori* grounds and especially in view of VII. 5. 5. The suppressor of a will, explicitly deemed subject to the penalty for falsification (II. 5. 12, VIII. 5. 2), certainly had to pay the beneficiaries what they stood to gain from it (thus the Chindasvindian II. 5. 14). Differently, however, VII. 5. 5, and cf. V. 5. 10, where giving the will after publication to someone other than the major beneficiary involved double payment of the sum which that beneficiary stood to gain.
[5] VII. 5. 2: cf. VI. 1. 6 for accusation to the king.
[6] VII. 5. 1. The unattributed Novel VII. 5. 9 carries a general ban on the copying of orders, laws etc. by unauthorised persons, and provides severe corporal penalties for infringement.
[7] VI. 1. 2: 'Habeat *prius* fiduciam conprobandi quod obicit...Quod si probare non potuerit...inscriptio fiat, et sic questionis examen incipiat': cf. VII. 2. 23: 'Quod si servus non convincitur, inscribatur'.

accordance with Germanic custom,[1] and it was no doubt because of this that the earlier Roman regime underwent many changes in the interests of protecting an accused person against injustice.[2] The legislators had a grim confidence in the efficacy of torture in extracting a confession of guilt,[3] but precisely for this reason carefully regulated its use: the utterances of a man put to the question were not to be relied upon. The safeguards were such that any accuser in doubt about the outcome of the case would proceed to the use of torture only at his extreme peril. An oath that he did not act maliciously towards the accused was a preliminary condition,[4] but a more effective deterrent was the penalty which awaited the unsuccessful accuser. Torture was permitted only after the accuser had presented a subscribed and witnessed *inscriptio* to the judge in which he recognised that in the event of failure he himself would be liable to suffer the fate which would have befallen his opponent, if proved guilty: he would escape only death, in lieu of which he would be enslaved to his innocent victim if composition could not be arranged.[5] A further defence was provided for the accused by the requirement that the accuser deliver secretly to the judge a written account of the circumstances of the crime: only if there was no discrepancy between this account and any confession forced from the victim was guilt held to be established.[6] Commonsense demanded that if the accused already knew the details torture should not be allowed,[7] and since these must often have been disclosed at an earlier stage of the trial it is doubtful whether question was often permissible at all. In any case, its possible use against ordinary freemen was restricted to capital cases and to those involving a sum of 500 *solidi* or more, while nobles could be tortured on the accusation of their equals only when a capital charge was involved and on that of their inferiors not at all.[8] When the

[1] Torture – always closely connected with strong central authority – disappeared for centuries in the disturbed conditions after 711: see G. Martínez Díez, 'La tortura judicial en la legislación hist. esp.', *AHDE*, xxxii (1962), 249–50.
[2] The Roman system is sketched by Martínez Díez, 'Tortura', pp. 224–33, with pp. 229–33 on the Breviary.
[3] vi. 1. 2: 'Quia dubitari non potest, quod per tormenta sibi crimen inponat...'.
[4] vi. 1. 5.      [5] See ii. 3. 4, vi. 1. 2, vii. 1. 1, 5, and below, p. 115, n. 6.
[6] vi. 1. 2.                            [7] Ib.
[8] Ib. By no means did the law forbid ordinary freemen to lay charges against nobles, as Thompson, *Goths*, pp. 137, 258, holds. The use of torture by a Jew against a Christian was forbidden: xii. 2. 9.

accuser was represented by a *mandatarius,* the torture of nobles was ruled out altogether and that of ordinary freemen was permitted only when the mandatory was not a slave.[1]

If, despite the prospect facing him in the event of failure, the accuser decided to inscribe his adversary, it became his personal responsibility to inflict the torture.[2] Further dangers awaited him here, even if his case was just, for although the judge who supervised the three-day proceedings had considerable interest in ensuring that the accused did not die under torture, since he himself then escaped death only if he and the *honesti viri* who were also present swore that no corruption or malice on his part had been responsible and since even then he had to pay the enormous composition of 500 *solidi* for his 'indiscretion', it might well happen that the accuser, inexperienced or desperate, would push his victim too far – a literally fatal mistake, for he was then delivered to the power of the relatives of the dead man, to be killed by them.[3] It is no wonder that before a *mandatarius* could demand torture he needed special authority from his principal, for the latter was the one who would suffer in the event of failure.[4]

When manifest proof was lacking and torture either not permitted or not proceeded with, a final resort consisted in the oath. The use of oaths in Visigothic society was understandably widespread, for what better means could be found of ensuring the reliability of a man's profession than its investment with a religious solemnity and binding force which left the declarant in no doubt as to the eternal sanction threatening untruth or breach of promise?[5] Indeed, it was the very strength of the binding power of oaths which led Egica, made fearful of conspiracy by Sisbert's plot, to menace anyone who took an oath with a co-jurant 'citra fidem regiam vel propria causarum negotia'

---

[1] II. 3. 4.

[2] Differently, Dahn, *Studien,* p. 284, n. 1. But 'coram iudice...accusator penas inferat' can bear no other meaning.

[3] VI. 1. 2. No separate penalty was provided for grave injury, against the infliction of which the torturer was also warned. Talion? But VI. 1. 5 provided the same punishment for causing grave injury to a slave by torture as for torturing him to death.

[4] II. 3. 4.

[5] For excellent examples of the terms of oaths, see XII. 3. 15 and *FV* 39. The difficulties presented when it was expedient for an oath to be broken are well illustrated by VIII Tol. 2: see also XV Tol. (cols 520–4). Note further X. 1. 14: 'Si...aliquam dubietatem habuerint...ipsi, ut animas suas non condemnent, nec sacramentum prestent'.

with the penalties of treason.[1] Oaths may be conveniently divided
into two categories. There were, first, those as to present state and/or
future behaviour. Under this heading may be grouped most of those
oaths which have so far been encountered – the oath of the pursuer
to spare the claimant of sanctuary, that of the accuser forswearing
malice when proceeding to the use of torture, constitutional oaths –
and many others.[2] The second group was composed of oaths in confirmation of declarations concerning the past, oaths which had as
largely an evidentiary or probative purpose as had those of the first
category a promissory one. Numerous examples could be adduced:
the oath of the victim of an arsonist as to the value of the property
destroyed, that of the litigant who had suffered from unlawful
judicial delay as to the expenses he had incurred, that of the redeemer
of a slave captured by the enemy as to the price he had paid, and
so on.[3]

The supreme and certainly most important example of this second
group was the oath taken at the end of a case, with its function the
basic one of resolving the question of which party should emerge
victorious. No doubt this oath was couched in as awesome terms as
the two others which have survived: nevertheless, it was realistically
recognised that the distant sanction of lost salvation, although as
effective a deterrent as could be found, was no sure guarantee against
perjury, and the judge was therefore required always first to investigate witnesses and to examine documents, 'ut veritas possit certius
inveniri, ne ad sacramentum facile veniatur'.[4] When Ervig added
that it was up to the judge concerned to determine in which cases and
by whom an oath should be taken, he certainly did not mean to
countermand this, but rather to make it clear that the magistrate had
full discretion of decision as to when orthodox evidence was or was
not fully convincing, and also that the oath was not necessarily to be
taken by the defendant. This does not mean to say that an accuser or
plaintiff was regularly permitted to damn his adversary by oath alone.
Ervig no doubt had in mind the sort of case in which the defendant

[1] II. 5. 19. Sisbert may have taken advantage of the freedom from pre-trial imprisonment granted him by XIII Tol. 2 to try to bind those who would hear his case.

[2] II. I. 19, III. I. 5, VII. 2. 8 etc. For oaths confirming peace-treaties and sealing
friendships, see VIII Tol. 2.

[3] VIII. 2. I; II. I. 22; V. 4. 21: further examples in II. 4. 5, 5. 13, VII. 5. 2, VIII. I. 5,
X. 3. 5 etc.　　　　　　　　　　[4] II. I. 23.

was not in a position to swear with certainty to the facts, while his opponent was – the situation envisaged, for example, in v. 4. 13, where a lord attempting to reclaim property illegally alienated by his slave was obliged to swear, if he could not prove, that the property in contention had not been part of the slave's *peculium*.[1] Normally, we may be quite sure, the oath was required of the defendant: this was the general rule established in II. 2. 5, II. 2. 9 and VI. I. 2,[2] and confirmed in many particular laws.[3] Naturally, failure to take the oath when required led to an adverse verdict.[4]

On the basis of direct evidence, of torture or of the oath, then, judicial decision was eventually arrived at. We have already seen that when this went in favour of the defendant as a result of his failure to confess under torture, the penalties facing his accuser were very grim. The same penalties in fact faced the false accuser who had laid his charge before the king.[5] But in both cases the circumstances were exceptional. All that the successful defendant stood to gain from his opponent in other cases was the sum of five *solidi* – or more if a lengthy journey to court had been necessary – 'pro iniusta petitione'.[6] But he did also have a fair degree of assurance against vexatious revival of the suit, for he left the court armed with documentary confirmation of his success.[7] In more important cases the judge was

---

[1] Cf. also v. 2. 6, x. 1. 14.

[2] II. 2. 5 is worth citing: 'Tamen si per probationem rei veritas investigare nequiverit, tunc ille, qui pulsatur, sacramentis se expiet, rem, vel si quid ab eo requiritur, neque habuisse neque habere nec aliquid de causa, unde interrogatur, se conscium esse vel quidquam inde in veritate scire nec id, quod dicitur, et illi parti, cui dicitur, commisisse'. Cf. also VIII Tol. 2: 'Quod si et testis deficiat, innocentis fidem sola jurisjurandi taxatio manifestat'.

[3] E.g., II. I. 19–21, 29, V. 5. I–3, 7, VI. 5. 5, 7, 12, VII. 2. 8, 23, IX. I. 4, 9, 14, X. I. 6.

[4] VI. 5. 12: cf. *FV* 40, where it is probably the defendant who is asked, but does not dare, to take the oath: thus Bethmann-Hollweg, p. 214.

[5] VI. I. 6.

[6] See II. 2. 5, 6 (to be read together), 9, VI. I. 2, which rule out the common view that every unsuccessful accuser suffered the penalties which the accused would have undergone if found guilty. In fact, the special undertaking of the inscriber to submit to these penalties if torture failed would be inexplicable and absurd if they threatened the failed accuser in any circumstances. True, the latter suffered, according to VII. I. 5, 'penam et damnum...quod debuit percipi accusatus, si de crimine fuisset convictus', but the clear evidence of these other laws requires us to understand that the law assumed torture (which it later spoke of) to have been used. In VII. I. I torture is certainly supposed.

[7] For the following, see II. I. 25.

obliged to write out and subscribe two identical accounts of the proceedings and of his verdict, one for each side.[1] But in less significant matters the parties had to be content with a sworn protocol of the evidence of the witnesses of the victorious side.[2] Even when the case was a minor one and the defendant had conceded his adversary's claim at the outset, a written judicial declaration to this effect was required. The law stipulated that in all cases the judge should keep a copy of the appropriate document for himself.

It is not clear whether the compulsive execution of judgements was always the work of the judge and his helpers, although it is certain that the refusal of a defeated party to comply with a judicial decision could not lawfully be countered by unauthorised seizure by the baulked victor of what was his due or of a security for this.[3] A judicial grant of permission to act directly against the property of the obstructor was perhaps sometimes made.[4] But the usual answer to the problem of recalcitrance must certainly have been executive distress by the authorities.[5] The procedure here was that the judicial *saio* enforced the judgement, receiving payment – a tenth of the value of the goods involved – as well as the cost of the hire of horses from the man to whose assistance he came.[6] In criminal cases, a convicted prisoner was apparently kept in custody until payment of composition: if he had to be released in order to procure the necessary money or goods, it was the judge's responsibility to ensure that the due

[1] *FV* 40 furnishes an example.

[2] See *FV* 39, and note II. 4. 3. See now also the slate document discussed by Diaz y Diaz, 'Un document privé', pp. 61–6. This document seems the most valuable of those that have survived. For others, see M. Gómez-Moreno, *Documentación goda en pizarra* (Madrid, 1966), passim (with many plates), elaborating earlier remarks in *Boletín de la Real Academia Esp.*, XXXIV (1954), 25–58.

[3] See v. 6. 1. *FV* 38 does not argue for permissible private distraint, despite H. García, pp. 145–6.

[4] Cf., in another connection, II. 2. 7: 'Iudex...obsignatam petitori faciat iussionem, in qua pigneris quantitatem adnotet, per quam petitor presumendi sibi habeat potestatem'. The possibility is allowed for in the words of II. 1. 21: 'Ille, qui a iudice ordinatus ad tollendum fuerat destinatus'.

[5] The briefest glance through the code shows the frequency of references to the payment of compositions or surrender of property at judicial instance. See 'iudicis instantia' (II. 3. 7), 'iudicis executione' (VIII. 3. 15), 'insistente iudice' (v. 6. 6), 'a iudice coactus' (VIII. 3. 2) for random examples.

[6] See II. 1. 18, 21, 26.

amount was paid and his right to take one-tenth as reward.[1] It was by judicial authority that a prisoner unable to pay was enslaved to his victorious accuser and that a criminal sentenced to delivery *in potestatem* was handed over.[2] Sentences of flogging and scalping, not infrequently ordered to be inflicted in the presence of the judge,[3] can be assumed to have been carried out by a judicial servant,[4] and it was certainly the general rule that the punishment be suffered before the public gaze.[5] Judges were especially warned not to carry out executions in secret.[6] Deterrence of others was unquestionably a prime motive of this strong emphasis on publicity,[7] but fear of judicial corruption must also have played a part.

For the untrustworthiness of the judiciary is one of the persistent themes of the code. Although the kings, concerned to avoid judicial self-seeking and dependence upon others, no doubt followed Reccared's example by granting their appointees *conpendia*,[8] and although the judges were authorised to receive fees for cases which they judged and sentences which they enforced,[9] the frequency with which the laws exhorted the judges to uphold justice, showing favour to none, and threatened them with dire penalties for dereliction of their duty indicates the magnitude of the problem.[10] Bribery was the prime and constant danger,[11] but personal enmity or friendship, the obligations inherent in the workings of the patronage system, lethargy and ignorance all played their part in permitting injustice to flourish and

[1] VII. 4. 4, where the responsibility of accompanying the prisoner and supervising the payment is doubtless in mind. We may believe that a *saio* would normally have done this.
[2] See III. 3. 11, 6. 2, v. 6. 5 etc.
[3] III. 2. 2, VII. 2. 14, 20, VIII. 1. 3, 3. 14 etc.
[4] Note III. 4. 17: 'A comite CCC flagella suscipiat', IX. 1. 2: 'A iudice C flagella suscipiat' etc. VI. 4. 3. (last page of App. II) would appear exceptional.
[5] III. 4. 17, VI. 4. 2, VII. 3. 2, VIII. 1. 3, 10, IX. 3. 3 and very many others. The market-place was the location, to judge from IX. 2. 4: 'In conventu mercantium'.
[6] VII. 4. 7.        [7] Above, p. 30, n. 7.
[8] XII. 1. 2.
[9] II. 1. 26 (judgements: a twentieth), VII. 4. 4 (above, in text). See further Zeumer, XXIII, 99–100. Both laws provided penalties for overcharging. Occasional payments for contempt might also come their way (II. 1. 19, 2. 2, 4, 8, VII. 2. 22, 4. 1, VIII. 6. 2) and they might sometimes have the administration of the estates of exiles, to judge by VI. 5. 13 and 13*.
[10] For exhortation, see II. 1. 27, XII. 1. 1, and the *Tomi* of XII and xv Tol.
[11] Bribery which did not result in a false verdict was apparently not punished: Zeumer, XXIII, 93–5.

the laws to be flouted. An unjust judgement made in ignorance was not punished – although the verdict was rejected[1] – but severe penalties awaited judges guilty in other respects. The basic punishment for wilful misjudgement was payment to the victim of the injustice of whatever he had lost as its result:[2] the same penalty befell those judges who unlawfully refused or delayed hearings.[3] But sometimes such a consequence was inappropriate or inadequate, and other sanctions were laid down for particular offences: the corrupt execution of an innocent man, for example, was paid for with the judge's own life, and the venal acquittal of a wrong-doer guilty of a capital crime by sevenfold payment of the bribe to the accused's opponent, as well as loss of office.[4] Failure to take action to bring public criminals to justice, on the other hand, was usually penalised by fines, sometimes also by corporal sanctions: thus, the country judge who through negligence or bribery permitted a prostitute to ply her trade was not only mulcted in the sum of thirty *solidi* but sentenced to one hundred lashes into the bargain,[5] while the judge who turned a blind eye to the activities of a coiner was liable to lose a quarter of his possessions.[6]

To guard against these various dangers, the king naturally relied upon his more important judicial officers, but most heavily, like the Byzantine Emperor, upon the clergy. One is justified in doubting, given contemporary ecclesiastical standards, whether these watchdogs were not often tarred with the same brush as were the judges:[7]

[1] II. I. 21.
[2] Ib. ('per amicitiam vel cupiditatem aut per commodum quodlibet'): cf. II. I. 24, V. 7. 8 ('muneris acceptione corruptus'), VII. 4. 6 ('pro patrocinio aut amicitia'). But in VI. 4. 3 the judge ('amicitia corruptus vel premio') had apparently to pay an arbitrary composition, though he also lost office, and II. I. 21 in fact provided for the judge to suffer a mere fifty lashes if he had no property (!). For unjust decisions made in fear of the king, or at his order, see above, pp. 43, 44.
[3] II. I. 20 ('pro patrocinio aut amicitia...malignitatis obtentu vel quolibet favore aut amicitia'): cf. II. 2. 7, VII. I. I. But contrast VI. 5. 14. For delay during the hearing 'dolo aut calliditate', see pp. 98–9.
[4] VII. 4. 5: cf. VI. I. 2.
[5] III. 4. 17.
[6] VII. 6. 2. For judicial corruption, disobedience or negligence, see also II. I. 11, 18, 28, 30, 2. 4, III. 5. 2, IV. 5. 6, VI. I. 5, VII. I. 5, VIII. I. 8, IX. I. 9, 21 (Egica), 2. 5, XII. I. 2, and for judges and the Jews, below, p. 138.
[7] See below, pp. 150ff. Punishments for sacerdotal corruption or negligence in the discharge of governmental duties appear in III. 4. 18, 5. 2, IX. I. 21 (Egica), XII. I. 2, 3. 24: cf. XVI Tol. 2 (bishops and judges).

nevertheless, they constituted the best weapon available. Already in 589 Reccared had confirmed a canon of the Third Council which provided for annual meetings of the bishops with the *iudices locorum* and the *actores fiscalium patrimoniorum* so that these men might learn how to behave *pie et juste*:[1] the bishops, 'prospectatores...qualiter judices cum populis agant',[2] were to report all cases of oppression to the king if they were unable to bring justice about by their own representations.[3] Fiscal exactions and arbitrary seizures of property were here chiefly in mind, and it was these abuses also which were proceeded against in a law of Reccared where again the bishops were enjoined to notify the king of the excesses of the royal servants.[4] A Reccesvindian provision later in turn warned the judges that they were as much subject to the penalties of the law as was anyone else if they dispossessed others of their property or harmed them in any other way.[5] But oppression by way of the denial of justice doubtless came within the episcopal purview.[6] By Ervig's time, certainly, the bishops had been allocated a vital role in the system devised to protect the king's subjects, especially the ordinary freemen, against the miscarriage of justice. Regrettably, the texts are obscure, but the system was perhaps as follows.[7] In cases where a judge was deemed suspect – that is to say, partial – he and the bishop were required to sit together to hear the case and to deliver a common verdict.[8] Appeal from this to the king was possible, but only after execution of the terms of the judgement had been carried out, so that the victorious party should suffer no delay in gaining satisfaction. A successful appeal brought not only restoration of whatever had been lost as a result of the joint hearing, but also the payment of the value

[1] III Tol. 18. The document *De fisco Barcinonensi* is certainly connected.

[2] Cf. III Sar. *Praef.*: 'Speculatores...plebium' and the episcopal self-designation as the 'oculi' of the *ecclesia* (VIII Tol. 4).

[3] Cf. also IV Tol. 32. I cannot agree with G. Martínez, 'Función de inspección y vigilancia del episcopado sobre las autoridades seculares en el período visigodo-católico', *Revista esp. de derecho canónico*, XV (1960), 583–4, that III Tol. 18 allowed the bishops to deprive the secular authorities of office.

[4] XII. 1. 2.

[5] II. 1. 32: cf. VIII. 1. 5.

[6] Cf. IV Tol. 3 (below, p. 152, n. 7).

[7] Differently, Zeumer, XXIV, 79–88, Martínez, 'Función', pp. 585–8, Thompson, *Goths*, pp. 261–2.

[8] II. 1. 24. The earlier right of recourse to a higher court was apparently abused for the purpose of causing delay.

of this from the unjust judge and bishop: failure, on the other hand, was harshly penalised, for the *petitor* became liable to pay the same amount or to suffer one hundred lashes if he could not find it.[1]

This procedure was a fair one, but it applied only when the declaration of judicial partiality had been made before the case was ever heard,[2] or, at least, before decision was reached. When a litigant decided to appeal against a verdict delivered by a lower judge in the normal course of events,[3] the case was regularly heard in the next higher court, that of the city count, either by the count in person or by his appointees, one of whom might be the bishop.[4] The higher tribunal might be by-passed by appeal direct to the king, or appeal might be made to him from its finding or during the course of the hearing, but the penalties for the unsuccessful appellant were the severe ones already mentioned. No doubt failure in the count's court was penalised simply by the normal composition *pro mala petitione*, for the appeal took the form of a charge against the judge of first instance. But precisely because of the penalties of failure, the humbler members of society would frequently not have proceeded with appeals. It was in the protection of such persons that the bishop had a special role.[5] If a report of judicial injustice came to him, he was to summon the judge concerned and to try to prevail upon him to amend his verdict, so that a common judgement could be agreed upon. There was no question of punishment for the unjust judge here. But if the judge refused to relent, the bishop was permitted to draw up a document including an account of the judicial judgement and his own, and to forward this, together with the victim of the oppression, to the king for his decision. This was, again, a most equitable procedure, for while the victim avoided the risks of formal appeal, the pressure exerted upon a corrupt judge to do justice was considerable. A Judge who tried to hinder the procedure by refusal to

[1] Ib. The severity is in keeping with that for false accusations lodged with the king.
[2] Thus also Justinian's law: see Zeumer, XXIV, 86 – who, however, denies Visigothic borrowing in this respect.
[3] For the corrupt practice whereby judges unjustly bound litigants by *placita* not to reopen resolved cases, see II. I. 28.
[4] II. I. 31, the source also of the following. Appeals from the count were doubtless heard in the ducal court.
[5] For the following, see II. I. 30.

release to the bishop the unjustly treated party was punished by a fine of two pounds of gold, paid to the crown.[1]

One cannot but be impressed by the practicality, rationality, sophistication and justice of the Visigothic laws concerning procedure and evidence, especially when they are viewed in comparison with the regimes in force in the other barbarian kingdoms. The legacy of Rome was here most clearly to be seen, but the legislators were no slavish copyists of the past but went their own way, adopting what they considered valuable, rejecting what they found abhorrent or unnecessary, and not afraid to draw upon other sources, like Byzantine law or their own Germanic traditions. These last, however, played a very unimportant part. The emphasis now was upon reason, flexibility, judicial discretion,[2] not upon the crude, if elaborate, formalism of Germanic procedure. Only the widespread use of the oath recalled the typical Germanic hearing,[3] that and the single extraordinary law, probably of Wittiza and probably the last ever to be issued, where ordeal by boiling water made its primitive appearance.[4] And there is no better indication than that law of the declining standards of the kingdom as it neared its end.

[1] The alternatives of recourse to the duke or to the bishop are probably reflected in VI. 4. 3, dealing with a corrupt judge 'ab episcopo vel duce districtus'.

[2] Which is not to say that some judges did not stoop to the use of diviners in their investigations: below, p. 147.

[3] See H. Brunner, *Deutsche Rechtsgesch.*, I, 2nd edn (Leipzig, 1906), pp. 257ff. Levy, *Obligationenrecht*, p. 177, designates the oath of innocence 'typisch germanisch', but that is not to say that it was absent from late Roman judicial procedure, where ecclesiastical influence was probably largely responsible (see A. Steinwenter in *ZRG.KA*, LIV (1934), 58–61), but where Germanic influence was itself no doubt a factor: note the apparent rejection of oath-helpers in *LRB* 23. 1. Generally, see P. Merêa in *AHDE*, XXI/XXII (1951/2), 1163–8.

[4] VI. 1. 3 (of Wittiza in the view of Zeumer, XXIII, 511), on which see Martínez Díez, 'Tortura', pp. 247–8. The law is notoriously difficult, but seems to abolish Ervig's limitation of the use of torture against ordinary freemen to cases involving more than 500 *solidi*. The ordeal appears as a preliminary test of criminality: if unsuccessfully undergone by the accused, torture might be used, but success brought no penalty for the accuser but simply loss of the case. To my knowledge, the only other reference to ordeal in the Visigothic sources is II Sar. 2 (of as early as 592), ordering Arian relics to be put to the test of fire. Material on ordeals from different sources is gathered by J. Gaudemet in *Recueils de la Société Jean Bodin*, XVII: *La preuve* (part 2) (Brussels, 1965), pp. 99–112.

## Chapter 5

# THE CHURCH AND THE FAITH

The ideological fundament of the society ruled over by the Visigothic kings was its Catholic faith. The conversion of Reccared's reign brought the Goths and the Sueves to share with the Romans a common adherence to Nicaean Christianity which remained characteristic of the kingdom until its fall in 711.[1] It was indeed this cementing bond of faith which on the one hand constituted a desirable, if not essential, precondition for unity of law, itself based upon Christian principles, and on the other allowed the thoroughgoing apotheosis of the king entrusted with his position by the Christian God. It is assuredly no accident that theocratic elements are almost wholly absent from laws promulgated before the conversion, or that Leovigild, the first king to introduce ceremonial emphasising his supremacy over the people, should have sought to bring them to share a common faith. The very concept of society as a unitary body whose head existed by, and in order to fulfil, God's will, was indeed dependent upon the prior attainment of religious uniformity.

On a wider plane, of course, the inhabitants of the seventh-century realm were, by their Catholicism, members of the greater body which was the universal Church. But although no attempt was ever made to deny participation in this wider *ecclesia* or to reject the articles of its faith,[2] the fact is that the religious ethos of the kingdom was essentially particularist, isolationist, in spirit. The uniformity of liturgy, holy days and so on – even of tonsure – upon which the councils insisted was uniformity within the kingdom:

[1] Racial diversity within territorial unity is clearly in mind in XII. 2. 1, where Reccesvind's language also reflects the virtually complete identification of society and *ecclesia*.

[2] On the Trinitarian theology of the conciliar creeds, see J. Madoz in *RET*, IV (1944), 457–77. See also idem, *El símbolo del Concilio XVI de Toledo* (Madrid, 1946), passim, for the doctrinal orthodoxy of the Spanish position vis-à-vis the anti-Monothelete decisions of the Sixth Ecumenical Council.

Nec diversa sit ultra in nobis ecclesiastica consuetudo *qui una fide continemur et regno,*

declared one canon.[1] Relations with Rome, normal before 589, were distant indeed after that date: Gregory the Great's extensive correspondence contains only ten letters concerned with Spanish affairs, but not even that number was mustered by his successors during the whole of the period between 604 and 711.[2] The two exchanges which took place were acrimonious: if earlier papal sources were cited in the Visigothic canons and if Isidore was sturdily loyal to papal primacy,[3] a tone of prickly independence, resentful of the exercise of Roman authority, nevertheless underlay the missives dispatched to Honorius I and Benedict II by Braulio of Saragossa and Julian of Toledo.[4] It has been not implausibly suggested that by the

[1] IV Tol. 2: on this and the connection of liturgical uniformity and political unity, see Z. García Villada, *Hist. eclesiástica de Esp.*, II, part II (Madrid, 1933), 32–6. For uniformity, see III Tol. 2, IV Tol. 5–18, 26, 41, V Tol. 1, VI Tol. 2, XVII Tol. 2, 3, 6 etc., and for XI Tol. 3 and the disusage of the Romanised liturgy of Braga, P. David, *Études hist. sur la Galice et le Portugal du VIᵉ au XIIᵉ siècle* (Coimbra, 1947), pp. 106ff. Only seventh-century Spain and Byzantium knew internal unity centring on the monarch, as J. M. Lacarra, 'La iglesia visigoda en el siglo VII y sus relaciones con Roma', *Sett.*, VII (1960), 376, points out.

[2] For earlier relations, see A. C. Vega, 'El primado romano en la iglesia esp. desde sus orígenes hasta el siglo VII', *RET*, II (1942), 63–99. For papal letters, see E. Magnin, *L'église wisigothique au VIIᵉ siècle*, I (Paris, 1912), 2ff. Difficulty of travel was not a prime factor. The suggestion of Lacarra, 'Iglesia', pp. 367–8, that the connection of Rome with Byzantium was in part responsible for Visigothic hostility is wholly convincing.

[3] See Magnin, pp. 7ff., J. Madoz, 'El primado romano en Esp. en el ciclo isidoriano', *RET*, II (1942), 236ff. Relevant conciliar texts are III Tol. 1, II Sev. 2, IV Tol. 6, 17, VI Tol. 8, XI Tol. 10, 12: cf. Braulio, *Ep.* 14, Isidore, *Epp.* 6, 8 etc. I am inclined to accept the authenticity of the last letter despite P. Séjourné, *Saint Isidore de Séville* (Paris, 1929), pp. 94–5, and others: see A. C. Vega in *Ciudad de Dios*, CLIV (1942), 506ff., Madoz, 'Primado romano', pp. 240–2. But that the pre-eminence of St Peter was queried is in itself revealing. Note *DEO* II. 5. 5, where, after referring to St Peter as first to receive the power of binding and loosing, Isidore continues: '*Siquidem* et caeteri apostoli cum Petro pari consortio honoris et potestatis effecti sunt' – almost defensively. For royal relations with the popes, see *Reg.* IX. 227a, where Reccared spoke of St Peter's primacy of honour ('qui primus fulget honore'), and for Chintila, Vives, *Inscripciones*, no. 389: later, Chindasvind sent Taio to Rome to seek Gregory's *Moralia* (*CH* 28ff., J. Madoz, 'Tajón de Zaragoza y su viaje a Roma', *Mélanges Joseph de Ghellinck*, I (Gembloux, 1951), 345–60).

[4] For Braulio, see *Ep.* 21, which answered a (lost) accusation that the Spanish bishops were insufficiently concerned with the Jews: Braulio stressed that God worked through the king as well as through the pope. P. B. Gams, *Die Kirchengesch. von*

end of the century schism was near.[1] Certainly by then the metropolitan of Toledo had achieved a position of *de facto* primacy within the Visigothic Church similar to – and perhaps based upon – that of the patriarch of the Imperial city in the Byzantine Church.[2] For all that, he remained subordinate to the king. The riveting question of the relationship between monarch and *sacerdotium* in the period after Reccared's conversion cannot be dealt with here, but it must be said that the view, still sometimes maintained, that the Church dominated the king is woefully wide of the mark.[3] Far from being enthralled to the *sacerdotium*, the Visigothic king was its master.[4] The tone was set already by Reccared who not only con-

*Spanien*, II, part II (Regensburg, 1874), 224, rightly spoke of 'die Gereiztheit, ja Bitterkeit', of the letter. A more respectful tone has been discovered in it by, e.g., Lynch, pp. 101–2, 145–7 (though cf. ib., p. 56), Madoz, ad loc. in his edition, and A. C. Vega, *Ciudad de Dios*, CLIV (1942), 521ff. – whose designation of it as 'espontánea, franca, sincera, sin eufemismo, quizá con algo de ese noble rudeza y energía propia del carácter español, pero respetuosa y sumisa siempre a la autoridad del Papa' (p. 521) is in itself revealing! For Julian's second *Apologeticum*, see xv Tol. (cols 513–20) and Lacarra, 'Iglesia', pp. 379–84, who, following Gams, pp. 234ff., rightly stresses its offensive tone. See also Ziegler, p. 52. *Contra*, but unconvincing, F. X. Murphy, 'Julian of Toledo and the condemnation of Monothelitism in Spain', *Mélanges Joseph de Ghellinck*, I (Gembloux, 1951), 361–73.

[1] See Gams and Lacarra, 'Iglesia', locc. citt. last note.

[2] For the development of the Toledan see (rightly attributed to the royal status of the city by Magnin, pp. 101–4), see J. F. Rivera Recio, 'Encumbramiento de la sede toledana durante la dominación visigótica', *HS*, VIII (1955), 8–34. On Julian's part, see Gams, pp. 215ff. The primacy (never *de iure*) is most clearly shown by the metropolitan's right of episcopal ordination (subject to royal nomination) throughout the whole kingdom: see XII Tol. 6, which may have represented Julian's *quid pro quo* for his part in the Wamba affair. Earlier stages are marked by the *Decretum Gundemari* and *Constitutio Carthaginensium sacerdotum*, allegedly dating from the first years of the century but found at the end of the acts of XII Tol. (cols 482–6), and VII Tol. 6, requiring the neighbouring bishops to spend a portion of their time in the *urbs regia*: cf. the *synodoi endemousai* of Byzantium. Cf. also Mer. 4 and the later XIII Tol. 8. Papal apprehension about the Visigothic situation might account for the carping criticism of Julian's first *Apologeticum* in the Monothelete affair: was Benedict II probing the metropolitan's strength? If so, Julian's answer must have amply confirmed papal fears.

[3] See, e.g., Aubin, pp. 79–86, especially p. 85: 'Die Theokratie bei den Westgoten bedeutete weniger eine solche des Herrschers als der Bischöfe'. The view, associated above all with Dahn (see *Könige*, p. 492, e.g.), found fervent English expression in R. D. Shaw, *EHR*, XXI (1906), 213–14. In my sense, Ziegler, pp. 126–33: thus already Pérez Pujol, III, 351–64. See also the excellent comments of Sánchez-Albornoz, 'Aula', pp. 85–95, and now Thompson, *Goths*, pp. 280–2.

[4] See also above, pp. 46ff.

voked the Third Council 'propter instaurandam disciplinae ecclesiasticae formam' but attended throughout, directed the proceedings – even to the point of ordering the recital of the creed before communion during the mass, according to the Eastern custom[1] – and confirmed the acts.[2] Reccared, of course, occupied an exceptional position, since it was he who had brought the Goths and Sueves to conversion,[3] and the bishops recognised this in their extravagant acclamation:

Ipse mereatur veraciter apostolicum meritum qui apostolicum implevit officium.[4]

But Reccared's successors made good use of the flying start he had given them. They regarded themselves, and were regarded by the episcopacy, as divinely authorised to control ecclesiastical affairs: royal supervision and direction of all aspects of life within the kingdom was indeed inherent in the king's very position as head of a Christian community, responsible for the *salus* of its members and accountable to God for the welfare of the Church.[5] It was the king:

Cujus vigilantia et saecularia regit...et ecclesiastica plenius disponit.[6]

It is no exaggeration, the non-interference of the king in doctrinal matters once recognised,[7] to talk of caesaropapism in the Visigothic kingdom. Certainly the priesthood pronounced in the councils the

---

[1] But see Schäferdiek, p. 219.
[2] See Lacarra, 'Iglesia', pp. 355–6, Schäferdiek, pp. 238–9.
[3] Note his own words in the *Tomus*: 'Divino nutu nostrae curae fuit hos populos ad unitatem Christi Ecclesiae pertrahere'.
[4] III Tol. (col. 345c). Note further John of Biclar, 590. 1, who compares Reccared with Constantine at Nicaea and Marcian at Chalcedon: cf. E. Ewig, *HJ*, LXXV (1956), 26–8. For Reccared's (self-confessed) zeal, see III. 5. 2: 'Zelamus enim pro veritatem zelo Dei...'.
[5] See above, p. 50, n. 2.
[6] Mer. 23: cf. ib. *Praef.* (615b). For further examples of the same theme, note Reccared's words at III Tol. (350b): 'Non in eis tantummodo rebus diffundimus solertiam nostram quibus populi...pacatissime...vivant, sed etiam in adjutorio Christi extendimus nos ad ea quae sunt coelestia cogitare', Gundemar in XII Tol. *Decretum Gundemari* (483c/d): 'Nos enim talia in divinis ecclesiis disponentes credimus fideliter regnum imperii nostri...divino gubernaculo regi', IV Tol. *Praef.* (363d): 'Non solum in rebus humanis sed etiam in causis divinis sollicitus maneat', III Sar. *Epil.* (322b) etc.
[7] But no doctrinal dispute affected the seventh-century Visigothic Church. XIV Tol., concerned with approval of the canons of the Sixth Ecumenical Council, was summoned by the king.

norms of Christian behaviour and provided for disciplinary action against those who breached these rules.[1] But canons were decreed in councils not only held solely with royal permission but in the great majority of cases directly convoked by the king.[2] It is difficult to believe that many canons, if indeed any, were passed in defiance of the king's wishes:[3] often, indeed, the subject-matter of conciliar legislation was that suggested by the king in the written *Tomus* regularly presented, from the time of the Eighth Council onwards, before the deliberations began.[4] The king was present at part of, or throughout, nearly every general council held before 681, when the custom of royal retirement was introduced,[5] and the attendance of the great court dignitaries helped to ensure after that time, as before, that the royal wishes would not be flouted.[6] In any case, the bishops were the king's creatures, elevated by him even against the opposition of the leading churchmen.[7] The closeness of relationship between Church

[1] Ervig's words at XIII Tol. (*Tomus*, 489a): 'Ut et vobis praedicantibus et nobis implentibus quae divinis oculis complacent' do not signify the superior authority of the priesthood, but simply recognise the clergy as expert in matters concerning the faith. The king chose what to implement. Counsel was the function of the *sacerdotium*: see XII Tol. *Tomus* (also of Ervig): 'Testimonium paternitatis vestrae fortissimum in salutis nostrae advoco *adjumentum*, ut quia regnum fautore Deo ad salvationem terrae et sublevationem plebium suscepisse nos credimus, sanctitudinis vestrae consiliis *adjuvemur*'.

[2] See Magnin, pp. 51–5, 106ff., who is detailed, and on the gratitude regularly expressed by the bishops, Ewig, 'Königsgedanke', pp. 28–30. Only at XV Tol. is royal convocation not witnessed for a general council. See Mer. 7, where a reference to the summoning of annual provincial synods ends: 'Quae res non extra regiam agitur voluntatem', and XVI Tol. *Lex edita* (548a/b) for royal instructions concerning a provincial assembly. Bishops were excused attendance if the king so ordered: Mer. 5, XI Tol. 15. Braulio, *Ep.* 6, refers to a council postponed by Sisenand in 632. For the later use by the Norman Anonymous of Visigothic royal convocation (and direction) of the councils, see E. H. Kantorowicz, *The king's two bodies* (Princeton, N. Jersey, 1957), p. 51: Müller, 'Königssalbung', p. 321, n. 21 (cf. ib., p. 340, n. 134), wrongly accuses the Anonymous of misunderstanding.

[3] For an instance of disagreement, see above, p. 63, n. 2: it was the king's decision which appeared in the canons.

[4] But Reccared earlier presented a *Tomus* to III Tol., and Chintila delivered a programme to V Tol.: the bishops were explicit that they confirmed this latter 'ex praecepto ejus et decreto nostro' (*Praef.*).

[5] Magnin, pp. 58–9.          [6] See Thompson, *Goths*, pp. 294–6.

[7] See J. Fernández Alonso, *La cura pastoral en la Esp. romanovisigoda* (Rome, 1955), pp. 60–5. Despite III Tol. 1 and IV Tol. 19, royal appointment was accepted throughout the century: see II Barc. 3, Mer. 4, XVI Tol. *Tomus* (529c) and especially XII Tol. 6: 'Libera principis electio...quoscunque regalis potestas elegerit'. For the

and king in Visigothic times has often been remarked upon, but when the Church's bishops were nominated by the monarch, its metropolitans judged by him, its councils summoned by him and its measures subject to his scrutiny,[1] the relationship appears clearly as one between royal master and ecclesiastical subordinate.

The supreme position of the king as head of Christian society is by nothing exposed more clearly than by his employment of excommunication as a penalty for breach of the laws. If the punishment of *exilium* usually involved public penitence, then the number of occasions upon which excommunication was prescribed was quite large, for public penitence certainly involved excommunication.[2] But even if notice is taken only of explicit references to excommunication or penitence, it is evident that the spiritual sanction was not infrequently employed after its first appearance in the laws during the reign of Chindasvind.[3] In Ervig's code it was provided as a direct punishment for usurpers and their helpers,[4] for certain offenders against the anti-Jewish laws,[5] for heretics,[6] for those guilty of incest,[7] and for those who broke their religious vows.[8] Earlier, slave-owners who murdered or mutilated their slaves had been faced with it,[9] and in Egica's time it was the fate both of homosexuals and of those bishops who failed to enforce the new - and wholly secular - law on

appointment of Eugenius against the will of Braulio, see Braulio, *Epp.* 31–3, Ildefonsus, *DVI* 14, and Lynch, pp. 59, 80–1: for the background, see J. F. Rivera Recio, *HS*, 1 (1948), 259–68. (Eugenius would not seem to have been grateful, to judge by his remarks about Chindasvind in *Carm.* 25.) Another case in Braulio, *Epp.* 5, 6, where Isidore is shown to accept royal nomination as a matter of course. (For the citation of these last two letters by Manegold and other Imperialist writers of the eleventh century, see Lynch, pp. 143–5.) See also Braulio, *Epp.* 35, 36, *EW* 7 and *HW* 6, and for forced ordination and the uncanonical creation of a new bishopric by Wamba, xii Tol. 4. For the royal rearrangement of diocesan boundaries in Lusitania, see Mer. 8.

[1] ix Tol. 1, xiii Tol. 12 (judgement); Magnin, pp. 83–5 (scrutiny).

[2] See iv. 5. 6, and generally J. Fernández Alonso, 'La disciplina penitencial en la Esp. romanovisigoda desde el punto de vista pastoral', *HS*, iv (1951), 256–7, 305–6, *et saepe*. Penitential discipline was sometimes so severe that men preferred to commit suicide: xvi Tol. 4.

[3] But cf. already iii Tol. *Edictum regis* (358a/b).

[4] ii. 1. 6.          [5] xii. 2. 15, 3. 8, 22, 24.

[6] xii. 3. 1.          [7] iii. 5. 5 (cf. iii. 5. 1, 2), xii. 3. 8.

[8] iii. 4. 18, 5. 3.

[9] vi. 5. 12 (Chindasvind), vi. 5. 13 (absent from the code but later reintroduced by Egica as vi. 5. 13*).

runaway slaves.[1] Most revealing of the matter-of-fact attitude towards excommunication is its appearance in three other laws as an alternative punishment for those who could not pay financial penalties.[2] Only rarely did the kings expressly confirm canonical provisions rather than produce independent measures when they threatened wrong-doers with excommunication,[3] although several royal laws including the punishment later received conciliar reinforcement.[4]

It is only at first sight that such monarchical action appears extraordinary. It was in fact a natural consequence of the king's vicegerential status and supreme authority over the Christian body which was his kingdom that he should have felt able to exclude offenders from the Christian society with the government of which God had entrusted him.[5] It is at one and the same time a mark of the extreme but wholly logical loyalty with which the notion of theocratic monarchy was served and a telling indication of the subordination of the *sacerdotium* to the king that excommunication should have been imposed as the result of the royal *fiat*. That the bishops too decreed excommunication for various offences against the canons in no way detracts from the comprehensiveness and uniqueness of the king's vicariate authority over the *ecclesia*, for they acted with the tacit approval of the king, just as they acted upon his express instructions when they excommunicated in accordance with royal laws: it is powerfully eloquent of the royalsacerdotal relationship that subservient provision should have been made by the bishops for the automatic retraction of the sentences of excommunication imposed upon those offenders against the canons in whom the king had a particular interest – traitors – as soon as they

[1] III. 5. 7 (homosexuals), IX. 1. 21. After III Tol., excommunication figured as a penalty in the royal edicts confirming the decisions of XII, XIII, XVI and XVII Tol. Note also Egica's peremptory instructions in the *Tomus* to XVI Tol. that bishops guilty of usurping ecclesiastical property rightfully held by others and failing to proceed against idolaters should be excommunicated: the corresponding canons are 5 and 2. Cf. also III. 4. 13.

[2] IV. 5. 6, XII. 3. 19, 24. In IX. 2. 8 exile is an alternative, and in II. 1. 19 fasting on bread and water.

[3] III. 4. 18, 5. 3 (below, pp. 153–4), 7 (below, p. 235, n. 5). For the relation of IV. 5. 6 and XI Tol. 5, see p. 155, n. 2).

[4] XII Tol. 9 confirmed XII. 3. 1, 8, 19, 22, 24, and VIII Tol. 10 (but cf. already IV Tol. 75) the law II. 1. 6.

[5] Note Reccesvind in XII. 2. 15: 'A fidelium Christi societate divelli' and Ervig at XII Tol. (482a), where excommunication is 'a coetu nostro'.

were received back into royal favour.[1] When the supreme and mortal weapon of excommunication was employed or withdrawn at the pleasure of the king, there ruled a truly theocratic monarch. The king's position as head of society, however, like his use of excommunication as a punishment, depended upon the existence of a body united in its Christian faith over which he might rule and within which excommunication might effectively function. The king had as one of his necessary aims the prevention of activity which threatened to undermine the faith which bound society together, and thus to bring about the destruction of society itself: at the same time, it was his duty, as it was that of any Christian ruler, to proceed against the enemies of the faith and, if possible, to bring them to salvation.[2] It was to the fulfilment of these defensive and offensive obligations that nearly all the laws of the last book of the code were devoted. The king had hitherto issued measures to purify the *ecclesia* which was formed by the *fideles* of the realm, to bring peace and well-being to the faithful who dwelt in the house of the Lord: now he turned to deal with the *infideles*, that he might bring them 'ad concordiam religiose pacis' and enjoy his heavenly reward.[3]

Heresy struck unambiguously at the roots of the faith, and it is only to be expected that the king should have used the law to defend orthodox doctrine and to drive out error:

Et ea, que in luce fidei manent, a tenebris contradictionum edicto legali defendere et ea, que exoriri obvia forsitan error inpulerit, gestis legalibus propulsare.[4]

Open or secret attacks upon the one, true, Catholic faith were forbidden: biblical, patristic and contemporary orthodox writings were similarly protected. The excitation of controversy was an offence,

---

[1] See v Tol. 8, vii Tol. 1 (with reservations), and, particularly, xii Tol. 3: 'Quos regia potestas aut in gratiam benignitatis receperit aut participes mensae suae effecerit, hos etiam sacerdotum et populorum conventus suscipere in ecclesiastica communione debebit, ut quod jam principalis pietas habet acceptum nec a sacerdotibus Dei habeatur extraneum'. At xvi Tol. Sisbert was sentenced to lifelong excommunication 'excepto si eum principalis pietas *cum sacerdotali conniventia* delegerit absolvendum' (*Decretum judicii*): but cf. ib. c. 9, also concerning Sisbert: 'Excepto si regia eum pietas ante absolvendum crediderit'.

[2] See viii Tol. *Tomus*: 'Hanc [sc. fidem] cum fidelibus servans, ad hanc salvandos infideles advitans, in hac subjectos populos regens, hanc propriis gentibus tenendam insinuans, hanc populis alienis annuntians'. This is perfectly in accordance with *Sent.* iii. 51. 3.     [3] xii. 2. 1.     [4] xii. 2. 2.

as was – the 'moral' flavour of the stipulation is apparent – even the entertainment of thoughts contrary to the faith. The normal punishment for the individual who transgressed was loss of office, forfeiture of property and lifelong exile, under penitence:[1] punished additionally by *decalvatio* and flogging were the particular offences of blasphemy against the name of Christ or against the Trinity, and refusal either to accept or to consume the sacrament.[2] Harsh as these consequences appear, by later medieval standards they were moderate. Return from exile and repossession of property were in any case open to the heretic who recanted, while the man detected in error held by ignorance rather than defended in deliberate public statement was subject to penalty only if the efforts of the clergy failed to correct his fault.[3]

But the brevity with which heresy was treated in the code indicates that unorthodoxy had largely disappeared from the peninsula.[4] Certainly there is no evidence of great conciliar concern with the matter,[5] and already Reccesvind referred to its root-and-branch extirpation: his heresy law was designed to prevent its recrudescence.[6] But if heresy posed no real problem, Judaism did.[7] No less

[1] Ib., xii. 3. 1.
[2] xii. 3. 2. For refusal of the sacrament, see also xi Tol. 11, with sensible reservations: cf. xii Tol. 5.        [3] xii. 3. 1.
[4] Only xii. 2. 2, 3. 1, 2, deal with heresy. The last, *De blasphematoribus sancte Trinitatis*, was perhaps in part directed against Arianism: although there is no relic of conciliar attack upon the heresy, it played a part in the decision of iv Tol. 6 in favour of single baptismal immersion (on which see Séjourné, pp. 154–6, and A. Braegelmann, *The life and writings of Saint Ildefonsus of Toledo* (Washington D.C., 1942), pp. 85ff.). The fault of the Sintharius mentioned in Braulio, *Ep.* 3, does not appear. For Priscillianism, see Braulio, *Ep.* 44, and on it Lynch, p. 108: further, J. Fontaine, 'Isidore de Séville et l'astrologie', *REL*, xxxi (1953), 278–80. iv Tol. 41 refers to the Priscillianist style of tonsure. Generally on heretical elements, see Fontaine, 'Conversion', pp. 131–40.
[5] A bishop of Syrian origin, Gregory, was converted from Acephalism (a sort of Monophysitism) at ii Sev. (cc. 12, 13): see also *CH* 16 and on the matter M. Menéndez y Pelayo, *Hist. de los heterodoxos esp.*, 2nd edn, ii (Madrid, 1917), 192ff., and J. Madoz, 'El florilegio patrístico del II Concilio de Sevilla', *Miscellanea isidoriana* (Rome, 1936), pp. 177–220. The concern of xiv and xv Tol. with Monotheletism was, of course, entirely at papal instance.
[6] xii. 2. 2 (with a reference to ii Timothy 4. 3–4): cf. next note.
[7] As Reccesvind also recognised in xii. 2. 3: 'Nam cum virtus Dei totum universaliter acie verbi sui radicitus heresum extirpaverit surculum, sola Iudeorum nequitia ingemiscimus regiminis nostri arva esse polluta'. A similar theme in his *Tomus* at viii Tol.

than forty-three *capitula* were directly dedicated to matters concerning the Jews, laws which by their ferocity of language and punishment alike bear abundant and appalling witness to the disgust – and perhaps fear – in which the old religion was held and to the determination of some of the Visigothic kings to eradicate it. Jewish settlements had probably existed in Spain already in apostolic times, when St Paul planned a visit to the country,[1] and were certainly extensive by the beginning of the fourth century.[2] In the Visigothic period both the volume and the obvious ineffectiveness of the restrictive legislation indicate large numbers. Some of these Jews were very wealthy, to judge by the laws concerning bribery, and it will be suggested below that as a class they played an important role in the commercial life of the kingdom. The sanctions imposed upon unconverted Jews by Egica testify to their economic significance,[3] and when general enslavement was finally ordered, the reason alleged – that the Jews were in traitorous conspiracy with their brethren overseas – would have been totally unconvincing if they had not formed a rich and influential group.[4] The imposition of a special tax upon the Jews argues the same point.[5] But in the laws we catch glimpses of Jews of another and more humble sort:[6] sometimes to be found living in remote areas of the country,[7] they appear personally cultivating the fields and working as spinners and weavers,[8] serving as slaves for other Jews and acting as the stewards and clients of Christians.[9] And there is no hint anywhere in the sources of the time that economic jealousy, such a prominent feature of later anti-Semitism, provided motivation for Visigothic hostility.[10]

[1] Romans 15. 24, 28, and for the possibility that the visit took place, A. C. Vega in *BRAH*, cliv (1964), 12–20. But the earliest Jewish inscription is of the early third century: see S. Katz, *The Jews in the Visigothic and Frankish kingdoms of Spain and Gaul* (Cambridge, Mass., 1937), p. 141.

[2] On the Jews and the Council of Elvira, see B. Blumenkranz, *Juifs et chrétiens dans le monde occidental, 430–1096* (Paris–La Haye, 1960), p. 106.

[3] Below, p. 199.

[4] xvii Tol. *Tomus*, 8. Note also their probable implication in the revolt of 673: *HW* 5, 28.     [5] For the tax, above, p. 71.

[6] For Jewish *viliores*, see below, p. 184.

[7] xii. 3. 21: 'In locis illis, ubi sacerdotalis presentia defuerit'.

[8] xii. 3. 6.     [9] xii. 3. 16, 18; xii. 3. 19, 22.

[10] See J. Parkes, *The conflict of the Church and the Synagogue* (London, 1934), pp. 369–70. But confiscation certainly figured regularly among the punishments for breach of the anti-Jewish laws.

It was rather the hatred of the Christian for the people who had betrayed God's trust which inspired persecution. So much is amply clear from the constant employment in the laws and canons of condemnatory allusions to Jewish disobedience to the divine commandments, perversity in face of the Messiah and obdurate denial of the Christian interpretation of the Old Testament in spiritual terms.[1] It is not material envy but deep-seated emotional revulsion which is shown by the vehemence of the language used in description of the Jewish faith and people: *execranda perfidia, detestanda fides et consuetudo, perfida calliditas, detestabilis conversatio* and so forth.[2] That this religious repugnance did not find legislative expression before the reign of Reccared is not difficult to explain.[3] By the conversion of 589 there came into being a true *societas fidelium Christi*,[4] a unitary body bound together by a common faith and ruled over by a divinely sanctioned head. With the creation of such politico-religious unity, it is understandable that attention should have become focused upon the Jews who, by their very existence, stood in the way of a virtually absolute identification of *regnum* and *ecclesia* and detracted from the full theocratic character of the monarchy. The conversion provided the strongest impetus to persecution in that both the unitary and the Christian premises of Visigothic society were denied by the survival of a large group within the territorial boundaries of the kingdom but beyond its ideological confines.[5] But if the prime aim of legislation was always to bring the Jews to membership of the *societas fidelium* – from the Christian point of view, a benevolent policy – the notion

[1] See, e.g., XII. 3. 12 (cit. p. 137, n. 3), XVII Tol. *Tomus*: 'Qui ab initio...Christi nomen incredibili pravitate negaverunt', XII. 3. 4 (where Ervig brands the 'obstinata Iudeorum perfidia' in holding to the letter of the Law as the cause of the Crucifixion) and XII. 3. 5 (where Romans 7. 6 is referred to).

[2] Cit. from XII. 2. 14, 15, 3. 1, 7. Note also Ervig's inflamed appeal in XII Tol. *Tomus*: 'Exsurgite, quaeso, exsurgite...Judaeorum pestem quae in novam semper recrudescit insaniam radicitus exstirpate...'.

[3] 589 is, in the judgement of Blumenkranz, *Juifs*, p. 105: 'Le point de départ de la plus tragique aventure des Juifs pendant le haut moyen âge'. For the pre-conversion period, see Parkes, pp. 351–3, Ziegler, pp. 186–9.

[4] Reccesvind's phrase in XII. 2. 15.

[5] For the *regnum* = *ecclesia* notion, see VI Tol. 3, concerning Chintila: 'Christianissimus princeps ardore fidei inflammatus...nec sinit degere in regno suo eum qui non sit catholicus': cf. VIII Tol. 12: 'Indignum reputans [Reccesvindus] orthodoxae fidei principem sacrilegis imperare, fideliumque plebem infidelium societate polluere'.

of the perversity of the Jews as a people, branded with the *parentalis error* as rebels against God and crucifiers of Christ,[1] was never far away from the minds of the legislators and could only have been confirmed by the real obstinacy shown by the Jews in holding firm to their faith. The general enslavement of 694 was the exasperated result of a century of royal and ecclesiastical preoccupation with the problem of conversion and of the powerful reinforcement which the failure of the policies followed offered to the view of the Jews as a race condemned to the wilderness.

More than most did Ervig concern himself with the Jews. Already within three months of his accession he had had drafted an extensive series of new laws: presented to the Twelfth Council, which included the rubrics in its ninth canon, they were promulgated to the Jews of Toledo on 27 January 681.[2] Many older laws, included in the code of 681 and explicitly confirmed by the king, who abolished only the death penalty as a punishment for their breach, were in fact made redundant by the new measures.[3] Only twice before, during the reigns of Sisebut and Chintila, had the Jews been presented with the alternatives of baptism or punishment:[4] the influence of the *sacerdotium* had probably been against forcing men unwillingly to the font.[5] But Julian of Toledo now had the ear of the king, and Julian,

[1] Cf. XII. 2. 17 (*p. error*) and XII. 3. 12. Responsibility for the Crucifixion is a theme of, e.g., XVII Tol. 8: 'Plebs Judaeorum nequissima sacrilegii nota respersa et effusione sanguinis Christi cruenta' and '[Egica] qui...injuriam crucis Christi vindicare vult', XII. 3. 4 and XII. 3. 10, with reference to the thirty pieces of silver.

[2] See XII Tol. *Tomus* (468d), II. 1. 1 and XII. 3. 28, *in fine*: cf. XII. 3. 12, 13, 17, for particular dates from which laws were to operate.

[3] XII. 3. 1, with scriptural justification. Death by burning or stoning had been ordered as the regular punishment in Reccesvind's XII. 2. 11: cf. XII. 2. 16 and 17, where, with 'grausame Ironie' (Dahn, *Studien*, p. 55: cf. Deut. 13. 10), the baptised Toledan Jews had promised to stone (or burn) any apostate.

[4] For Sisebut, see *HG* 60 (next note), *Etym.* v. 39. 42, Isidore, *Chronica* 416, *CH* 15 and Blumenkranz, *Juifs*, pp. 107–9. The view that Heraclius inspired Sisebut's policy (thus P. Goubert, *Revue des études byzantines*, IV (1946), 120) finds no support in the evidence. Heraclius himself only coerced the Jews to baptism later and as an exceptional action in a century of comparative calm: A. Sharf, *Byzantinische Zeitschrift*, XLVIII (1955), 103–15. For Chintila, see VI Tol. 3, connected with Honorius's accusation (above, p. 123, n. 4). Dahn, *Könige*, pp. 650–3, contains the text of the *Confessio vel professio* made by baptised Jews at this time (and perhaps composed by Braulio: see Lynch, pp. 130–1): it is referred to in XII. 2. 17.

[5] Isidore showed his disapproval of Sisebut's policy in *HG* 60, but was able to fall back upon Phil. 1. 18. IV Tol. 57 (confirmed, together with the council's other provisions concerning the Jews, by VI Tol. 3 and VIII Tol. 12) condemned forced

despite his Jewish origin[1] – perhaps, indeed, because of it – was vigorous in his hostility to the Jews.[2] The result was an ultimatum: the Jews of the kingdom had the bitter choice of baptism within a year or exile, after flogging, *decalvatio* and confiscation of property.[3] It is the Jew constrained to baptism who is primarily denoted by the term *Iudeus* in Ervig's other laws,[4] for the king would certainly not have concerned himself to produce these if they were to lose applicability once the year's grace had expired. The king realistically accepted that many Jews, forced to baptism by fear of the cruel alternative, would continue to practise the faith and observe the customs of Judaism when they could, and it was to the prevention and punishment of such activities that he devoted himself. Celebration in the Jewish fashion of the Passover, the Feast of Tabernacles, the Sabbath and the lunar and other festivals was forbidden on pain of those same punishments which were imposed for the refusal of baptism.[5] It was the responsibility of the clergy to ensure that local Jews were under worthy Christian supervision at the times of the Jewish festivals so that secret worship could not take place.[6] The same determination to prevent Jewish circumvention of the law

baptism and forbade it for the future, but insisted that those baptised should not backslide (see also cc. 59, 62): baptised children were to be brought up as Christians (c. 60, without *baptizatos* in Migne, but see Katz, p. 50, n. 3; *contra*, Blumenkranz, *Juifs*, p. 111, with n. 178). I can see no 'manifest contradiction' here, as can A. Echánove, *HS*, XIV (1961), 270. On the interest of IV Tol. 57 for canon law, see the excellent article of S. Monzó, 'El bautismo de los judios en la Esp. visigoda. En torno al canon 57 del Concilio IV de Toledo', *Cuadernos de trabajos de derecho*, II (1953), 111–55. On Isidore and the anti-Jewish canons of the council (over which he presided), see Séjourné, pp. 253–5, and on his literary activity B. Blumenkranz, *Les auteurs chrétiens latins du MA sur les juifs et le judaïsme* (Paris–La Haye, 1963), pp. 88–101: see also L. Castán Lacoma in *Isidoriana*, pp. 445–56.

[1] *CH* 50. Not surprisingly, the contemporary *Vita* by Felix passed over this in silence.

[2] For Julian's anti-Jewish writings, see Blumenkranz, *Auteurs chrétiens*, pp. 118–27. I have not had access to P. à Wengen, *Julianus, Erzbischof von Toledo* (St Gall, 1891), who, pp. 30–9, argues for Julian as the instigator of Ervig's anti-Jewish policy but is opposed by Murphy, 'Julian and the fall of the Visigothic kingdom', pp. 13–14 (whence the reference). [3] XII. 3. 3.

[4] Thus generally: see, e.g., Katz, p. 19, Blumenkranz, *Juifs*, p. 123. Naturally, the unbaptised Jew would also have been subject to the laws during and after (while in exile) the one-year period.

[5] XII. 3. 4, 5: cf. XII. 2. 5.

[6] XII. 3. 20, 21: cf. IX Tol. 17, which also required baptised Jews to celebrate Christian feasts in episcopal company.

underlay the elaborate and surely unenforceable requirements concerning Jewish travel. The traveller was obliged to report to the local bishop, priest or judge when he arrived in a strange region: the cleric – or, presumably, the judge – was responsible for the Jew's good behaviour and had to give him, when he left, a letter detailing the times of his arrival and departure, as well as to notify the clerics who had charge of the areas through which he would pass. Evasion of these provisions, or failure to keep to his route, brought the offending Jew a lashing.[1] Flogging, scalping, confiscation of property and exile were further prescribed for the Jew who married or fornicated within the prohibited degrees:[2] marriage in any case had to be accompanied by the payment of dowry or (*vel*) clerical blessing.[3] The same penalties awaited the Jew who attacked Christianity, defended Judaism, fled the kingdom or hid himself away, and anyone who helped him.[4] Flogging and scalping alone attended the failure of a Jew to rest on Sunday and other, specified, holy days,[5] or his adherence to the Jewish dietary laws.[6] The same punishment was meted out to the Jew who possessed or read anti-Christian literature, and to the teacher of anti-Christian doctrines: a second offence, in breach of the special *placitum* which followed the first, involved confiscation of property and exile as well.[7] Circumcision was prohibited on pain of genital amputation for the circumcisor and the willing proselyte alike: a female circumcisor, or a woman who provided the proselyte for circumcision, lost her nose. In both

---

[1] XII. 3. 20.

[2] XII. 3. 8: cf. XII. 2. 6. But confiscation was conditional upon the absence of sincerely Christian children of a prior and licit union.

[3] XII. 3. 8 (below, p. 225, n. 2): cf. XII. 2. 6. For the condemnation of sexual relationships between Christians and Jews, see XII. 2. 14, III Tol. 14, IV Tol. 63 and Katz, pp. 89–90, Lombardía, 'Matrimonios mixtos', pp. 87–107.

[4] XII. 3. 9: cf. XII. 2. 4, 15.

[5] XII. 3. 6: cf. already Narb. 4, forbidding Sunday work to all. The first festival noted in XII. 3. 6, the Annunciation (assigned the fixed date of 18 December by X Tol. 1) was particularly objectionable to the Jews: see Blumenkranz, *Auteurs chrétiens*, pp. 111–12, in his discussion of Ildefonsus' *De virginitate perpetua* – written with the Jews partly in mind. Further on the *DVP* see Braegelmann, pp. 119–53: pp. 125–7 concern the Marian cult and pp. 154–6 discuss the mass composed by Ildefonsus in the Virgin's honour (see Cixila, *Vita s. Hildefonsi* 6). Isidore also took issue with the Jews over the Virgin Birth: *De fide catholica* I. 10. 3.

[6] XII. 3. 7: cf. XII. 2. 8. Further, below, p. 141, n. 2.

[7] XII. 3. 11, excepting only children under the age of ten.

cases, the property of the offender was confiscated.[1] Successful Jewish missionaries were punished in the same way.[2]

The objective of these provisions was the total eradication of the rites and ceremonies of Judaism and the universal observance of certain Christian practices. The Jew was to be constrained to the acceptance, in some measure, of a Christian life, just as he had been constrained to baptism. In this way, it must have been hoped, the old religion would die away and the Jews become reconciled to the new: at the same time, the outward dignity of the Christian kingdom would be maintained. What deserves to be stressed is the absence of any naïve belief that the ritual of baptism wrought some magical transmutation of the Jew so that he underwent automatic metamorphosis into a sincere Christian. In Ervig's eyes, the baptised Jew remained a *perfidus*, an *infidelis*, an *Antichristi minister*.[3] As such he was subject to legal disabilities in his relations with the *fideles*. Not only might a Jew not employ torture against a Christian in the courts, but he might not even testify against him. The children of a baptised Jew were permitted the right of testimony, but even then its concession was dependent upon prior examination of their faith by the authorities.[4] These were Reccesvindian laws, but the notion underlying them – that the baptised Jews were not *membra Christi* but *adversarii eius* – was precisely that of the Ervigian legislation. Nor might a Jew, except by express permission of the king, hold any official position which involved the control of Christians: his authoritative action against a *fidelis* brought the confiscation of half his property or scalping and flogging, while the Christian responsible for permitting the exercise of such power underwent severe financial or corporal penalty.[5] The appointment of a Jew to control over the Christian slaves of private estates was more harshly punished still, for the Jew suffered both the loss of half his property and the pains of *decalvatio* and flogging: the estates and personnel concerned

[1] XII. 3. 4: cf. XII. 2. 7, 16, IV Tol. 59 and – concerned solely with the circumcision of Christian slaves – XII. 2. 12, 13, 14, III Tol. 14. Deut. 23. 1 made the penalty the more terrible for the believing Jew.
[2] XII. 3. 4. The penalties for the defence of Judaism (XII. 3. 9) must surely also have applied?
[3] E.g., XII. 3. 10 (*perfidi*, contrasted with *fideles*, *christiani*), XII. 3. 24 (*infideles*), XII. 3. 12. For *infideles*, see also XI Tol. 11.
[4] XII. 2. 9, 10: cf., more judiciously, IV Tol. 64.
[5] XII. 3. 17: cf. already III Tol. 14, IV Tol. 65.

were forfeit to the fisc when a layman had made the appointment, while an offending cleric or monk had to pay their value from his own pocket or undergo exile, under penitence. In this way, Ervig added grimly, the offender might learn 'quam sit inpium infidos fidelibus preponere christianis'.[1]

The same notion of the impropriety of Jewish authority over Christians was the justification for further laws which, by forbidding Jews the possession of Christian *mancipia* – a favourite theme of earlier legislation and of the canons[2] – struck, like those above, at their means of livelihood.[3] Two months were granted in which the Jew could either dispose of his *mancipia* – though not by manumission, since it was deemed unworthy for a Christian to receive his freedom at Jewish hands[4] – or make a solemn profession of Christianity, in which case he was permitted to keep them.[5] Advantageous sales would hardly have been possible in these circumstances, especially since a potential buyer would have known that the illegal retention of a Christian slave after the period of grace would involve the Jew in the loss of half his property or, if he was a *vilior*, in scalping and flogging, as well as the loss of the slave.[6] Christian slaves were obliged to declare their faith: those who had neglected to do so by the end of the period allowed were given by the king to whomever he wished.[7] Non-Christian slaves of the Jews who underwent a sincere conversion were automatically granted their freedom from a master whom they showed to be a Jew.[8]

The task of enforcing these numerous and detailed measures would have been an alarmingly difficult one even if the king could have

---

[1] XII. 3. 19.

[2] See XII. 2. 12, 13, 14, III Tol. 14, IV Tol. 66, x Tol. 7, and generally Katz, pp. 98–100, Blumenkranz, *Juifs*, pp. 197–202, 329–33.

[3] The general prohibition is XII. 3. 12 (but cf. XII. 3. 13, 16, 18), where the opening words refer to the 'inportabile...flagitium' that the 'gens Iudaica, contra Dominum rebellis semper et inpia, christiana mancipia suis habeat servitiis religata, et... honorabile Christi membrum humilietur ante filios perditorum, et portio dicata Christo...perfidorum obsequiis subiugetur, sicque corpus Christi videatur obsequi Antichristi ministris'. (For ministers of Antichrist, see also IV Tol. 66.) The organological principle leads logically to the view that the body as a whole is affected by the subjection of one of its parts. For impropriety, see also XII. 2. 14: 'Abominanda sunt ergo in christianis funesta Iudeorum imperia, et reducenda est sub amore catholico plebs Deo sacrata in gratia'.

[4] XII. 3. 1, 12.     [5] XII. 3. 13.     [6] XII. 3. 12, 13.

[7] XII. 3. 13, 16.     [8] XII. 3. 18.

relied upon the positive support of the population at large and upon the services of a willing and honest judiciary and clergy. But it is quite clear that he could not. There is no reason for believing the relations of the people with the Jews to have been bad: Judaising Christians and actual conversions were not unknown,[1] and the evasion of the laws which took place throughout the century could hardly have occurred if the mass of the *fideles* had been anti-Jewish zealots.[2] Ervig in fact found it desirable both to maintain the older law forbidding all Christians to render assistance to Jewish transgressors and also to introduce new measures of his own, penalising the acceptance of bribes from Jews or the exercise of patronage on their behalf.[3] Nor was the judiciary dependable, as Ervig frankly admitted.[4] It was to the clergy therefore that the task of enforcement was entrusted.[5] Either the bishop or his representative should be present at the hearing of every case against a Jew where, without concern for money or patronage, he should apply the laws together with the judge.[6] But who was to guard the guardians? Venality and apathy – and tolerance too, no doubt – were not the prerogatives of laymen,[7] and in a law which bore explicit witness to his recognition of the fact, Ervig set bishop to watch over bishop and envisaged even then the possibility that *perfidia* would go unchecked and that he would have to take action himself.[8]

The fact is that enforcement was quite beyond the royal resources: there was, as one author has put it, an 'approach to totalitarian con-

---

[1] See XII. 2. 16, 3. 4 and Julian of Toledo, *Insultatio* 2. For the early case of Froga, see *EW* 20 and the scholion published by W. Gundlach, *NA*, XVI (1890), 46–7. But it is not demonstrable that Froga was a neophyte: see W. Giese, *HJ*, LXXXVIII (1968), 412. It was partly to combat Jewish missionary activity that Isidore's two anti-Jewish works were written, and Julian's *De comprobatione aetatis sextae* had perhaps the same end: Blumenkranz, *Auteurs chrétiens*, pp. 90, 120, with n. 13. For the immediately post-Visigothic period, see A. C. Vega, *Ciudad de Dios*, CLIII (1941), 57–100.

[2] See Parkes, p. 349.

[3] XII. 2. 15 (Reccesvind), XII. 3. 10 (bribery), 22 (patronage): cf. IV Tol. 58.

[4] XII. 3. 24, 25.

[5] XII. 3. 23: 'Ut cura omnis distringendi Iudeos solis sacerdotibus debeatur'. For particular duties, see XII. 2. 10, 3. 12, 20, 21 and 28, requiring them to promulgate the new *corpus* to their local Jews.

[6] XII. 3. 25.   [7] See XII. 3. 10, IV Tol. 58, for bribery.

[8] XII. 3. 24, where a defence against the charge of neglect was 'obstruction' (patronage?). Bishops were not responsible unless offences were reported to them by their subordinates: XII. 3. 26.

trols, without the means of a totalitarian state'.[1] The contrast between the theory and the practice of Visigothic government is arguably nowhere more clearly demonstrated than in the anti-Jewish legislation. In the production of the imposing complex of laws the king fulfilled his theocratic – which is necessarily to say, totalitarian – role: he pronounced from on high what in his judgement was beneficial to the Christian society placed in his care. But royal *dicta* remained so many words if the king's servants chose not to act upon them. Theoretically supreme, the monarch had, governmentally speaking, feet of clay, as Ervig's concern with corruption and sloth by his judges and bishops makes abundantly clear. What a remarkable illustration it is of the gulf between the ideal and the real that the vice-gerent of God should have been compelled to exhort one bishop to repair the damage caused by the negligence or avarice of another,[2] that the guardian of Christian morality should have been forced openly to prohibit the supervision of Jewesses by clerics during the Jewish festivals lest misbehaviour take place,[3] that the interpreter of justice and giver of law should have been driven to insist that his judges should not hear a Jewish case in the absence of a cleric for fear of bribery!

Alongside the baptised *Iudei* dealt with in the laws just discussed, there existed another class of Jews who received scant attention. It is self-evident that sincere conversion to the Christian faith must from time to time have been experienced by Jews,[4] and the laws say just enough to show that such converts were regarded as *christiani*, no longer as *Iudei*. Two of the laws contain, in fact, the profession of faith and the elaborate oath by which individuals 'ex Iudeis ad fidem venientes' discarded their Jewish character and assumed that of the Christian.[5] The *professio* was no simple form of words, but a solemn abjuration and pledge, made before the bishop and afterwards

---

[1] S. W. Baron, *A social and religious hist. of the Jews*, 2nd edn, III (New York, 1957), 43.
[2] XII. 3. 24.
[3] XII. 3. 21. Not only those who see religion as a sublimation of the sexual urge will find delight in the terminology: 'Quod si quemlibet sacerdotum contigerit, ut zelum, quo pro Christi nomine uti debet, frequenter ad libidinis sue sibimet occasiones usurpet...'!
[4] Apart from Julian (above, p. 134), Taio of Saragossa (who bore the forename Samuel) may have been of Jewish origin: see Lynch, p. 60, Madoz, 'Tajón', pp. 347–8. [5] XII. 3. 14 (profession), 15 (oath).

retained in the local church archives,[1] in which the convert renounced the rites and observances of Judaism, recited the creed, promised never to return 'ad vomitum superstitionis Iudaice' and declared that he would thenceforth live 'christiano more', avoiding the company of Jews, consorting with Christians, going to church and so on. The accompanying oath was packed with references to the God of Old and New Testaments alike. The Jewish proselyte was not permitted an easy transition to Christianity: the history of his heritage was paraded before him, and out of his own mouth he had to condemn his erstwhile faith as error and superstition. That the Jew undergoing baptism in accordance with Ervig's ultimatum, XII. 3. 3, made also this sworn profession of faith, and that it was such a Jew who was designated by the term *Iudeus* in the remainder of the king's legislation is a general but unwarranted assumption.[2] There are no grounds for linking baptism with the *professio*: nothing in XII. 3. 3 even implicitly refers to an act of profession, while there is similarly nothing in the profession which alludes to baptism.[3] That the *professio* involved much more than baptism is clearly shown by the promise in the former that the convert would shun the company of the *Iudei*. There is nothing about such an obligation in any other law, while the implementation of such a promise, if it had been taken by, and if it had referred to, all of Jewish origin undergoing baptism, would have had social effects of unimaginable ramifications. In fact, the sincere convert promised here not to consort with those Jews who were simply baptised, or who had remained unbaptised.[4]

By the *professio*, the Jew became a *christianus* and as such was not

[1] Cf. XII. 3. 13, 28.

[2] Held by, e.g., J. Juster, 'La condition légale des juifs sous les rois visigoths', *Études d'hist. juridique offertes à Paul Frédéric Girard*, II (Paris, 1913), 288ff., Melicher, *Kampf*, p. 205, Parkes, p. 365, Katz, pp. 17–18.

[3] The laws containing the profession and oath do not even follow that concerning baptism, but appear after XII. 3. 13, where the profession (mentioned for the first time) is viewed as proof that the Jew has become a Christian. Katz, p. 18 (following Juster, p. 289, n. 3: Katz's general reliance on Juster is startling), holds that XII. 3. 28 'proves that every baptized Jew had to sign the formulas': presumably he bases this upon the phrase: 'Professionum atque conditionum scripturas, quas *quisque ille Iudeus* sacerdoti...obtulerit'. But 'any Jew' is meant, as a little earlier: 'Sed in quocumque fuerit postea *quisque ille* prevaricator inventus, in nullo erit harum legum sententiam evasurus'.

[4] Already in IV Tol. 62 the baptised Jew was required not to mix with the unbaptised. But now all were ordered to be baptised.

the direct object of the laws concerning his ex-brethren, the *Iudei*,[1] although he was liable to the penalties of *decalvatio*, flogging, confiscation of property and exile if he broke his oath or relapsed into Jewish
ways.[2] The identification as a Christian of the Jew who made the profession is clear from two laws concerning slaves. Jews were given sixty
days in which to sell their Christian *mancipia* or face the rigour of the
law. But Christians were entitled to Christian workers, and Ervig
provided that Jewish masters who claimed to be Christians should
make a sworn profession within the sixty days and thus 'se christianos
ostendant'. The profession made, the masters, 'utpote christiani',
might hold Christian *mancipia*:

Nam non aliter poterunt christiana mancipia illorum dominio subiugari,
nisi et ipsi evidenter conprobentur verissimi christiani et frequenter
christianorum societate coniungi.

By making the sworn profession, the master 'christianum se esse
devoverit'.[3]

Profession and baptism – unmentioned in the law – were quite
distinct here: indeed, it is clear that the beneficiary of the measure
was the already baptised Jew,[4] for not only would no other be able
to claim with any plausibility that he lived as a Christian,[5] but the
period of sixty days' grace was altogether too short to permit the

1 How, e.g., could XII. 3. 19, forbidding *Iudei*, the *infidi*, control of Christian slaves
on private estates, have applied also to the Jew who had shown himself to be
a *verissimus christianus* by sworn profession and who was allowed authority over his
own Christian *mancipia* (XII. 3. 13)?
2 XII. 3. 13. But the rejection of pork 'natura...fastidiante' was not seen as an indication of relapse in the case of a Jew who had made the profession (XII. 3. 7: 'Si
...christianitatis ab eis non defuerit *votum*', where the conditional clearly points to
the existence of others who had not made it). Compare also the phrases: 'Qui
*fideles*...approbantur...Quos manifesta operum Christi nobilitat fides' with the
designation of (baptised!) Jews elsewhere as *infidi*, *perfidi* etc. An exemption concerning pork appeared already in the *placita* of Chintila's and Reccesvind's reigns:
see *Confessio vel professio* C1, XII. 2. 17.
3 XII. 3. 13.
4 Thus, Parkes, p. 363. The view of Katz, p. 19 (and Juster, p. 290, n. 3), is that Ervig
here gave a reward to those Jews who became baptised (and thus, in Katz's view,
swore the profession) within sixty days.
5 The legislator attempted in XII. 3. 13 to guard against the fraud of the Jew who
claimed to live 'christiano more' and 'ob hoc dicat, non se amittere debere
christiana mancipia, quia et ipse christianam videatur ducere vitam'. While Ervig
did not want 'astuta fraus' to win the day, neither did he wish 'sincera conversio'
to be unjustly penalised.

lengthy catechumenical preparation prescribed for the Jewish proselyte by the Council of Agde.[1] Ervig's purpose was to establish the criterion by which the sincere convert might be recognised. The same distinction of baptism and conversion occurs in another law. XII. 3. 3 required that all Jews be baptised, masters and slaves alike. But XII. 3. 18 provided that a slave should be freed as soon as he had shown himself to be a Christian by the sworn profession – 'mox ut se et professione et iusiurandi adtestatione christianum ostenderit' – and his master not to be – 'dominorum suorum prevaricationes manifeste prodiderit'. Unless we are to make the wholly unjustified assumption that this law applied only until the one-year period of grace was up,[2] we have to suppose that Ervig was here allowing a distinction between the converted slave – who was to be treated in precisely the same fashion as the Christian slave – and the simply baptised one, over whom his master, similarly baptised, was to keep control.[3]

The distinction appears yet again in a third law in which Ervig dealt with royal clemency towards an offender guilty of breach of one of the various measures which provided for loss of property and exile – a baptised Jew in the great majority of cases.[4] It was the prerogative of the king to recall such an offender from exile and reinvest him with his property when the priest or judge of the area in which he lived had testified to his good behaviour, and the Jew himself had sworn a profession of Christian faith.[5] The profession here was unconnected with baptism, for there could be no question

[1] c. 34 – eight months.

[2] Thus Katz, pp. 99–100. Parkes, p. 364, recognised the problem of reconciliation with XII. 3. 3 and considered XII. 3. 18 to refer to slaves acquired after the one-year period. This suggestion does not, in fact, resolve the difficulty.

[3] The title of XII. 3. 18 refers to conversion: 'Ut Iudeorum servi necdum adhuc conversi, si ad Christi gratiam convolaverint, libertate donentur'. The law ends: 'Sicque proveniet, ut in omnibus omnino rebus ordo ille omnis in eum inpleatur, qui de christianis mancipiis est constitutus'. That the baptised Jew was not considered a *christianus* is beyond doubt. Is it perhaps the case that the phrase *Christi gratia* here is used to indicate the acceptance of Christianity as opposed to that simply of baptism (the phrase of XII. 3. 3 being *gratia baptismi*)?

[4] XII. 3. 27.

[5] 'Postquam eorum professio cum iurisiurandi adtestatione regie agnitioni claruerit ...postquam se professus fuerit christianum...'. There is no indication of an earlier oath and profession. Note also XII. 3. 5, providing for the return of confiscated goods to the Jew 'perfecte converso'.

of rebaptism, universally reprobated by the Church. And the profession may be seen to have had legal effects which were quite distinct from those of simple baptism and which it is reasonable to view as based upon a recognition of the transformation of the *Iudeus* into the *christianus*.

The distinction between converted and other Jews was retained in later Egican measures.[1] Just twelve years after the code of 681 was published – when, that is to say, all the Jews living freely within the kingdom would, or should, have been baptised[2] – Egica held out to those prepared to undergo true conversion the prospect of avoiding payment of the special tax apparently paid up to that time by all of Jewish origin: at the same time he imposed severe commercial restrictions on those who did not sign a profession of faith and bought in all the slaves and property which they had at any time received from Christians.[3] Such action spelled the end of what had been

[1] See Blumenkranz, *Juifs*, p. 131.

[2] There are no grounds for believing Egica revoked, or chose not to enforce, XII. 3. 3, although Katz, p. 20, is obliged to believe this, since he identifies baptism and conversion and cannot otherwise explain the existence of non-converted Jews. That in 688 a Jewish messenger was dubbed *infidus et a cultu fidei alienus* by Idalius (*Responsio*, in Julian of Toledo's *Prognosticon*) by no means indicates that Jews were then free to practise their religion: rather, the terminology fits that of Ervig's laws concerning the baptised Jews, and the messenger's name, Restitutus, may well have been baptismal.

[3] XVI Tol. *Tomus*, I, and XII. 2. 18. The law removed the burden of taxation from the Jew who 'ad catholice fidei rectitudinem per veram conversationem sive professionem redierit omnemque suorum rituum errorem vel ceremonias abnuens christianorum more tramitem vite sue duxerit', for it was unjust that those Jews should bear the special levy 'qui iugum Christi dulce eiusque onus leve per dignam conversationem noscuntur excipere'. Opposed to such men were the *ceteri Iudei* who 'in perfidia cordis sui perseverantes, ad catholicam fidem converti neglexerint'. Note that baptism here finds no mention. Why should it, since all were now – officially, at least – baptised? The talk is all of conversion and the profession, as it is throughout the law. Similar language is used in the *Tomus*: 'Ex quibus igitur Hebraeis...si quis deinceps ad catholicae fidei regulam integerrima devotione conversus exstiterit, abnegans ex toto genuinae praevaricationis errores vel caerimonias omnesque parentalium rituum sectas, ab omni exutus jugo maneat functionis, quam pridem in errore praestitutus...exsolvere consuevit' and in c. 1, where the bishops decree: 'Ut quicunque eorum ad Christum plena mentis intentione converterint et fidem catholicam absque aliquo infidelitatis fuco servaverint, ab omni functione...securi extorresque persistant'. They continue: 'Ipsi vero qui ab errore suo conversi exstiterint, suis tantum utilitatibus ut caeteri ingenui vacent, et...quidquid...a principe eis fuerit imperatum ut veri Christicolae expediant. Nam id aequitatis ordo deposcit, ut qui fide Christi decorantur coram omnibus nobiles atque honorabiles habeantur'.

a policy not without merit, for while Ervig had attached few material benefits to conversion, so that this had remained voluntary, Egica in effect coerced the Jews to conversion. Naturally, many of them would have been insincere, and it is no surprise that a year later the king enslaved all Spanish Jews, 'converted' or not.[1]

In the pretence of constrained baptism or in the truth of voluntary conversion, then, Christ was preached.[2] That Ervig was guilty, in insisting upon the former, of denying what many today would consider a basic human freedom should not blind us to the realism and sense of justice which he showed in allowing for the second. At least the genuine convert was not proceeded against simply because Jewish blood ran in his veins; at least, in Ervig's time, the sins of the fathers were not visited upon all the sons.[3] Nor should our moral condemnation prevent us from recognising the strength of the case for forced baptism which Ervig had, given the premises of the day. It is easy to see how total certainty that salvation depended upon faith could lead a responsible Christian ruler to practise intolerance towards the enemies of that faith: men of the time did not, as we do, admire conviction in belief but repudiate the concomitant coercion of dangerous disbelievers. The protective function of the king was served when he effectively countered with *salutifera remedia* the diseases which might debilitate the Christian society divinely committed to his care.[4] As God's chosen instrument of government, the zealous Christian king naturally felt outraged by Jewish rejection of his faith. Constraint, Augustine had argued, was justifiable when it was constraint to good:[5] even biblical warrant was held to exist for it.[6] And constraint to baptism had its own particular justification, for the sacrament brought its recipient into a state of grace regardless of his character and wishes,[7] and without it not even the infant could

---

[1] xvii Tol. *Tomus*, 7, 8.

[2] Phil. 1. 18 is in fact quoted in xii. 3. 18 and 2. 18 (Egica).

[3] It is salutary to recall that only in 1865 did Jewish blood cease absolutely to be an impediment to office in Spain: H. Kamen, *The Spanish Inquisition* (London, 1965), p. 135.          [4] See xii. 2. 14 and note the 'medical' references in xvi Tol. 1.

[5] Augustine, *Ep.* xciii. 16: 'Non esse considerandum quod quisque cogitur, sed quale sit illud, quo cogitur, utrum bonum an malum'.          [6] Luke 14. 23.

[7] Cf., in another connection, viii Tol. 7: 'Licet inviti perceperint quod non merebantur habere, libenter tamen ob hoc coeleste retineant praemium...ut tandem inviti appetant bona diligere quae sponte videntur desides impugnare', where the reasoning is equally valid for baptism – in fact, referred to earlier in the canon.

enter the kingdom of heaven.[1] At least the possibility of redemption was open to the baptised Jew. From the Christian standpoint, indeed, Ervig's policy could justifiably be viewed as positively benevolent.[2]

The religious unity of Ervig's reign was, then, formal rather than real, for it was not a unity of faith. And it may be questioned how firmly the faith sat upon the shoulders even of the alleged *fideles*. Certainly it is not to be expected that Christianity should have swept away all opposition in the remoter areas where a priest, if he was to be found at all,[3] would often have possessed little more learning than his flock, and where the tenacious conservatism of the countryside would have posed a daunting problem even to the most vigorous cleric. It is in fact clear from the sources that underneath the Christian surface of Visigothic society there throve a profusion of primitive beliefs and observances to which many, as a matter of conviction, cautious insurance or simple habit, remained profoundly attached. Generally speaking, it had been the custom of the Church to come to terms with the traditional practices of the areas which it penetrated when it could do so without sacrifice of the integrity of the faith. But the exclusive and totalitarian demands of the Christian God made impossible a syncretic solution: there could be no compromise with idolatry, sorcery and divination, which in any case were the works of devil-worshippers and to be shunned as sacrilegious by any true Christian.[4] The extent of the problem in sixth-century

---

[1] *Sent.* I. 22. 2, *DEO* II. 25. 7, echoed in Ildefonsus, *Liber de cognitione baptismi* 113: John 3. 5 is cited by both, though conflated with ib. 3. 3 by Ildefonsus.

[2] According to the much later Solomon Ibn Verga, *Schevet jehuda* 9 (I use the German translation of M. Wiener, Hanover, 1856), Sisebut (ruling here in Rome c. 800!) argued that it was his duty to force baptism on the Jews, since the unbaptised would surely suffer everlasting death: they should be compelled to receive spiritual blessings for their own good, as a child should be compelled to learn its lessons. Note that the clergy are exhorted in XII. 3. 23 to instruct the Jews 'pro eorum salvatione': VIII Tol. 12 had generously recognised that Christ died 'ut pro nobis ita quoque pro illis': therefore, 'necessarium duximus summam pro eis impendere curam pro quibus suam Christus ponere non dedignatus est animam'.

[3] Cf. XII. 3. 21.

[4] I Cor. 10. 20 was the basic source for the identification of idolatry and devil-worship, for which see XII Tol. 11: 'Cultores idolorum...qui diabolo sacrificare videntur', XVI Tol. *Tomus* (529c). For the connection of sorcery and idolatry, see already the Council of Elvira, c. 6, and for the requirement that Christians avoid the magical and divinatorial arts 'in quibus omnibus ars daemonum est', *Etym.* VIII. 9. 31. Consultation of diviners and magicians was sacrilege in IV Tol. 29: so was idolatry in III Tol. 16, XII Tol. 11, XVI Tol. 2.

Galicia, where the Sueves were only a century removed from paganism and where the magical and astrological arts had received reinforcement and respectability from the prevalence of Priscillianism, is revealed by St Martin's *De correctione rusticorum*,[1] but it is doubtful whether the situation was a great deal better in the contemporary Visigothic kingdom, for the Arian Goths were tolerant of paganism, even considering it no sin 'si inter gentilium aras et Dei eclesiam quis transiens utraque veneretur' and themselves maintaining the pagan custom of burying grave-goods.[2] In 589, at any rate, the bishops at the Third Council roundly declared that the sacrilege of idolatry was implanted throughout almost the whole of Spain and Septimania.[3] They themselves censured the chanting of funeral dirges and immodest singing and dancing on Church festivals,[4] while both divination and the practice of rest on Thursdays in honour of Jupiter came under attack at Narbonne in the same year.[5]

To what extent the problem had become a lesser one by Ervig's day we have no means of knowing. But certainly it had not disappeared. It is remarkable, in view of the powerful Christian ethos of the time, that the code contained no express denunciation of idolatry or of pagan superstitions. These last had been proceeded against earlier by the Fourth Council, which attempted to counter them by ordering New Year's Day to be spent in fasting,[6] and both the Twelfth and the Sixteenth Councils concerned themselves with

[1] On which see S. J. McKenna, *Paganism and pagan survivals in Spain up to the fall of the Visigothic kingdom* (Washington D.C., 1938), pp. 88–107. The *DCR* could be cited as an additional reference in many of the notes in this section.
[2] See *HF* v. 43 and further F. J. Dölger, *Antike und Christentum. Kultur- und Religionsgeschichtliche Studien*, VI (Münster, 1950), 69–70. For grave-goods, see the *Antiqua* XI. 2. 1 and Melicher, *Kampf*, pp. 22–3 (on the Germanic *Totenteil*): H. Zeiss, *Die Grabfunde aus dem spanischen Westgotenreich* (Berlin–Leipzig, 1934), passim, is basic on the finds, but there is a valuable brief account in Thompson, *Goths*, pp. 147–51. For the *LRV* and Catholic activity, see McKenna, pp. 111–13.
[3] III. Tol. 16, ordering judges and bishops to take joint action and slave-owners to eradicate it in their *familiae*.
[4] III Tol. 22, 23. For Gothic lamentation of the dead Theodoric I, see Jordanes, *Getica* 214.
[5] Narb. 14, 15. Sunday rest was correspondingly ordered in c. 4.
[6] IV Tol. 11: cf. *DEO* I. 41. But *LO* 450–1 shows 2 January as the day of abstinence: had the Church given up the struggle? On the pagan practices associated with the calends, see McKenna, pp. 47, 95–8, and on 1 January as the Feast of the Circumcision, Kottje, pp. 84–6.

the continued worship of the fountains, stones and trees which had been sacred objects to the Celt-Iberians and to the Germans.[1] The reality of idolatrous worship in Galicia towards the end of the century is revealed by Valerius's autobiography.[2] But if idolatry received no attention in the code, soothsaying did. Divination was forbidden because it was a *mendacium*, the work of the Devil who was a liar from the beginning: those who consulted diviners were 'Dei spiritu vacui, erroris spiritu pleni', the diviners themselves 'odibiles Deo'.[3] Divination was clearly of powerful allure, for clerics availed themselves of its services and judges had to be warned not to consult augurs for assistance in the cases they heard.[4] It was also a dangerous practice from the royal point of view, for prophecies about the health or future fate of the ruler might easily lead to disaffection within the kingdom. Chindasvind's concern was reflected in vi. 2. 1, where he forbade the consultation of diviners 'de salute vel morte principis vel cuiuscumque hominis' and provided that both client and diviner in such a case should suffer lashing, forfeiture of property and enslavement if they were freemen, or sale overseas after punitive torture if they were slaves.[5] These punishments were in fact those which awaited anyone who consulted a diviner for any reason, but the diviner in other cases himself escaped with fifty lashes, accompanied by *infamia* if the offence was repeated.[6]

More dangerous than augury, however, was sorcery, for the evil results of this could directly harm the health or property of any one of the king's subjects.[7] For deterrent effect, a convicted sorcerer was ordered to be paraded about the neighbouring areas after he had endured two hundred lashes and scalping, and then either to be kept in prison or to be sent to the king for a decision as to his fate: in any

[1] xii Tol. 11, xvi Tol. *Tomus* (529c), 2. On the autochthonous cult of the fountains and stones, see McKenna, pp. 7–9, and for the Germans' holy places as woods and groves, Tacitus, *Germania* 9.

[2] Valerius, *Replicatio* 1. For clerical profanity see idem, *Ordo querimoniae* 6.

[3] vi. 2. 2.          [4] Ib., and for the clergy, iv Tol. 29.

[5] For the *ariolus* and the *aruspex* in vi. 2. 1 see *Etym.* viii. 9. 15–17, and on the second as an astrologer, Fontaine, 'Isidore et l'astrologie', pp. 280–2. For conciliar condemnations of inquiry into the fate of the king, see v Tol. 4 ('religioni inimicum et...superstitiosum'), vi Tol. 17.

[6] vi. 2. 2.

[7] See Mer. 15 for clerics attributing illnesses to spells cast by members of their households.

case, he suffered *infamia*. His client received just the flogging.[1] The laws showed the sorts of activity which were feared when they referred to the conjuration of hailstorms to strike vineyards and crops,[2] to the invocation, by nocturnal sacrifices, of demons who might be used to make men mad,[3] and to the employment of ligatures and magical writings to destroy property or to bring dumbness, injury or death to men or animals.[4] The astonishing forms which ecclesiastical sorcery might take are revealed by the canons of two late councils which condemned the practice whereby priests suspended divine service, removed the altar vessels and donned mourning garments in an apparent attempt to force God into punishment of their enemies and the even greater abuse which was the celebration of a requiem mass for someone still alive, with the intention of causing his death.[5] These allusions offer a bare glimpse into the twilight world of magic and superstition which was never far away, we may believe, from the attention of a large number of people, especially among the lower classes,[6] and in terms of which the religious history of the period should ideally be largely written: the Church's heavy reliance upon its own form of magic, miracles, shows the temper of the age. Belief in the efficacy of the magic arts was certainly strong in king and churchman alike, and naturally so, for the reality of divine and diabolical intervention in the affairs of the world was universally accepted: the invocation of the powers of the Devil by the sorcerer was simply the other side of the coin to the appeal for heavenly intercession by the saint.

But magical practices did not always depend upon recourse to the powers of darkness. An *Antiqua* which punished the man who 'mortui sarcofacum abstulerit, dum sibi vult habere remedium' with a fine of twelve *solidi* if he was a freeman or with one hundred lashes

---

[1] VI. 2. 4, 5. Dahn, *Studien*, p. 234, McKenna, p. 124, unjustifiably see talion in the latter. For *infamia*, see II. 4. I (where *sortilegi* appear: on these see *Etym*. VIII. 9. 28 and McKenna, p. 113) and for the execution of *malefici* VI. 5. 16.

[2] VI. 2. 4.

[3] Ib.: cf. VI. 5. 16, and for demons as the cause of madness, XI Tol. 13.

[4] VI. 2. 5.

[5] For the first, see XIII Tol. 7, and on its suggested purpose McKenna, pp. 131–2. For the mass, see XVII Tol. *Tomus* (554a/b), 5.

[6] Slaves appear as a prime target of III Tol. 16, Mer. 15, XII Tol. 11 and VI. 2. 4.

if he was a slave[1] – penalties much less severe than those for grave-robbing for gain, where the freeman paid a pound of gold and was lashed and the slave was executed[2] – shows that they might take the relatively harmless form of the superstitious attribution to a particular object of medicinal properties. And they might also rest upon the calculated use of scientific knowledge, for potions, and particularly poisons, were still, as they had been among both the Romans and the Germans, regarded as in some way magical: it is significant that Chindasvind's law on poisoning is preceded in the code by two on divination and followed by two on sorcery. The horror felt at the use of malefactory potions is illustrated by the provision that the poisoner should die a *turpissima* death, apparently after suffering torture, and that even the attempt at poisoning should have as its consequence the delivery of the offender into the power of his intended victim, to be treated – though presumably *vita reservata* – at the latter's pleasure.[3] In the same way, the administration of an abortifacient potion was a capital offence, while abortion brought about by a blow or some other means was penalised only by a fine – though a heavy one.[4] It is difficult to believe that intelligent men attributed the harmful effects of potions in such cases to the supernatural art of the magician rather than to the natural and constant properties of the ingredients. But it is clear from another law,[5] referring to magical preparations by which adulteresses managed so to affect their husbands that these were unable to accuse their wives or even to stop loving them, that potions were not regarded in what even approached a scientific manner, for here they were seized upon as the explanation for behaviour which so shocked contemporary notions of marital propriety that the love, lethargy, jealousy or whatever which was the true cause had to be accounted for as the result of some magical agency.[6]

It is salutary to remember that the paganism and superstition referred to above occurred in a realm whose king could boast that

---

[1] XI. 2. 2, where, pace McKenna, p. 125, I can see neither necromancy nor robbing a coffin. One of the stones used to form a coffin (for an illustration, see *Gallia*, XVII (1959), 163) or perhaps a head-stone is to be thought of.
[2] XI. 2. 1. For violation of tombs, see also IV Tol. 46.
[3] VI. 2. 3: cf. II. 4. 1 (*infamia*).     [4] See below, pp. 238–9.     [5] III. 4. 13.
[6] Though the use of aphrodisiacs to keep a husband charmed by his adulterous wife should not, I suppose, be wholly discounted.

throughout almost the whole world men spoke of the fullness of faith which flourished in Spain,[1] and whose great churchmen stood head and shoulders above their foreign counterparts. The truth is that, despite the sophistication of a few, the great mass of men who made up Visigothic society remained wedded to the primitive and continued to act, when they were not restrained from so doing, in the self-interested, anarchic, vicious, violent and corrupt fashion of the primitive. And this is as true of the clergy as of anyone else. To say that Visigothic civilisation was a civilisation of the minority is to utter a truism, but what would be a gross misjudgement would be the identification, by and large, of the whole of the clergy with this minority. Not only the lesser clergy but the bishops too were guilty of behaviour far from reconcilable with either the ethics of the faith or the discipline of the canons. Whatever the reasons – and the *Eigenkirche* system, on the one hand,[2] the 'Germanisation' of the episcopate by a king dependent upon faction support, on the other,[3] can hardly have helped matters – the Visigothic clergy were guilty of the same lawlessness and unscrupulousness as their lay *subiecti*.

The most damning evidence comes from the canons of the councils where the greater figures of the day had their opportunity of acting against the malefactors. Ignorance,[4] simony and sexual incontinence

[1] xvii Tol. *Tomus* (553a).

[2] See R. Bidagor, La '*iglesia propia*' *en Esp.*, Analecta Gregoriana, iv (Rome, 1933), passim, but especially pp. 70–6, and Martínez Díez, *Patrimonio*, pp. 70–9. For ill-effects, see Fernández Alonso, *Cura pastoral*, pp. 220–3, with reference to the one case of which we are informed in detail and which appears in Valerius, *Ordo querimoniae* 5ff.: on this see also I. Arenillas, *AHDE*, xi (1934), 468–78.

[3] See J. Orlandis, 'El elemento germánico en la iglesia esp. del siglo VII', *Anuario de estudios medievales*, iii (1966), passim, but especially pp. 48–57, and Thompson, *Goths*, pp. 289–96. 'Gothicisation' and decline are certainly linked by Orlandis (pp. 57–64). Nevertheless, Fructuosus was a Goth: thus, convincingly, Thompson, 'Fructuosus', pp. 54–8. So probably was Ildefonsus: see Braegelmann, pp. 5–6.

[4] On this and measures to counter or eradicate it, see iii Tol. 7, Narb. 11, iv Tol. 25, 26 (on the *libellum officiale* of which see García Villada, pp. 34–5), viii Tol. 8, xi Tol. 2, iii Braga 1, xvi Tol. 6. The matter was closely connected with uncanonical transition to the religious estate, on which see iii Tol. 1, ii Barc. 3, iv Tol. 19 (listing impediments to elevation to the episcopate), 54, and for the case of Agapius, ii Sev. 7. Ignorance was no new problem: in the 590s Licinianus of Cartagena had written to Gregory the Great (*Reg.* 1. 41a) that the papal command that the ignorant should not be ordained might well mean no ordinations at all in his area. For parish, episcopal and monastic schools, see Riché, pp. 326–8, 331–6, 339–50: generally on clerical education, Fernández Alonso, *Cura pastoral*, pp. 71–118.

all appear here as prevalent vices of the contemporary clergy.[1] Penalties had to be laid down for episcopal treason,[2] murder, wounding and *invasio*,[3] and feuding bishops threatened with excommunication.[4] Clerics were wont to mutilate their slaves,[5] to condemn their inferiors unheard or in secret hearings,[6] even to inflict the death penalty.[7] We have just seen that they sometimes consulted magicians and diviners and perverted even the most solemn rite of their faith in practising sorcery themselves. The picture is black.[8]

Little of this appeared in the laws, and there is no reason why it should have done, for those offences which did not fall within the province of purely ecclesiastical discipline involved the transgressor in punishment in accordance with the universally binding laws of the kingdom. Canonically, clerics were required to present disputes amongst themselves for settlement by the bishop,[9] and it is clear from the preoccupation of the councils with matters concerning the valid manumission of ecclesiastical slaves and the circumstances in which freedmen might be recalled to slavery that ecclesiastical courts also enjoyed jurisdiction over the slave and freed *subiecti* of the Church, for none of the numerous provisions found its way into the code exclusively used by the secular judges.[10] Several texts witness judge-

---

[1] For simony see II Barc. 1, 2, IV Tol. 19, VI Tol. 4, VIII Tol. 3, Mer. 9, XI Tol. 8, 9, III Braga 7, and Martínez Díez, *Patrimonio*, pp. 32–8. For incontinence, see below, in text.

[2] Many of the texts cit. p. 47, n. 5, take episcopal treason into account: some of them (e.g., IV Tol. 30, 45) are concerned solely with clerical sedition. Sisbert of Toledo is the supreme example of an episcopal traitor, but see Thompson, *Goths*, p. 226, for the bishops participating in Paul's rebellion against Wamba.

[3] All in XI Tol. 5, a canon which more than any other demonstrates the turpitude of the higher clergy.          [4] XI Tol. 4.

[5] Mer. 15, XI Tol. 6. Clerics above the rank of deacon might not be whipped by their superiors except for the gravest offences: III Braga 6.

[6] II Sev. 6, XI Tol. 7.

[7] XI Tol. 6, 7: cf. IV Tol. 31, cautioning bishops not to act as judges in treason trials unless the king had sworn not to inflict the death penalty.

[8] Further comments in the following pages. See also Fernández Alonso, *Cura pastoral*, pp. 173–6, and Thompson, *Goths*, pp. 296–305. The various abuses are welcome grist to the mill of K. D. Schmidt, *Die Bekehrung der Germanen zum Christentum*, I (Göttingen, 1939), 302–4: astonishingly indulgent, on the other hand, is H. Leclercq, *L'Esp. chrétienne* (Paris, 1906), pp. 359–61.

[9] III Tol. 13. The canon, confirmed by Reccared, declared that an offender should lose his case, but nothing in the code supported this.

[10] For the texts, see above, p. 67, n. 5, and below, p. 179, n. 6. I Sev. 1, II Sev. 8 and X Tol. *Aliud decretum* are particularly significant.

ment and sentence by bishops of those under their authority,[1] although an offender might alternatively be handed over for secular trial,[2] and two canons order that Church slaves should be tried by the regular judges.[3] By no means, however, were cases between laymen and those in the service of the Church required to be heard in ecclesiastical courts,[4] even if recourse was no doubt often had to the bishop as a suitable arbitrator. Legal and conciliar texts alike bear certain witness to the subjection of bishops and other clerics to the general laws of the kingdom and to their appearance in the ordinary courts:[5] most revealing is the law which warned the bishop that his sacerdotal dignity did not free him from the obligation to send his representative to court in obedience to a judicial summons and that contumacy would cost him fifty *solidi*.[6] Only for the very special case of treason do we know that bishops were tried by their peers in a council of the Church, and the evidence for this in fact dates from the period after Ervig.[7] Moreover, clerics who had been unjustly treated by their bishops or metropolitans were granted the right of recourse to the king.[8]

Although Visigothic kings did not always identify the interests of the ecclesiastical establishment with those of society at large,[9] it is wholly in keeping with the unitary and Christocentric premisses of Visigothic society that legal provision *pro utilitatibus ecclesiarum* should have been considered beneficial to the kingdom as a whole.[10] Certain royal laws were therefore explicitly aimed at the correction of clerical shortcomings proceeded against in the canons, while others offered protection and privilege to the Church and its per-

---

[1] E.g., III Tol. 20, II Sev. 6, Mer. 17, III Braga 6, XI Tol. 6, XIII Tol. 8, 11, 12.
[2] XI Tol. 7.
[3] Mer. 15 (but sentence by the bishop), XI Tol. 5.
[4] See IX Tol. 1 and below, in text, on IV. 5. 6.
[5] See II. 1. 6, 9, 24, 3. 3, IX. 1. 21 (Egica), 2. 8, IX Tol. 1, XI Tol. 5 etc.
[6] II. 1. 19.
[7] See XVI Tol. 9 and *Decretum judicii*: XIII Tol. 2 had stated the rule. Pace Hinojosa, 'La jurisdicción eclesiástica entre los visigodos', *Obras*, I, 13, IV Tol. 30 does not establish the council as the competent court for the judgement of a seditious cleric: the conciliar penalty is to be taken as additional to the secular one. That IV Tol. 3 provides for cases against bishops (as well as *potentes* and judges) to be heard before the councils naturally in no way excludes secular hearings.
[8] XIII Tol. 12: cf. ib. 8 for bishops failing to answer a summons from king or metropolitan.
[9] One recalls, e.g., Wamba's IV. 5. 7.        [10] V. 1. 2.

sonnel. One such measure was III. 4. 18, which placed the weight of the secular law behind the frequent and apparently futile fulminations of the councils against the sexual failings of the higher clergy.[1] Either the judge or the bishop was to take action to break any illicit union: the woman concerned was to be flogged by the judge and prevented from continuing in the liaison,[2] while the cleric was to be delivered to his bishop to undergo penitence in accordance with the canons.[3] In this way, thought Reccesvind, might God's will be done. No doubt the secular reinforcement of the canonical prohibition had some deterrent effect, but that the bishops were lukewarm in their zeal to enforce celibacy is clear from the need the king felt to lay down the large fine of two pounds of gold for a bishop whose lethargy prevented him from inflicting due punishment. The same impression of episcopal unconcern is given by a law of Reccared, where the even larger sum of five pounds of gold was

[1] Generally on the councils and celibacy, see Fernández Alonso, *Cura pastoral*, pp. 153–70. Extra-marital relations were forbidden to all (I Sev. 3, IV Tol. 43), but clerics of the rank of deacon and above (later subdeacon, as in III. 4. 18) were obliged to celibacy even if already married (III Tol. 5, II Sar. 1, Council of Toledo of A.D. 597, c. 1 (Vives, *Concilios*, p. 156), IV Tol. 21, VIII Tol. 4–6) and those below might marry only with episcopal approval and certainly not a prostitute, widow or divorced woman (IV Tol. 44). Keeping a concubine, marriage with a divorced, widowed or loose woman and marriage for a second time were impediments to certain ranks of the higher clergy (II Sev. 4, IV Tol. 19). Children of illicit unions were to be enslaved (thus IX Tol. 10: but see above, p. 17, n. 3). To prevent suspicion and temptation, the only women allowed to live under the same roof as a cleric were close blood-relations (III Tol. 5, IV Tol. 42: III Braga 4 went so far as to exclude all but a mother if there were no respectable witnesses), and deacons and their superiors were required to have respectable people living with them who might testify to their chastity (IV Tol. 22, 23). Priests and deacons had to make a special profession that they would live 'caste et pure' (IV Tol. 27): cf. the episcopal *placitum* required in Mer. 4 and the general profession required from all clergy in XI Tol. 10. It was an episcopal responsibility to ensure clerical chastity (thus, e.g., the Councils of Huesca and Egara). But for fornicating bishops see the *Decretum pro Potamio* of X Tol., the staggering XI Tol. 5, and *EW* 1. Fornication was one of the charges against Marcianus of Ecija in the 620s: see *Exemplar judicii* and Thompson, *Goths*, p. 288.

[2] By sale if she was an *ancilla* (of the Church): this is the effect of Reccesvind's words: 'Servata...sententia, que canonum decretis agnoscitur ordinata', where the reference is doubtless to VIII Tol. 5: 'Mulieres vero seu liberae sint seu ancillae...separentur aut certe vendantur'. When earlier canons provided for the sale of a woman involved in an immoral relationship with a cleric (III Tol. 5, I Sev. 3, IV Tol. 43), it was doubtless an *ancilla* of the Church whom they had in mind: thus Schäferdiek, p. 220, n. 261.          [3] See VIII Tol. 4–6.

required from the bishop – or judge – who neglected to take action against an incestuous union or one to which someone in breach of his or her religious vows was party.[1] Secular support for the canons concerning breach of vows was further provided by a Chindasvindian law which punished with infamy and confinement in houses of religion, under penitence, all those who had vowed themselves or been vowed to the religious life but had abandoned it.[2]

It was the positive corruption rather than the apathy of the bishops, on the other hand, which prompted Wamba in 675 to issue IV. 5. 6, a law again in support of the canons. On numerous occasions the councils found it necessary to warn bishops against unpermitted exactions from the churches, monasteries and personnel of their dioceses: the episcopal entitlement was one-third of the income of each parish church, but this was to be employed upon the maintenance of the fabric of the building itself and might only be used for another purpose if repairs were unnecessary.[3] But, relying no doubt upon the general canonical declaration that the administration of the goods of diocesan churches was in the episcopal power,[4] the bishops were wont even to usurp the endowments of the *Eigenkirchen*.[5] It was to prevent this that Wamba's law was promulgated. Episcopal appropriation of the endowments of churches or mon-

---

[1] III. 5. 2: see below, p. 233. Remarkably, the seventh-century councils did not deal with the matter of incest: for earlier provisions, see Fernández Alonso, *Cura pastoral*, p. 422. But concern with the breach of vows, especially by widows and penitents, was marked: see, e.g., III Tol. 10, 12, II Barc. 4, IV Tol. 49, 52, 55, 56, VI Tol. 6, 7 (where also an allusion to sacerdotal corruption in enforcement), VIII Tol. 7, X Tol. 4–6, XII Tol. 2 and, for an exception, VI Tol. 8.

[2] III. 5. 3: cf. III. 5. 6 (Egica).

[3] See III Tol. 20, II Sev. 10, IV Tol. 33, 51, VII Tol. 4, IX Tol. 9, X Tol. 3 (appointment of lay connections to religious offices), Mer. 16, XVI Tol. 5 and texts cit. in the following notes. Apparently at variance, IX Tol. 6 ('Tertiam...ecclesiae cui elegerit conferre decreverit'), but the absence of need for repair must be supposed. Mer. 14 deals with the details of the division of offerings (generally on which see Martínez Díez, *Patrimonio*, pp. 19–38, who rightly denies an obligatory tithe). Note that annual episcopal visitation was prescribed so that the state of repair of the churches and the state of life of the clergy might be ascertained: IV Tol. 36. Generally on thirds and usurpation see Bidagor, *Iglesia propia*, pp. 101–6 (who, however, holds that the thirds were at free episcopal disposal), and Martínez Díez, *Patrimonio*, pp. 83–94.

[4] III Tol. 19: cf. III Tol. 9, IV Tol. 33. See Bidagor, *Iglesia propia*, pp. 70–1.

[5] IV Tol. 33, IX Tol. 1.

asteries was condemned as sacrilege. Accusation of a bishop for such an offence was open in the first instance to the founder of the establishment, or to his heirs, but finally to all.[1] The problem revolved in large part around the thirty-year prescription period, which the bishops used to defend their acquisitions. The protection afforded by this was now removed: only in cases where a bishop had already successfully possessed the property throughout thirty years was judgement piously left by the king to the divine court. In all other cases where usurpation had already taken place, the property was simply to be restored. But in future cases the offending bishop was to pay, in addition to restoration, a *legitima satisfactio* – presumably an equivalent sum, as in the event of *invasio* – out of his own resources: if unable to meet this demand, he was to be subject to twenty days' penitence for each ten *solidi* owed.[2] The opportunities for fraud were finally diminished by the requirement that a bishop should render to a newly inducted priest subscribed copies of those documents which related to the church put in his care and to its property, so that neither the priest's ignorance nor the bishop's avarice might result in loss for the church. A similar device was employed to protect the goods of the Church against alienation or appropriation into a cleric's own property. Every bishop, priest or deacon was to make a witnessed inventory of the possessions of the church which he took over. Losses indicated by the inventory of his successor were to be made good from the private estate of the dead incumbent.[3] Property validly disposed of would naturally not have been included among these losses, and when the law authorised the new office-holder to reclaim sold property, with whatever improvements it had undergone, on payment of the purchase price, it was no doubt sales made without reference to the canonical regulations that were in the legislator's mind. The provision was in general harmony with another law which declared invalid a sale or donation

---

[1] The canons cit. in the last note talk only of complaint by the founder or his heirs: on this right of vigilance, see Bidagor, *Iglesia propia*, p. 72, Fernández Alonso, *Cura pastoral*, pp. 218–20. For the right of presentation (possessed by the founder alone according to Martínez Díez, *Patrimonio*, pp. 75–6: but see Valerius, *Ordo querimoniae* 5ff.), see IX Tol. 2, and for priority in charity from the Church, IV Tol. 38.

[2] Explicitly in accordance with the general ruling of XI Tol. 5, of a few weeks before.

[3] V. 1. 2.

of Church property made without the knowledge of the clergy or uncanonically.[1]

Further protection was offered to Church property by the requirement of the law that children commended into ecclesiastical *obsequium* by their clerical fathers should straightway lose lands or any other possessions held from the Church if they were to leave its service. The danger here guarded against was that by long possession in the hands of a non-cleric who fulfilled no obligations towards the Church, property might be lost for ever by the workings of the thirty-year limitation period.[2] And other laws again favoured the Church or the clergy by comparison with the laity. Revocation *causa ingratiae* was ruled out in the case of donations made voluntarily and validly – 'votive ac potentialiter' – to the benefit of the Church, for these were declared eternally irrevocable.[3] The rights of a *patronus*

[1] v. 1. 3. On alienation, see Martínez Díez, *Patrimonio*, pp. 125–46. Despite earlier canons providing for the validity of alienations made good from a cleric's own property, Mer. 21 insisted upon at least threefold compensation (though single compensation sufficed in the case of the alienation of slaves (1 Sev. 2) as it did in that of their manumission: see below, p. 179, n. 6). Further on alienation or appropriation, see Narb. 8, IX Tol. 4, 7 (regulating the respective rights of a bishop's personal and episcopal successors), 8, and for a case of illicit testamentary alienation, x Tol. *Aliud decretum*, with Martínez Díez, *Patrimonio*, pp. 129–31. For payment from Church goods, see IV Tol. 37, IX Tol. 3, Mer. 21. Profanity rather than alienation was the chief target in III Braga 2, XIII Tol. 7 and XVII Tol. 4. Connected with alienation were the provisions permitting limited episcopal donations to, or endowments of, diocesan churches and monasteries (III Tol. 3, 4, IX Tol. 5). The charitable support of clerics, monks, strangers, the poor and those who had given to the Church was, of course, an episcopal duty: see III Tol. 3, IV Tol. 38. For usurpation of Church labour, see III Braga 8. Some check on a rapacious bishop, as well as some help to a conscientious one, was provided by the *economicus*, a steward and administrator who acted at the order, and by the decision, of the bishop (Isidore, *Ep.* 1: but cf. J. Fontaine, *Isidore de Séville et la culture classique dans l'Esp. wisigothique* (2 vols, Paris, 1959), I, 335, n. 1): no bishop might operate without one, but a layman might not be appointed (II Sev. 9, IV Tol. 48). On the *economicus*, see Fernández Alonso, *Cura pastoral*, pp. 199–200, but cf. Martínez Díez, *Patrimonio*, pp. 110–11.      [2] v. 1. 4: see p. 61, n. 2, above.

[3] v. 1. 1: cf. VI Tol. 15. But the view of G. Vismara, 'La successione volontaria nelle leggi barbariche', *Studi di storia e diritto in onore di Arrigo Solmi*, II (Milan, 1941), 195, n. 2, that the law's object was to declare irrevocable even donations *post obitum* in favour of the Church, cannot be ruled out. For gifts to the Church, especially as *Seelteile*, endowments etc., see IV. 2. 18, 5. 1, 2, 6, v. 1. 1 ('pro remediis animarum'), 7. 16 ('pro animabus suis'), *FV* 8, 9, 21, 25, and, in addition to the texts just cited in the comments on IV. 5. 6, III Tol. 15, Council of Toledo of A.D. 597, c. 2 (Vives, *Concilios*, p. 156), Mer. 19, III Sar. 1, and below, in text, on *liberti*. Generally, see Martínez Díez, *Patrimonio*, pp. 39–46.

and his heirs over a freedman disappeared in their entirety when the
*libertus* had passed into ecclesiastical *patrocinium* or had himself
become a cleric: 'Quod enim gloriosius Deo adherere censetur,
obsequiis hominum religari honestate nulla sinitur'.[1] The Church
might appoint any slave as a mandatory and had certain privileges
in the matter of inheritance.[2] A cleric other than a bishop who was
guilty of contumacy towards a judicial summons was sentenced to
fast rather than to be flogged if he could not pay the resulting fine.[3]
We have already seen that an incontinent cleric escaped the lashing
meted out to his female partner in sin.

The privilege and protection witnessed in these and other laws
were no doubt seen by the king as in part a *quid pro quo* for the responsibilities of the clergy in general, and the bishops in particular,
in the governance of the kingdom. Their most significant duties
were indubitably those connected with the prevention and correction
of injustice and oppression and with the supervision of the Jews. But
in many narrower fields also the king made use of their services.
We have seen that clerics played a part in the publication and probate
of wills and will note later their role in the protection of minors and,
occasionally, in the manumission of slaves. In matters of morals,
the bishop was expected to act against those guilty of incest or breach
of vows of chastity.[4] Men convicted of sodomy were placed in the
episcopal charge: so too, before and after Ervig's day, were masters
who had mutilated their slaves.[5] Joint action of bishop and judge was
urged by the councils in cases of idolatry.[6] Occasionally the king
would delegate to a bishop the hearing of a trial for treason,[7] and it
was to him that a royal order addressed to a judge who had died
might be delivered.[8] He was, too, an executive officer to whom
a minor judge might appeal for help in the constraint of those whom
he could not himself force to court.[9] It was even to the local *sacerdos*
that notification of animals found straying might be made.[10]

The employment by the king of the services of the *sacerdotium* in

[1] v. 7. 18: contrast the earlier IV Tol. 73 and see also III Tol. 6, IV Tol. 72.
[2] Above, p. 102; below, p. 249.   [3] II. I. 19.
[4] III. 4. 18, 5. 2.                [5] III. 5. 4; VI. 5. 13, 13*.
[6] III Tol. 16, XII Tol. 11, XVI Tol. *Tomus*, 2. III Tol. 17 and 23 also urged joint action
against infanticides and those guilty of immodest singing and dancing.
[7] At an earlier stage, at any rate: IV Tol. 31.
[8] VII. 5. I.              [9] VII. I. I.              [10] VIII. 5. 6.

these various governmental tasks is in no way surprising. It stemmed naturally from the character of the clergy as, so to speak, Christian professionals, possessed – or assumed to be possessed – of a more specialised knowledge of faith and morals, a more compassionate concern for the interests of the weak and oppressed, a more profound personal integrity and a more advanced degree of learning than the members of the lay estate. Certainly the kings cannot be criticised for their course of action: what better fitted body of men did they have at their disposal? But enough will have been said above to indicate that royal trust in ecclesiastical personnel, although necessary, was often misplaced. It would be a grave error indeed to judge the quality of the episcopate in the Visigothic kingdom, let alone the quality of the clergy at large, on the basis of the impressive standard achieved by such lights of the Church as Isidore, Braulio and Ildefonsus.[1]

[1] There are some stark comments on these and others of the greater figures in C. M. Aherne, *Traditio*, xxII (1966), 435–44. Most recently on Ildefonsus see A. C. Vega in *BRAH*, cLxv (1969), 35–107.

*Chapter 6*

# SLAVES, FREEDMEN AND NOBLES

One arresting and basic feature of the society mirrored in the Visigothic law code is its class stratification. This is hardly surprising. Any wistfully romantic notion that there had reigned among the pre-entry Goths the principle of democratic egalitarianism is quite insupportable: at the one extreme they had their optimates, at the other their slaves.[1] The social divisions they knew both received reinforcement and underwent refinement once the Goths had entered the Empire and come into everyday contact with a class-dominated society in which the social inequalities among freemen were increasingly the matter of *de iure* – as they had long been that of *de facto* – legal distinction.[2] The differences between the estates became, if anything, more pronounced during the centuries which followed.[3] Christian rationalisation justified the vertical composition of society,[4]

---

[1] See Thompson, *Visigoths in the time of Ulfila*, pp. 43ff., and the same author's general comments in 'Slavery in early Germany', *Slavery in classical antiquity*, ed. M. I. Finley (Cambridge, 1960), pp. 191–203. But slavery is not likely to have been a significant institution.

[2] Basic is G. Cardascia, 'L'apparition dans le droit des classes d'*honestiores* et d'*humiliores*', *Revue hist. de droit français et étranger*, 4th series, xxviii (1950), 305–37, 461–85, but see now also the valuable study of P. Garnsey, *Social status and legal privilege in the Roman Empire* (Oxford, 1970), passim. For late Roman patronage, see J. Gagé, *Les classes sociales dans l'empire romain* (Paris, 1964), pp. 417ff.

[3] That the distinction of *honestiores* and *humiliores* does not appear in the *CE* should be considered wholly coincidental, despite d'Ors, *Código*, p. 7: only if an *Antiqua* corresponding to an Eurician law mentioned the distinction would we have to explain its earlier absence, and none does. But several other *Antiquae* do. So too does *CEB* 2 – strangely, not discussed by d'Ors, *Código* – on which note the comment of Zeumer, xxiii, 108, that the Bavarian law otherwise did not know the principle of distinction of penalty according to status. D'Ors's explanation of the alleged absence of the *honestior/humilior* distinction from the *CE* – that the Goths as a whole enjoyed superiority and were therefore the *honestiores* – is quite unconvincing: Romans like Leo of Narbonne (Euric's chief minister) and Victorius (duke and count) would hardly have been *humiliores*, and rude Gothic warriors not!

[4] See, e.g., Isidore, *Synonyma* ii. 74 and *Sent.* iii. 47. 1 (cit. p. 179, n. 2). Further, Ullmann, *Individual*, pp. 13ff.

159

and the quasi-philosophical organological principle buttressed it yet more strongly.[1] This hierarchical ordering was not a matter of simple social prestige. The individual's activities were both dictated and circumscribed by his membership of a particular estate: he ventured outside the limits set at his legal peril. Responsibilities, like activities, varied according to personal status. The distinctions of class were enshrined in the penal law: while the more important freeman was dealt with in one way, the ordinary *ingenuus* suffered differently for the same offence, and the slave differently again. But despite the rigid class divisions, there existed a remarkable social mobility. The paradox is only apparent. For although the place of an individual in society had its defined consequences, that place was not necessarily permanent. The ease with which – willingly or not – transition could be effected from one estate to another is indeed striking: the nobleman of one year might be the slave of the next. While birth was unquestionably the crucial element in determining the class in which any certain individual found himself, a variety of factors – his own wealth, talent or criminality, for example, or the hostility or patronage of another – might be responsible for establishing that to which he eventually belonged. There was nothing static about this society, despite its stratiform structure. Subject always to luck, the resourceful man could rise high: conversely, an incautious step could plummet the *potentior* to the very depths.

It was the slaves – the *servi* and *ancillae*, the *mancipia*, of the texts – who of course occupied the lowest grade in the social scale.[2] That the number of slaves in the Visigothic kingdom was very large is perfectly clear from the very frequency of reference to them in the code and other sources.[3] It is very likely that their abundance is in large part to be attributed to the inclusion within their ranks of those

[1] See ib., pp. 40–3.
[2] But see XII. 2. 14, 3. 12, for *mancipium* used of a man *in patrocinio*. On Visigothic slavery see above all C. Verlinden, *L'esclavage dans l'Europe médiévale*, 1: *Péninsule ibérique–France* (Bruges, 1955), pp. 59–102 (elaborating earlier comments in *AHDE*, XI (1934), 322–64). Of little value is J. M. Mans Puigarnau, *Las clases serviles bajo la monarquía visigoda y en los estados cristianos de la Reconquista esp.* (Barcelona, 1928).
[3] The scanty statistics confirm this. If the smallest church with its own minister had ten *mancipia*, but was 'pauperrima' (thus, XVI Tol. *Tomus*), the greater establishments must have numbered their slaves in hundreds or thousands: note Ricimer's wrongful alienation of over 500 slaves (X Tol. *Aliud decretum*).

*coloni* taken over by the Goths on their settlement in Spain and probably also, by the late seventh century, of those *coloni* who served Roman masters. The great importance of the colonate as an institution of the late Empire needs no commentary here, and *coloni* clearly survived in Spain into the Visigothic period, for they are mentioned in a conciliar source as late as 619.[1] But not a single *Antiqua* refers to the colonate either by name or in fact,[2] and perhaps not a single law of the whole code.[3] Since already in the fifth-century *Interpretationes* there are signs of the deterioration of the status of the *colonus* from that of a bondsman to the soil to that of a bondsman to a *dominus*,[4] it seems much more probable that the Goths ignored the slender practical distinction between half-free and unfree than that they elevated the *coloni* to the free estate.[5]

Most slaves in the late kingdom, whatever the original standing of their forbears, were certainly such by virtue of their birth: the application of the general rule propounded by Isidore:

Semper enim qui nascitur deteriorem parentis statum sumit[6]

is witnessed by several laws,[7] and was indeed taken fraudulent advantage of by some slave-owners, who lied about the status of

---

[1] II. Sev. 3. The *coloni* are treated at length in the *LRV*.

[2] I disregard the *tributarii* of *Fragmenta Gaudenziana* (cc. 16, 19, 20), for the *Fragmenta* do not, in my estimation, belong to the history of Visigothic legal evolution: see Merêa, *Estudos*, pp. 121–47, though differently G. Vismara, *Fragmenta Gaudenziana*, IRMAE, part I, 2b *bb β* (Milan, 1968), passim. The *edictum regis* to which the *Fragmenta* refer was perhaps one governing the Ostrogoths: cf. *Excerpta Valesiana* 60, Cassiodorus, *Variae* VII. 3.

[3] The only possible reference is that of v. 4. 19, *in fine*: 'Nam plebeis glebam suam alienandi nullam umquam potestas manebit', where Zeumer's note reads: 'Plebei vocantur coloni glebae adscripti'. But this, I believe, is surmise: nowhere else in the code is *plebei* used in this sense. Chindasvind might with more plausibility be thought to have meant slaves (thus also Gama Barros, IV, 104–11): note the striking similarity of terminology and regime between v. 4. 19 and Chindasvind's v. 4. 13, forbidding slave alienation of immovables and *mancipia*. There is no reason to think that the tenant-farmers of X. 1. 13 and 15 were *coloni*, as Schultze, *Eherecht*, p. 111, holds.                    [4] See Pérez Pujol, IV, 232.

[5] In this sense, Bethmann-Hollweg, p. 219, n. 57. Verlinden, *L'esclavage*, p. 85, holds the view that the colonate was legally suppressed once the *LRV* was abrogated in the mid-seventh century. See M. Torres, *Lecciones de hist. del derecho esp.* (2 vols, Salamanca, 1933–4), II, 220–2, for the view that the *coloni* rose in status. *Sui generis*, Pérez Pujol, IV, 231–45.

[6] *Etym.* IX. 5. 18: cf. IV. 5. 7: 'Inferioris parentis adsequens sexum'.

[7] III. 2. 3, 4, 3. 9, IX. 1. 15, 16.

their slaves and married them to free or freed persons with the object of later claiming the children.[1] But freemen might sell themselves into slavery or be sold into it against their will,[2] and the foundling was in fact treated as a slave until, if ever, redeemed by its parents.[3] Freedmen and their descendants might lose their liberty for offences against the patronal family, as we shall see. Prisoners-of-war became slaves if they were not ransomed,[4] and slave-trading was certainly carried on.[5] A most important source of new slaves, finally, was provided by the operation of the law. Not only did several particular offences involve enslavement as a direct penalty,[6] but it existed as a general legal principle that the criminal unable to pay the composition demanded was to suffer permanent enslavement.[7] Numerous laws confirm this for specific crimes,[8] although sometimes, even when quite large sums were involved, floggings were ordered as the consequence of non-payment.[9] The insolvent debtor was similarly enslaved.[10] These severe rulings must have brought a steady flow of poorer freemen into the slave class. How far their movement downwards was counterbalanced by the escape, legal or otherwise, of slaves from their servitude, cannot, of course, be estimated.

Slaves by no means constituted a homogeneous class. Of the crown slaves and of the considerable power which the more notable of these exercised we have already spoken. The king was wont, as a Toledan

[1] III. 2. 7, where Chindasvind declared slave and children alike to be free.
[2] For a document of self-sale, see *FV* 32, and on it Levy, *Obligationenrecht*, p. 282. The sale or gift of a free person (into slavery is to be understood) against his will was severely punished: see V. 4. 11, VII. 3. 3, 5, 6, and on these conflicting laws d'Ors, *Código*, pp. 96–9. In cases of fraudulent collusion between the freeman sold and the vendor, the former remained in servitude unless the full purchase-price was repaid (V. 4. 10).
[3] See below, p. 239, for this and the prohibition of the sale etc. of children.
[4] See Verlinden, *L'esclavage*, pp. 62–5.
[5] Below, pp. 195, 199.  [6] E.g., III. 3. 1, 4. 2, 17, VI. 3. 1 etc.
[7] V. 6. 5, VII. 1. 5.
[8] E.g., II. 4. 9, VI. 1. 2, 5, VII. 2. 13, IX. 1. 2 etc.: further cases are cit. in Thompson, *Goths*, p. 137, n. 4.
[9] II. 1. 19, 21, 2. 10 (Egica), 4. 3, VI. 4. 4, IX. 1. 21 (Egica) etc.: further cases in Thompson, *Goths*, p. 137, n. 5. No regular exchange rate for the substitution of lashes for unpaid *solidi* is discernible here: thus, in VIII. 3. 14 fifty lashes are suffered instead of a composition of five *solidi*, but in XII. 3. 17 *decalvatio* and one hundred lashes take the place of a fine of no less than five pounds of gold.
[10] V. 6. 5. A criminal or debtor owing satisfaction to several became their joint property.

canon makes disapprovingly clear, to take slaves and freedmen from the service of others into his own, as members of the *palatinum officium* or as administrators of his estates,[1] and this is eloquent witness of the skills possessed by the more able slaves of the kingdom, and of the heights to which they might aspire. The king could not have gained knowledge of the ability of these men, however, if they had not already held important managerial positions – as the *actores, procuratores* and *villici* who looked after a lord's estates, for example,[2] or as majordomos or secretaries in the household.[3] No doubt it was such dominating figures as these who were principally in mind when the legislators laid down punishment for the slave who sold a freeman into servitude.[4] The *servi idonei* who occasionally appear in the laws and whose status entitled them to a degree of preferential treatment and protection as compared with the ordinary slaves, the *vilissimi*,[5] must certainly have included these slave administrators in their number, but the category was no doubt more widely construed. *Idoneus* was probably taken to describe any slave who enjoyed a position involving special skill, favour or trust – like the *artifex* whose replacement when he suffered death or grievous injury under torture, though innocent, is discussed in VI. I. 5, like the *ancilla*-concubine,[6] the lady's maid,[7] the legal representative,[8] the judicial surrogate,[9] and so forth. Such able or trusted slaves would have been the natural objects of the envy of other lords, and some of these were not above the use of fraud to gain their services for themselves. One law for-

---

[1] XIII Tol. 6 forbade the practice, since those elevated 'in necem dominorum suorum vehementius grassaverunt, et...dominis suis regio jussu tortores existunt'.

[2] References to these functionaries in VI. I. I, 5, 2. 4, VIII. I. 5, IX. I. 9, 21 (Egica), XII. 3. 19: cf. also 'rationales' in X. 2. 6. Although none of these laws indicates that they were slaves (but cf. VIII. I. 5, cit. below, n. 4), it is unlikely that the Roman usage would have disappeared. Slave administrators appear in II. 2. 9 and are partly in mind in V. 4. 13.

[3] Note the allusions to 'scriniis domesticis' in II. 5. 17 and to the papers and books of a *de cuius* in II. 5. 12.

[4] V. 4. 11, VII. 3. 6. Note too that Chindasvind found it necessary to forbid any 'vilicus, prepositus, actor aut procurator seu quilibet ingenuus adque etiam servus' to anticipate legal judgement by the seizure of property 'post nomen...dominorum suorum aut suum' (VIII. I. 5).

[5] Cf. III. 3. 9, VI. 4. 3, 7, Mer. 17, and note III. 4. 15 (below, p. 178, n. 5).

[6] III. 5. 5.

[7] The sort of person figuring, one imagines, among the 'suitable' *ancillae* whose presence authorised a doctor to treat a freewoman in the absence of her relatives (XI. I. I).      [8] Above, p. 102.      [9] II. I. 18.

bade clerics to prevail upon owners to sell slaves who had fled 'quorumdam sollicitatione' to the churches, for the masters were likely later to find the slaves in the possession of enemies,[1] and other measures, commented upon later, took into account the possibility that a slave would be persuaded to commit an offence which would compel his master to hand him over to the apparent victim. The closeness to their owners which some 'suitable' slaves enjoyed doubtless brought its rewards, but it had its drawbacks too, for such individuals, often trusted confidants, would have been those who above all stood to suffer on those occasions when the law permitted the torture of slaves 'in capite domini vel domine'.

The *servi idonei* were a minority group, however. The bulk of the slave population was constituted by the *inferiores*, menial slaves in the household and agricultural workers on the land. It was certainly at these individuals that the large number of laws dealing with the flight of slaves was directed. The problems presented by runaways were great. Both prevention of escape and recovery of an absconder were primarily, of course, the responsibility of the slave-owner, and there survives in fact the model of a mandate in which an owner instructed a third party to undertake the task of bringing a fugitive back to his servitude.[2] The law could not effectively assist owners in the prevention of escapes – except by provision for the punishment of those who incited flight – and concentrated its efforts upon ensuring that a fugitive, deprived of succour, would be swiftly caught and returned. On the one hand, an inducement was held out: the man who apprehended a runaway and brought him back to his master was entitled to reward, the amount of this depending upon the length of the journey which he had been obliged to make.[3] On the other, threats were used to make those prepared to harbour fugitives, for humanitarian or whatever reasons, think twice. A major problem here must have been the identification of a fugitive slave. Long hair was, it seems, the mark of the slave class, for the freeman who cut the hair of a stranger slave was punished in the same way as one who actively incited a slave to flee or who knowingly gave an

[1] v. 4. 17.
[2] *FV* 43: cf. IX. 1. 18. Rights remained in slaves (and other property) seized by the enemy: see v. 4. 21 and IX. 2. 7 for details of the financial arrangements for the return of slaves and goods rescued or ransomed.
[3] IX. 1. 9, 14: a *tremis* for thirty miles or under, a *solidus* for one hundred miles.

absconder hospitality: he was obliged to pay to the fugitive's master three slaves, in whose number the original slave was himself to be included if he could ~till be found.[1] Freemen also wore their hair long, but in a particular style,[2] and what the legislator was concerned with was no doubt the assumption of this fashion by the slave.[3] But not every slave travelling through the kingdom could be treated forthwith as a fugitive, for slaves must frequently have gone on lawful journeys on behalf of their masters. The law provided therefore that any stranger who was given hospitality for more than a day and a night – all that a *bona fide* traveller would require, it was perhaps thought – should be brought before the local authorities within a week:[4] in the outlying districts, indeed, notification had to be made on the day when the stranger arrived or on the following day.[5] Failure to comply with this regulation, or the deliberate concealment of a stranger who turned out to be an absconding slave, rendered the free offender liable to pay the fugitive's master two slaves, including, where possible, the runaway himself.[6] It was advisable, in fact, to notify the authorities as swiftly as possible, for if a stranger who proved to be a runaway disappeared after twenty-four hours but before notification, his luckless benefactor had either to find and to restore him to his owner or to establish the identity of those who had next helped him, when legal responsibility passed to them: failure in both quests meant payment of a substitute slave, returnable if the

[1] IX. I. 5.
[2] On the hair-style, see C. Barrière-Flavy, 'Le costume et l'armement du wisigoth aux Ve et VIe siècles', *Revue des Pyrénées*, XIV (1902), 137–9: further, Schramm, pp. 218ff., with illustrations and remarks on Alaric II, Theodoric the Ostrogoth etc., and for the coin evidence Miles, p. 48. Freemen apparently wore their hair cut straight across the forehead and nape of the neck, but falling over their ears and then curling up: cf. Sidonius, *Ep.* I. 2. The long hair of the laity is mentioned in IV Tol. 41.
[3] Or is the clerical tonsure perhaps in mind?
[4] IX. I. 9: cf. IX. I. 3, 4, 6, and for 'stranger' rather than 'slave', IX. I. 12. The time limit mentioned appears also in XIII Tol. 11, dealing with fugitive clerics and monks, where other aspects of the laws are also reflected. For fugitive ecclesiastics, see also II Sev. 3, Braulio, *Ep.* 17 (with Lynch, pp. 63–5), and for an intending monk's promise not to abscond, *FV* 45.
[5] IX. I. 6.
[6] For failure to notify, see IX. I. 3, 6, 9, and for concealment, IX. I. 1 and 3, where in the first the penalty for a concealing slave (and for the fugitive) is one hundred lashes. IX. I. 11 is directed against the fraud of a slave-owner who might send his slave 'propter lucrum capiendum' to conceal himself elsewhere.

fugitive was later recaptured.[1] Presentation of the stranger to the authorities was followed by his examination and restoration, if he was a fugitive, into the hands of whoever had brought him to court, whose duty it then became to return him and claim the reward. Documentary evidence of the date and place of the slave's apprehension, together with other information, was provided by the authorities, doubtless to ensure that the correct reward was paid and that the slave was back in his master's possession within the week – or longer, if a great distance was involved – which was permitted.[2] If the fugitive managed to escape, his custodian was not held liable as long as he could swear that he was innocent of complicity.[3] A slave who refused to name his master had to be brought before the king himself for identification. Any judge who neglected his duties with regard to the investigation of suspected fugitives suffered like the man who failed to report a stranger's presence.[4] There was, naturally, no penalty for the employment of a fugitive when this was done in good faith, on the basis of a judicial decision which turned out to have been mistaken.[5]

Despite laws like these and others which penalised the man who freed a captured slave from his bonds or the slave who pointed out the road to his fellow on the run,[6] many a slave doubtless made good his escape and succeeded in passing himself off as a freeman. It must often have been a precarious life that he led, however, for only after fifty years did his *de facto* status receive *de iure* recognition.[7] He might take refuge in the household of a freeman, even a *potens*, only to be discovered and claimed by his former master: the mere allegation that a household worker was a runaway slave entitled the claimant to immediate possession of the suspect's person, provided that he pledged himself to inflict no punishment before judicial decision had been given on the question of status.[8] The runaway might succeed in acquiring property of one sort or another, only to see it all pass

---

[1] IX. I. 4.
[2] IX. I. 9. Torture of the stranger appears only in the later IX. I. 21 (Egica).
[3] IX. I. 14.  [4] IX. I. 9.
[5] IX. I. 12: a finding of innocence is probably also the presupposition of IX. I. 8 (absent from the code).
[6] IX. I. 2; IX. I. 7.
[7] X. 2. 2: cf. X. 2. 5 (Egica).
[8] IX. I. 13.

into the ownership of his lord when he was reclaimed.[1] He might even contract a marriage with a freewoman only to have to suffer separation from his wife and the sight of his children reduced to the bondage which he believed he had escaped.[2]

The lengthy and detailed preoccupation of the laws with the flight of slaves points to a problem of very large proportions,[3] and that conclusion is convincingly borne out by the extraordinary law issued by Egica in the last months of 702,[4] a law which attempted to organise the whole of society in a campaign against what the king called the *increscens vitium* of abscondence, but which both explicitly, in the confession that runaways were spread throughout the land:

Ut non sit penitus civitas, castellum, vicus aut villa vel diversorium, in quibus mancipia latere minime dignoscantur,

and implicitly, in the very severity of punishment provided for those who failed to fulfil its elaborate demands, admitted that the problem had escaped control. The terms of the law in practice required every individual to hale immediately before a judge any poorly dressed stranger whom he might meet locally: excommunication, a fine of three pounds of gold and 300 lashes were among the punishments meted out for breach of its various provisions. The law represents, in fact, the supreme exemplification of the lack of realism and the wildness – born, one might think, of desperation – which characterise many of the legislative enactments of the last years of the kingdom. It is as if the kings, knowing in their hearts that the situation was beyond their grasp, sought furiously to prove themselves wrong by the production of more and more complex provisions, the presupposition of whose effective application was a degree of public obedience and governmental command which the extravagant

---

[1] IX. 1. 12, 17. Stolen property had naturally to be returned, while the slave's concealer was responsible for compositions etc. Cf. also IX. 1. 20, providing that the *iudex* keep property found on a fugitive for later delivery to its owner.

[2] IX. 1. 16: the *peculium* of the children also passed to the lord. The *coniunctiones* of fugitive *ancillae* and freemen were treated in the same way. But the *Antiqua* IX. 1. 15, providing for the freedom of the children of a union where the freewoman had married in good faith, still appears in the code, and two MSS of Ervig's IX. 1. 16 have similar references. Cf. also the MS V17 of III. 2. 7. In any case, III. 2. 3 conceded freedom to children of slave–free unions who could prove that they and their parents had enjoyed *de facto* freedom for thirty years.

[3] Note that the poorly dressed Fructuosus was taken for a runaway: *VSF* 11.

[4] IX. 1. 21.

167

penalties imposed showed did not exist. Fantasy and extremism went hand in hand.[1]

One is obliged to speculate upon the origins of these fugitive slaves and upon the reasons for the prevalence of flight.[2] No doubt some runaways were domestic servants, hoping to escape cruelty or simply to take advantage of opportunities not open to them in the household. But in an agricultural society it is agricultural slaves whom we should expect to have made up the majority of the fugitives. Now, if Spain had followed the general European pattern of development established in the late Empire, the social and economic position of the agricultural slave had tended more and more in practice to become that of a bound tenant-farmer.[3] But it is difficult indeed to believe that a slave population chiefly involved in exploitation of the land on its own account would have been so prone to flight as was that of the Visigothic kingdom. Leaving out of account those who might have fled to take up a life of crime,[4] in what way could such slaves have hoped radically to improve their material conditions of life? Economically, the most that the fugitive might reasonably have expected would have been his own smallholding as the tenant of some free landowner. The conditions of tenancy might well have been better than those he abandoned, of course, and the stigma of servitude, together with its legal disadvantages, would have been lost. But only to those farmers who worked particularly poor soil or held on particularly unfavourable terms and to a few adventurous souls would these uncertain incentives have presented sufficient allure to overcome the innate reluctance of the conservative countryman to leave the land he knew and farmed – probably the

[1] Verlinden, *L'esclavage*, p. 95, rightly remarks: 'Une législation pareille ne peut être nécessaire que dans un État dont tous les cadres craquent'.

[2] That much of the legislation is Euric is not to the point: the earlier laws remained of paramount relevance to the society of the sixth and seventh centuries, being amended and added to by kings from Leovigild to Egica. The problem got worse, not better.

[3] See, e.g., A. H. M. Jones, 'Slavery in the ancient world', *Slavery in classical antiquity*, pp. 14–15, who wrote (p. 15) of the later Empire: 'Where agricultural slavery survived it was a heritage of the past, and the social and economic position of slaves on the land had become indistinguishable from that of free persons'. For slaves in direct exploitation of their masters' lands, see Salvian, *De gubernatione Dei* IV. 14 ('servi...*etiamsi* stipendia usitate praestentur'), 15, and A. Piganiol, *L'impôt de capitation sous le bas-empire romain* (Chambéry, 1916), p. 68.

[4] Cf. IX. 1. 19, where *latrones = absconsi*.

most significant factor making for acceptance of the *status quo* – and to outweigh the immediate and practical sacrifices and fears which the fugitive would have to face – the loss of the *de facto* security offered by his holding, the break-up of his family, the certainty of punishment if his escape was unsuccessful, and so on.

It seems very much more likely that it was slaves in the greatly more depressed position of simple farm-labourers on a home farm who would have felt impelled to run the risks of flight in the hope of rising in the world to farm their own lands: at the same time it seems far more likely that the law would have taken the constant and close interest which it did if the problem was the flight of farm-workers rather than that of virtual tenant-farmers, for the former brought about a more positive and expensive economic loss to the slave-owners. The implication, therefore, is that large numbers of slaves in the Visigothic kingdom were employed in the direct exploitation of their masters' lands. The frequency of reference in the laws to slaves who committed offences *domino iubente* argues in general favour of their being under immediate control,[1] and brief but valuable textual support is to be found in Ervig's army law, where the king spoke of slave-owners who, intent on working their fields, thrashed their multitudes of slaves.[2] Men enduring the lowly life of agricultural drudges would have needed no especial stimulus to escape, but particularly favourable conditions would have been provided if, as seems more than likely, the kingdom shared in that general decline in population which affected Europe as a result of the plague in the second half of the sixth century and throughout the seventh.[3] Certainly the country was sporadically struck by the plague: there was a severe outbreak in Septimania as late as the 690s

[1] Cf., particularly, vm. 5. 3.

[2] ix. 2. 9: 'Laborandis agris studentes servorum multitudines cedunt'.

[3] J. C. Russell, *Population in Europe, 500–1500*, Fontana economic hist. of Europe, ed. C. M. Cipolla, I, sect. I (London, 1969), 19, tentatively suggests a decline by 650 of some half a million souls from the four million which he attributes to the peninsula in 500, and although accurate demographic appraisal of the period is impossible (compare, e.g., the figure of 4 mill. with that of 7 to 8 mill. suggested by Reinhart, 'Tradición visigoda', p. 537, and with that of 9 mill. suggested by Valdeavellano, *Curso*, p. 177), it is difficult to believe that there was no decline. Most recently on the plague see J.-N. Biraben and J. Le Goff in *Annales: économies, sociétés, civilisations*, xxiv (1969), 1484–1510.

which in fact prevented the Narbonnese bishops from attending the Sixteenth Council of Toledo in May 693.[1] If man-power was short, it is understandable that owners should have been concerned to preserve their standard of living, on the one hand by protecting themselves – through the king and his law – against the successful flight of their slave hands, and on the other by working their labour force the harder in order to compensate for its depletion: it is equally understandable that slaves should have shown a greater propensity to take to flight as a result of these conditions, and that other lords, short of labour, should have been tempted to take them on, as free workers – *mercennarii* – or tenants, no questions asked.[2]

However this may be, it is clear that many slaves – especially, no doubt, the erstwhile *coloni* – did work the land free from the direct control of their lords: those laws which allude to the payment of composition by slaves themselves are significant in this respect,[3] while one law refers specifically to a slave's acquisition of immovables on the estate of someone other than his owner.[4] The property which such a slave possessed, his *peculium*, might consist of lands, a house, animals – even other slaves – as well as the bits and pieces he had gathered around him,[5] and might be added to by inheritance or payment from outsiders.[6] But such property was not his to dispose of at will. For the slave was a chattel, to be used as his master might

[1] See XVI Tol. *Lex edita* (548a). Cf. also *CH* 53 (for 693), and the reference in XVII Tol. *Tomus* (553d). A funerary inscription from Narbonne, dating from 688–9 and recording the deaths of three Jewish children of various ages, perhaps reflects the work of this outbreak: see Katz, pp. 148 (for the inscription), 151. Anti-Jewish action (thus Blumenkranz, *Juifs*, p. 131, n. 236) really cannot be seen here: executions are otherwise unknown, and why should the children alone have been the victims? Earlier references to plague in the kingdom in *Chron. Caesaraug. reliquiae* ad a. 542 and *HF* VI. 14, 33, IX. 22 (the 580s) and probably IV. 5 (the 550s): a possible allusion in *EW* 4 (the 610s).

[2] The repressive anti-slave legislation was linked with the plague by T. de Sousa Soares in Gama Barros, IV, 416–17, but the point was not developed. It may well be that a searching examination would reveal the plague as the decisive factor in the crisis of the final years of the kingdom.

[3] See below, p. 175, n. 1. Note also v. 4. 15, assuming a lord's ignorance of the extent of his slave's *peculium*, and VI. 1. 1, assuming a slave to be living well away from lord, *villicus* or *actor* (or is prior flight in mind?).

[4] X. 1. 17.

[5] v. 4. 13: cf. X. 1. 18.

[6] v. 7. 13 (inheritance from a freed relative), VII. 6. 1 (reward from fisc) etc.

lawfully desire:[1] as such, he might be sold, bartered or given away almost at will.[2] Even the union of slaves in the relationship still known as *contubernium*, to distinguish it from true marriage,[3] might remain in existence only so long as the owner or owners concerned wished:[4] children born to slave parents belonging to different masters were divided equally among the lords, with financial compensation when there was an odd number.[5] It followed from the character of the slave as an object of his master's property that anything he might acquire passed, in strict law, into his master's ownership.[6] Hence, the owner had the right to take possession of the *peculium* when he sold a slave without knowledge of the extent of this; hence, also, the 'sale' of a slave for money which in fact came from the *peculium* was, if the owner was unaware of this, no sale, for no true payment had taken place.[7] Moreover, agreements and transactions undertaken by the slave without the consent of his lord were, as a general rule, invalid.[8] In no circumstances might he validly alienate immovables or slaves on his own authority.[9] But over animals, ornaments and

[1] Note the series of terms in v. 4. 7: 'Ut seu res aliquas vel terras seu mancipia vel quodlibet animalium genus venditur': similarly, v. 4. 8. The freeman selling himself in *FV* 32 declared: 'Quicquid in meam vel de meam personam facere volueris, directa tibi erit per omnia vel certa potestas'.

[2] III. 1. 5 (dowry!), v. 4. 7, 14, 15 etc.: *FV* 11 records a slave sale. Restrictions: above, p. 137, below, p. 195, n. 2.

[3] Thus x. 1. 17, but note *matrimonium* in III. 2. 3 (where also *contubernium*), 4 etc., and *uxor* for the slave wife in III. 2. 5 and *FV* 8 (following later Roman usage: Gama Barros, IV, 72, n. 3).

[4] See Verlinden, *L'esclavage*, pp. 89, 93. Differently, in some degree, Pérez Pujol, IV, 249–50, Melicher, *Kampf*, p. 114, Gama Barros, IV, 72, 79, and especially A. E. de Mañaricua, *El matrimonio de los esclavos*, Analecta Gregoriana, XXIII (Rome, 1940), 201, 207. But x. 1. 17 did not forbid a lord to dissolve the union of his slave with a slave belonging to another lord after a year had passed, but simply warned him that the offspring would after that time be shared equally between the masters. It was a union undertaken independently by the slaves which was regulated ('postquam ad dominorum cognitionem contubernia servorum pervenerint'): unions agreed to by the lords would have been the subject of *placita*, while a lord who joined his slave to another's without the knowledge of the latter's owner forfeited both slave and claim to the children (III. 2. 5). Cf. also III. 3. 10, where the slave abductor of an *ancilla* suffered lashing and scalping and had to separate from her 'si dominus ancille voluerit'. [5] X. 1. 17.

[6] See Levy, *Obligationenrecht*, pp. 71–2, and note VII. 1. 4: 'Dominus servi substantiam eius sue vindicet potestati'. That lawful acquisitions made by fugitives passed to their lords has been noted above. For acquisitions on campaign, see below, p. 238.

[7] v. 4. 15, 16.          [8] II. 5. 6: see also v. 5. 6, x. 1. 10.

[9] v. 4. 13: see also above, p. 161, n. 3. For *servi fiscales*, see p. 64, above.

other lesser objects of the *peculium* the law did grant him, for the sake of convenience, full power of lawful disposal.[1] Already in this concession is apparent a characteristic ambivalence of legal attitude towards the slave, who was neither wholly thing nor wholly person.

The independent personality of the slave received recognition also in the laws' treatment of offences committed against him or his *peculium*. Since these were injuries to his master's property, it was the slave-owner's ultimate right and responsibility to seek remedy. Regularly, this took the form of payment by the offender to the master. The deliberate and cold-blooded killing by a freeman of another's slave, for example, was satisfied by the simple delivery of two substitutes,[2] beating by the payment of one *solidus* for each blow,[3] induced abortion in an *ancilla* by the fixed composition of twenty *solidi*.[4] Sometimes, but infrequently, corporal punishments were imposed in addition to economic: thus, the freeman who forced intercourse upon an *ancilla* suffered fifty lashes as well as a fine of twenty *solidi*, and the freeman who scalped a 'suitable' slave one hundred lashes as well as a fine of ten *solidi*.[5] Comparison of these penalties with those inflicted upon free persons guilty of the same offences against members of their own estate tells its own story of the slave's lowly status.[6] No doubt a master would often permit a slave victim to take possession of the penalty exacted from the offender, but in only one case – when an innocent slave had suffered grave injury under torture – was benefit for the victim expressly provided for, and that benefit was more apparent than real, for freedom *in patrocinio* would have been at best worth little to a maimed man, and at worst the equivalent of a death sentence.[7] But although the laws regularly speak of prosecution by the master and payment to him, a plaint might in certain circumstances be lodged by the slave himself.[8] He was permitted to bring an action on his own or on his master's behalf – the distinction being, of course, a *de facto* one – if

[1] v. 4. 13.
[2] vi. 5. 12 (Chindasvind's version of which had ordered lifelong exile in addition): cf. vi. 1. 5 (death or grave injury to an innocent slave under torture).
[3] vi. 4. 3: but at judicial discretion in some cases, and see also vi. 4. 1.
[4] vi. 3. 4.      [5] iii. 4. 16; vi. 4. 3.
[6] Cf. vi. 4. 3 (beating, scalping), vi. 3. 2–3 (abortion), iii. 4. 14 (forced intercourse), and below, p. 259 (killing). Examples could easily be multiplied.
[7] vi. 1. 5.
[8] For the improbability of slaves as accusers in public cases, see above, p. 89, n. 4.

his master was more than fifty miles away. No written authorisation was necessary, as it was when the owner was closer at hand. A free-man was forbidden to refuse to present himself as defendant in a suit originated by a slave and was assured of his entitlement to the full composition *pro iniusta petitione* or, in cases concerning less than ten *solidi*, to half of this if the allegation was not proved.[1] The slave's master was, of course, finally responsible for the payment. If a case handled by a slave was lost as a result of his fraud or negligence, opportunity existed to reopen the matter.[2]

With the exception of torture, which could not be used against a freeman,[3] the slave could avail himself of the usual means of proving his claim. But it must often have been the case that he was obliged to pin his hopes on the reluctance of his opponent to submit to the oath of innocence,[4] for only rarely was the testimony of those who in the nature of things would frequently have been in the best position to support him, his fellow-slaves, accepted as admissible. The general rule was that the evidence of slaves was accorded no credibility,[5] and exceptions were few and minor. The more im-portant slaves of the *palatinum officium* were exempt by virtue of their office, and lesser palatine slaves might be exempted at the royal will.[6] The testimony of other slaves was acceptable when there were no independent free witnesses in cases concerning unimportant objects or inextensive landed property and in cases of killing, but only in these last might evidence given to the disadvantage of a freeman by a slave who was himself very poor or who had a criminal record be believed.[7] Finally, testimony extracted from a slave under torture was accepted when certain serious crimes – killing, adultery, treason, coinage offences or sorcery – were alleged against his owner.[8] The

[1] II. 2. 9. For a slave as *interpellator* in a case of theft, see VII. 4. 1.

[2] II. 2. 9.  [3] *Arg. ex* II. 3. 4, VI. 1. 2.  [4] Envisaged in II. 2. 9.

[5] II. 4. 4: cf. *FV* 40, with judicial rejection of slave (and freed) evidence. But slave testimony to an oral will might be accepted: II. 5. 13. How remarkable it is that a slave might act as a judge (II. 1. 18)!

[6] II. 4. 4.

[7] My interpretation of II. 4. 10, where the last sentence is very difficult. I cannot agree with Zeumer, XXIV, 105, that there is any definite earlier allusion to disputes about slaves.

[8] III. 4. 10, 13, VI. 1. 4, VII. 6. 1: III. 4. 11 declared invalid manumission made so that a slave would not have to give evidence under torture. Since torture 'in priorum dominorum capite' was also unlawful (V. 4. 14), alienation for the same reason was doubtless also invalid.

slave might not himself accuse his owner,[1] but he was expected to disclose what he knew before he was put to the question: if he did not, and his torture revealed his owner's guilt, he was punished as an accessory by the king.[2]

Greatest account of the independent personality and will of the slave had perforce to be taken when he himself was an offender. The law took the view that responsibility for an offence committed by a slave at the orders or with the knowledge of his master lay entirely at the latter's door, except on very rare occasions when the slave was also held punishable.[3] The slave-owner suffered the consequences of his slave's act as if he himself had been the actor. But how, one may ask, would a slave have been able to incriminate his owner, if the latter chose to deny prior knowledge? An unscrupulous lord could literally get away with murder, for even if an accused slave held fast under torture to the allegation that he had acted under orders, his uncorroborated testimony was of no avail against his owner's oath of innocence.[4] In such a case, and, of course, when the slave had in truth acted *domino nesciente*, the law had no choice but to accept the slave not as a juristic extension of his master but as an independent actor, personally accountable for his offences.[5] The practical difficulty lay in the matter of punishment, for the imposition of compositions and fines to the crown upon a criminous slave in fact directly penalised his master. Very frequently, therefore, punishment took a corporal form when the same offence committed by a freeman involved payment of some sort.[6] But financial penalties for offending slaves did occur, particularly when loss or damage to property had been caused: sometimes these would have been paid from the slave's

[1] Cf. v. 4. 14, providing that a slave charging his ex-master be returned to him 'ut ipse in servo suo crimen, quod sibi obiectum est, inquirere vel vindicare studeat', where malice seems to be assumed.

[2] VI. 1. 4.

[3] The general rule, stated by VIII. 1. 1 (below, p. 189, n. 2), is confirmed in numerous individual laws – III. 3. 8, 12, 4. 16, VI. 4. 2, 4, VII. 2. 5, 22, 23, 3. 5, VIII. 5. 3, IX. 1. 2, XI. 2. 2 etc. Note the liability of a judge for the misdeeds of his slave surrogate: II. 1. 18. Exceptions occur to my knowledge only in III. 3. 11 ('sollicitatores adulterii') and VI. 5. 12 (murder). But an accused slave who incriminated his master only under torture suffered punishment for the crime: VI. 1. 4.

[4] VI. 5. 12.

[5] Note 'proprie volumtatis excessus' in VI. 2. 1.

[6] There are numerous examples – II. 2. 7, V. 6. 1, VI. 4. 2, 3, VII. 3. 1, 4 (cf. 2), 4. 1, VIII. 3. 14, 15, IX. 1. 1, X. 3. 2, 5, XI. 2. 2 etc.

peculiar resources,[1] but more often than not it would have been the slave-owner's task to pay what was required, and in normal circumstances it was always his ultimate responsibility to do so.[2] But always also he had an alternative, delivery of the slave himself.[3] His decision would naturally have rested largely upon the amount of the sum demanded – usually less and never more than that required from a freeman for the same offence[4] – and upon the worth of the slave to him.[5] We have no direct information on slave-prices in the Visigothic kingdom, but an indication is to be found in the reward of eighteen *solidi* paid to an informant slave whose master declined to free him in return for compensation from the fisc:[6] a value of about twenty *solidi* agrees well with what is known of prices elsewhere.[7] But the value of any individual depended upon the variables of age, sex and utility,[8] and many slaves were worth much more than this: one law, indeed, envisaged the possibility that a master might pay as much as one hundred *solidi* to prevent the loss of a *servus idoneus*.[9] Even when the laws ordered the transfer of a slave offender without further ado,[10]

[1] References to direct payments by the slave occur in VI. 4. 3, VII. 1. 1, VIII. 3. 10, and perhaps in VII. 2. 9, 23, VIII. 3. 6 etc.

[2] Responsibility lay with the lord under whose dominion the slave stood when he committed the offence (see V. 4. 18, with details of the slave's recovery if since alienated), except when the slave had since been freed, when – in cases of theft, at least – he answered for himself, as a slave, although retaining his liberty (VII. 2. 2). For fugitives, see above, p. 167, n. 1.

[3] See III. 3. 9, V. 4. 18, VI. 1. 5, 4. 10, VII. 2. 4, VIII. 1. 8, IX. 1. 18 etc. Strangely, this rule might result in a lesser penalty for the slave than for the freeman: see p. 203, with n. 3, below.

[4] Cf. VI. 4. 1, 3, VII. 2. 13, IX. 1. 18 etc. Conversely, the slave was often flogged more severely (and never less severely) than the freeman for the same offence (III. 4. 15, VII. 2. 20, VIII. 1. 3, 6, 9, 2. 2, 3. 6, 4. 15 etc.) and might be executed when the free person kept his life (III. 3. 1, 8, 4. 14, VI. 4. 3, XI. 2. 1). But identical punishments are not rare: see II. 2. 8, III. 2. 3, VIII. 1. 11, IX. 1. 19 (flogging), III. 3. 11 (delivery *in potestatem*), VI. 2. 3 (death, delivery *in potestatem*), VI. 3. 7 (death, blinding), VI. 5. 10 (composition) etc.

[5] Note VIII. 2. 2: 'Si pro eo dominus conponere noluerit, cum duplum vel triplum damni fecerit, quam quod eundem servum valere constiterit, ipsum servum pro facto tradere non retardet'.

[6] VII. 6. 1. In VI. 3. 4, where a freeman responsible for the miscarriage of an *ancilla* is required to pay twenty *solidi*, a punitive element is probably present. For the price of slave labour, see below, p. 198.

[7] See Jones, 'Slavery', p. 13, and for Gaul, Claude, 'Merowingische Geldgesch.', p. 239.  [8] Cf. VI. 1. 5, X. 1. 17.

[9] III. 3. 9: cf. VII. 3. 6 (a pound of gold).

[10] In, e.g., V. 4. 11, VI. 3. 5, 4. 3, VII. 5. 2.

the master was no doubt at liberty to come to an agreement about composition if he could. Clearly, however, a system where the independent misdeed of a slave brought financial loss to his master was not a satisfactory one: if a slave committed a crime involving a large enough composition, his master would often have been obliged to transfer him to the injured party, and fraudulent arrangements for the commission of such crimes against colluders, although severely punished, could have been neither rare nor easy to expose.[1]

Slave-owners had, therefore, a direct interest in the outcome of a case against one of their *mancipia*, and from the first were involved in the proceedings. An accused slave might be arrested and examined by the judge if his master was not at hand,[2] but the normal procedure was for the owner or his representative to be summonsed to present the defendant in court: if recalcitrant, the master or agent was himself arrested and kept in custody until he gave way.[3] During the case the slave's defence must have rested largely in the hands of his master. No doubt the composition *pro iniusta petitione* was paid if his innocence was proved without the use of torture, but there was in fact little to deter an accuser from proceeding to the use of this. No limitations with respect to the gravity of the case appear,[4] and the sanction which threatened the inscriber if the slave turned out to be innocent, or was proved so by his lord after inscription[5] – namely, the payment of another slave of equal value – was not so fearful that it would have served to frighten off anyone other than the poor freeman. Indeed, even if torture was excessive and the slave died or suffered serious injury, the accuser had only to pay two slaves in composition.[6] If the slave was found guilty, he either received the corporal punishment prescribed or was kept in prison until his owner had decided whether to pay up or to forfeit the slave.[7]

No doubt a slave who involved his master in financial loss was

---

[1] See VII. 2. 6, VIII. 1. 5 and, for a slightly different example of the problems of the system, VII. 2. 3.
[2] VI. 1. 1, VIII. 1. 8. A special case also in VI. 4. 10.
[3] VI. 1. 1.
[4] Despite the rubric of VI. 1. 5. Cf. also VII. 2. 23. Slave mandatories might demand torture against other slaves: II. 3. 4.
[5] One wonders if masters did not sometimes keep their silence until after inscription.
[6] VI. 1. 5: cf. VII. 2. 23. The supervising judge had also to pay one slave (for negligence) in the event of death.
[7] VII. 2. 14: cf. VIII. 1. 8.

often made to suffer domestic punishment as a result. In fact, the law presented no real obstacles to a sadistic or vindictive master who wished to inflict death or injury on one of his slaves, and the savagery of some corporal punishments is indicated by the provision that a master was legally liable for the death of a slave as the consequence of a disciplinary flogging only if malice was involved.[1] There was no question of punishment for a freeman who killed his own slave, or someone else's, in anger or reaction to some or other injury.[2] Even the ban on the mutilation of slaves, justified on the grounds of their creation in the image of God, disappeared under Ervig, although it was to re-emerge in the following reign.[3] If a master ordered his slave to kill one of his fellows – or anyone else, for that matter – we have already seen that a perjured oath would allow him to escape conviction for murder if there was no evidence but that of the slave involved. In any case, a slave-owner had jurisdiction over offences committed by his slaves against one another or against him,[4] and in Ervig's time could even execute an offender guilty of a capital crime. He might have to explain the execution before a judge who had got to hear of it, but proof of the justice of his action could be furnished by oath alone.[5] Even if, by some means, an owner was convicted of the malicious killing of one of his slaves 'extra culpam', the punishment, previously the stern one of forfeiture of property and lifelong exile, was reduced by Ervig to loss of the right of testimony and a fine of a pound of gold.[6] There was scant security here for the hapless slave who ran foul of a cruel-hearted and unscrupulous master. It was not so much upon the law as upon his own economic worth to his owner that the slave had chiefly to rely for protection against arbitrary brutality.

The depressed status of the slave before the law was not simply the result of the application in practice of the basic principle that he was nothing but a piece of the property of his master: it had its origin also in a clearly felt notion of the inherent depravity of the slave and

---

[1] VI. 5. 8. The punishment of fugitives is mentioned in IX. I. 13 and that of fornicating *ancillae* in III. 4. 15.

[2] VI. 5. 12. But a *servus alienus* no doubt had to be replaced, as did an animal killed in the same circumstances: below, p. 216.

[3] VI. 5. 13, 13*, where note 'imaginis Dei plasmationem'. For the mutilation of Church slaves, see above, p. 151.     [4] To generalise from VII. 2. 21 (theft).

[5] VI. 5. 12.     [6] Ib.

moral superiority of the freeman. It was this social prejudice which underlay, for example, the restrictions on the admissibility of slave evidence and the provision that the unprovoked insolence of slaves towards freemen should be punished by flogging.[1] But it found its most palpable expression in the laws governing sexual relations between members of the two classes. Totally abhorrent was the idea of a sexual liaison between a freewoman and her own slave: both parties to such a union were flogged and then burned. At the best, the freewoman could hope for enslavement if she succeeded in claiming sanctuary, but there is no indication that any concessions were extended to her lover. Nor was it possible to evade the law by first manumitting the slave, for the prohibition applied equally to unions of freewomen with their own *liberti*.[2] The union of a freewoman and a *servus alienus* was punished by lashings for both and by the freewoman's eventual delivery into the power of her family if she persisted in the relationship after three such warnings – punishments which show that the offence was seen as one against the *mores* of society and the honour of the family rather than against the slave's master.[3] A freeman was forbidden, on pain of the same treatment, to cohabit with someone else's *ancilla*.[4] Unacceptable here was not the simple matter of sexual relations between the two, for elsewhere in the code fornication with an *ancilla aliena* was expressly stated not to involve legal consequence for the freeman if it took place outside the girl's master's house,[5] but rather, we may think, the permanent and public nature of the union. There was nothing to prevent a slave-owner from enjoying a relationship with one of his own *ancillae*.

Although Christian theory did not admit the equation of servitude

[1] vi. 4. 7, where 'persone nobili et inlustri' in the text is simply 'ingenuo' in the title. For *nobilis* meaning simply 'free', see iv. 5. 7, *in fine*, v. 7. 17, x. 2. 4 etc.

[2] iii. 2. 2, on which see Zeumer, xxiv, 589–92, with the sources. Children of the union were expressly forbidden rights of inheritance. Cf. also iii. 3. 1, 2: but in iii. 4. 14 enslavement, not death, appears.

[3] iii. 2. 3, on which see Zeumer, xxiv, 592–4, with Roman and Germanic parallels. The woman was enslaved to the slave-owner only if her family rejected her. But the children became his, except in special circumstances (above, p. 167, n. 2). Manumission is presumably envisaged in the last sentence of ix. 1. 15.

[4] iii. 2. 3.

[5] iii. 4. 15. Intercourse 'in domo domini' brought the freeman fifty or one hundred lashes, depending on the 'quality' of the slave girl.

and turpitude,[1] the Visigothic Church in no way attacked the institution of slavery itself, regarding it, in traditional fashion, rather as a necessary consequence of, and curb upon, the vitiated nature of man since the Fall.[2] Far from advocating what would have amounted to social revolution, the churches were centres

ubi castigationis disciplina et obtemperandi predicantur exempla

– as Leovigild put it, in terms which would not have met with St Paul's disapproval.[3] The councils concerned themselves very little with improving the lot of the slaves of the kingdom, but a great deal with ensuring that the Church's own holdings did not diminish. Christian humanitarian influence was present in the laws concerning slavery, but by no means a predominant feature.[4] In one respect, however, the Church profoundly affected for the better the fortunes of the slaves: by encouraging manumission as an act pleasing in the eyes of God and worthy therefore of heavenly reward,[5] it allowed the *servus* some prospect of liberation from his bondage and elevation into the ranks of the freed, the *liberti*.[6]

Freedom as the direct result of the law's penalisation of an owner or concession of reward or pity to a *mancipium* was not unknown,[7]

---

[1] But cf. IV Tol. 74, referring to the elevation of Church slaves to the clergy 'non dignitate naturae sed temporis necessitate'!

[2] Generally, see Verlinden, *L'esclavage*, pp. 30ff., with literature. Both notions appear in *Sent.* III. 47, 1–3: 'Aequus Deus ideo discrevit hominibus vitam, alios servos constituens, alios dominos, ut licentia male agendi servorum potestate dominantium restringatur... Unus enim Dominus aequaliter et dominis fert consultum, et servis. Melior est subjecta servitus quam elata libertas. Multi enim inveniuntur Deo libere servientes sub dominis constituti flagitiosis, qui, etsi subjecti sunt illis corpore, praelati tamen sunt mente'.     [3] V. 4. 17.     [4] A sensible account in Gama Barros, IV, 82–7.

[5] Note the religious motivation evidenced in the *cartulae libertatis*, *FV* 2–6.

[6] Paradoxically, a Church slave stood less chance of manumission than did a secular one. The Church required compensation from the manumitting cleric (I Sev. 1, IV Tol. 67, 69: a case of uncanonical manumission in X Tol. *Aliud decretum*) and only if this was double the value of the slave and his *peculium* were the *libertus* and his descendants free from *obsequium*: even then, recall to slavery was possible (IV Tol. 68, 74). The thirty-year rule was inapplicable when manumission was uncanonical (Mer. 20) and the period in any case ran from the date of the death of the manumittor, not the date of the manumittory document (IX Tol. 12). Church slaves elevated to the clergy had first to be manumitted, but even these could be recalled to slavery (IV Tol. 74, IX Tol. 11, Mer. 18). Generally, see Martínez Díez, *Patrimonio*, pp. 133–6.

[7] Cf. III. 2. 7, IX. 1. 10 (penalty), VI. 1. 5 (pity!), VII. 6. 1, XII. 2. 14 (reward). Nor should the part of prescription be forgotten. In a category of their own are the laws prohibiting Jewish possession of Christian slaves.

but the slave's main hope of liberty undoubtedly lay in the willingness of his master to grant it to him as an act of grace.[1] Manumission could be validly effected only when the manumittor possessed exclusive rights over the slave concerned.[2] The means of emancipation might be either a testamentary disposition, 'per scripturam aut presentibus testibus',[3] or a written grant, delivered to the slave in the presence of a priest or deacon and two or three witnesses.[4] Particular conditions might be attached to the manumission.[5] Most often, these would have had to do with the extent of the freedman's control over the *peculium* frequently conceded to him at the time of his liberation.[6] Alienation of this in breach of the conditions of the manumittory grant was, naturally, invalid, with the property reverting to the patronal family. But if no restrictive provisos had been imposed, the freedman was at liberty to dispose of it as he wished, and only if he died intestate and *sine prole* did it pass automatically to the manumittor or his heirs.[7]

Particular conditions apart, the grant of freedom itself was regularly revocable on the count of ingratitude:[8] in other words, the freedman had imposed upon him certain defined obligations towards his patron and the patronal family.[9] Chief amongst these was that of remaining in the service of the manumittor as long as this individual should live.[10] During this period, one half of the goods which the freedman might in some way acquire passed to the patron. On the manumittor's death, however, the freedman might retain his liberty if he sought another patron.[11] The freedman's children were apparently not subject to this restriction,[12] but in other respects they too were

1 'Gratie dono' (v. 7. 17), 'libertatis gratiam' (v. 7. 19).
2 v. 7. 2, with punishment for an offender. But later agreement with the owner or co-owner could bring validation.
3 v. 7. 1: cf. *FV* 21.
4 v. 7. 2, 9. Cf. C. G. Mor, *RSDI*, 1 (1928), 110–11.
5 v. 7. 9.
6 For grants, on death or not, see IV. 2. 18, 5. 1, 2, v. 6. 6, 7. 1, 13, 14, *FV* 2, 5, 6, *VPE* v. 12. 4 etc. Cf. also XII. 2. 13, 3. 12.
7 v. 7. 13, 14.
8 For a grave case by a Church freedman, see II Sev. 8.
9 But for exceptions see v. 7. 18 and XII. 2. 13, 14, and cf. IX. 1. 10.
10 v. 7. 13.                                    11 Ib.
12 But the Egican v. 7. 20 ordered the children to remain obedient and in the *patrocinium* of the manumittor and the three generations which followed him, on pain of enslavement.

limited by their status. No freed person or descendant of a freed person should dare presume, declared a scandalised Reccesvind, to attempt to marry the manumittor or any descendant of the same: nor might the former molest the latter with unjust court actions or otherwise harm him or her, on pain of enslavement to the offended party.[1] This comprehensive measure in fact went further than older provisions retained in the code, which stated in particular terms the grounds permitting revocation of freedom.[2] Only the earlier law which pronounced that a freedman and all his descendants were not to be believed but rather enslaved if they bore witness against their original patron or his children or grandchildren was not included within its scope.[3]

The status of the *libertus* was, in fact, very different from that of the *ingenuus*. The freeman was characterised, as Reccesvind put it in justifying the marriage prohibition just referred to, by his *generosa nobilitas*, his *claritas generis*, the freedman by his *ingenita libertas*, his *abiecta conditio*. It is understandable that the depravity of the slave should not have been deemed to metamorphose overnight into the rectitude of the freeman. Hence, the evidence of a *libertus* – although not that of his heirs – was admissible in the courts only in those special circumstances in which slave testimony was given credence.[4] Very occasionally the laws put the freedman on a par with the freeman.[5] But when the former received independent treatment he was both punished more severely and revenged less drastically than the latter. The full composition for the manslaughter of a *libertus*, for example, was only half that exacted when a freeman was the victim,[6] while if a freedman misused the person of an *ingenuus*, he was punished with one hundred lashes in addition to the normal penalty suffered by a free offender – and that, explicitly, 'pro eo, quod equalem statum non habet'.[7] The *libertus* might be more easily put to the torture than the freeman – in cases concerning more than two hundred and fifty *solidi* if he was an *idoneus* or more than one hundred

---

[1] v. 7. 17.            [2] v. 7. 9, 10.

[3] v. 7. 11. But the prosecution of *iusta negotia sua* against patrons was permitted: see also v. 7. 17.

[4] v. 7. 12. It was unfitting that 'libertorum testimonio ingenuis damna concutiantur'. Cf. *FV* 40.           [5] E.g., II. 4. 9, III. 2. 7.

[6] VIII. 4. 16: for misuse of the person, see VI. 4. 3, and for *raptus* compare III. 3. 8 with III. 3. 9.           [7] VI. 4. 3.

*solidi* if he was an *inferior* – and compositions alone were paid if he suffered grievous harm or death as a result.[1] On the other hand, he usually, although not always, received preferential treatment by comparison with the slave,[2] for *servus* and *libertus* also were not of the same condition – 'non iam unius conditionis esse noscuntur'.[3] A slave–freed union might take place with the permission of the slave's lord, but persistence in an unapproved match after three formal warnings brought enslavement of the freed partner, while even children born before a warning was issued became the property of the slave-owner.[4] Marriages between free and freed were not generally forbidden, but were doubtless frowned upon as *inhonestae coniunctiones*.[5]

Naturally, the law was concerned to ensure that a man enjoyed the status which was his due. A man serving as a slave but claiming he was a freedman was given judicial protection and a period of time in which witnesses might look for the documents which supplied proof.[6] An extrajudicial confession of servile condition made under duress was not admissible in later court proceedings: on the other hand, a man who attempted to claim another as his slave after earlier declaring in court that he was freed not only lost his case but was obliged to pay a slave in penalty to his adversary.[7] Another law provided that a litigant should give back before the hearing whatever he might previously have taken from the man he was reclaiming as his slave:[8] the object was perhaps to curb a sharp practice whereby a potential claimant took money as a *quid pro quo* for not proceeding with his suit and then reneged on the arrangement. An ostensible freedman claimed as a slave (but not as a runaway) in any case retained his freedom until the hearing, although the judge might require him to provide a guarantor of his appearance.[9] A case

---

[1] VI. I. 5. 300 *solidi* were paid by the accuser, 200 by the judge, or half these sums if the freedman was an *inferior*.

[2] E.g., VI. I. 5, 4. 3, VIII. 4. 16. But cf. IX. I. 21 (Egica) for their parity of treatment in contrast with the *ingenuus*, and note that the *libertus* composed as a slave for theft (VII. 2. 2) – in fact to his advantage!

[3] III. 3. 9.

[4] III. 2. 4: for a particular prohibition see III. 3. 9. Note the application of III. 2. 7 (above, p. 162, with n. 1) to slave–freed unions.

[5] With legal consequences in, e.g., v. 2. 5.

[6] V. 7. 3.  [7] V. 7. 7; V. 7. 6.

[8] V. 7. 5.  [9] V. 7. 4.

concerning status was to be judged on the evidence of the 'meliores adque pluriores', and the judge was expressly warned that if he gave a false decision as the result of bribery, both he and the *petitor* – assumed to be the briber – would face the penalties laid down for unjust judgement.[1]

The men most amply possessed of the means with which to coerce and to bribe their way to the appropriation of the persons of others were those greater freemen of the kingdom who appear described by the various equivalent terms *maiores*, *potentiores*, *honestiores* and *nobiliores* and contrasted with the ordinary freemen, the *minores*, *inferiores*, *humiliores* and *viliores*.[2] The standing of these nobles – for such we may call them[3] – was of more than simply social signifi-cance, for the laws frequently accorded them treatment quite distinct from that prescribed for the *inferiores*. For this reason, judgement as to a man's status was often a necessary precondition of correct judicial action. But any attempt to define the nobles in precise terms is futile.[4] Certainly one can point to certain general features of the nobility and to certain defined groups who belonged to it, but no clear-cut, formal statement of what identified the *nobilior* can be achieved. No doubt a compound of social, economic and political factors which can only in the broadest outlines now be isolated served as the raw material of decision. And we should probably be right to think that general public opinion was often as important as particular personal assets in the matter of identification.

Nevertheless, qualificative characteristics can be recognised in the form of birth, office, wealth and power. It would be very wrong to view these as in practice frequently possessed in isolation one from another. The superior members of the *palatinum officium*, the *primates palatii*, were certainly *potentiores*,[5] but their position was itself no

---

[1] v. 7. 8.

[2] In vɪɪɪ. 4. 24, the contrast is between the *potentior* and, simply, the *relique persone*, and in vɪɪ. 6. 2 between the *ingenuus* and the *humilior* – who is not a slave.

[3] Cf. ɪɪɪ. 6. 1: 'Nobiles...minoris loci persone', x. 2. 7: 'Nobilis adque inferior ingenuus', ɪv. 2. 20, xɪɪ. 3. 17, xvɪ Tol. 2.

[4] In ɪx. 2. 9, the 'maioris loci persona' appears as the *dux*, *comes* or *gardingus*, but the concern is solely with military standing, where precision is attainable. 'Qui in loco maior est' in ɪx. 1. 6 is simply the local judge, while in vɪ. 1. 1 the *seniores loci* are those in charge of an estate. In x. 3. 5, *seniores* means simply 'the older men'.

[5] vɪ. 1. 2: 'Nobiles...potentioresque persone, ut sunt primates palatii nostri eorum-que filii'. The *comes civitatis* is contrasted with a 'minor persona' in vɪɪɪ. 4. 29.

doubt often the result of material strength, military, financial or territorial, and certainly a cause of it, while more often than not any distinction between birth and wealth as qualifications for office would be unfruitful, since the social claim of distinguished ancestry and the economic claim of material possessions would have co-existed in the same persons.[1] But not all *potentiores* were in the royal service: even a despised Jew might be found among their ranks.[2] To judge from a law of 645, the old aristocracy of blood continued to survive distinct from that of service,[3] and there is no reason to think that by Ervig's day it had either disappeared or lost the wealth and strength which we are obliged to attribute to it.[4] On the other hand, the children of the *primates palatii* enjoyed by their birth the status of *nobiles*.[5]

It is wealth, in fact, which appears as the supreme characteristic of the *potentior*.[6] When Reccesvind, dealing in II. 1. 33 with contempt of a royal command, contrasted the *nobilior*, who had to pay three pounds of gold, with '[is qui] talis sit, qui non habeat', who was to suffer one hundred lashes, the terminology is significant. Certainly the law does not permit the inference that the *nobilior* was defined, in wholly financial terms, as any man able to pay 216 *solidi*: elsewhere in the code 'minime...vilioresque persone' were envisaged as being

---

[1] Note *VPE* v. 10. 1: 'Quosdam Gotorum, nobiles genere opibusque perquam ditissimos, e quibus etiam nonnulli in quibusdam civitatibus comites a rege fuerant constituti': cf. ib. v. 12. 2.

[2] *Arg. ex* XII. 3. 12, 13, where Jewish *viliores* appear as a distinct category: cf. also XII. 3. 8.

[3] III. 1. 5: 'Quicumque ex palatii nostri primatibus vel senioribus gentis Gotorum': cf. VI. 1. 2 (also Chindasvindian): 'Si...equalem sibi nobilitate vel dignitate palatini officii quicumque accusandum crediderit...', although *nobilitas* does not necessarily result from birth here. At III Tol. the *gentis nostrae primores* (344d) or *seniores Gothorum* (350a) were the nobility of blood – *majores natu* (346a) – which does not of course mean that they were not office-holders. For 'primatus totius gentis', see IV Tol. 75 (of 633). Note also VI. 1. 2 (cit p. 183, n. 5, above), where 'ut sunt' = 'as are, for example'.

[4] Sánchez-Albornoz, 'Aula', pp. 27–32, holds that the aristocracy of blood disappeared after Chindasvind's purge, when 200 of the *primates Gotorum* and 500 *mediogres* met their deaths (Fredegar, IV. 82). But the words of III. 1. 5 and VI. 1. 2 cit. in the last note remained in Ervig's elsewhere drastically amended versions. Great wealth is an obvious inference from III. 1. 5.

[5] VI. 1. 2.

[6] The implication of III. 1. 5 is that even freemen who were not nobles of blood or office might be possessed of fortunes of as much as 10000 *solidi*.

sometimes able to find no less than five pounds of gold, when the *nobiles* paid ten.[1] But it does indicate that the king found it natural to think of the *nobilior* in terms of wealth. The connection of *nobilitas* or *honestas* with riches is, in fact, apparent in several laws, where, although the possibility that the *humilior* might be able to pay a stipulated composition was accepted, the legislators assumed as a matter of course that the *honestior* would always be able to do so.[2] The postulate of a close relation between honourableness, *honestas*, and wealth is not foreign to our own society, but was basic to Visigothic where the opposite of *nobilis* was *pauper* and where even the weight attached to a freeman's testimony in the courts depended upon his means.[3]

The kings sensibly took into account the superior wealth of the *honestiores* when they established the penalties for certain offences. Occasionally they provided that the noble should pay a higher composition than the lesser freeman, but that the latter should also be flogged.[4] Whether in such cases the *humilior* able to meet the higher charge was allowed to pay it and so to escape corporal punishment we do not know. But it seems a likely assumption that this was the case, and that the penalty was thus conceived of as a single one, with the possibility of part-payment with the body taken into account.[5] From the lower freeman's point of view, the regime was positively merciful, for slavery was the regular alternative to non-payment. As for the nobleman, he was no more privileged than is the rich man in our own society who by using his wealth to pay a fine avoids the imprisonment which faces his poorer neighbour. Privilege was not the deliberate creation of the law, but

[1] XII. 3. 17.

[2] Cf., e.g., II. 4. 3: 'Si honestior persona fuerit...dupla...satisfactione conpellatur exolvere. Si certe inferior est persona et unde duplam rem dare non habeat...C flagellorum hictus...accipiat', II. 4. 6, VIII. 3. 14, IX. 3. 3, XII. 3. 12, 13.

[3] For the *nobilis/pauper* distinction, see II. 3. 4 (where also *humilior*), and for *potens/pauper* II. 3. 9. *Pauperes* probably means 'ordinary freemen' also in other laws (e.g., II. 1. 30, III. 4. 17), but is certainly also used to mean the poverty-stricken (e.g., V. 7. 16). For well-off witnesses, II. 4. 3.

[4] VIII. 3. 10, 4. 29.

[5] Note II. 1. 33, cit. above in text, and the texts cit. in n. 2, above, where (II. 4. 6 apart) lashings are ordered for the *vilior* unable to pay. The same rule perhaps applied in those cases where a financial penalty was laid down for the *maior*, a corporal one for the *minor*, without further ado: see VIII. 3. 6 and the texts cit. below, p. 186, n. 3.

rather the inevitable result of the economic inequalities of the members of society.

More often, however, the kings contented themselves with simply fixing two distinct sums, a higher one for the *honestior* and a lower one for the *inferior*.[1] Far from being privileged, the noble here suffered from obvious discrimination. This deliberate policy of class inequality before the law was based on a realistic recognition of the enhanced financial status of the noble and made very good sense from the royal point of view: what more reasonable and at the same time advantageous to the king than to curb those from whom he might expect the most frequent and defiant breaches of the law by the imposition of more severe penalties? The same interest in striking directly at the power of overmighty subjects underlay the provision of separate punishments for the *honestior* and the lesser freeman who tampered with royal documents or forged the royal seal: here, the *honestior* lost half his property, but the *minor* his hand.[2] It may be that the superior freeman thought himself privileged in such a case, but in terms of hard cash he certainly was not: half his estate would assuredly have been worth more than the one hundred *solidi* at which the loss of a hand was elsewhere rated.[3]

The common view that the Visigothic noble enjoyed considerable privileges at law is, in fact, unfounded. His *de iure* privileges consisted solely in restrictions upon the use of torture against him, and although these gave him unquestionable advantages, one can still speak with greater justification of the anti-aristocratic flavour of the laws. It is significant that nowhere is there any indication that higher compositions were required from offenders against nobles.[4] Certainly their rank did not exempt them from corporal punishments.[5] Moreover, on not one occasion were the financial penalties imposed upon the noble without doubt lower in real terms than those imposed

---

[1] VII. 2. 22, VIII. 3. 12, 4. 24, 25, IX. 3. 3, XII. 3. 17. Cf. VII. 5. 2.

[2] VII. 5. 1.

[3] VI. 4. 3. Note further II. 1. 33 (three pounds of gold/one hundred lashes), 2. 8 (two pounds of gold/fifty lashes), XII. 3. 8 (one hundred *solidi*/one hundred lashes) and cf. XII. 2. 18 (Egica), 3. 17.

[4] Differently, Sánchez-Albornoz, *Orígenes del feudalismo*, pp. 197–207, for killing in the Egica/Wittiza period.

[5] See VII. 2. 20, 5. 2, VIII. 1. 10 etc.

upon the humbler freeman.[1] In general, it is true to say that the status of *potentior* involved extra legal responsibilities rather than extra legal privileges, that the noble was more severely constrained to obedience to the law, not more widely entitled to protection and favour from it.

Part and parcel of the activity of the self-respecting *potentior* was the exercise of patronage.[2] Cliental relationships involving economic favour by the patron, service by the dependant, were directly regulated by the laws. The *buccellarii* received from the patron to whom they commended themselves land on which to live[3] – sometimes, no doubt, land originally their own but surrendered to a lord and accepted back in grant[4] – and arms with which to fight.[5] As freemen, they were at full liberty to leave the service of one lord and commend themselves to another, but they had then to restore to their first patron all that he had granted them.[6] Their right to these possessions would otherwise appear to have been hereditary, in daughters as well as sons,[7] although conditional upon their continuing obedience and loyalty.[8] The *buccellarii* of the late Empire had formed private war-bands, and there is no reason to doubt that these Visigothic retainers had the same character. Certainly they stood to gain property while in their patrons' service, for the law stipulated that they should leave half of their acquisitions behind if they were dismissed or themselves chose to cut the voluntary links which bound them to their lords.[9] Although it was on campaign that such gains would most often have been made, private feuds between great men were no doubt another source. In effect, these men had the military characteristics of later feudal vassals. The existence of groups of free individuals commended to patrons,

---

[1] Doubtful cases are II. I. 9 and XVI Tol. 2: cf. also the edict in confirmation of III Tol. To my knowledge, only in II. 4. 2 does the *minor* in any terms suffer more severely than the noble: both lose their right of testimony, but the *minor* is also flogged. The *maior* had to pay more for the services of the judicial *saio*: II. 1. 26.

[2] See on the following Sánchez-Albornoz, *Estudios*, pp. 29–45. For freemen in ecclesiastical *patrocinium* see V. 1. 4 (and cf. VI Tol. 5).

[3] Cf. V. 3. 4: 'Ille, cui se conmendaverit, det ei terram'.

[4] Cf. V. 2. 6, *in fine*, and Sánchez-Albornoz, *Estudios*, p. 529.

[5] V. 3. 1. Cf. the reference to patronal *beneficia* in IV. 5. 5.

[6] V. 3. 1, 3, 4.         [7] V. 3. 1.

[8] Ib., V. 3. 3: see also above, pp. 60ff.

[9] V. 3. 3, clarifying V. 3. 1.

receiving arms and land from them and fighting in their service is evidence enough of the *de facto* power deployed by the *potentiores* of the kingdom.

Perhaps more akin to the original Germanic 'companions', who lived with their patron and received their sustenance at his table rather than from land granted to them, were the *saiones*. Again, the *saio* was in the patronage of a lord from whom, 'pro obsequio', he received arms. Unlike the *buccellarius*, however, the *saio* had no right to keep any weapons which he might acquire during his service.[1] That he was a soldier seems from this to be clear, but only in one law does he not, in fact, appear as an officer of the court, concerned with the execution of judicial commands.[2] It is not difficult to see how an executive and police function exercised in the name of a judge should have developed out of his original military role as 'companion' of a great man.[3]

The relationship of patron and client was a means to power, profit and prestige for the former, to profit and protection for the latter. But inevitably it presented a threat to law and order, for a private army composed of free *commendati* and swelled by the inclusion of the slaves and freedmen bound to a lord's service could as easily be used against another of the king's subjects as against a rebel or foreign enemy. There is little evidence of such activity but the laws do show that patrons were not averse from using their men to whip up mobs to the danger of others and from personally leading their retainers in forcing entry to private houses and in robbing, manhandling and even killing their occupants.[4] Clearly, the king could not allow great lords *carte blanche* to use their private soldiery for the despoilation or terrorisation of others.[5] He was either unable or unwilling to strike at the institution of clientage itself:

[1] V. 3. 2, where 'illa' must refer to 'arma', given the right of the *saio* to receive fees as an executive officer (II. 1. 26).

[2] See II. 1. 18, 21, 26, 2. 4, 10 (Egica), VI. 1. 5, X. 2. 6: cf. II. 1. 13 (*exsecutor*), 19. I cannot agree with Zeumer, XXIII, 102–3, who saw the *saio* as an officer independent of the judge.

[3] There was the same use of *armati*, *satellites*, as agents and executors of justice in Merovingian Gaul: see P. Guilhiermoz, *Essai sur l'origine de la noblesse en France au MA* (Paris, 1902), pp. 50–2. For a *saio* as a bishop's executive officer, see Mer. 8: perhaps the *domestici* of III Sar. 4 were also *saiones*?

[4] VI. 4. 2, VIII. 1. 3, 4. Cf. VIII. 1. 6, 10.

[5] Perhaps in the extortion of documents to the benefit of the *potentior*: cf. II. 5. 5, 9.

indeed, he accepted the obligation of all those in a lord's service, free, freed or slave, to obey his orders and expressly absolved them from criminal responsibility when they acted in accordance with these.[1] Rather, he acted against the lawlessness which might ensue by holding the patron personally accountable for crimes committed by his men in his name.[2] Just as the value of a client to his patron was impaired by this ruling, so the value of a lord to his dependant was rendered less by the insistence of the law that a *potentior* might not act as the legal representative of a lesser freeman, except when the opposing party was of an equivalently high status,[3] and that he might not attempt to influence a decision – *patrocinare* is the term – by making his presence felt in court.[4] A man who commended himself to a patron in order to gain advantage in an impending suit in fact lost his case, even if it was good.[5]

The problem was recognised, then, but how effective these laws were in practice is another matter. For the higher judges who were required to enforce them were of the same social class as the *potentiores* themselves, and must frequently have had close connections with them. The claims of friendship, patronage or family could have been of no less appeal to the lower judge, while his vulnerability to the threats of another's patron put his strict judicial impartiality in further jeopardy. In personal power and possessions, certainly, the lesser magistrate could have been no match for the *potentior*. Bribery, of course, was a potent weapon in the noble's armoury.[6] In one way or another, the *potentior* was in a very strong position *de facto* to enjoy privileges which *de iure* he did not possess. And when the *potentior* was also a high officer in the palatine service, the sky was the limit: the throne itself was not an impossible goal.

[1] In keeping with this, a patron might discipline those *in patrocinio*: VI. 5. 8.
[2] VIII. 1. 1: 'Ut omnis ingenuus adque etiam libertus aut servus, si quodcumque inlicitum iubente patrono vel domino suo fecisse cognoscitur, ad omnem satisfactionem conpositionum patronus vel dominus obnoxii teneantur'. The men themselves were not blameworthy 'quare non suo excessu, sed maioris inperio id conmisisse probantur'. Cf. VI. 4. 2, VIII. 1. 3, 4, and above, in text, for slaves.
[3] II. 3. 9.
[4] Above, p. 100. Nor might he block the bringing to court of one of his clients: VII. 1. 1.          [5] II. 2. 8.
[6] On all this, above, pp. 117–18. The personal material weakness of some judges is graphically indicated by the provision in II. 1. 21 of fifty lashes for the judge unable to pay *anything* in composition.

*Chapter 7*

# THE ECONOMY

Spain had been among the most productive and prosperous of the Roman provinces, and we do not have to take at face value Isidore's encomiastic *De laude Spaniae* to recognise that it remained a rich country, at least by comparison with its Western neighbours, in the seventh century.[1] Naturally, there had been change. As elsewhere, there had occurred a general decline in urban life, and it is difficult to believe that industry had not also suffered: the mineral products for which Roman Spain had enjoyed fame, for example, find but rare mention in the Visigothic sources. On the other hand, the land hunger of the new settlers had almost certainly had as its effect an increase in the productive acreage of the country as a result of disafforestation and the clearing of wasteland for the purposes of tillage, pasturage and viticulture.[2] We should be right to think in terms of a considerable ruralisation of life and economy, a state of affairs reflected in large measure in the code, where preoccupation with the resolution of agricultural problems is a predominant feature. It would be a gross error, however, to conceive of the economy as based so completely upon the land that external trade had virtually dried up and the towns taken on the character of mere markets for the interchange of bartered goods. Not only direct evidence bearing on urban and commercial life but also the constant role which money compositions and transactions play in the code militates conclusively against any such view.[3]

The largest single sum which appears in any source is truly stagger-

[1] J. C. Russell, 'That earlier plague', *Demography*, v (1968), 176, is not justified in using the eulogy as evidence of recovery after plague. On the *DLS* and its influence, see J. A. Maravall, *El concepto de Esp. en la edad media*, 2nd edn (Madrid, 1964), pp. 19ff.

[2] For the extension of economically productive land, see VIII. 4. 24, 28, X. 1. 6, 7, 9, 13 etc.

[3] See also L. G. de Valdeavellano, 'La moneda y la economía de cambio en la península ibérica desde el siglo VI hasta mediados del siglo XI', *Sett.*, VIII (1961), 211.

ing: 200000 *solidi* paid to Dagobert for Frankish troops to help Sisenand in his successful bid for the throne.[1] But it is the clear implication of the dowry law that even those who were not *primates palatii* or nobles of the blood sometimes enjoyed the possession of property worth over 10000 *solidi*,[2] and not long after the Arabs invaded they were able to exact no less than 27000 *solidi* from a certain Athanagild.[3] To put these sums in perspective it should be borne in mind that a man could probably survive on some three to four *solidi* a year, for a single *solidus* was certainly considered adequate for the annual keep of a child under the age of ten.[4] Such a consideration in turn highlights the largeness of the financial penalties which so frequently appear in the code. Rarely was provision made for payment of less than a *solidus*, and when it was the circumstances envisaged were usually such that the total composition still amounted to several *solidi*.[5] Certainly it is not to be supposed that the ordinary freeman would easily, if at all, have been able to find the sums required in composition for more serious offences, even assuming financial assistance from his near kinsfolk. But it would be to attribute to the legislators either a grotesque lack of realism or the deliberate aim of bringing about the mass enslavement of the free population to suppose that the mulcts imposed for lesser offences could not normally have been met. Sometimes we come across freemen unable to find ten *solidi*, or even five, with which to pay a composition – and in fact sentenced to flogging rather than enslavement in place of the fine[6] – but anyone who possessed a couple of slaves was probably worth about thirty or forty *solidi* even before his land, buildings, livestock, tools and so on were taken into account. Of course, the fact that a composition was expressed in monetary terms does not mean that it was necessarily paid in coin. But even if payment was often made in kind, by the delivery of land or slaves, the commodity concerned could fulfil its role as a substitute for cash only if it had

[1] Fredegar, IV. 73.
[2] III. I. 5.          [3] CH 75.
[4] IV. 4. 3. See generally the statistics gathered in Jones, *Empire*, I, 447–8: the apparent correspondence of Visigothic slave-prices with those elsewhere has been remarked upon above. It is understandable that a poor woman should have been filled with joy at the gift of two *tremisses* (*VPE* v. 7. 6).
[5] E.g., a *tremis* for each fence-pale destroyed (VIII. 3. 7), every two animals wrongfully impounded (VIII. 4. 11, 26) etc.
[6] E.g., VI. 4. 2, VIII. 1. 6, 3. 14, IX. 1. 2.

a monetary value put upon it as a result of the willingness of someone, somewhere, eventually to exchange coin for it. When, on the other hand, the laws provided for payment in kind, they occasionally added that payment of the value of the object was an acceptable alternative.[1] Regularly, the laws took for granted the availability of money for cash sales – when they provided for a forfeited pledge to be sold and money surplus to the debt to be handed back to the erstwhile debtor, for example, or for the proceeds from the sale of an abductor to be divided between his victim and her betrothed.[2] All the emphasis, indeed, was upon sale: barter, as we have seen, was treated with unconcern.

It is clear, moreover, that the apparatus for a developed economic and commercial life based upon money transactions existed and needed regulation.[3] Sales on part-credit are witnessed,[4] and loans at interest were dealt with by the law, which established the maximum rate of interest on money at twelve and a half per cent per annum and threatened those who extorted *cautiones* providing for a higher rate with the forfeiture of all profit.[5] No interest was paid on money lost by no fault of the borrower, although the capital had, of course, to be repaid.[6] That loans of money were sometimes used in capitalist fashion to produce more wealth, rather than simply to stave off

---

[1] E.g., VIII. 4. 13, 21. Note also 'servum aut pretium scrvi' in VI. 4. 11, and the movement in VIII. 4. 8 from 'alium eiusdem meriti' to 'pretium pecodis'.

[2] V. 6. 3; III. 3. 5.

[3] Briefly on loans and deposits, see J. Martínez Gijón, *AHDE*, XXXIV (1964), 43–7. The classical distinction of *mutuum* and *commodatum* does not survive in Visigothic law, where the treatment of loan is usually not distinguished from that of deposit – *commendatum*, itself a vulgar law term. For the often casuistic laws on these two matters, see V. 5 passim.

[4] Above, p. 105.

[5] V. 5. 8. For the difference between this percentage and the classical *centesima usura*, see Levy, *Obligationenrecht*, pp. 160ff. For Bishop Masona's lending-bank in the late sixth century, see *VPE* v. 3. 9, and for a Visigothic IOU, *FV* 38, providing for double payment of capital and interest if the loan were not repaid at maturity. Agreements of all sorts regularly contained penalty-clauses: II. 5. 5. But only *placita* made with the king were exempt from the ruling (II. 5. 8) that clauses binding the person or providing for more than double payment of the property or triple payment of the money concerned invalidated the agreements containing them. For debt-recovery by a *mandatarius*, see *FV* 42, and for the use of a slave by the lender (also acting as a pledge?) in lieu of interest, *FV* 44. Remarkably, the seventh-century councils do not deal with usury.

[6] V. 5. 4. If profit equivalent to the loan had first been made, however, interest had also to be paid.

disaster, is clear.[1] In connection with such loans should be noted the measures concerning the redemption of secured debts. A deposited security had to be kept for ten days after the expiry of the time limit laid down in the *cautio*, and within this period the creditor had, if possible, to request the debtor to pay what was due, with interest for the extra period. If the debtor failed to pay, the local judge, with three 'honest men', assessed the extent to which distraint might be exercised upon the pledge: what remained of the price fetched when this was sold was returned to the debtor.[2] The failure of the creditor to return the security on redemption of the debt obliged him to eventual payment of one and a half times the value of the *pignus*.[3] Such provisions make most sense if seen against the background of commercial, rather than agricultural, interests, although they also had their application in the latter, of course. In fact, the law regulated the amount which might be taken as interest on the loan of agricultural products – wine, oil and cereal crops are mentioned – at fifty per cent, in accordance with Roman law.[4]

The natural concern of the kings to ensure the purity of the coinage is the more understandable in view of the extensive use of money. Only gold *tremisses* are known to have been minted in the seventh-century kingdom,[5] but coins of lower denomination must also have circulated,[6] and *solidi* certainly did, for it is in terms of them that even a seventh-century law dealing with coinage offences, VII. 6. 2, is expressed. But these *solidi* were almost certainly older coins, for an effective embargo upon the export of gold from the East appears to have been in operation from the reign of Heraclius.[7] Adulteration, clipping and counterfeiting were punished in the Visigothic laws with either the confiscation of half the property of a free offender or his

[1] Ib.
[2] v. 6. 3, on which see Levy, *Obligationenrecht*, p. 196: but why does he write of private sale of the pledge?          [3] v. 6. 4.
[4] v. 5. 9. For the loan or deposit of animals, see v. 5. 1, 2, 6, VIII. 4. 2.
[5] See Miles, p. 154, with a list of the seventy-nine mints at pp. 70ff.
[6] P. Grierson, in his review of Miles in *Numismatic chronicle*, 6th series, XIII (1953), 184, notes the absence of archaeological evidence for such coins. But how could the four *siliquae* in VIII. 5. 7 or the $12\frac{1}{2}\%$ interest rate (expressed as three *siliquae* to the *solidus*) have been paid if they had not existed? Cf. also the references to *siliquae* in the *De fisco Barcinonensi* and the comments on prices, above in text.
[7] See P. Grierson, 'Coinage and money in the Byzantine Empire, 498–*c.* 1090', *Sett.*, VIII (1961), 448–51: significantly, perhaps, it was in the reign of Heraclius that the Byzantines were finally expelled from Spanish soil.

enslavement: the slave suffered amputation of the right hand for a first offence and whatever fate the king might decide upon for a second.[1] The accusation *pro falsa moneta* was one of the particular few which might be substantiated against a freeman by the torture of his slaves, and the laying of information against an offender carried a reward.[2] Less serious than counterfeiting or maltreatment and punished only by a mulct of three *solidi*, paid to the aggrieved party, was the refusal to accept unadulterated *solidi* or *tremisses*, of whatever origin, when these were of correct weight, or the demand of a fee for their changing.[3]

It is very likely that the *tremisses* minted in Spain were, at least in part, coined from native gold: the large number of mints in Galicia suggests the continued exploitation of the mines there,[4] and there are references in Isidore to the auriferous rivers and to apparently contemporary panning for alluvial gold.[5] But gold was also imported, for it figured as one of the commodities – the others were silver, clothing and ornaments – mentioned in the *Antiqua* xi. 3. 1 as the possible objects of purchase from overseas merchants: the law was concerned to safeguard a native buyer if it should later transpire that what he had bought in good faith had been stolen.[6] What goods were shipped out of Spain in return – for the merchants would not

[1] vii. 6. 2.
[2] vii. 6. 1: for accusation to the king, cf. vi. 1. 6.
[3] vii. 6. 5. For the possible connection between the law and Leovigild's return to the minting of heavy-weight *tremisses* – which were, however, debased – see Grierson, 'Visigothic metrology', p. 81.
[4] For the Galician mints (nearly half the total number), see Miles, pp. 72–4. But A. R. Lewis, *The northern seas. Shipping and commerce in northern Europe, A.D. 300–1100* (Princeton, N. Jersey, 1958), p. 130, n. 113, is mistaken in citing O. Davies, *Roman mines in Europe* (Oxford, 1935), pp. 95–106, as saying that Galician gold was mined in this period, and why the discovery of an Egican gold piece in a mine (ore unknown: see Davies, p. 99, n. 10) at Corunna should seem to suggest that the Asturian mines were still operating (thus Lewis, p. 124) escapes me.
[5] *Etym.* xiii. 21. 33 and xvi. 22. 1: see also his *De laude Spaniae*. Goldsmiths are mentioned in vii. 6. 3 and 4.
[6] See F. Dahn, 'Über Handel und Handelsrecht der Westgothen', *Bausteine. Gesammelte kleine Schriften*, ii (Berlin, 1880), 324, for purchase in good faith as the implication of 'conpetenti pretio'. Normally, a good-faith purchaser lost the article without compensation if neither he nor the owner could find the thief-vendor: vii. 2. 8. The law is not explicit that the goods had been imported, but to think otherwise presents too many problems. Theft from other merchants is no doubt in mind – especially since the next law deals with disputes among merchants, ordering these to be heard by their own judges.

have gone home unladen – is almost entirely a matter for speculation.[1] The sale of slaves into foreign hands certainly occurred, although it was frowned upon and restricted, seemingly in the interests of the slaves themselves.[2] *Garum*, the famous fish-sauce, was still produced in Isidore's time, and probably exported, for Gregory of Tours reports the docking of ships – unfortunately unidentified – in Marseilles with cargoes of *liquamen* – apparently an equivalent term – and oil, another traditional Spanish export.[3] Corn was exported in the sixth century,[4] and a document from 716 records that Cordovan leatherware was to be found in Gaul.[5] But although there are plenty of allusions to viticulture, swine-keeping and horse-rearing in the code, we do not know if the overseas markets were still supplied with the products of these activities. As for the metallurgical industries, Isidore offers tolerable evidence of the continued extraction of silver and lead,[6] but the other rich mineral resources are not known even to have been worked.[7]

However this may be, evidence of trading relations between Spain and other countries – or, at least, of maritime links which argue for the strong probability of trade – is considerable. The early

[1] I. González Gallego, 'Apuntes para un estudio económico de la Esp. visigoda', *Archivos leoneses*, XXI (1967), 107, is altogether too dogmatic in his unqualified and unsubstantiated assertion of cereals, metals, salt, wine, vinegar, honey and oil as objects of export – and of silk, purple, cloth, ivory, gems and manufactured utensils as those of import. The article has a wretched footnote apparatus, and has to be read with a caution the greater for the author's uncritical attitude towards the *Etym.* as a source.

[2] A slave received his freedom if, after escaping and returning home, he was sold abroad a second time: IX. 1. 10. In keeping with this was the appearance of sale into foreign hands as a punishment in VI. 2. 1. If IX. 1. 10 was concerned with loss of manpower (thus Melicher, *Kampf*, p. 93, Verlinden, *L'esclavage*, p. 66), why was the slave freed rather than confiscated, and why was there no general prohibition of sales abroad? See also VII. 3. 3 (removal from the country of kidnapped freemen). For slave-imports, see the reference to Moors in the text, below, and the later comments on the Jews.

[3] Cf. *Etym.* XX. 3. 19, 20, and *HF* IV. 43. For earlier oil exports, see E. S. Bouchier, *Spain under the Roman Empire* (Oxford, 1914), p. 82: in fact, one need only think of Monte Testaccio. But references to olives, mustered below, are rare in the code.

[4] Cassiodorus, *Variae* v. 35: see L. Ruggini, *Economia e società nell'Italia annonaria* (Milan, 1961), pp. 291–2.

[5] See H. Pirenne, *Mahomet et Charlemagne*, 3rd edn (Paris–Brussels, 1937), pp. 71–2.

[6] *Etym.* XVI. 22. For silversmiths, see II. 4. 4, VII. 6. 4.

[7] But the prevalence of bronze ornaments etc. argues for the continued production of copper and tin: for alleged post-Roman slag-heaps from tin-mining, see Davies, p. 105.

use of Spanish authors, particularly St Isidore, in Ireland has been shown to be the result of direct transmission, necessarily by sea.[1] African connections, explicitly evidenced for the sixth century,[2] can hardly be thought to have disappeared in the seventh:[3] if Moorish slaves were imported into Gaul towards the middle of the century, it would be strange indeed if they were not to be found also in Spain.[4] Trading communications with Italy are attested by the finds of bronze jars in Majorca and Catalonia:[5] moreover, it was from Italy – Ravenna at the end of the sixth century, the south and Sicily in the second half of the seventh – that came the powerful Byzantine influence upon Visigothic architecture.[6] Taio, later bishop of Saragossa, certainly voyaged to Rome in the reign of Chindasvind.[7] On the other hand, no evidence of trade or of maritime relations with Gaul has survived from the seventh century,[8] although both are

[1] See J. N. Hillgarth, 'The East, Visigothic Spain and the Irish', *Studia patristica*, IV, Texte und Untersuchungen zur Gesch. der altchristlichen Literatur, LXXIX (Berlin, 1961), 442–56, and idem, 'Visigothic Spain and early Christian Ireland', *Proceedings of the Royal Irish Academy*, LXII (1961–3), sect. C, pp. 167–94. Both articles have a wealth of information bearing upon Spain and international trade in general.

[2] Procopius, III. 24. 11: cf. Cassiodorus, cit. For voyages rather than trade, see Procopius, IV. 4. 34–8, *VPE* III. 2 and Ildefonsus, *DVI* 4: a special case in *VPE* V. 11. 14–15.

[3] Generally on African influence on Spain, see Fontaine, *Isidore et la culture classique*, II, 857–9, and Lacarra, 'Península ibérica', pp. 240–3.

[4] Cf. *Vita Eligii* I. 10 and Verlinden, *L'esclavage*, pp. 66–7. For a probable seventh-century African inscription from Baetica, see Vives, *Inscripciones*, no. 325. Pace L. G. de Valdeavellano, 'La moneda', p. 215, the mention of camels in *HW* 30 does not argue for their import: the beasts may have been bred in Spain for many years. The context implies that they were regarded as lowly animals, and this, perhaps, that they were common. Note *HF* VII. 35 for their use in Gaul as pack-animals.

[5] See Hillgarth, 'Visigothic Spain and early Christian Ireland', p. 176, n. 45. For the sixth century see Cassiodorus, cit., *Reg.* IX. 227a and XIII. 47, and cf. Procopius, VI. 12. 29.

[6] See H. Schlunk, 'Relaciones entre la península ibérica y Bizancio durante la época visigoda', *AEA*, XVIII (1945), 177–204, especially 195ff.

[7] Above, p. 123, n. 3.

[8] But for 716 see above, in text. Lewis, pp. 123–4, builds far too much upon the only major find of Visigothic coins (not *solidi*, as he holds) outside Spain, that at Bordeaux (but see in any case Miles, p. 165, for doubts about the hoard's integrity). See the generally cautionary comments of P. Grierson, 'Commerce in the Dark Ages: a critique of the evidence', *Transactions of the Royal Hist. Society*, 5th series, IX (1959), 130ff., and in *Sett.*, VIII (1961), 330–1. For a convenient summary of the few finds outside Spain (which is also corrective of Lewis), see Hillgarth, 'Visigothic Spain and early Christian Ireland', p. 177, n. 47. No Visigothic coins were found at Sutton Hoo, despite Lewis, pp. 120, 124.

witnessed for the Arian period.[1] As for the East, links are amply attested for the sixth century, when Spanish clerics voyaged to Constantinople and Greek merchants and monks to Septimania and the peninsula.[2] Greeks and Syrians were in sufficient numbers at Narbonne – an important trading centre – to have been singled out for mention alongside Goths, Romans and Jews in the canons of the council of 589.[3] A Syrian bishop appeared at the Second Council of Seville in 619,[4] and Syrian influence operated in both the liturgical and the legislative fields.[5] Those Greek inscriptions found in the peninsula are all located in cities where a trading role is certain, like Merida,[6] or can be assumed, like Ecija.[7] Contact with the East was made the easier, of course, by the Imperial occupation of the south-east of the country until the 620s, and much of the extreme Byzantine influence upon Visigothic Spain must certainly be attributed to this.[8] But it is unlikely to have ceased after the expulsion of the Easterners, despite the dearth of direct evidence. Fructuosus is not reported to have had difficulty in finding a boat to take him to the East in Chindasvind's time,[9] and there is a reference

[1] See *HF* VIII. 35 (Gaul–Galicia), IX. 22 (Spain–Marseilles: 'Cum negotio solito'), and for a possible reference above, p. 195, with n. 3. Further, Thompson, *Goths*, pp. 23–4.

[2] See Gregory of Tours, *Liber in gloria martyrum* 77, *Reg.* v. 53a, *VPE* IV. 1. 1 and IV. 3. 2, Isidore, *DVI* 22, 29, 31. Further, Fontaine, *Isidore et la culture classique*, II, 846–8. *Contra* Lewis, p. 130, the grain-ship mentioned in Leontius, *The life of St John the Almsgiver* 10, sailed to Britain, not the peninsula: see Hillgarth 'Visigothic Spain and early Christian Ireland', p. 178, with n. 57.

[3] Narb. 4, 14.     [4] Above, p. 130, n. 5.

[5] For the liturgy see García Villada, pp. 37–8, and the literature cit. by E. F. Bruck, *Kirchenväter und soziales Erbrecht* (Berlin–Göttingen–Heidelberg, 1956), p. 162, n. 26, where pp. 157–63 concern legislative influence (the *Seelteil*).

[6] Vives, *Inscripciones*, nos. 418 (p. 141), 425, 426: cf. *VPE* IV. 3. 2 for trade. *VPE* V. 3. 12 shows the use of silk garments in the Meridan church: these would surely have come from the East. Cf. *Etym.* XIX. 22. 21: 'Exotica vestis peregrina deforis veniens, ut in Hispania a Graecis'.

[7] Vives, *Inscripciones*, no. 427. Other Greek inscriptions come from Trujillo (419), Mertola (420, 524), Cartcia (421) and Solana de los Barros (424). Nos. 422 and 423 are from Byzantine Cartagena.

[8] Generally on this influence see Stroheker, *Germanentum*, pp. 224–35: less satisfying is Goubert, pp. 111–33. For monasticism see A. Mundò, *Sett.*, IV (1957), 84–6. But architectural influence did not stem from the occupied territories: see Schlunk, 'Relaciones', passim.

[9] *VSF* 17. On the episode see Thompson, 'Fructuosus', pp. 58–63. But Egypt or Syria, rather than Byzantium, may have been the saint's destination: Hillgarth, 'Visigothic Spain and early Christian Ireland', p. 169, n. 10.

elsewhere to storms which affected travel to Libya and the Orient about the same time.[1] It is tempting to speculate that the fleet said by Isidore to have been formed by Sisebut was later used for the protection of the sea lanes around the coasts,[2] although its immediate purpose was no doubt to assist in the campaign against the Byzantines. A fleet was certainly still in existence in the reign of Wamba: according to a late and unverifiable source, indeed, it succeeded in destroying a Saracen force of no less than 270 vessels.[3]

In 693 ships from overseas were still putting in to the Spanish ports:[4] Ervig was assuredly not preserving older legislation for its own sake when he included in his code of 681 the *Antiquae* dealing with overseas merchants.[5] These men were no doubt generally subject to Visigothic law when they came into contact with the natives of the kingdom, but they were certainly free from its rule when they fell out among themselves: their own law was then applied by officials known as *telonarii*, who may also have acted as collectors of the custom-duties.[6] The merchants employed native slaves 'pro vegetando conmercio', hiring them from their masters at a statutory rate of three *solidi* per annum, but strictly forbidden, on pain of lashing and fine, to remove them abroad.[7] As for the native merchants with whom they dealt, indirect evidence points to the Jews as the merchant class *par excellence*.[8] It has been noted above that Jews formed an important element of the population of Narbonne in 589, together with Greeks and Syrians,[9] and Tarragona, certain to have been prominent in trading activities, was later to be known by the Arabs as 'the city of the Jews'.[10] The canons and laws which, as we saw earlier, throughout the century repeatedly forbade

---

[1] Ildefonsus, *DVI* 14. According to the unconfirmed report of *Crón. Alfonso III* c. 3, Ervig was the son of a Greek refugee.

[2] *HG* 70: 'Sed postquam Sisebutus princeps regni sumpsit sceptra...non solum terras, sed et ipsa maria suis armis adeant'. In fact, a fleet of sorts was already in existence in Leovigild's day: see C. Torres, 'Mirón', p. 200.

[3] See above, p. 76, and *Crón. Alfonso III* c. 3.

[4] See, e.g., XII. 2. 18 (Egica).

[5] XI. 3. 1–4.         [6] XI. 3. 2: see Thompson, *Goths*, p. 126.

[7] XI. 3. 3, 4.

[8] But cf. the general reference of IV. 2. 16: 'Quod vero maritus...de extraneorum lucris...conquisivit'.

[9] The Jews were still in Septimania a century later: cf., e.g., Julian of Toledo, *Insultatio* 2, *HW* 28, XVII Tol. *Tomus* and the inscription mentioned above, p. 170, n. 1.         [10] J. M. Millas Vallicrosa, *Sefarad*, XVII (1957), 9.

Jews the purchase and possession of Christian slaves were perhaps the more frequently infringed because the slave-trade was traditionally in Jewish hands.[1] If the Jews were constantly on the move throughout the land, engaged in their commercial dealings, particular point is given to Ervig's detailed regulation of their travel.[2] Egica's law denying unconverted Jews the right to engage in foreign or internal commerce appears against this background as a drastic attempt to cut away the very roots of Jewish economic well-being.[3] One might speculate that the chaotic state of the currency in the last years of the kingdom's existence was not unconnected with a dislocation of overseas trade effected by anti-Jewish legislation which eventually forced the Jews into treason.[4]

Of internal trade we know next to nothing.[5] Travel by river, in those places where the geography permitted, was not fast – it took Fructuosus three days to travel down the Guadalquivir from Seville to Cadiz, a distance of nearly one hundred miles overland[6] – but no doubt safer than that by road, with the danger of brigands.[7] Free navigation of the larger rivers, used by fishing-boats and trading-vessels, was insisted upon in the code, which forbade a riparian owner to erect an obstruction extending more than halfway across the waterway or blocking the only channel.[8] The maintenance of the

[1] III Tol. 14 seems to except the purchase of slaves for trade, since it only forbids Jewish purchase 'in usos proprios'. But the actual evidence of Jewish slave-trading in the Visigothic kingdom is slim: apart from XII. 2. 14, with an allusion to Jewish possession of foreign slaves, there is only, to my knowledge, *Reg.* VII. 21, concerning the purchase of slaves in Narbonne *c.* 597 by Jews, who were perhaps traders.

[2] Above, p. 135.

[3] XII. 2. 18: see also above, p. 143. The law permitted truly converted Jews 'mercandi usu properare ad cataplum et cum christianis agere christiano more commercium', but warned others that 'nec ad cataplum pro transmarinis commerciis faciendis ulterius audeant properare nec cum christianis quodcumque negotium...peragere'. Cf. also XVI Tol. *Tomus.* For the term *cataplus*, see also *HF* IV. 43 and generally F. Vercauteren, *Bulletin du Cange*, II (1925), 98–101, who considers that in the Toledan text it signifies 'un endroit où l'on traite des affaires commerciales, une espèce de bourse' (p. 101): see also the discussion printed in *Sett.*, VI (1959), 395–6.

[4] For the currency, see Grierson, 'Visigothic metrology', pp. 82, 86.

[5] 'In conventu mercantium' in IX. 2. 4 has nothing to do with merchants, but means simply 'in the market-place'.

[6] *VSF* 14.

[7] For *latrones* see IX. 1. 19 and for the robbery of travellers below, in text.

[8] VIII. 4. 29, on the vulgar law context of which see Levy, *Law of property*, p. 124. When two riparian owners were involved, hindrances had to be staggered to allow thoroughfare.

post argues for the continued upkeep of the roads, possibly by corvées:[1] it was an offence to bar the public highways by fences or other hindrances or to encroach upon the sixty-foot stretch of land which had to be kept clear on either side of the road.[2] Several laws were concerned with the rights and responsibilities of travellers.[3] A traveller might pull down a fence or wall which he found obstructing the highway,[4] and was entitled to use unenclosed land, and even uncultivated land marked off as private by ditches, for pasturing his animals: permission from the owner was required only when he stayed for more than two days. Small, non-glandiferous trees might be felled for fodder, and the branches of others lopped, and the owner of the land was penalised if he impounded or drove out the animals.[5] If cultivated land near a river-crossing was not enclosed, the traveller was not responsible for damage which he or his animals might cause,[6] and the same probably applied when the land was near a highway.[7] It is understandable, then, that the destruction of fences was treated seriously.[8] In any case, the traveller was not liable for damage caused by his entry on to cultivated land when passage was otherwise impossible.[9] He might light a fire with wood from the place where he rested, although he had to be careful to prevent it from spreading and causing injury or damage, for which he was, of course, accountable.[10] He received some compensation for injuries inflicted by snares or pits,[11] and was extended protection against unlawful detention, manhandling, theft or robbery.[12] It is tempting to see these provisions as evidence of a considerable volume of internal trade, and the traveller with his pack-animals is, indeed, perhaps directly referred to in one law.[13] But the traveller for whose

[1] Above, pp. 64–5, 71.

[2] VIII. 4. 24, 25. In both cases the amount of the fine (paid to the fisc) depended upon status.

[3] On the following, see Melicher, *Kampf*, pp. 183–4, Levy, *Law of property*, pp. 125–6: parallels and later developments are discussed in J. Beneyto Pérez, *Estudios sobre la hist. del régimen agrario* (Barcelona, 1941), pp. 109ff.

[4] VIII. 4. 24.   [5] VIII. 3. 9, 4. 26, 27.   [6] VIII. 4. 28.

[7] Cf. VIII. 4. 25, requiring the fencing or ditching of land adjoining the clear stretches on both sides of the roads. But the immediate aim was probably to prevent the encroachment of cropland.

[8] Cf. VIII. 3. 6, 7 – but with difficulties of reconciliation.   [9] VIII. 3. 9.

[10] VIII. 2. 3.   [11] Below, p. 216, n. 6.   [12] Cf. VI. 4. 4, VII. 2. 17, VIII. 1. 12.

[13] VIII. 4. 27: 'Iter agentibus...deponere sarcina et iumenta vel boves pascere non vetentur'. Dahn, *Bausteine*, pp. 312–13, related the laws to foreign travellers.

benefit the laws were chiefly intended should probably rather be identified as the herdsman moving periodically with his animals from the lowlands to the summer pastures in the hills and back again.[1] That preference for the interests of graziers over crop-raisers which was to be such an arresting feature of later Spanish history was already, it would seem, in evidence.

That there was an overall decline in town life in the Visigothic kingdom can hardly be doubted.[2] Many towns had been devastated already during the third-century invasions, and although only the north-west suffered to any significant extent in the attacks two centuries later, the economic dislocation brought about by the break-up of the Empire could scarcely have failed to affect the trading towns of the eastern littoral.[3] Several towns in the south and east, Cartagena among them, were ruined as the result of Visigothic conflict with the Byzantines in the early seventh century,[4] and others in Baetica and Carthaginensis became mere shadows of their former selves during the century's course:[5] the plagues of locusts which ravaged the second province were no doubt in part a cause.[6] It is difficult to believe that the rise of Islam did not have some adverse effect upon urban life in the peninsula. Nevertheless, Toledo, considerably expanded from the twelve acres or so of Roman times, was restored 'mire et eleganti labore' as late as the reign of Wamba.[7] Merida flourished also, at least in the late sixth century, when its church was the richest in Spain, and there is no evidence of its decline in the seventh.[8] Both Leovigild and Svintila

[1] J. Klein, *The Mesta* (Cambridge, Mass., 1920), pp. 18, 301, clearly agrees.
[2] Generally on the sixth- and seventh-century towns, see J. M. Lacarra, 'Panorama de la hist. urbana en la península ibérica desde el siglo V al X', *Sett.*, VI (1959), 331–45. Hispano-Roman towns had in any case been small by comparison with their counterparts of Gaul: Merida, the largest, was no more than 300 acres at the very most (ib., p. 321). For the cities of Septimania see A. Dupont, *Les cités de la Narbonnaise Première depuis les invasions germaniques jusqu'à l'apparition du Consulat* (Nîmes, 1942), pp. 225–45.
[3] See Lacarra, 'Panorama', pp. 322–30; to the literature concerning the third-century invasions on p. 322, in n. 2, add J. M. Blázquez, 'La crisis del siglo III en Hispania y Mauritania Tingitana', *Hispania*, XXVIII (1968), 5–37.
[4] Fredegar, IV. 33, *Etym.* XV. 1. 67 (Cartagena).
[5] Lacarra, 'Panorama', pp. 340–2.          [6] See below, p. 211.
[7] Lacarra, 'Panorama', pp. 321, 339, *CH* 46. See also P. de Palol, *Arte hispánico de la época visigoda* (Barcelona, 1968), pp. 100–2 (in the English version).
[8] Lacarra, 'Panorama', pp. 337–8, *VPE* IV. 5. 3. The dearth of seventh-century inscriptions is not in my view evidence of decline, as Riché, p. 323, suggests.

actually refounded towns, and not in every case for a military purpose.[1]

Government in the towns was in the hands of officers who have already been mentioned – the *comes civitatis* and his vicar, the *defensor* and the *numerarius*: alongside these stood, of course, the bishop. The curials perhaps still had some minor functions to perform in the early seventh century, but they appear after that time in only one law, of Chindasvind, where their rank is not shown to have been anything but honorary, and they can justifiably be assumed to have disappeared altogether by Ervig's day.[2] We are ill-informed as to the quality of life in the towns. The games still flourished in the first quarter of the seventh century,[3] but the probable erection of a church in the amphitheatre at Tarragona in the late sixth century shows the change which the moral climate was undergoing:[4] the severity of punishment meted out to the town prostitute is a further measure of that change.[5] The requirements of the poor had no doubt not altered greatly by Ervig's reign from what they had been a century before, when Bishop Masona of Merida had dispensed wine, oil and honey.[6] The two chief hazards faced by the town-dweller were, as they had long been and were long to remain, fire and disease. The town house of a man like the *dominus* of III. 4. 17, with his *villa* in the country, was doubtless a substantial affair, but most houses, we may believe, would have been humble structures of wood, or wood and

[1] Both Victoriacum (John of Biclar, 581. 3) and Ologicus (*HG* 63) were part of the military complex guarding the north against the Basques: see Vigil and Barbero, pp. 319–21, who suggest the first to be the modern Iruña, near Vitoria, and the second Olite, south of Pamplona, and both to have been refoundations. For the large city of Reccopolis (John of Biclar, 578. 4, *HG* 51), also a refoundation and situated near Zorita de los Canes, sixty kilometres east of Madrid, see the three articles entitled 'Studien zu Reccopolis' by, respectively, K. Raddatz, D. Claude and L. Vázquez de Parga in *Madrider Mitteilungen*, V (1964), 213–33, VI (1965), 167–94, and VIII (1967), 259–80, where the archaeological finds, historical evidence and question of identification are exhaustively discussed.

[2] See above, p. 66, n. 2.

[3] Cf. *EW* 7 (where Lacarra, 'Panorama', p. 336, n. 21, suggests *taurorum* for *faunorum*), and note also VIII. 4. 4: 'Animal aut quemcumque quadrupedem, qui ad istadium fortasse servatur...vel bovem'.

[4] On the church and its suggested date see S. Ventura Solsona, *AEA*, XXVII (1954), 273–80. For the militarisation of the amphitheatre at Nîmes, see Dupont, p. 229.

[5] III. 4. 17. The free prostitute received 300 lashes – the highest number of the code – and was banished from the town: a further offence brought another lashing and enslavement. The *ancilla* suffered scalping in addition.        [6] *VPE* V. 3. 7.

stone, like those of contemporary Gaul,[1] and therefore at severe risk in the event of fire. Precisely because of the disastrous general effect which his action might therefore have, the fire-raiser operating in the *civitas* was treated with extreme harshness: execution by burning was his fate, with compensation paid from his estate to the victims of his activities.[2] His counterpart of the countryside escaped more lightly, being required to make good the damage and to suffer one hundred lashes.[3] The other great danger, disease, especially plague, must have kept the doctors busy, for the law insisted that only in the case of a charge of killing should the community be deprived of their services by their pre-trial imprisonment.[4] The statutory establishment of twelve *solidi* as the fee to be paid to the doctor who undertook the training of a student was perhaps an attempt to ensure that the supply of physicians would not be cut off as the result of overcharging by the doctors:[5] it is difficult to find any other reason for this unusual provision. The medical profession was lucrative, to judge from the fee of five *solidi* laid down for the removal of a cataract,[6] although when treatment was consequent upon a written agreement, payment was dependent upon success.[7] But it was also potentially dangerous,

[1] See R. Latouche, *The birth of Western economy* (London, 1967), pp. 115–16.

[2] VIII. 2. 1. But perhaps he could purchase his life, for if a victim was found to have exaggerated the extent of the damage, he was required to deliver double the value of the excess to the original payer of compensation. Is the arsonist meant, or rather his heir?

[3] Ib., VIII. 2. 2: but cf. VIII. 3. 5 for vineyards and VIII. 3. 6, 7, for fences. That the slave should escape execution, wherever the scene of his operations, if his master paid compensation for the damage, but suffer it if his master did not, appears remarkable, but is in fact wholly reasonable, for the master could not be made to pay – for he could always deliver the criminous slave – and clearly would not if he was also to lose the slave. The slave was always lashed, however.

[4] XI. 1. 8.                              [5] XI. 1. 7: see also Riché, p. 298.

[6] XI. 1. 5. But why should only this operation have been dealt with by the law? Were cataracts particularly common? Cf. *HF* v. 6 for a Frankish case. Apart from phlebotomy, the only other operation appearing, to my knowledge, in the Visigothic sources is the Caesarean performed by Paul of Merida (of Greek origin) to remove the dead fetus of what appears to have been an ectopic pregnancy: see *VPE* IV. 2 passim. The episode shows that the practice of medicine was forbidden to the clergy: Fernández Alonso, *Cura pastoral*, pp. 178–80. For a hospital founded by another bishop of Merida, Masona, see *VPE* v. 3. 4–6, and for a doctor's epitaph from (perhaps sixth-century) Merida, Vives, *Inscripciones*, no. 288. For Isidore, see W. D. Sharpe, *Isidore of Seville: the medical writings*, Transactions of the American Philosophical Society, new series, LIV, part II (Philadelphia, 1964), with a translation of the relevant parts of the *Etym*.                              [7] XI. 1. 3, 4.

for the doctor who bled a free patient and thereby caused his death suffered the extreme penalty of delivery into the power of the deceased's family, to be treated at their pleasure.[1] Whatever may be thought of the role of the towns in the Visigothic kingdom, there can be no doubt that the centre of the economic picture was occupied by the villages and *villae* of the countryside. It seems very likely, from the appearance in Ervig's code of Eurician provisions concerning the original division of lands between Goths and Romans in Aquitaine, that the movement of the barbarians into Spain had been followed by a division along the same lines.[2] The details of this are, however, far from clear.[3] The laws refer to the 'two parts' taken by the Goths as their *sortes*, and to the 'thirds' of the Romans:[4] as in the Burgundian kingdom, therefore, the settlers took the lion's share of each estate divided.[5] Wasteland and wood-

[1] XI. 1. 6. Other laws insisted that a doctor be accompanied when he tended public officials in prison, lest they should seek death at his hands (XI. 1. 2), and that he should not bleed a woman in the absence of witnesses, except in emergency (XI. 1. 1). For brief comments on the Visigothic laws see J. L. Cassani, 'La medicina romana en Esp. y su enseñanza', *CHE*, XII (1949), 63, 67.

[2] The usual view: see, e.g., Torres, *Lecciones*, II, 93–4, Jones, *Empire*, I, 253, Thompson, *Goths*, p. 133. But d'Ors, *Código*, p. 174, is doubtful. Compare *Chron. Caesaraug. reliquiae* ad a. 497: 'Gotthi intra Hispanias sedes acceperunt' with Hidatius, 69, concerning the 418–419 settlement: 'Gothi...sedes acceperunt'. But I do not agree with Thompson, loc. cit., that Ervig's addition to X. 1. 6 has anything to do with *hospitalitas*: indeed, the original law is not necessarily to do with it.

[3] The fullest discussion is in A. García Gallo, 'Notas sobre el reparto de tierras entre visigodos y romanos', *Hispania*, I (1940–1), no. IV, 40–63. But I do not follow his view (pp. 53–63) that the division was on the same lines as that alleged for the Burgundians by Lot (see below, n. 5). In particular, his interpretation of the (enormously difficult!) VIII. 5. 2 is unconvincing: much better is d'Ors, *Código*, pp. 187–8 – although I can see no reason why the *consortes* of the law should be thought of only as a Roman and a Goth.

[4] X. 1. 8: *tertiae* also in X. 1. 15, 16, 2. 1.

[5] *LB* 54. 1: 'Populus noster mancipiorum tertiam et duas terrarum partes accepit'. For the Burgundians see F. Lot, 'Du régime de l'hospitalité', *Revue belge de philologie et d'hist.*, VII (1928), 975ff. But Lot's view that the Burgundians took two-thirds of the land farmed by tenants and one-third of the domain, and that this approximated a fifty–fifty division overall, I find unconvincing. For different interpretations of the disparity between the proportions of land and of slaves taken over, see Jones, *Empire*, I, 252, n. 32, and R. Koebner in *CEH*, I, 32. But is the disparity not easily explicable in terms of the Burgundian leaders' need to settle their clients and the Romans' need for more slaves on their other lands at a time when many had taken to flight? The divisions have not been sufficiently considered from the point of view of their possible economic benefit to Roman landowners faced with a depleted labour force and high taxes.

land sometimes remained undivided and in common use,[1] but when they were apportioned, either by agreement or as the consequence of individual initiative in assarting or enclosing, there is no reason to think that the allocation was of equal shares rather than in these same proportions.[2] Once made, the division could not be overthrown: usurpation was, of course, forbidden, but a fifty-year limitation period strengthened the prohibition.[3] As for *coloni*, slaves, livestock, dwellings and so on, we are wholly uninformed, although undoubtedly the Goths took over a proportion of these with the lands.

It is not to be thought that each and every Roman landowner in Spain suffered the loss of two-thirds of his land:[4] it would have been quite impossible for the small peasant farmers to have borne such a deprivation, and it is the larger landowners alone whom we should believe to have been affected, and they not on all their estates.[5] In any case, the archaeological evidence quite clearly shows that the original Gothic settlements were restricted to northern-central Spain,[6]

[1] VIII. 5. 5, X. 1. 9.

[2] X. 1. 9 by no means necessarily indicates a fifty–fifty division, as in the Burgundian kingdom (*LB* 54. 2). It declares that if part of the undivided woodland is brought under cultivation by Goth or Roman – 'si adhuc silva superest, unde paris meriti terra eius, cui debetur, portioni debeat conpensari, silvam accipere non recuset. Si autem paris meriti, que conpensetur, silva non fuerit, quod ad culturam excisum est dividatur'. The law establishes that the land taken by the non-cultivator be of the same quality as his partner's, but says nothing of the extent of the area of the portion. The object was to prevent – say – the Roman from taking a third composed entirely of good land and leaving poor-quality land to the Goth. A 2:1 ratio is shown, on the other hand, in X. 1. 8, without distinction of arable and woodland: 'Divisio...facta de portione terrarum sive silvarum nulla ratione turbetur...ne de duabus partibus Goti...aut de tertia Romani...sibi aliquid audeat usurpare aut vindicare [Romanus aut Gotus]'. See also VIII. 5. 2 and on it d'Ors, *Código*, pp. 177, 187–8. Further, Pérez Pujol, II, 149 and IV, 350–1, and d'Ors, *Código*, pp. 176–8, whose argument from X. 1. 6 I do not, however, accept. [3] X. 1. 8, 15, 16, 2. 1.

[4] As thought by Torres, *Lecciones*, II, 92–3, and apparently by C. Verlinden, 'Le grand domaine dans les états ibériques chrétiens au MA', *Recueils de la Société Jean Bodin*, IV: *Le domaine* (Wetteren, 1949), p. 179.

[5] For southern France see García Gallo, 'Reparto de tierras', pp. 44–51, and M. Garaud, 'L'occupation du Poitou par les wisigoths', *Bulletin de la Société des Antiquaires de l'Ouest*, 3rd series, XIV (1945), 555–6. Cf. for the Burgundians Marius of Avenches, *Chron.* ad a. 456: 'Terras...cum Gallis *senatoribus* diviserunt'. Were some fiscal (emphyteutic?) lands also divided? Cf. X. 1. 16, with its allusion to clearly non-private *villici*.

[6] See W. Reinhart, 'Sobre el asentamiento de los visigodos en la península', *AEA*, XVIII (1945), 124–39: further, idem, 'Territorialität', pp. 351–2, and d'Abadal, 'Legs visigothique', pp. 545ff. The appearance at III Tol. of Arian bishops from the

although garrison troops and administrators would naturally have been found elsewhere. Again, it is really inconceivable that each and every Gothic warrior received land at the expense of an individual Roman: there would not have been enough land to go round.[1] It may well be that the barbarian war-leaders settled their men on the *sortes* which they themselves received,[2] either giving them land as *buccellarii* or keeping them in their households, in Germanic fashion, as *saiones*,[3] and that those Goths who were not clients took group possession of *sortes* on other large estates or established settlements of their own,[4] perhaps taking up residence in areas from which the Romans had fled or been driven, perhaps bringing back under cultivation lands abandoned at an earlier time.[5] It is perfectly clear that the *vicini* referred to in several *Antiquae* – laws originally addressed to the Goths alone – were not neighbouring landowners with considerable estates, but men in close and constant relationship with one another, villagers, and therefore that many Goths lived in village communities.[6] What is not evidenced in any law is the existence of a Germanic *Markgenossenschaft* system, compulsory regulation of the arable by the villagers and the like.[7]

But the original division between Goths and Romans could certainly no longer have been of pressing relevance in Ervig's day,

cities of other areas – Barcelona, Tortosa, Valencia, as well as Galician cities (for a map of all the bishoprics represented see Fontaine, 'Conversion', facing p. 124) – is in my view best explained in terms of Leovigild's campaign for religious unification – and perhaps of its success. One cannot believe that Gothic garrison troops alone constituted the flocks. The toponymical evidence shows the vast majority of Gothic place-names to occur in the north and north-west, but both E. Gamillscheg, *Romania Germanica*, I (Berlin–Leipzig, 1934), 360–1, and J. M. Piel, 'Toponimia germánica', *Enciclopedia lingüística hispánica*, ed. M. Alvar et al., I (Madrid, 1960), 541–3, place the movement into these areas in the post-711 period (although they disagree as to the date).

[1] Garaud, loc. cit. p. 205, n. 5, and Thompson, *Goths*, p. 133.
[2] See Thompson, 'Fritigern to Euric', pp. 120–1, on the Aquitaine settlement. But not *only* the optimates received lands, I think.
[3] Note *buccellarii* and *saiones* already in *CE* 310, 311.
[4] See Torres, *Lecciones*, II, 94.
[5] For the absence of *agri deserti* from the barbarian compilations, see Levy, *Law of property*, pp. 124–5.
[6] Cf. VIII. 3. 13, 15, 16, 4. 16, 17, X. 3. 2 etc.
[7] The texts adduced by Melicher, *Kampf*, pp. 232–42, do not support his thesis to the contrary. See also Beneyto Pérez, *Estudios*, pp. 63–4, and note in particular VIII. 5. 5, where a *consors* gained rights of private ownership simply by enclosure of his share of the waste.

especially after a century of intermarriage between the two races, and only four laws in the chapter *De divisionibus et terris ad placitum datis* are in fact expressly concerned with it.[1] It might be considered that the divisions in mind in the chapter were in part those made by groups of Goths at the original settlement or by bands of men who had together attacked and cleared virgin forest and waste,[2] but the apportionment of chief, because constant, significance must have been that of a decedent's estate among his heirs.[3] Sometimes division was not made in such a case but the arable farmed as a joint concern: this must most regularly have occurred when the heirs were the dead person's children.[4] And even when the arable was divided, the woodland and pastureland were sometimes – perhaps usually – left unapportioned for the common use of the *consortes*.[5] Division agreements were often reduced to writing, but the written record was solely probative, and the evidence of witnesses served perfectly well in its stead.[6] When several individuals were involved in a division, the twin features of superiority of status and majority of numbers

[1] X. 1. 8, 9, 15 (above, p. 66), 16. It should be stressed that the appearance of the term *consortes* does not indicate that the law containing it is necessarily connected with the Goth/Roman division. *Consortes* meant nothing but 'partners', in the sense of those who shared in something: Reccared and Hermenegild were 'consortes regni' (John of Biclar, 573. 5), and a thief's *consors* was his accomplice (VII. 1. 3). For X. 1. 4 see n. 4, below. I know no text (X. 3. 5 included) where *consortes* is indubitably used to designate the Goth and Roman in a relationship of *hospitalitas*. But this is not to deny that its general scope included such partners, even though in VIII. 5. 5 the phrase 'consortes...vel ospites' points to two separate categories, *hospites* being (see Jones, *Empire*, I, 250) the term used of both partners in a barbarian/Roman division.

[2] Cf. especially X. 1. 3: 'Si plures fuerint in divisione consortes, quod a multis vel melioribus iuste constitutum est, a paucis vel deterioribus non convenit aliquatenus inmutari'. *Meliores* and *deteriores* weigh against a division between a deceased's children, though differently Melicher, *Kampf*, p. 260.

[3] Cf. the Ervigian addition to II. 1. 26: 'Quod si divisionem quisque cupiens celebrare dilationem ab erede suo pertulerit...'.

[4] Cf. III. 1. 8: '[Soror] portionem suam, sive divisam sive non divisam, quam de facultate parentum fuerat consecutura, amittat' and on this, and generally, L. G. de Valdeavellano, *La comunidad patrimonial de la familia en el derecho esp. medieval* (Salamanca, 1956), pp. 23–4 (with pp. 9–23 on Roman and Germanic precedents). Melicher, *Kampf*, pp. 258–61, is exaggerated. Note that several *consortes* own a slave in common in V. 7. 2 and that X. 1. 4 abrogates the earlier provision that all *consortes* (= *coheredes*) should appear in court cases 'pro comunibus rebus'. See also X. 1. 14.      [5] VIII. 5. 2, 5.

[6] X. 1. 1, 2 (but why only *divisio inter fratres* in the latter?): see *FV* 33 for a document recording the division of a parental estate.

were apparently decisive in establishing its terms.[1] Breach of the division agreement was punished in accordance with the general laws on *invasio*.[2] But genuine mistakes as to the ownership of land could easily occur between *consortes*, and the law took care to provide that a man who built a house or planted a vineyard in the portion of his *consors*, wrongly believing the land to be his own, should suffer no ill-effects but keep the exploited plot on payment to the true owner of a parcel of equivalent basic value: only if he acted in deliberate defiance of the owner's representations did he forfeit all right to the product of his efforts.[3] The man who planted a vineyard on the property of someone whose *consors* he was not, on the other hand, lost it without further ado, being regarded by the legislator as fortunate not to be punished for *invasio*.[4]

*Invasio* was the deliberate and unauthorised occupation of immovables in the possession of another. If the *invasio* was of property to which the offender had no claim, his obligation was to restore what had been usurped and additionally to hand over property of equal value: if, on the other hand, it was of property to which the invader had a right, his extrajudicial action resulted in the loss of his claim, to the benefit of the man who had previously held wrongful possession.[5] It was no excuse, in other words, to plead mere anticipation of a court order.[6] These were severe consequences which show the determined concern of the kings both to protect property-holders against the open greed of others and to prevent the anarchy which would have threatened if private individuals had been permitted to take the law into their own hands. Precisely the same penalties befell the man who conveyed land in his possession but owned or rightfully claimed by another, or land in the possession of another, to a third. The general rule in such cases was that the deceived recipient, obliged to yield up the property, received back from the *auctor* of the transaction the purchase price, together with compensation for his labour in exploiting the land and whatever *pena* might have been established

---

[1] Above, p. 207, n. 2.  [2] X. 1. 5.
[3] X. 1. 6.
[4] X. 1. 7: cf. X. 1. 13. See on X. 1. 6, 7, Levy, *Law of property*, pp. 94–5, who, however, relates the former only to the Goth/Roman division.
[5] VIII. 1. 2: cf. V. 6. 1, VIII. 1. 4, 5, X. 1. 5, 14, 3. 4, 5, and *FV* 35. Penalties were harsher when the *invasio* was of a house *absente domino*: VIII. 1. 7.
[6] Cf. also VI. 5. 14, *in fine*.

for the event of eviction.[1] But the sole Ervigian contribution to the chapter *De divisionibus* made an important amendment to this rule, providing that when an owner delayed court action to recover his property – as it was clearly in his interests to do, since the longer he waited the more developed the property would become, at no cost to himself – the estate should remain with its holder, the alienator paying double its value to the owner.[2] This represented an equitable concession to the interests of the exploiter of the land, who no longer stood to lose what he had produced by months or years of labour and yet perhaps to receive no compensation but the enslaved person of an impecunious alienator.[3]

The related matter of tampering with the boundaries of estates naturally also received the attention of the legislators. The boundaries were marked by special landmarks (*arca*), banks of earth, inscribed stones or trees with the letter 'X' cut into them.[4] These markers were of paramount importance in the resolution of disputes, and not only legal but conciliar texts refer to their examination by boundary-inspectors.[5] The rule was that all markers be left 'sicut antiquitus videntur esse constructi',[6] and deliberate tampering with them was harshly treated: a guilty freeman paid no less than twenty *solidi* for each marker which he destroyed or moved, while a slave received fifty lashes.[7] When a marker was accidentally overthrown – during ploughing, for example – it had to be replaced by the man responsible in the presence of the *vicini*.[8] New markers might be set up as the result of the sworn evidence of the older and more knowledgeable inhabitants when boundaries were not clearly indicated, but to erect one in the absence of the neighbouring party involved (*consors*) or the inspector was punishable as *invasio*.[9]

Not all freemen held their lands in full ownership. We have already had occasion to mention the royal, ecclesiastical and patronal concessions of property in return for services. But other grants were

[1] See v. 4. 8, 9, 20, and below, pp. 254–5.
[2] X. 1. 6.
[3] It was also, incidentally, in the interests of the alienator, for he escaped payment of compensation and of the penalty for eviction.
[4] X. 3. 3: for 'X's (*decuriae*), see also VIII. 6. 1.
[5] X. 3. 4 (on which difficult law see d'Ors, *Código*, pp. 196–9), X. 3. 5, II Sev. 2, Mer. 8.
[6] X. 3. 1.
[7] X. 3. 2. For the even more severe Roman penalties see d'Ors, *Código*, p. 195.
[8] X. 3. 2.          [9] X. 3. 5.

made in the direct economic interests of the landlord. Leases for a determined number of years were certainly made,[1] leases for life or lives almost certainly and perpetual leases very probably.[2] Services, rent – normally, it appears, a tithe of the produce of the holding – or both were required from the tenant, who forfeited the *beneficium* in the event of non-fulfilment of his obligations.[3] Such a provision strongly implies that the owner had no right to dispossess the lessee if he was not in breach of the terms of the agreement by which he held,[4] and it is significant in this respect that the law says nothing of forfeiture as the penalty for a tenant who exceeded his rights by bringing under cultivation land which was not the subject of the *placitum*: the landlord had a simple choice between repossessing the land and leaving it with his lessee on payment of an increased *canon*.[5] A detailed law provided for an oath by the grantor or his heirs as to the extent of the land leased when dispute arose about this – for tenancy agreements were not necessarily in writing[6] – or, if they were unable or unwilling to take such an oath, for a fixed amount of the whole estate to be deemed the lessee's rightful holding.[7]

'Bene pascere et bene arare', the two activities in which Isidore declared the wealth of the ancients to have consisted,[8] were no less

[1] x. 1. 12: 'Si per precariam epistulam certus annorum numerus fuerit conprehensus....'.
[2] I cannot agree with Levy, *Law of property*, pp. 90–2, that perpetual leases are evidenced by certain *Antiquae*, particularly x. 1. 11: see Merêa, *Estudos*, pp. 186–9, and on the general character of x. 1. 11 idem, 'Sobre a precária visigótica e suas derivações imediatas', *RPH*, IV (1949), 288–9, and Gama Barros, VII, 114. The most shown by the letter of the laws x. 1. 13 and 14 is a lease of fairly long duration and valid despite the landlord's death. But no law denies the existence of perpetual leases, which, on the grounds of the prior Roman regime and of the situation elsewhere, should be accepted as very probable: see Gama Barros, VII, 117, 119, and Levy, *Law of property*, pp. 43–9 (late Roman), 92–4 (Vandals and Franks). No time limit appears in *FV* 36 and 37.
[3] x. 1. 11 speaks of expulsion only in the event of non-payment of the annual *canon placiti*: but cf. x. 1. 19, providing for double payment of the tithe or services due in the case of delay (as penalty or as alternative to expulsion?). A tithe appears also in *FV* 37 (where it stands alone as 'prisca consuetudo') and 36 (where it is combined with *exenia* as payment 'ut colonis est consuetudo', and where the tenant promises also to assist the grantor's interests, accepting expulsion as the penalty for breach of these terms, like the lessee of *FV* 37).
[4] But cf. Merêa, 'Precária', p. 290, n. 11.
[5] x. 1. 13: but cf. x. 1. 14, *in fine*.      [6] x. 1. 19.
[7] x. 1. 14. The size of the land-unit described here as an *aratrum* is unknown, although clearly greater than fifty *iugera*.
[8] *Etym.* XVII. 2. 1.

the essential bases of economic well-being in his own day. It goes without saying that the principal crop raised on the cultivable lands of the kingdom was corn, but it is the sad, although hardly surprising, fact that despite many references to the arable lands (*terrae*), to the standing crops (*messes*), to threshing-floors (*areae*) and so on, the code gives precious few details of the system of cultivation practised,[1] so that if there had been innovations since Roman times we do not know of them.[2] It is to be assumed that the basic regime continued to be that imposed by the climatic features of most of the country – dry-farming, with half the land left fallow every other year so that it might regain strength and, in particular, retain moisture. The repeated ploughing which this method of husbandry demanded was undertaken by the traditional ox or, on the lighter soils, by the ass or perhaps the cow.[3] The bulk of the sowing would have taken place by the end of November and, barring misfortunes like hailstorms – whether or not attributable to the incantations of sorcerers[4] – or the intrusion of animals, the crops would normally have been ripe for the reaping by the following June. Harvest-time was in fact between 18 July and 18 August – except in the province of Carthaginensis, where the devastations of the locusts made necessary an earlier harvest, between 17 June and 1 August – and of such fundamental significance in the life of society that, as we have seen, the period was treated, subject to certain qualifications, as a legal holiday:[5] even the bishops in the neighbourhood of Toledo were excused from their duty of attendance upon the metropolitan at harvest-time.[6] The use of horse- and ox-power for threshing the corn was well established: the comparative lightness of the penalty imposed for the use of someone else's animal for this purpose is probably to be explained as the consequence of a sensible recognition that great speed was necessary at the threshing stage, lest rain or windstorm should destroy the fruits of a man's labours, and that this was a considerable factor in extenuation of the offence.[7] Both theft from, and damage to, the

---

[1] The *Etym.* are virtually worthless, despite Pérez Pujol, IV, 364–6.

[2] An excellent account of Roman cereal husbandry now in K. D. White, *Roman farming* (London, 1970), pp. 173–89.

[3] See below, in text.      [4] Cf. VI. 2. 4.

[5] II. 1. 12. But why the longer period in Carthaginensis? To provide for cases where the crop was late? For locusts in Carpetania, see *HF* VI. 33, 44.

[6] VII Tol. 6.     [7] See below, p. 217, for unlawful use, and White, p. 184, for speed.

mills were dealt with in the code.[1] The diversion of water was a serious matter less because it removed the power-source of some of these mills than because it affected the irrigation system upon which much farming wholly depended.[2]

A further legal holiday – and a further consequent dispensation from the episcopal duty of attendance in Toledo – occurred during the period of the vintage, from 17 September to 18 October.[3] Vineyards rival arable lands in frequency of mention in the code, and were clearly of outstanding importance. The vine received, indeed, especial protection from the law, which provided that the deliberate destruction of a vineyard render the offender liable to hand over two others of the same value, with the affected land remaining with its owner. Grapes which were unlawfully gathered had to be restored *in duplo*, the amount taken being established by the oath of the vintagers.[4] Even allowing for the steady demand provided by the Church and for a perhaps considerable export trade, it is difficult to resist the impression that wine had become the staple drink.[5] In those areas where it could not be produced, Isidore tells us, the people drank *caelia*, a traditional alcoholic beverage made from wheat.[6]

The third principal crop raised in Roman Spain had been the olive,[7] but there are surprisingly few references to it in the code and other sources. Nevertheless, its role was – and is – such a basic one in the Mediterranean diet that it is highly improbable that the extent of the land given over to its cultivation had diminished, and what allusions there are bear witness to its continuing function as a dietary essential. A sure indication of this is provided by the appearance of

---

[1] VII. 2. 12 (theft) and VIII. 4. 30, providing that if the damage was not repaired within twenty days the culprit should be flogged and pay twenty *solidi* on top of the original twenty.

[2] For water-mills, see VIII. 4. 30: 'Eadem et de istagnis, que sunt circa mulina, et conclusiones aquarum precipimus custodiri'. Irrigation in the areas of low precipitation is expressly referred to in VIII. 4. 31: 'De furantibus aquas ex decursibus alienis': cf. also *FV* 8, 21: 'Aquarum...ductibus'. One *solidus* had to be paid for every four hours' supply of water diverted when the flow was considerable, and one *tremis* when it was less so, while the water had also to be replaced.

[3] II. I. 12, VII Tol. 6.     [4] VIII. 3. 5.

[5] It had not been popular among the natives earlier, according to Bouchier, p. 81.

[6] *Etym.* XX. 3. 18: cf. Bouchier, loc. cit.

[7] It is worth noting that even in modern times over 60% of the cultivated land of Spain is devoted to olives, wheat and vines: thus J. M. Houston, *The western Mediterranean world* (London, 1964), p. 198.

olive oil both among those agricultural commodities envisaged as the most likely objects of loan and among the provisions distributed to the poor by Masona of Merida.[1] As we have seen, there is probable evidence of its export in the sixth century.[2] Later, Ervig referred to the construction of new olive-yards, and Egica to their possession by Jews.[3] But perhaps most revealing is the valuation of the olive-tree in an amended *Antiqua* at five *solidi*, more than any other tree.[4] Next in value to olives came fruit-trees, *pomiferae*, assessed at three *solidi* each.[5] The only fruit-trees mentioned by name in the code are figs,[6] but no doubt the other fruits grown in Roman Spain – apples, pears, plums, dates and quinces[7] – were also cultivated in the orchards. Distinct from these *pomaria* and used for the production of vegetables and herbs, of which the Roman world had known a wide variety, were the *(h)orti* or kitchen-gardens.[8] In defence against pilferers and roaming animals, these were usually enclosed,[9] but it is a remarkable feature of the law that a freeman (but not a slave !) who inflicted damage upon the plants escaped with the simple payment of compensation.[10] This rule, like the similar one concerning the felling of trees,[11] underlines the privileged position held by the vine.

While fruit, herbs and vegetables provided variety of diet, honey provided virtually the only sweetening-agent.[12] The importance of apiculture was reflected in three laws, which dealt with the matters of theft from an apiary,[13] damage caused by the bees and rights to wild swarms:[14] the rule in the last case was that the man who found the colony should mark its location with a device of three crosses and by that means gain legal right to the swarm.[15] It is a justifiable guess that

[1] v. 5. 9; *VPE* v. 3. 7.     [2] *HF* iv. 43.     [3] x. 1. 6; xii. 2. 18 (Egica).
[4] viii. 3. 1. But the law concerns compositions for felling, and the very slow growth of the olive was doubtless taken into account.
[5] Ib.     [6] viii. 2. 2.     [7] The list of R. E. Smith in *CEH*, i, 441.
[8] The distinction appears in x. 1. 6. For a *pomarium* see also viii. 2. 3 and some MSS of x. 3. 2. On Roman *horti* and *pomaria* and their products, see White, pp. 246ff.
[9] viii. 3. 7.
[10] viii. 3. 2: cf. viii. 3. 7, and note the omission of reference to *horti* in viii. 3. 10.
[11] Below, in text.     [12] Note its distribution to the poor: *VPE* v. 3. 7.
[13] viii. 6. 3 (below, p. 251).
[14] viii. 6. 2 (damage: see below, p. 220), viii. 6. 1 (rights).
[15] Breach of this right involved restitution *in duplo* and twenty lashes. For similar methods of establishing rights in other times and places, see G. Clark, 'Bees in antiquity', *Antiquity*, xvi (1942), 213.

the ancient habit of mixing wine with honey was still practised,[1] especially when the wine was of poor quality, and that the wax from the combs was used, like oil, for the lighting of the churches and the houses of the better-to-do. Bees were an incidental benefit of the woodland, however. Of prime importance there were the glandifers, the acorns and nuts of which provided pannage for swine and food for humans alike. Woodland owners could profitably exploit their property, for their entitlement was to one-tenth of the number of pigs which they agreed to receive on their land for the period of the mast, and to one-twentieth of those that remained after that time.[2] Rules were laid down governing the number of pigs which might be accepted from an outside party on to woodland held in common and concerning the distribution of the *decimae* among the *consortes*.[3] From the woodland trees would come also the timber required for buildings, fences, vine-stakes and so on, and owners were naturally entitled to compensation from those who destroyed their trees,[4] although it was only when trees were carried away after felling or were deliberately burned down that a strictly penal consequence faced the offender.[5] The foliage of the trees offered fodder for the working animals when the supplies of regular green forage gave out, and twigs and branches furnished fuel for the fire: a sensible law ordered the forfeiture of the cart and oxen of a man caught making off with firewood or wood for cooperage.[6]

The importance of the woodland for the sustenance of the swine was matched by that of the waste for the nourishment of the cows, sheep and other animals, and agreements concerning pasturage rights are witnessed, apparently made on the same terms as those *pro*

---

[1] See C. Parain in *CEH*, I, 169, and *Etym.* XX. 3. 13: note also the Bronze Age example from Denmark cit. in Clark, pp. 210–11.

[2] VIII. 5. 1 (where *voluerit* is surely to be read for *noluerit* in the penultimate line): for *decimae* see also VIII. 5. 2–4. To remove the pigs before payment was treated as theft: VIII. 5. 3.

[3] VIII. 5. 2.

[4] Cf. VIII. 2. 2, 3, 3. 1, the last of which fixed the value of trees at five *solidi* for an olive, three for a *pomifera* and one or two, dependent on size, for a glandifer. Two *solidi* were paid for trees of other sorts (e.g., the pines, 'piceas arbores', of VIII. 2. 2?) when they were sizeable and in fair numbers. Injury or damage caused to persons or property by felling had also to be paid for: VIII. 3. 3, though note VIII. 3. 4.

[5] Cf. VIII. 2. 2 (burning: one hundred lashes), VIII. 3. 1 (carrying away: double payment).

[6] VIII. 3. 8.

*glandibus* for the pigs.[1] Stock-raising played a very significant role in rural life,[2] as the laws regulating the privileges and duties of travellers will already have shown. But there is no evidence of the exploitation of any breed of larger animal other than the pig for the purpose of meat-production. Oxen and other cattle figure frequently in the laws, but their function, when it appears, is regularly a work-aday one around the farm – drawing the plough or the cart, bearing burdens, treading the corn on the threshing-floor.[3] Since cattle, especially oxen, were expensive to maintain, however, and often unsatisfactory for work on the lighter soils, as in Baetica, we must assume the extensive use of donkeys and mules in their stead as well as alongside them.[4] Quite remarkably, there is not a single allusion in the code either to the useful and economical ass or to the mule, but they do appear in other texts,[5] among them a *formula* which includes ten mules and ten horses among the objects given by a nobleman in *Morgengabe* to his bride.[6] Both this *formula* and the later law which lists twenty horses among the goods which the *primates palatii* and *seniores Gothorum* were specially privileged to give in dowry[7] confirm what is indicated by other references – namely, that the horse was the most highly prized of all animals.[8] Spanish horses had always enjoyed fame,[9] and it may well be that they were still exported. But the use made of them within the kingdom was in any case extensive. It is likely that their importance stemmed primarily from their military role, but they were certainly used for the post and for personal travel,[10] for threshing and for carrying.[11] Nor can horse-racing be ruled out, in view of the survival of the games. Herds of mares kept for the breeding of mules and horses would no doubt have

[1] Compare VIII. 5. 5 with VIII. 5. 1 and 4.
[2] But it was not the preferred occupation of the Goths before 376, despite the apparent acceptance of this view by J. Vicens Vives, *An economic hist. of Spain*, trans. from 3rd Spanish edn (Princeton, N. Jersey, 1969), p. 88: see Thompson, *Visigoths in the time of Ulfila*, pp. 27–8.
[3] Cf. v. 5. 2, VIII. 3. 8, 4. 9, Narb. 4 etc. But note VIII. 4. 4.
[4] On the importance of these animals in Roman farming, see White, pp. 293ff.
[5] Cf. *VPE* v. 7. 7, Valerius, *Replicatio* 14 etc.
[6] *FV* 20.  [7] III. 1. 5.
[8] Cf. VIII. 4. 3, 5, 6 (below, p. 217, with n. 5). The *caballus* is often mentioned by name in the laws when other animals are not.
[9] Sánchez-Albornoz, 'Cabellería', p. 96.
[10] Cf. v. 4. 19 (post), II. 1. 26 (travel).
[11] Threshing: VIII. 4. 10. Carrying: v. 5. 2, *VPE* v. 7. 4, Valerius, *Ordo querimoniae* 9.

been among the principal transhumants, but sheep would have rivalled them. Whether wool was still exported in Visigothic times we cannot say, but the native working of the product naturally continued.[1] The laws rarely mention sheep, but large flocks must have been kept, for the animal was a profitable investment, yielding milk as well as its fleece, and cheap and easy to feed: it is significant that even such an important man as Fructuosus' father took a personal interest in his flocks, going up into the mountains to inspect them and to hear his shepherds' reports.[2] Of other agricultural livestock we read nothing in the laws, although camels were known,[3] and the ubiquitous goat was certainly not absent from the scene:[4] poultry, too, must have been kept for eggs and the occasional meat dish. Pork and the odd lamb apart, the only other fresh meat likely to have been available to the average man was that from domestic stock which died, or which had to be killed during the winter for want of fodder, and that from wild animals. There is silence about the chase in the code,[5] but references do appear to the digging of pits and setting of snares for trapping.[6] Fishing is mentioned in only one law, and there it is netting from boats in the larger rivers which is the matter of interest.[7]

The importance of livestock in the rural economy is perhaps best illustrated by the large number of laws which concern themselves with breaches of a man's rights in his animals and with damage or injury caused by them. The general rule was that the man who deliberately caused the death or injury of an animal should replace the beast – which he himself kept – and also pay a mulct of five *solidi* (or receive fifty lashes if he was a slave), unless his action had been provoked by damage or injury caused by the animal, when he escaped the penal saction.[8] But individual laws established a variety

---

[1] Note 'laneficia faciens' in XII. 3. 6. The importance of sheep-rearing for wool was hardly now beginning (thus González Gallego, p. 97): see Bouchier, p. 78, for earlier exports.    [2] *VSF* 2.    [3] Above, p. 196, n. 4.
[4] For goats see *VSF* 10.    [5] But cf. *VSF* 5, 10.
[6] Cf. VIII. 4. 22 (no compensation for injury to an intending thief from traps etc.), 23 (safeguards when a landowner or hunter dug pits or set snares: no indemnification for neighbours previously warned, one-third for strangers, full compensation for animals).    [7] VIII. 4. 29.
[8] VIII. 4. 8, read in conjunction with VIII. 4. 13: cf. also VIII. 3. 13, 17. Simple compensation was payable also when injury or death was brought about by negligence: cf. V. 5. 1, 2, VIII. 3. 3, 4. 23 etc.

of distinct consequences for particular offences. The killing of animals 'nocte aut occulte', for example, was treated as theft and involved ninefold restitution,[1] while that of strays whose owner was unknown made necessary repayment *in duplo*.[2] A beast's castration was similarly punished by twofold restitution.[3] To dock the tail or to cut the mane of a horse obliged the offender to payment of another horse of the same value, the injured one remaining with its owner, although if some other animal were involved composition of a single *trians* sufficed.[4] When a mare was caused to miscarry, the offender had to deliver a yearling foal, but when some other animal was involved the rule was different: a cow, for example, passed to the offender, who was required to hand over in its place a sound beast together with its calf.[5] One particularly odd misdemeanour dealt with was the tying of a skull or something similarly frightening to a horse in order to panic it: fifty lashes were inflicted on the guilty freeman, who was further obliged to replace the horse if it was injured or died as the result of its bolting.[6]

A similar complexity is to be found in the laws governing the wrongful use of another's animal. To untether it was a minor offence, involving composition of one *solidus*, but to take it away and use it was another matter: the offender had to give a further animal of the same value or, if the beast was not found by its owner within three days, to compose as a thief, which meant ninefold restitution.[7] Delivery of an additional animal appears also in another law as the penalty for the unauthorised use of an ox,[8] but only a *solidus* had to be paid if an animal was unlawfully employed on the threshing-floor.[9] Borrowed animals always had to be replaced if they died as the result of their work,[10] but a separate penalty of one *solidus* for every ten miles travelled threatened the borrower who used a beast for tasks not agreed to by its owner.[11] Rights remained in animals

---

[1] VII. 2. 23.  
[2] VIII. 5. 7.  
[3] VIII. 4. 4.  
[4] VIII. 4. 3.  
[5] VIII. 4. 5, 6. The different regimes illustrate the greater importance and value of the horse, for the mare's owner received very positive benefits. Not only could the mare which he kept be used as a foster-mother, but the colt which he received would be past the dangers of early life, already weaned and halfway, towards the age at which training might begin.  
[6] VIII. 4. 15.  
[7] VIII. 4. 1: see below, p. 253.  
[8] VIII. 4. 9.  
[9] VIII. 4. 10, for a suggested explanation of which see above, p. 211.  
[10] V. 5. 2.  
[11] VIII. 4. 2.

which had strayed. We shall see later that the impoundment of another's animals was sometimes permitted, but their unlawful detention when they had caused no damage, even though they were trespassing, was punished by a composition of one *tremis per duo capita*.[1] Naturally, this law did not concern the man who found and cared for strays until their owner turned up to collect them. Such a man was obliged to make public the fact that he had found strays, by announcement to the priest or local judge or before a meeting of the *vicini*, and then carefully to look after them as his own. Failure to publicise his find or alienation of the animals rendered him liable to pay the composition for theft,[2] while killing them meant restitution *in duplo*.[3] Marking the animals as his own brought a fixed fine of three *solidi*.[4] The finder and custodian of strays was naturally compensated for his expenses, but he also received a reward for their safe keeping.[5]

As frequently dealt with as the rights of an owner of livestock, however, were his responsibilities.[6] The rule was that damage or injury caused by animals had to be made good or compensated for, but that a penal sanction was involved only when the animals' owner was directly responsible, by wilful action, for the ill-effects of their behaviour, or when he could be held so, by his gross negligence in refusing to heed warnings of a beast's vicious or mischievous propensities. The owner of animals deliberately sent into a meadow of young grass, for example, had to repay the hay-crop which would otherwise have been produced and pay in addition one *tremis* or one *solidus*, according to his standing, for every two beasts: different only in detail was the treatment of the man who sent his animals into a vineyard or onto arable land.[7] But when animals strayed onto another's property, only the damage had to be made good,[8] although the owner had always the alternative of surrender-

---

[1] VIII. 4. 11.    [2] VIII. 5. 6, 8. For the special case of VIII. 4. 14 see below, p. 258.
[3] VIII. 5. 7.    [4] VIII. 5. 8.    [5] VIII. 5. 4, 5, 7.
[6] Although the laws talk of a *dominus*, a borrower (and no doubt a keeper in general) was responsible for the misdeeds of the animals in his charge: see V. 5. 2 and A. B. Schmidt, *Die Grundsätze über den Schadensersatz in den Volksrechten*, Untersuchungen . . . , ed. O. Gierke, XVIII (Breslau, 1885), 55–6. No doubt it was he also who received compensation when they came to grief, just as a custodian received the composition for the theft of an article left with him (V. 5. 3).
[7] VIII. 3. 12; VIII. 3. 10.
[8] VIII. 3. 11, 13.

ing the beasts.[1] The procedure for dealing with trespassing animals was carefully regulated. The landowner was empowered to impound those found on cultivated land, but had then to notify their owner so that an estimate of the damage could be jointly made. This was done by measuring the affected area so that the extent to which it had suffered could be accurately assessed by comparison of the crop it later produced with that from an equal area of land undamaged by the intrusion.[2] But animals might not be impounded if they were not found on the damaged land or if, although trespassing, they had done no damage,[3] and their death or injury as the result of the land-owner's deliberate action or during his angry expulsion of them from his land obliged him to replace them with sound stock.[4] Failure to notify their owner or later refusal to release them to him was pun-ishable by a composition of one *solidus* or one *tremis* for each head.[5] If the animals' owner did not appear within three days to make assessment of the damage, so that he might reclaim his stock, the animals – watered, but not fed – had to be released, but the damage, assessed in his absence by the *vicini*, had then to be made good *in duplo*.[6] Double payment was also required from the owner who took back his animals without permission, before or after impoundment, while he was further subject to a fine or lashing.[7] In the case of pigs found in the woodland, or sheep, cows or other animals found on the waste, the law made no distinction between strays and animals deliberately introduced: one animal might be impounded, and this became forfeit unless the stock-owner entered into an agreement with the property-owner to pasture his beasts, on the usual terms, on the latter's land.[8]

Injury caused by an animal to the person of a man or to another animal was treated in much the same way. Either the offending beast was transferred or composition was paid: the choice was that of the owner.[9] But there were sensible exceptions. No liability existed

---

[1] VIII. 4. 12.     [2] VIII. 3. 13: cf. VIII. 3. 15 and Dahn, *Studien*, pp. 85–6.
[3] VIII. 3. 16; VIII. 4. 11.
[4] VIII. 3. 13, 17, 4. 8. Half their value had to be paid if they suffered wholly accidental injury in the process of expulsion (VIII. 3. 13). Expulsion by their owner (or anyone else) naturally did not absolve him from the obligation to make good the damage (VIII. 3. 16).     [5] VIII. 3. 15.
[6] Ib.     [7] VIII. 3. 14.
[8] My interpretation of the confusing laws VIII. 5. 1, 4 and 5.
[9] VIII. 4. 12. For injury by one animal to another, see VIII. 4. 7.

when an animal was provoked,[1] and if a dog bit someone – or, no doubt, some animal – its master was liable only if he had egged it on and even then not so if its victim was a criminal whom he was trying to arrest.[2] On the other hand, an unavoidable financial liability existed for an animal whose dangerous qualities were known to its owner. If he failed either to kill such a beast or to expel it, warning his neighbours that he had done so, and if the animal then killed or injured someone, he was given no choice but to pay the full composition – an enormous 500 *solidi* in the case of the death of a free person.[3] A second offence by a dog which had previously shown itself to be a worrier of sheep or other animals but which its owner had declined to kill involved him in double compensation.[4] Special provision was also made for the case of bees: a beekeeper who failed to obey a judicial order to remove his swarms *in abdita loca* was required not only to restore *in duplo* an animal the bees might later kill or to replace an injured beast – which he took – with a sound one, but also to pay a fine of five *solidi* for contempt.[5]

Tedious reading though the various rulings recounted in the last few pages may make, their inclusion has been of value for two principal reasons. First, they illustrate supremely well some of the characteristic features of Visigothic legislation: its range, its thoroughness and detail, its reasonableness, its concern with the practical and concrete, its liking for the particular provision, not the general principle. Virtues and vices jostle here side by side. Second, they are of intrinsic importance for their relevance to the realities of rural existence. Behind the starkly informative words of the laws may be glimpsed, though darkly, the animate society of the countryside, concerned with marauding animals and ruined crops, with malicious neighbours and careless herdsmen, with vicious dogs and ferocious bulls – in short, with the perennial problems of agricultural communities.[6] It was laws such as these which

[1] VIII. 4. 18.  [2] VIII. 4. 19.
[3] VIII. 4. 16, 17.  [4] VIII. 4. 20.
[5] VIII. 6. 2.
[6] One need only glance through the provisions of the Animals Bill now (January 1971) passing through Parliament to realise the constancy of the problems – and of some of the solutions. I am grateful to the Member for Harborough, Mr John Farr, for a copy of the Bill.

impinged most constantly and pertinently upon the ordinary man going about his ordinary business of exploiting the land for survival. That they do not reflect the rigorous routine of his daily toil follows from the nature of law itself. But they remain our chief point of contact with the everyday actualities of life for the overwhelming majority of the inhabitants of the Visigothic kingdom.

*Chapter 8*

# THE FAMILY

There is precious little trace in Ervig's code of the all-important position which, at an earlier Germanic stage, the kindred had held in society. The stresses and strains of the migrations, accompanied by and assisting the growth of the institution of the retinue, had no doubt drastically weakened the effective force of the kindred as a cohesive unit already before 376, and the different customs the Goths found and adopted in the Empire, together with their further wanderings, could only have served to debilitate it still more.[1] The most severe counterforce to the kindred appeared, however, in the developed monarchy, for the growth of a strong royal power, the links postulated between this and God and the consequent erection of a theocratic and unitary *Ordnungsstaat* left no room for populism in the form of the continued survival of the kin's most characteristic activity, the enforcement of law. In the seventh century the individual faced the world, as far as can be seen, for the most part bereft of the comforts and liabilities of an operative kin system. It was cold written law which now protected or threatened him, not the hot blood of feud; it was the evidence of documents and witnesses which vindicated or damned him, not the oaths of his relatives. The kindred had receded, and the social horizon become filled rather by the close-knit family. That particular blood relationships loomed large in importance goes without saying: kinsmen assumed the guardianship of minors, arranged their marriages, inherited from each other. But this occurs in any society and can no more be seen as evidence of corporate kin solidarity than can the provisions which – understandably, given the accusatorial principle – suppose kinsmen as prosecutors and beneficiaries in cases of killing, kidnapping and so on.[2]

[1] Differently, Melicher, *Kampf*, p. 215, who holds the post-376 wanderings responsible for keeping the kin system alive and only the settlement to have brought about its *Erblassung*.

[2] Melicher's account (*Kampf*, pp. 214–22) of the kin's role is marred by a failure to take these points into account: see also Phillpotts, pp. 4ff.

Kinsmen as a body had very little power, and what they had was in any case always subordinate to that of the parents. It was the monogamous family which now constituted the basic social group.

By no means, however, was the character of this family that of the classical Roman unit. Just as the kin had lost its vigour, so too had the old Roman concept of the almost unlimited authority of the head of the family, already much weakened in the late Empire, suffered attenuation under the twin influences of Christian humanitarianism and contrary Germanic custom.[1] Paternal authority in the seventh-century kingdom was the barest shadow of what it had been in classical times. The total and lifelong sovereignty which had been the *patria potestas* of the old days had disappeared, to be replaced by a restricted and temporary domestic control possessed by the father of each separate household and in fact hardly distinguishable from that exercised by his widow after his death. *Pietas* rather than *potestas* was now the keyword,[2] and the kings were at pains to ensure that children who did not enjoy practical benefits as the result of the voluntary parental exercise of the former were guaranteed these by operation of the law. Parallel to the striking theme of royal concern for children and similarly responsible for radical change in the character of the family unit was that of the improvement in the status of women. In all fields was this noticeable but in none more so than that of the law of succession, where the old Roman preference for agnates and the Germanic refusal to allow women the inheritance of immovables disappeared, although not without trace. Against the frequent cruel severity of the Visigothic code must be weighed the remarkably enlightened efforts made by the kings to ameliorate the lot of these weaker members of society. We should be right to recognise here the implementation in practice of the paternalist principle characteristic of theocratic monarchy.

Marriage is the obvious starting-point. It must be made clear at the outset that the *coniugium* of Ervig's code was not, as marriage normally is today, a legal relationship created by the fulfilment of certain prescribed formalities. Rather, *coniugium* described, as it had

---

[1] For a brief account of its decline, see A. Otero, 'La patria potestad en el derecho hist. esp.', *AHDE*, xxvi (1956), 210–16.

[2] Quite in accordance with Christian–Roman developments: see M. Roberti, '*Patria potestas* e *paterna pietas*', *Studi in memoria di Aldo Albertoni*, i (Padua, 1935), 257–70.

done in Roman times, a state or union existing as a matter of social fact and created solely by the will, manifested in action, of particular individuals.[1] Naturally, this is not to say that marriage did not have legal consequences upon both participants and outsiders: nor does it mean that *coniugia* might not be dissolved, because contrary to the law, or otherwise penalised, although allowed to continue. But particular marriages were invalidated or punished because the parties, by contracting them, broke the law rather than because of procedural defects.

Nevertheless, it would be perverse to suggest that marriage did not usually come about as the end-product of an accepted procedure. Three stages can be usefully distinguished as normal preliminaries – the suit (*petitio*), the betrothal (*disponsatio*) and the wedding (*nuptiae*). The first, of a formal nature,[2] came from the man's side,[3] and if received favourably no doubt led to discussion concerning the important matters of the financial arrangements to be made, the date of the wedding and so on. Once agreement had been reached, the parties were ready to proceed to the next step, by which for the first time legal obligations were created, the betrothal. This took the form of a witnessed undertaking – either written or signified by the delivery and acceptance of a ring as pledge – that the marriage would take place and was accompanied by the transfer or promise of transfer by the groom's side of the dowry settled on the bride.[4] At some later date the wedding was celebrated: although we have no information on the matter, it is reasonable to suppose that the principal feature was the ceremonial delivery of the bride to the groom's house – the

[1] The Roman concept is excellently summarised by R. Bidagor, 'Sobre la naturaleza del matrimonio en S. Isidoro de Sevilla', *Miscellanea isidoriana* (Rome, 1936), pp. 258-9. For the Germans see R. Köstler, 'Raub-, Kauf- und Friedelehe bei den Germanen', *ZRG.GA*, LXIII (1943), 92-136, with the view that the 'offenkundig begründete, dauernde Haus- und Geschlechtsgemeinschaft' (p. 133) was the criterion for judgement as to the existence of marriage. But Ervig's dowry law (below, p. 225, n. 4) shows that the need was increasingly felt for a precise procedural means of distinguishing marriage from concubinage. A concubine appears only in III. 5. 5, but is doubtless in mind in III. 4. 7 (below, p. 231, n. 3): cf. also *HG* 37, 57, III Tol. 14 etc.

[2] III. 1. 1: 'Petitione dignissimam', *FV* 18: 'Nuptiarum solemnium festa petitio'.

[3] III. 1. 1, 5, 7, 8 (with rejection envisaged in the last two): cf. III. 2. 8.

[4] III. 1. 3: 'Cum...pro filiorum nuptiis coram testibus precesserit definitio, et anulus arrarum nomine datus fuerit vel acceptus, quamvis scripture non intercurrant', III. 4. 2: 'Dato pretio et, sicut consuetudo est, ante testes facto placito de futuro coniugio', III. 1. 4, 6. 3. On the *arrae* see below, p. 227, n. 1.

old Roman *deductio in domum* and Germanic *Heimführung*.[1] Whether it was normal or simply occasional practice to precede this with a religious ceremony we have no means of knowing.[2]

Two aspects of the procedure here cursorily sketched deserve lengthier treatment. The first is the highly significant matter of the dowry. The giving of *dos* by the man's side was a practice with origins rooted both in Germanic custom and in the late Roman institution of the *donatio ante nuptias*,[3] and quite clearly a normal feature of Visigothic marriage. Indeed, *dos* served as the chief identifying token by which marriage might be distinguished from other relationships of a less binding nature, and although its provision was not an essential condition for the validity of a union, Ervig certainly regarded its omission as wholly improper.[4] Since the dowry was,

[1] See T. Melicher, *Die germanischen Formen der Eheschließung im westgotisch-spanischen Recht* (Vienna, 1940), pp. 74–5. Note 'nuptiarum...festa celebritas' in III. 1. 3 and the mention of ornaments, clothes etc. loaned to a girl 'pro dignitate nuptialium federum' in IV. 5. 3.

[2] Clerical benediction at marriage was certainly known: see *Ep. Siricii ad Eumerium* 4, 9, and *DEO* II. 20. 5, 7. The sole reference in the laws appears in XII. 3. 8, where Ervig commanded Jews to celebrate their marriages 'non aliter quam cum premisso dotis titulo, quod in christianis salubri institutione preceptum est, vel sacerdotali benedictione intra sinum sancte ecclesie percepta' – although infringement did not bring nullity, as Gama Barros, VI, 458, pointed out, but fine or lashing. The section of the *LO* (cols 433–43) concerning marriage is post-Visigothic: see ib., col. 431, n. 1. To speak of the Christianisation of Germanic law as particularly apparent in the Visigothic marriage laws (thus Aubin, p. 83) is in all respects unjustifiable: see below for divorce by consent. I do not know on what grounds M. García Garrido, 'El régimen jurídico del patrimonio uxorio en el derecho vulgar romano-visigótico', *AHDE*, XXIX (1959), 422, talks of the marriages of nobles as those blessed by the Church.

[3] For the Germans see Köstler, pp. 119ff. Schultze, *Eherecht*, passim, but especially pp. 39–44 (dealing with the terms *pretium* and *mercatio* in the sources), denies that *Kaufehe* is reflected in the *Antiquae* (against, particularly, Melicher, *Formen*, pp. 51ff.), but it was no doubt precisely here that Gothic custom was affected by the character of the *donatio ante nuptias* (the Roman *dos* being *ex parte sponsae*), on which see especially the comprehensive study of L. Anné, *Les rites des fiançailles et la donation pour cause de mariage sous le bas-empire* (Louvain, 1941), pp. 235–486. There is a convenient brief account in García Garrido, pp. 397–400. Merêa, *Estudos*, p. 23, rightly describes the Visigothic *dos* as 'o produto da confluência do dote *ex marito* ...proprio do direito germânico...com a *donatio ante nuptias*'.

[4] Cf. Ervig's addition to III. 1. 9: 'Ne sine dote coniugium fiat...Nuptiarum opus in hoc dinoscitur habere dignitatis nobile decus, si dotalium scripturarum hoc evidens precesserit munus. Nam ubi dos nec data est nec conscripta, quod testimonium esse poterit in coniugii dignitate futura, quando nec coniunctionem celebratam publica roborat dignitas, nec dotalium tabularum hanc comitatur

subject to certain conditions, at the free use and disposal of the woman, it was of high economic significance, and negotiations about its size were doubtless the major concern of the two sides before the betrothal.[1] There was, nevertheless, a statutory maximum: as it appeared in Ervig's code, this was established as one-tenth of all the property which a man owned or stood to inherit, although the nobles of the blood and the *primates palatii* were privileged by being allowed to add to this ten slave boys, ten slave girls, twenty horses and ornaments to the value of 1 000 *solidi*.[2] Ervig maintained Chindasvind's provision that the prescribed limit might be exceeded as long as the surplus was matched by an equivalent gift *ex sponsa*.[3] *Dos* might be handed over before the marriage – to the girl's father, mother or other relatives,[4] or to the woman herself[5] – or simply promised in writing.[6]

honestas?' This hardly justifies the usual view that *dos* was essential for lawful marriage (thus Zeumer, xxiv, 587, A. Lemaire, 'Origine de la règle *Nullum sine dote fiat conjugium*', *Mélanges Paul Fournier* (Paris, 1929), p. 421, Merêa, *Estudos*, pp. 29–30 – but cf. ib., p. 165): the law is not coercive command but concerned exhortation (note the absence of penal or other consequences), as already Gama Barros, vi, 429–32, held. Jewish marriages without *dos* were valid, though penalised, as we have seen. But note the significance of *dos* in iii. 2. 8 and 4. 7.

[1] Cf. iii. 1. 2: 'Si pater...de pretio convenerit', iii. 3. 3 etc.
[2] iii. 1. 5 (to which iii. 4. 7 does not establish an exception, as García Garrido, p. 424, holds): cf. iii. 1. 9. It is not certain that the ornaments alone might make up the sum stated: but see Schultze, *Eherecht*, p. 47, n. 162. The additional gifts (slaves etc.) correspond closely with references in *FV* 20 (which itself shows half of a man's possessions given in dowry, but dates from before Chindasvind's version of iii. 1. 5, the first restrictive law we have) and are to be identified as the constituents of the originally independent *Morgengabe*: see, exhaustively, Schultze, *Eherecht*, pp. 44–54.
[3] This is the sole reference to a gift *ex sponsa* (although gifts *ex uxore* appear in iii. 5. 3, v. 2. 3, 4), and in no way justifies talking of 'la obligatoriedad del equilibrio entre dote y *donatio*', as does A. Otero, 'La mejora', *AHDE*, xxxiii (1963), 26. Idem, 'Liber Iudiciorum iii. 1. 5', *AHDE*, xxix (1959), 545–55, further declares that the Visigothic *dos* is exclusively the Roman *donatio a.n.* and that the existence of the *Morgengabe* is not secure: he prefers not to discuss *FV* 20 ('Ordinis ut Getici est et *morgingeba* vetusti') and suggests that 'la Patrística' can perhaps explain the 'supuesta morgengabe' of iii. 1. 5. Romanist zeal goes here rather too far. But the Roman *dos* was in mind in iii. 1. 5: the law referred explicitly to the *leges Romanae*,
[4] iii. 1. 6 (below, p. 244).
[5] See below, in text, on female freedom of marriage. Payment to the woman would also apply in iii. 1. 8.
[6] iii. 1. 5: 'Dotis titulo conferat vel conscribat' (where also a dotal *sacramentum*), iii. 1. 9, 2. 7 etc. For dotal *scripturae*, although of an earlier date and Roman in character, see *FV* 14–19 (where *FV* 15 is in favour of a *coniux*: see iii. 5. 3 for *dos* given after the wedding): *FV* 20 is a similar Gothic formula.

The betrothal once concluded, the parties became subject to considerable legal obligations. *Disponsatio* bore little relation to the flexible, casually assumed and as casually rejected engagement of today or even to the stricter one of the recent past. It was a binding contract from which unilateral withdrawal was not permitted[1] – given that the other party had not committed some offence justifying repudiation – except in the particular cases of the betrothal of a woman to a man younger than herself, when either party could withdraw,[2] or the imminence of death, when the religious life might be assumed.[3] If, for example, more than the two years stipulated by the law were to elapse between betrothal and wedding and this was due not to mutual consent or lack of interest – in which case the betrothal was voided – and not to the unavoidable absence of one of the parties, then the side which dragged its heels not only had to pay the penalty provided in the betrothal agreement but remained committed to the match.[4] It is true to say that betrothal was regarded, no doubt as the result of ecclesiastical influence,[5] as all but marriage, as creating a relationship which gave to those involved most of the rights, and imposed upon them most of the obligations, which attended marriage. The legal relations of *sponsus* and *sponsa* can therefore best be dealt with below, where those of husband and wife are discussed, but it may be noted here that the abduction of a *sponsa* was punished more severely than that of an uncommitted woman – by death, in fact, if she was actually

---

[1] III. I. 3, 6. 3. J. García González, 'El incumplimiento de las promesas de matrimonio en la hist. del derecho esp.', *AHDE*, XXIII (1953), 618ff., should be read with caution. For *arrae* as a binding pledge, see Zeumer, XXIV, 580–2, whose argument for an earlier regime where the groom who had given *arrae* could withdraw without penalty (see above, p. 106, for *arrae* and sale) is to be accepted despite Merêa, *Estudos*, p. 98, n. 43.

[2] III. I. 4. If marriage came about, however, it was not invalid.

[3] III. 6. 3. Cf. *VSF* 15, where a *sponsa* fleeing from her parents (note the implication of forced betrothal) and becoming a member of a religious community is permitted to remain so by the *comes* sent to investigate by the king on the complaint of the *sponsus*, a *gardingus*, but dies shortly afterwards.

[4] III. I. 4. See Zeumer, XXIV, 583–4, with Roman precedents: further, García González, p. 625, n. 30.

[5] See Fernández Alonso, *Cura pastoral*, pp. 423–5. Note *Etym.* IX. 7. 9: 'Coniuges autem verius appellantur a prima desponsationis fide, quamvis adhuc inter eos ignoretur coniugalis concubitus', where Isidore cites the case of Mary and Joseph. The notion is basic to Isidore, as Bidagor, 'Naturaleza del matrimonio', pp. 270–83, shows.

raped[1] – and that the parents who consented to the marriage of their betrothed daughter with her abductor had to pay no less than four times the value of the dowry to the injured *sponsus*.[2]

The most difficult question of Visigothic marriage law is that of determining the character and extent of the power which parents or relatives possessed in the matter of the betrothal of a child. The right of arranging a child's marriage belonged in the first instance to the father: on his death it passed to his widow, and when she died or remarried, to the brothers of the child or, if they were not of sufficient age, to a paternal uncle.[3] There is no reason to think that either the father's or the mother's power of decision in the matter of marriage was in any way limited by surviving kin authority:[4] certainly a betrothal once lawfully arranged by either of the parents might not be overthrown by the other relatives, even after the parent's death.[5] In contrast, a family council was required to decide upon the acceptability of a suitor for the hand of an orphaned girl once her brothers or uncle had assumed the *potestas de coniunctione*, so that 'aut communi voluntate iungantur, aut omnium iudicio denegetur'.[6]

By far the more important question, however, and one where dogmatism is wholly out of place, is this: how far was this *potestas* enforceable against an unwilling child? One must beware here of laying too much emphasis upon the legal, as opposed to the actual, state of affairs, for in the majority of cases, especially in an age when children married young, no problem would have arisen: most children would have taken for granted the right of a parent or close relative to make matrimonial arrangements for them, just as most children did until very recent times – and still do, in many parts of the world. The notion of filial duty and obedience was stronger then than now. Similarly, it would be flying in the face of what we know

[1] III. 3. 5. For simple abduction the *raptor* forfeited all his property or, if he had little or none, was sold as a slave: in either event the proceeds were shared by the betrothed couple.     [2] III. 3. 3.

[3] III. 1. 7. The brothers' age had doubtless to be twenty: see IV. 3. 3. Other male relatives can be assumed to have taken on the right after the *patruus*: see Schultze, *Eherecht*, pp. 16–19.

[4] Ib., pp. 25ff., 33. That marriage was to be accompanied 'prosapie sollemniter consensu comite' (III. 1. 1: see Zeumer, XXIV, 575–6) means, I believe, nothing more than that the consent of the holder of the *potestas de coniunctione* was to be obtained.

[5] III. 1. 2: cf. II. 5. 4.       [6] III. 1. 7.

of human nature to believe that parents would not frequently have consulted their children's wishes and have desisted from making a match violently opposed. Mutual agreement was no doubt the rule rather than the exception.[1] Nevertheless, situations must have arisen where the wishes of a child and of its controlling relative were at variance, and the question remains: how were such disputes resolved? The indications are that the possessor of the *potestas de coniunctione* enjoyed a right of betrothal over a young girl which was not limited by the need to gain her approval, except in very special circumstances,[2] but that the woman who had reached the *perfecta aetas* of twenty became entirely responsible for her own matrimonial fate.[3] A reference to the possibility of renewal of a betrothal contract by the couple themselves 'si profecte sunt iam etatis' points to the likelihood of independence for the older woman,[4] and other texts which allude to women arranging their own marriages offer support.[5]

[1] Note 'parentum tuorum tuusque consensus' in *FV* 15: cf. *FV* 14, 18.

[2] The strong implication of III. 1. 2: 'Si quis puellam cum voluntate patris aut aliorum propinquorum parentum, quibus...potestas tribuitur, sponsatam habuerit, et ipsa puella, contemnens voluntatem parentum, ad alium tendens, parentibus contradicat...Et si fratres [etc.]...male voluntati eius consenserint, ut eam illi traderent, quem ipsa sibi contra paterna voluntate cupierat...'. If the girl had previously given her consent, the law says nothing of it. Comparison of III. 3. 3, 4 and 7 suggests that the parents (alone) could marry their daughter to a *raptor* against her will. The view expressed here is that generally accepted, at least with regard to the father: see Merêa, *Estudos*, pp. 6–7, with literature at n. 12, to which add Schultze, *Eherecht*, pp. 25ff. The opposing view, found, e.g., in the highly tendentious G. Merschberger, *Die Rechtsstellung der germanischen Frau* (Leipzig, 1937), at p. 6, rests almost entirely upon a challengeable interpretation of III. 3. 11.

[3] See J. Ficker, 'Über nähere Verwandtschaft zwischen gothisch-spanischem und norwegisch-isländischem Recht', *MIÖG*, Ergänzungsband, II (Innsbruck, 1888), 532–5, and the cautiously favourable remarks of Merêa, *Estudos*, pp. 40ff. (though he is more assertive than the evidence justifies in denying a woman's freedom *patre vivente*), against whom Schultze, *Eherecht*, p. 20, n. 53, is unconvincing. III. 1. 7, showing the orphaned *puella*, in contrast to the *puer*, bound by the decision of her relatives when she had passed the age of fourteen, does not prove that control continued indefinitely. III Tol. 10: 'Nec extra voluntatem parentum vel suam cogantur [virgines] maritos accipere' perhaps points to the alternatives. (But see Melicher, *Formen*, p. 66, for the view that the canon required both parental and the girl's consent.)

[4] III. 1. 4: 'Non amplius quam biennium expectetur, nisi aut parentum aut cognationis vel [!] certe ipsorum sponsorum, si profecte sunt iam etatis...adfuerit consensio'.

[5] Thus, III. 1. 3: 'Cum inter eos, qui disponsandi sunt, sive inter eorum parentes aut fortasse propinquos pro filiorum nuptiis...precesserit definitio', III. 1. 5: 'Nec erit ultra licitum puelle parentibus seu etiam puelle vel mulieri ab sponso vel ab sponsi

A widow enjoyed freedom from control over her remarriage, it is true,[1] but in at least two cases it is the union of a *puella*, a never-married woman,[2] which is envisaged. And when we find mention in III. 4. 2 of agreement about a future marriage concluded 'inter sponsum et sponse parentes aut cum ipsa forsitan mulierem, que in suo consistat arbitrio', it is difficult to believe that the last phrase is nothing but a circumlocution for *vidua* or refers to what must have been the comparatively rare phenomenon of a woman who had no surviving male relatives to whom the power of arranging her marriage might have passed.[3] As for male children, it is certain that a young man over the age of fourteen could not be betrothed against his will when both his parents were dead, since the law expressly allowed him the right to marry as he chose.[4] *E contrario*, we can assume that he had no such right during the lifetime of either of his parents, and although this does not involve as a necessary corollary the belief that his consent was of no legal importance, it may be thought likely that he too could be the unwilling subject of an arranged match. Probably the attainment of the *perfecta aetas* brought him also freedom from this subjection, but it should be borne in mind that, legal right or no, a son would, while his parents were both alive, have little or no property from which he might present a dowry to his intended.

Although a young woman certainly had no general legal *right* to marry without the consent of the relative possessing the *potestas de coniunctione* over her, it was nevertheless within her *capacity* to contract a valid and permanent marriage without that consent.[5] If a woman wishing to marry the man of her choice simply presented

---

parentibus plus...petere' (concerning *dos*), III. 3. 7: 'Quod si cum puelle parentibus sive cum eadem puella vel vidua de nuptiis fortasse convenerit [raptor], inter se agendi licentiam negari non poterit', and III. 4. 7 (below, p. 231, n. 3).

[1] III. Tol. 10, Schultze, *Eherecht*, pp. 68–9.

[2] In general, *mulieres* is used to mean women as a sex, but sometimes women as opposed to girls, and *puella* (sometimes *virgo*, palpably misused in III. 2. 2 !) to mean a never-married woman, but sometimes, more particularly, a girl.

[3] On the text, see Merêa, *Estudos*, pp. 40–5. Schultze, *Eherecht*, p. 69, holds that a widow is meant.

[4] III. 1. 7. It seems clear from the context that the *proximi* whose care the adolescent boy is allowed to reject do not include the parents: thus Zeumer, XXIV, 576, although Merêa, *Estudos*, p. 7, is doubtful, and Schultze, *Eherecht*, p. 30, includes the mother among them.

[5] Generally on the matter see Merêa, *Estudos*, pp. 157–83.

her family with a *fait accompli*, her partner was none the less her husband – *maritus* – for the lack of parental consent.[1] But she could not take such a step with impunity: as a consequence she forfeited all right to her share of the parental inheritance.[2] What was really punished here was her dishonourable behaviour, her loss of chastity, for precisely the same penalty befell the woman who slept with a man *in domo aliena*, regardless of whether the liaison led to marriage.[3] That it might not is clear: a man was under no obligation to marry an *ingenua* with whom he had intercourse, nor was he normally subject to punishment for his action.[4] The law was careful, however, to protect an orphaned girl against the greed of her brothers, who might misuse their *potestas de coniunctione* in the hope of forcing her in desperation to marry without their consent: once three suitable candidates had presented themselves and had been rejected by the

---

[1] III. 2. 8.

[2] Ib., where disinheritance is 'si...eam parentes in gratia recipere noluerint'. Note that the orphaned and brotherless daughter of a *buccellarius* suffered the equivalent of disinheritance if she married against the will of her patron: V. 3. 1. On disinheritance for sexual misbehaviour, see the valuable comments of Zeumer, XXIV, 596–9. The notion is nicely Germanic, but Merêa, *Estudos*, pp. 169–81, and 'Le mariage *sine consensu parentum* dans le droit romain vulgaire occidental', *Revue internationale des droits de l'antiquité*, V (1950), 203–217, has argued for a similar vulgar law rule.

[3] III. 4. 7: 'Si puella ingenua sive vidua ad domum alienam adulterii perpetratione convenerit, et ipsam ille uxorem habere voluerit, et parentes, ut se habeant, adquiescant: ille pretium det parentibus, quantum parentes puelle vellint, vel quantum ei cum ipsa muliere convenire potuerit. Mulier vero de parentum rebus nullam inter fratres suos, nisi parentes voluerint, habeat portionem'. The law presents grave problems, for it appears to attribute to the *parentes* the right of consent to the marriage of a widow and to designate them as the receivers of the dowry. (To Merschberger, p. 47, and Schultze, *Eherecht*, pp. 40–1, the *pretium* here is a penalty paid to the *parentes*: but it is absurd that the amount might be fixed by the offending woman, and we know that no such penalty threatened a man who did *not* marry a woman with whom he had had intercourse. See also R. Gibert, *AHDE*, XVIII (1947), 722, with n.★.) The law is badly drafted, but I believe that both the agreement of the *parentes* and the payment to them applied only when a girl was still subject to the *potestas de coniunctione*. Melicher, *Formen*, p. 67, agrees with this to the extent that he holds the *pretium* to have been paid direct to the *vidua*. But in fact the 'mulier' of the phrase 'cum ipsa muliere' may not refer to the *vidua* alone, but also to the unmarried woman free from control. In my view, the law lays down the normal procedure for translating a simply sexual relationship into marriage and the regular punishment for any unchaste woman, including the widow, whose virtue, if not her marriage, remained the affair of her *parentes*. Fornication within the family house was a more serious affair, as we shall see.

[4] III. 4. 8: see Gama Barros, VI, 435, n. 1.

brothers, the girl was entitled to choose a husband for herself without loss of her rights of inheritance, provided that her choice fell upon someone who was her social equal.[1] What is quite clear is that a woman was protected by the law against being forced into marriage by the sole will of some outsider – with the exception of the king alone.[2] In early Germanic society the abductor of a woman had often enjoyed what amounted to an automatic right to retain her as his wife on payment of composition for his offence.[3] Such a right was explicitly denied by Visigothic law,[4] where even the *raptor* who yielded up his victim unharmed stood to lose to her half of his property. If he forced intercourse on the woman he had seized, on the other hand, he lost everything which he owned and was enslaved, either to her or to her *parentes*, who in fact always took possession of his person if they had been obliged to use force to achieve her recovery.[5] But lawful marriage could come about between *raptor* and *rapta* if agreement was reached between them or between the *raptor* and the holder of the *potestas de coniunctione*.[6] When the latter was not the woman's father or mother, however, her consent was necessary for the validity of the union, and the

---

[1] III. I. 8: see Zeumer, XXIV, 576–8, with a remarkable Icelandic parallel. Equality of status was doubtless basic to the notion of *honesta coniunctio* (III. I. I etc.): cf. III. I. 7.

[2] III. 3. 11: cf. III Tol. 10. On the law see Zeumer, XXIV, 604–5, with references also to III. 2. I, 5. I, 6. 2, which also concern special royal powers in matrimonial matters: further, Melicher, *Formen*, pp. 30–2. See Fredegar, IV. 82, for Chindasvind's delivery to his *fideles* of the wives and daughters of his exiled and executed opponents, together with their property – although slavery may be meant.

[3] See Melicher, *Formen*, pp. 11ff., especially p. 19, and Köstler, p. 115.

[4] See below, n. 6. Generally on Visigothic *raptus* see Zeumer, XXIV, 600ff., with the Roman sources, and d'Ors, *Código*, pp. 140ff.

[5] III. 3. I, 2. The penalties facing a *raptor*, with the exception of death, faced also a girl's brother who, *patre vivente*, consented to, or participated in, an abductor's action: III. 3. 4. For assistance to a *raptor* by others, see III. 3. 12.

[6] III. 3. 7 (cit. p. 229, n. 5), which stands in only apparent contrast with III. 3. I: 'Si vero ad inmunditiam, quam voluerit, raptor potuerit pervenire, in coniugio puelle vel vidue mulieris, quam rapuerat, per nullam conpositionem iungatur', where the object is the rejection of the old *Raubehe*: see Zeumer, XXIV, 600–2. Melicher, *Formen*, pp. 28–9, holds that once intercourse had occurred lawful marriage was impossible: thus too Gama Barros, VI, 422. But the title of III. 3. I: 'Si ingenuus ingenuam rapiat mulierem, *licet* illa virginitatem perdat, iste tamen illi coniungi non valeat' argues powerfully against this. Lawful marriage was not, of course, possible after the enslavement of the *raptor*: see III. 3. I, 2 and above, p. 178. Cf. also III. 4. 14.

relative concerned was punished if he agreed that the *raptor* should keep her against her will.[1]

However contracted, certain unions were unlawful and not only punished but forcibly dissolved. Those between members of different classes have been discussed elsewhere, and bigamous matches, and those in disregard of a prior betrothal, will be referred to below. But a further group of particular interest was comprised by those which sinned against the incest laws.[2] Sexual intercourse, outside or within marriage, was forbidden to those who stood to each other within the sixth degree of kinship, the relationship being determined by counting up to the common ancestor and down again: thus, second cousins might not lawfully marry. Kinship by marriage was also taken into account, with relations prohibited between an individual and a relative of his or her spouse. The censure of the law even extended to intercourse between a man and his father's, brother's or son's concubine or casual mistress: indeed, it went so far as to categorise a relationship between a man and his father's betrothed as incestuous. The scope of the net cast by the incest laws was therefore very wide and must have offered ample opportunity to blackmailers, for the penalties were severe: the couple were separated, lost their property to their heirs and were confined in houses of religion for the rest of their lives. Unions involving a man or woman who was vowed to chastity were treated in the same way.[3]

There can be no question but that the husband was the dominant partner in the marriage union. Biblical sanction reinforced what was both Germanic and Roman practice in affirming the subjection of wife to husband,[4] and one need look no further than to the provisions

---

[1] III. 3. 4 deals only with the case of the brothers but applies *a fortiori* to the other relatives: the penalty was loss of half the offender's property and lashing. Cf. III. 3. 3 for the parents.

[2] On the following see Zeumer, XXIII, 104ff., XXIV, 613ff.

[3] See III. 5. 1, 2, 5, and above, p. 154: cf. XII. 3. 8. On the concession in III. 5. 2 of inheritance rights to children born of such unlawful unions (but 'unda sacri baptismatis expiati'), see Zeumer, XXIV, 614–16, and Melicher, *Kampf*, pp. 176–7. Differently XII. 3. 8 (Jewish children!). Note the explicit exclusion of the children of slave–free unions from inheritance in III. 2. 2, 3.

[4] Cf. IV. 2. 15: 'Vir, qui uxorem suam secundum sanctam scripturam habet in potestate' (where apart from Gen. 3. 16, Eph. 5. 22–4 may be in mind) and 'coniugalis obsequii' in III. 1. 5. Note also *DEO* II. 20. 6, 13, 14, and Chindasvind's use in III. 1. 4 of *Etym.* XI. 2. 17 as justification for repugnance at the prospect of the marriage of a woman with a man younger than herself.

concerning adultery to recognise discriminatory treatment by the law.[1] By marriage a woman entered the household power of her husband,[2] to whom she became responsible for her sexual chastity and to whom others had to answer for their attempts, successful or not, upon it.[3] The horror with which her adultery was viewed is witnessed by the maintenance in the code of the old provision that the husband who caught his wife *in flagranti* with her lover might kill them both without further ado.[4] If the offence was proved in court, the sentence was delivery of the couple, together with all their goods, into the power of the outraged husband, to be dealt with as he might wish.[5] Forfeiture of property and enslavement were the corresponding penalties for the *sponsa* and the man with whom she had sexual relations or to whom she even promised herself in marriage[6] – unless her betrothed should find her in the act of inter-course, when he too was empowered to execute summary punishment.[7] Forgiveness by a husband did not free a peccant wife from fear of punishment, for accusation was eventually open to all: if she passed into the power of anyone other than her husband or her sons she might not be killed, but the law is explicit that she might be flogged and her body mutilated.[8] A husband's adultery, on the other hand, was far more lightly treated. He might in certain circumstances be punished if he slept with a slave girl belonging to someone else,[9] but there was nothing to prevent his free enjoyment of an *ancilla* of his own. Relations with a freewoman were punishable for him only if he went so far as to contract a marriage with her, even if the

---

[1] Contrast Isidore's lack of distinction between the adulterous wife and husband in *DEO* II. 20. 12.

[2] Schultze, *Eherecht*, p. 63.

[3] For enticement, e.g. The 'sollicitatores adulterii' were delivered to the arbitrary vengeance of the husband (III. 3. 11, where Ervig put the *sponsus* on the same footing as the *maritus*). The same penalty faced the man who forced another's wife into adultery: III. 4. 1.

[4] III. 4. 4. The provision was *gemeingermanisch* (Zeumer, XXIV, 606–7), but for the vulgar law see d'Ors, *Código*, pp. 144–5.

[5] III. 4. 1, 3, 12, 6. 1, 2 etc.: but see final note of chapter. The same penalty befell the woman who remarried, wrongly thinking her husband dead: III. 2. 6.

[6] III. 4. 2: cf. III. 4. 1. 2, 4. 12.   [7] III. 4. 4.

[8] III. 4. 13. Zeumer, XXIV, 612, rightly comments: 'Die maßlose Leidenschaftlichkeit, mit welcher die westgothischen Gesetzgeber die Verletzung der Familienehre strafen, findet hier ihren Höhepunkt'.

[9] Above, p. 178, with n. 5.

woman herself was in all circumstances liable to be delivered to the vengeance of the insulted wife, 'vita tantum concessa'.[1]

The subject of adultery brings us to the interesting provisions concerning the dissolution of marriage – and, *mutatis mutandis*, of betrothal. Death, of course, ended the union: there were no restrictions upon the right to remarry of a widower or widow,[2] with the exception of the requirement that the widow wait one year, the *tempus luendi*, after her husband's death.[3] Divorce was a complicated story.[4] Visigothic law did not know of a petition for divorce as such, but there were certain offences on the part of the husband – homosexuality,[5] the giving of his unwilling wife in adultery to another man or the conclusion of a second, naturally unlawful, marriage – which justified his wife's remarriage, just as her adultery justified his. Statutory grounds apart, there existed also divorce by mutual consent 'aut scriptis aut coram testibus': Roman notions clearly died hard in the face of Christian ideas of indissolubility.[6] The danger was that men would force or trick their wives into the unwilling or unintended provision of written consent to their husbands' wishes. A document extorted in this way was declared invalid, and the husband punished by loss of all his property to his children or, in

[1] See below, in text, and for the woman III. 4. 9, 6. 2 (which excludes killing).

[2] The express permission to remarry granted the widow at the end of III. 1. 4 (where I cannot recognise any limitation as to her groom's age, as could Zeumer, XXIV, 582) perhaps suggests the survival of prejudices based upon earlier restrictions: one recalls Tacitus, *Germania* 19. See p. 153, n. 1, above for ecclesiastical hostility to vidual remarriage.

[3] III. 2. 1. But there were economic and domestic consequences of remarriage for a widowed mother, as we shall see.

[4] I follow the essential and convincing account of Zeumer, XXIV, 619–30. The relevant texts are III. 6. 1 and 2: III. 6. 3 extends the penalties of these to betrothed persons 'coniugale fedus contemnentes'.

[5] For which see also III. 5. 4. On the relationship of the later III. 5. 7 (Egica) with XVI Tol. 3, see Zeumer, XXIV, 618–19.

[6] See Zeumer, XXIV, 629–30, against whom Ziegler, pp. 152–5, does not convince. III. 1. 3, 4, allowed the dissolution by mutual consent of a betrothal which in its legal character was virtually the same as marriage. XII Tol. 8 cited Matt. 19. 9 in prohibiting a husband's abandonment of his wife 'excepta causa fornicationis' (see also *DEO* II. 20. 11, 12), but divorce by consent was compatible with this and no more difficult to reconcile with a reference to God's joining of the couple than was divorce on the statutory grounds mentioned. See IV Tol. 19, 44, for allusions to divorced women. Even in the Eastern Empire divorce by mutual consent was forbidden only in 542, and it was re-permitted after 566: M. Kaser, *Das römische Privatrecht*, II: *Die nachklassischen Entwicklungen* (Munich, 1959), p. 123.

their absence, to his wife, together with forfeiture of his reversionary claims on the *dos*. These claims alone disappeared if he simply repudiated his wife without justification – that is to say, not *fornicationis causa* – but if he went so far as to contract a second marriage, he suffered flogging, scalping and either exile or enslavement. There was no way, then, in which a husband could with impunity escape the obligation to remain with his wife, unless she willingly agreed to dissolution of the marriage or committed adultery. Without her consent he could not even enter the religious life: nor was he allowed to remarry if he persuaded her to do so. The woman, on the other hand, was equally committed to her husband. Even his enslavement did not free her from the obligations of the marriage bond: if she elected not to stay with him 'in coniugali consortio', she was required nevertheless to remain faithful to him until his death.[1] And if her husband went missing, she had to gain certain evidence of his death before she might remarry in safety.[2] What problems arose from this and how they were solved, we cannot begin to imagine, for mistakes of identification could not have been difficult to make in the heat of battle.

The will of the husband was not, therefore, the decisive factor in bringing a marriage to a *de iure* end: nor was it as dominant during the course of the union as one might perhaps assume. Most revealingly is this shown in the provisions concerning the control of the wife over property which had accrued to her, provisions which governed also her economic status after her husband's death. A husband exercised no more authority over the *dos* than he did over property which his wife brought into the marriage or acquired during it,[3] even if it was no doubt often the case that, as a matter of convenience, he controlled his wife's and his own estates as an economic whole.[4] The woman's rights of disposal at death of the dowry and of gifts from her husband – for Visigothic law, in contrast to Roman, allowed donations *inter coniuges*, although only after a year of the marriage had elapsed, unless death was imminent[5] – were limited not by her husband but,

---

[1] But this would surely not have applied to the *sponsa*?
[2] III. 2. 6: see Zeumer, XXIV, 594–6.    [3] See Merêa, *Estudos*, pp. 35–6, 59, n. 35.
[4] The husband's *de facto* control is assumed in III. 6. 1, 2. See above, p. 102, n. 5, for a husband as his wife's legal representative.
[5] III. 1. 5, which has all the air of a compromise between the earlier Roman and Gothic regimes, on which see King, pp. 183–9. For conjugal gifts see also v. 2. 4, 5, 7 and above, p. 107.

as we shall see, by the existence of children of the marriage. But one-quarter of the dowry and one-fifth of marital donations *extra dotem* – including those *mortis causa* – were hers to dispose of as she wished,[1] and in any case she enjoyed lifelong possession of the whole of both sets of property, of which only sexual misconduct, during or after the union, could normally deprive her.[2] One-fifth of the *res propriae* which she brought into the marriage with her or inherited after it had begun was similarly at her free disposal.[3] In the case of all three groups of possessions, however, the absence of issue entitled her to full rights of disposal: only if she died intestate did the dowry and marital gifts revert to her husband or pass to his heirs.[4] A husband had corresponding powers over gifts from his wife or his family property.[5]

But children had no guaranteed successory rights to parental property acquired in some fashion other than by inheritance or conjugal gift.[6] The regime concerning acquisitions made by the marriage partners during the union is not easy to determine, but it was probably the general rule that the fruits or profits stemming from a specific piece of property or from an individual action passed to the particular spouse involved, and that only when joint activity was responsible or when difficulties of allocation arose – as they were bound to do, given the fact of a common household and the likelihood that the husband frequently exercised everyday control over the combined estates – were acquisitions divided, on the death of either partner, in proportion to the extent of the property held by each.[7]

---

[1] IV. 5. 2; V. 2. 4.

[2] V. 2. 5 ordered forfeiture of goods stemming from a husband – *dos* etc. – for a widow's fornication or unsuitable marriage: similarly III. 5. 3 for breach of vows. The economic consequences of adultery have been discussed above.

[3] IV. 5. 1: cf. IV. 2. 18. On the origins and character of the Visigothic *Seelquoten* see Bruck, *Kirchenväter*, pp. 147–63, holding Syrian influence responsible. For property transferred to children upon marriage cf. IV. 5. 3 and below, in text.

[4] III. 1. 5, IV. 2. 18, 20, 5. 1, 2 etc. But note that in V. 2. 4 the fate of gifts *extra dotem* is dependent upon the benefactor's instructions: cf. V. 2. 5.

[5] IV. 5. 1, V. 2. 4. Sexual sanctions applied to him only in isolated cases, but see III. 5. 3, 6. 1, 2.

[6] See, convincingly, Zeumer, XXVI, 142–3, arguing from IV. 2. 16, 5. 1, V. 2. 2. II. 1. 6 provides strong support: cf. also IX Tol. 4 and Martínez Díez, *Patrimonio*, p. 193.

[7] I follow Merêa, *Estudos*, pp. 49–61, especially pp. 59–60. Given the separation of ownership of estates, separation of the ownership of proceeds seems most likely. IV. 2. 16 would then give the procedure when division of a common fund was

Direct gifts were certainly held personally by the donee, and gifts to the couple in accordance with the provisions of the donation.[1] One exception to the rule was provided by the stipulation that a wife had no claim on property gained by her slaves when they were in her husband's service – during campaigning, for example.[2] Intestate inheritance apart, it was only when a woman ran foul of the law by committing adultery or by marrying or sleeping with a man during the first year of widowhood that her husband or his heirs stood to gain these acquired goods, in whole or in part.[3] When it is added that a widowed mother also enjoyed the usufruct, held till death or remarriage, of a share of her husband's estate equal to that of each of the children,[4] it can be seen that both during and after marriage she was remarkably well catered for by the law, which permitted her rights of control and disposal of an extensive nature. Direct intestate inheritance of wife to husband, or *vice versa*, was, however, rare.[5]

There remains to be discussed the matter of parental authority over the children of the marriage.[6] That this was substantial is undeniable: it is enough to recall the power of arranging a child's marriage and to mention that at a parent's pleasure a young child might be obliged to enter the religious life.[7] But the emphasis of the laws was rather upon duties than upon powers, and the safeguards they offered children against possible *impietas* correspondingly extensive. Far from there being any question of the survival of a parental *ius vitae ac necis*,[8] the child received protection even while still within the womb. Abortion was punished by the execution or blinding of the offending woman, together with her husband if he had ordered her

---

called for – 'de omnibus augmentis et profligationibus *pariter* conquisitis'. Certainly the husband alone had ownership of what he gained 'de extraneorum lucris aut in expeditione publica'. A different view of IV. 2. 16 in Zeumer, XXVI, 122–3.

[1] IV. 2. 16: but García Garrido, p. 444, interprets 'in amborum nomine...scripture' as agreements between husband and wife. For royal gifts see also V. 2. 3.

[2] IV. 2. 15.

[3] For the *Trauerjahr* see III. 2. 1, ordering forfeiture of half the *res suae*: Roman parallels in Zeumer, XXIV, 588–9.     [4] IV. 2. 14.     [5] Below, p. 249.

[6] Sadly, Merêa, *Estudos*, pp. 1–22, closely followed by Otero, 'Patria potestad', pp. 216–21, is less detailed than one would wish.

[7] See III. 5. 3, IV Tol. 49, 55, and X Tol. 6 (no child over ten against its will): cf. *LO* 38–40.

[8] On parricide in its broadest sense see VI. 5. 17–19: but see p. 240 for a permissible case. Generally on what follows see Melicher, *Kampf*, pp. 14–19, with references also to the Fueros.

to commit the crime, or consented to it: Chindasvind's sense of outrage at such guilty parents, 'pietatis inmemores', led him to subject slaves also to the penalties of the law, no doubt to the dismay of slave-owners, who thereby had loss heaped upon loss.[1] The attempted concoction of an abortifacient potion brought enslavement, or lashing if the woman was already a slave, and its actual administration to a pregnant woman the death penalty,[2] while abortion caused by a blow or some other means was heavily punished by a composition of one hundred and fifty *solidi* if the child had reached the fetal stage, or of one hundred *solidi* if it had not.[3] The terms of Chindasvind's abortion law applied also to infanticide, where the custom of exposure, 'the prevailing and stubborn vice of antiquity' in Gibbon's words, must have been a principal target. But even if an exposed child was found and cared for, legal consequences threatened the parents, for they were bound to redeem it by the payment of a slave or a slave's price: if they neglected to fulfil their obligation, the local judge redeemed the child from their property and exiled them, while if they were unable to meet the cost, the exposer was enslaved in place of the child.[4] The sale, donation or pledging of children was also forbidden, although, remarkably, no penalty was laid down for offenders.[5] Certainly children were frequently given by their parents for upbringing by others, for the law found it desirable to establish a statutory rate for this arrangement – one *solidus* a year until the child was ten, when it was deemed able to earn the expenses of its keep:[6] if the parent failed to pay the sum

[1] VI. 3. 7: cf. III Tol. 17 ('fornicationis avidi, nescii pietatis'), but with no death penalty. Note in the canon the characteristic justification of marriage as 'causa propagandae prolis': cf. IV. 5. 2, *FV* 17 etc.

[2] VI. 3. 1, where the *facere* of 'mulier, que potionem ad aborsum facere quesibit' inclines me against 'a woman who seeks a potion' (thus McKenna, p. 122, d'Ors, *Código*, p. 123).

[3] VI. 3. 2, 3: cf. VI. 3. 4–6 for slave offenders and slave victims.

[4] IV. 4. 1: for exposure of slave children see IV. 4. 2.

[5] V. 4. 12. The recipient lost his *quid pro quo* – to the parents?! The sale of children – preferable to exposure – was conditionally permitted by Roman law: see on the whole matter T. Mayer-Maly, 'Das Notverkaufsrecht des Hausvaters', *ZRG.RA*, LXXV (1958), 116–55.

[6] IV. 4. 3: 'Usque ad decem annos per singulos annos singulos solidos pretii... percipiat'. Not, therefore, two *solidi* p. a. (d'Ors, *Código*, pp. 152, 223), three (ib., p. 131, n. 344), ten (Zeumer, XXVI, 137) or thirteen (Dahn, *Studien*, p. 58): *aliquando boni dormitant Homeri*! Pace Jones, 'Slavery', p. 13, the law does not concern children exposed or sold as infants.

due, it was he or she, not the child, who was enslaved.[1] We are a very long way here from the sovereign authority of the classical Roman father. No doubt abortion and the exposure and sale of children continued, but due credit must be accorded the legislators for their attempts to check the practices. It is not the least mark of the level of Visigothic civilisation that it upheld the right to live even of the unborn child.

As the child grew up in the family household, it was naturally subject to the disciplinary authority of its parents and grandparents: filial obedience was the other side of the coin to parental *pietas*. There is nothing to show that the physical chastisement of a child *in familia* was denied a parent even when the child had reached mature years,[2] while we shall see later that in certain specified and extreme cases of offensive behaviour any child might be disinherited. Particularly serious were breaches of the sexual code by a woman, for here not just parental pride but family honour also was injured. The texts talk therefore of the *parentes* – a vague term, meaning either 'parents' or 'relatives' – or of the *propinqui* as responsible for the bringing to book of an unbetrothed or unmarried woman guilty of sexual offences, and at the same time offer no evidence that any distinction was made between the *puella* and the widow.[3] In the most serious case – for it also involved defilement of the family house, the sanctity of which is elsewhere reflected in the code[4] – the father who found his daughter in the sexual act under his own roof might kill both her and her lover or, if he wished to spare their lives, treat them as he

---

[1] Ib.: 'Quod si hanc summam qui repetit dare noluerit, mancipium in nutrientis potestate permaneat'. The 'natural' reading of this suggests that the child remained a slave: thus Zeumer, cit. last note. But as he himself points out, this would mean that the child could in practice be given away, despite v. 4. 12. I suggest the possibility that the parent who is the subject of the first clause is the subject also of the second. This would square well with both IV. 4. I, with its penalty of enslavement for the parent unable to redeem his exposed child, and v. 6. 5, the general provision of enslavement for non-payment of debt. 'Permaneat' is not so difficult as it might seem: cf. VI. I. 5: 'Ille, qui debilitatus est, ingenuus in patrocinio... permaneat', where the *ille* is in fact a slave and where *permanere* has therefore the sense of 'to become and to remain'.

[2] IV. 5. I: 'Flagellandi...et corripiendi eos, quamdiu sunt in familia constituti ...potestas manebit'.

[3] See Schultze, *Eherecht*, pp. 64ff. But a widow's offences – even those committed before her husband's death – were also the concern of her relatives by marriage: see III. 2. I, 4. 13, V. 2. 5.          [4] Below, p. 258, n. 8.

desired: after his death the same right of summary punishment was allowed the woman's brothers or paternal uncles.[1] It was the *parentes* who were apparently primarily responsible for taking action against a woman guilty of marrying a slave and who might take possession of her person as a result.[2] We have already seen that fornication *in domo aliena* brought forfeiture of the profectitious inheritance and that this applied even after the death of the parents. On the other hand, the parents and other relatives also had the duty of pursuing those who attempted to besmirch a kinswoman's honour:[3] we find them rescuing an abducted woman by force and taking possession of the person of the *raptor* in III. 3. 2, and empowered to deal as they like with the enticer whom they have successfully prosecuted in III. 3. 11. Some parents obviously did not prize so highly the chastity of a daughter, for the law found it necessary to threaten with a hundred lashes those who allowed her to become a prostitute and lived off her earnings.[4]

Since children enjoyed a statutory right of inheritance to the estates of their parents, it was imperative that they should receive adequate protection against the greedy designs of others when they were orphaned of one or both of their parents at an early age.

Discretio pietatis est sic consultum ferre minoribus, ut iuste possessionis dominos damna non patiamur,

began a law of Chindasvind.[5] A detailed law established the duties and rights of a father bereft of his wife.[6] He was obliged to preserve the *bona materna* intact for his children – although the fruits might be used for the common expenses of the household – and on a child's marriage or attainment of the age of twenty to hand over two-thirds or half, respectively, of the share due, keeping the rest for himself in life usufruct. This did not mean, in fact, that he necessarily lost con-

---

[1] III. 4. 5: cf. III. 4. 6 and Zeumer, XXIV, 607, who points out the Roman and Germanic parallels. A comparative treatment of this widespread ruling, and of related matters, is to be found in T. Melicher, 'Das Tötungsrecht des germanischen Hausherrn im spanischen, französischen und italienischen Recht', *Zeitschrift für vergleichende Rechtswissenschaft*, XLVI (1930–1), 379–409.    [2] See above, p. 89, n. 3, and p. 178.
[3] Note here XI. 1. 1 (above, p. 204, n. 1) where the danger of 'ludibrium' is in mind and where the composition of ten *solidi* goes to the relatives (or husband).
[4] III. 4. 17.    [5] IV. 3. 1.
[6] IV. 2. 13. For an excellent discussion of this law, which exists in different forms as CE 321, an *Antiqua*, a Novel of Wamba (IV. 2. 13*) and in its final Ervigian shape, see Zeumer, XXVI, 110–19.

trol of the whole, for it is evident that sons sometimes – we might even think, usually – did not leave the parental household when they married and that they sometimes allowed the father to retain administration of the portion which was their due.[1] Remarriage in Ervig's day no longer brought any change in the position of the father – although the legislators were aware of the dangers inherent in the introduction of a stepmother onto the scene, and insisted that an inventory of the goods reserved for the children be drawn up – but if he declined continued *potestas* over his children, a *tutor* was appointed by the judge from among their maternal relatives.

Rather different was the position of the widowed mother. A law of Chindasvind provided that only those children under the age of fourteen who had lost both parents were to be designated *pupilli*[2] – and therefore to be considered in need of the appointment of a guardian – so that the widow held a true *potestas* over her children and was not subject to the complex tutorial regime laid down in the laws. The reality of this *potestas* already at an earlier stage is clearly implied by the references to both father and mother in *Antiquae* forbidding the sale, donation or pledging of children and denying parents any claim on a child's acquisitions,[3] and the particular vidual *potestas de coniunctione* is witnessed in III. 1. 7. But legally the widow was a guardian before Chindasvind's time, and vestiges of this earlier role survived in the *Antiqua* IV. 3. 3, which still spoke of her *tutela* over the children. The widowed mother had to provide an inventory of the *bona paterna* and also to yield both power and control of these goods on remarriage. Although there is no evidence that the possession of her usufructuary portion was ever dependent upon her

---

[1] Cf. IV. 2. 18.

[2] IV. 3. 1: 'Licet actenus a patre tantum relicti parvuli filii pupilli nuncuparentur, tamen, quia non minorem curam erga filiorum utilitatem matres constat frequenter inpendere, ideo ab utroque parente, hoc est patre vel matre, infra XV annos [Zeumer's note: Id est usque ad annum 14. completum] filios post mortem relictos pupillos...decernimus nuncupandos'. In my sense, Dahn, *Studien*, p. 59, Ficker, p. 523, and S. Minguijón Adrián, *Hist. del derecho esp.*, I (Buenos Aires, 1927), 49–50, 53. *Contra*, Merêa, *Estudos*, p. 15, following Zeumer, XXVI, 134, takes the 'vel' to mean 'or'. But this would mean that the father of a motherless minor possessed the power of a guardian, and IV. 2. 13 contradicts this.

[3] V. 4. 12; IV. 5. 5. In my view, only one section of the latter might be held to justify the rejection by Merêa, *Estudos*, pp. 11–17 (followed by Otero, 'Patria potestad', pp. 217–19), of a *materna potestas*: on this, see p. 244, n. 3. In support of a *materna potestas* see, additionally to the text, IV. 4. 1, 3, V. 1. 4, XII Tol. 6.

acceptance of responsibility over the children – for she could decline this if she wished – it seems very likely that the chief function of the portion was in fact to reward her for her duties – the more so, since it too had to be surrendered upon her remarriage. At what time the children received from her their shares in the *bona paterna* does not appear, but it is probable, since she possessed *potestas* like her husband, that she transferred these when he did: certainly it should not be thought that she was entitled to keep them longer than he was.

That marriage brought the child escape from parental control is certain.[1] But it is clear that the age of twenty was also of significance in the matter of emancipation: not only is it very probable, as was argued earlier, that children of that age had the right freely to contract marriages on their own initiative, but in the laws just discussed we have seen them at that same age taking full control of their shares of the *bona materna* and probably also of the *bona paterna*. It is not unreasonable to conclude that twenty was therefore the age at which a child achieved full freedom from paternal or maternal *potestas*: the designation of this age as the *perfecta aetas* in IV. 3. 3 is wholly in harmony with this.[2] Such a hypothesis explains why *CE* 300 earlier dealt only with those over twenty when it provided that men who fraudulently sold themselves into slavery should be held to the sale: if they were below this age, their persons would not have been theirs to dispose of. The much-discussed law IV. 5. 5 did, it is true, allow children the right to alienate property which they might have acquired,[3] and we have no reason to think that only those over the

[1] See Merêa, *Estudos*, pp. 164ff.
[2] For *perfecti anni* see also *FV* 34 – a Roman formula of emancipation: further, Merêa, *Estudos*, pp. 19–21.
[3] 'Filius, qui patre vel matre vivente aliquid adquisierit, sive de munificentia regis aut patronorum beneficiis promeruerit...in ipsius potestate consistat' – where I take 'aliquid' to be general in scope. The suggestion of Merêa, 'A lei IV. 5. 5', pp. 63–81, that the ruling applied only to the child who had left the parental household has primarily against it the failure of the legislator to say so. But a valid alternative reading of the law might connect both verbs with 'aliquid', and 'aliquid' with royal and patronal munificence alone, and the denial of parental rights in the particular case of these acquisitions would then argue for their existence in other circumstances: the final section on the sharing of property gained in military service (below in text) might then be explained in terms of an amendment, brought about by universal though irregular military obligations, of the Roman institution of the *peculium castrense*. On the general character of *leudes* in this last section, see above, p. 58, n. 3.

age of twenty were meant, even if it is clear that children under the age of fourteen were not.[1] But this law should be seen as a special concession, permitting the child a *peculium* of its own, and that view is strengthened by the fact that the legislators found it necessary to instruct parents that they had no claims on children's acquisitions – hardly a point which would have been made unless grounds for such a claim had at an earlier stage existed. In fact, apart from royal or patronal *beneficia* – expressly mentioned in the law, and understandably so, for they totally lost their point if they passed straight into the control of someone other than their recipient – few acquisitions could normally have been made by the child under twenty. Compositions constituted one source, and there are references to show that these passed direct to unmarried *puellae* when there is no reason to suppose that their parents were dead.[2] A share of the booty for sons performing their military service may have been a further source, for there is no certain evidence that only those over the age of twenty were obliged to fight. In fact, the father had the right to take one-third of the trophies of war borne home by his son *in familia*, no doubt on the sensible principle that some compensation was due him for the loss of his son's labour.[3] By no means was the dowry included among the acquisitions freely alienable by a child: the parents had over this the *potestas conservandi* – if the hypothesis put forward here is correct, until their daughter's marriage or attainment of the *perfecta aetas* of twenty.[4]

As we have seen, the appointment of a guardian was only necessary when a child was orphaned of both parents while still under the age of fourteen. This was the age of majority,[5] when a child became free to testify in the courts and to make valid wills and contracts.[6]

---

[1] Cf. II. 5. 11.                                  [2] Cf. III. 3. 1, 5, 4. 14 etc.

[3] IV. 5. 5. The omission of the mother here can plausibly be put down to careless drafting.

[4] III. 1. 6. When the law continues: 'Quod si pater vel mater defuerint, tunc fratres vel proximi parentes dotem, quam susceperint, ipsi consorori sue ad integrum restituant', it means simply to say, I believe, that the brothers etc. were not to regard the *dos* as part of the parental inheritance or to usurp what was their sister's due.

[5] IV. 3. 4: cf. *Etym.* XI. 2. 3, 4.

[6] II. 4. 12, 5. 11. But IV. 3. 3 shows that a male could not become a guardian until he had reached the age of twenty. The importance of age in the code is fully discussed by Melicher, *Kampf*, pp. 71–86. Germanic custom was doubtless responsible (ib.,

Nevertheless, children could be under tutelage after this age, for twenty years were taken as the maximum number spent in those *pupillaribus annis* which IV. 3. 2 declared were not to be counted towards the thirty-year limitation period when orphans wished to litigate about matters originating during the lifetime of their parents, while IV. 3. 4 expressly referred to a child over fourteen whose person or property was still in tutorial power. The child over fourteen may itself have had the right to decide whether it should remain in, or be placed under, tutelage, but an alternative explanation, based on the analogy of the probable regime in the matter of betrothal, is that male and female children were treated in distinct fashions, the first gaining freedom from tutelage at fourteen – no doubt only if they so wished – and the second remaining under control until they had reached the age of twenty, which must in any event be seen as the upper limit.

It well agrees with this second view that the relatives who might assume the guardianship are the same, and appear in the same order, as those entrusted with the *potestas de coniunctione*. The office fell first to the brother who had reached the *perfecta aetas*, next to the paternal uncle, and then to his son.[1] Failing all these, a tutor was chosen by the remaining relatives in the presence of the judge – an indication, perhaps, not so much of a surviving, if vestigial, kin authority as of the natural interest of the relatives in the protection of property which might one day pass to them. The safeguards against abuse of power by the guardian were detailed. A witnessed inventory of the inheritance held for the child had to be lodged with a bishop or priest on the assumption of office, and any property lost, by corruption or negligence, had to be made good from the guardian's own possessions. As long as a child, or a child's property, was in the power of a guardian, any document subscribed by the child at his instigation was invalid. Only when all the inheritance had been accounted for by the *tutor* before a priest and (*vel*) judge and he had received written

pp. 33–5, 77–8) for the attribution of significance to the age of ten. A child over that age might make a will if *in extremis*, although it was invalidated by his recovery (II. 5. 11, IV. 3. 4): for ten, see also above, p. 135, n. 7, p. 238, n. 7, and p. 239. For the separation of a slave child from its mother at twelve, see X. 1. 17, and for that of a Jewish child at seven, XVII Tol. 8.

[1] For this and the following, see IV. 3. 3, 4. Episcopal *tutela* protected orphans entered upon the religious life: IV Tol. 24.

acquittance from the child were his responsibilities and liabilities at an end. If an action was entered upon against his charge, the guardian could defend it or not as he chose: it was only just that in the latter event the petitioner should receive what he claimed, but the child could revive the case when he came of age – for tutorial negligence or fraud might have been involved – and if successful stood to gain from the original claimant not only what had been lost, but also the fruits and services stemming from it during the intervening years, and in addition the sum of ten *solidi* 'pro presumptione'. The guardian might also choose to prosecute actions on his ward's behalf, but cases lost through negligence might be reopened at a later date. On the credit side, the *tutor* might claim one-tenth of the fruits of the property administered.

That the kings took seriously their duty as Christian monarchs to care for the interests of children will already have become apparent. But the most striking evidence of the practical form in which their concern was manifested is to be found in the introduction of statutory restrictions, operating in favour of the children, upon the freedom which parents had previously enjoyed in the disposal of property. By Ervig's time, children who behaved themselves were guaranteed inheritance of the lion's share of nearly all parental property, whatever the parent's feelings about the matter. Four-fifths of all those goods, excepting the dowry, which had been received by one spouse from the other were assured to them,[1] and four-fifths also of the family inheritance held by, or due to, each parent.[2] Of the *dos*, three-quarters had to be reserved for the

[1] v. 2. 4.
[2] IV. 5. I: cf. IV. 2. 18. It was the work of Chindasvind to restrict a previously total freedom of disposal: 'Abrogata legis illius sententia, qua pater vel mater aut avus sive avia in extraneam personam facultatem suam conferre, si voluissent, potestatem haberent, vel etiam de dote sua facere mulier quod elegisset in arbitrio suo consisteret...'. The view that this freedom was that of the Romans (thus, e.g., Bruck, *Kirchenväter*, pp. 151–3) is misconceived. No Roman 'legis sententia' permitted such freedom, and Roman children were entitled to a fourth. The view that the permitted disinheritance of children was in mind (thus Otero, 'Mejora', p. 13) does not take into account that the 'legis sententia' also allowed a woman to dispose of her *dos* at will: the Roman woman was obliged to preserve all property coming from her husband, including the *donatio ante nuptias*, for her children (see King, pp. 195–8). See also H. Brunner, 'Beiträge zur Gesch. des germanischen Wartrechtes', *Festgabe für Heinrich Dernburg* (Berlin, 1900), pp. 43–6.

children.[1] Even the *donatio mortis causa* made by one spouse of a childless marriage in favour of the other – or, presumably, anyone else – became invalid once a child was born: only if the *testatio* was made before the marriage did it stand.[2] Both the dowry and other conjugal gifts were, we may assume, shared equally among the children, and no grounds for disinheritance were given in the laws. But the other property due to the children was divided equally among them only after the parent had taken advantage, if he or she so wished, of the right to bestow one-third of the whole estate on any one or more of them,[3] while a child could be disinherited if he or she had been convicted of physical assault upon, or had lodged a (presumably false) accusation against, the parent.[4] Baptism was the sole juridically significant criterion of a child's right to inherit, with the earlier stipulation that it must have lived for ten days nullified, in inane fashion, by the addition of the words 'sive amplius vel infra'.[5] A posthumous child enjoyed the same rights of inheritance to the paternal estate as did his brothers and sisters: why, if he was an only child and his father had disposed of his property by will, his claim should have been reduced to only three-quarters of the estate is difficult indeed to fathom.[6]

These valuable rights of the children against their parents were maintained in the persons of the grandchildren and greatgrand-

[1] IV. 5. 2: cf. III. 1. 5, IV. 5. 1, V. 2. 5. This restriction, also Chindasvindian, was new (see IV. 5. 1, in last note, and IV. 5. 2: 'Quibus *dudum* concessum fuerat de suis dotibus iudicare quod voluissent'): quite perverse is Otero, 'Mejora', pp. 60–1. On the originally free disposal by Visigothic wives of their *dotes* and of other gifts stemming from their husbands, see King, pp. 192–5. The view that such freedom was allowed in the interests of the Arian Church (thus Melicher, *Kampf*, pp. 221, 258, Bruck, *Kirchenväter*, pp. 147–9) is seductive. Rights of expectancy were doubtless sometimes ascribed to the children already before Chindasvind's reform, but the Visigothic formula *FV* 20 does not show this, as it provides alternatives: 'Relinquas …posteris…aut inde facere vestra quodcumque voluntas elegerit'. But cf. *FV* 15, 17.　　　　[2] IV. 2. 19. Cf. *FV* 23, 24.

[3] The amount was a tenth in Chindasvind's version of IV. 5. 1. For an elaborate hypothesis upon the origin of the so-called *mejora* of Visigothic law (mentioned also in IV. 2. 18, 5. 4), see Otero, 'Mejora', pp. 5–73, where the author's determination to discover a Roman principle lurking concealed behind every text relevant to his theme makes necessary a frequently remarkable argumentation.

[4] IV. 5. 1.

[5] IV. 2. 18: cf. IV. 2. 17 and III. 5. 2. For the Germanic background, see Melicher, *Kampf*, pp. 20–1.

[6] IV. 2. 19.

Law and society in the Visigothic kingdom

children,[1] and to this extent the regime corresponded with that established for intestate succession. The children who were first in line of succession inherited equally and, as in all successory matters, there was no distinction of sex: as Chindasvind remarked:

Iustum omnino est, ut, quos propinquitas nature consociat, hereditarie successionis ordo non dividat.[2]

In the total or partial absence of children, the grandchildren inherited per stirpem, with the greatgrandchildren next in line:[3] these were followed by the parents and they by the grandparents.[4] The inheritance of greatgrandparents was not dealt with in the code, presumably because of the rarity of the combination of circumstances which could have made it possible, but no doubt followed that of the grandparents.[5] Equality of share in the inheritance would appear also to have been the rule in the succession of ascendants, subject to the highly important proviso that property which had passed to the de cuius through a particular line should be returned to the representatives of that line – the so-called truncal principle.[6]

We are not informed in detail about succession by collaterals, but IV. 2. 3 shows that brothers and sisters had the first claim, and it is

[1] IV. 2. 20 allows general freedom of disposal 'de rebus suis' to the individual 'qui filios vel nepotes aut pronepotes non reliquerit', even though IV. 5. 1 mentions only children and grandchildren. It is a reasonable assumption that the dos was also reserved for greatgrandchildren, despite the silence of IV. 5. 2. Cf. also IV. 2. 18 and Zeumer, XXVI, 142. The mejora could not be to the benefit of a grandchild patre vivente, according to A. Otero, 'La mejora del nieto', AHDE, XXXI (1961), 391–4.

[2] Thus IV. 2. 9: cf. IV. 2. 1 and 10, with Zeumer, XXVI, 104–7, on the latter. For sexual successory equality (based on the law of nature) in Justinian's law, see B. Biondi, Il diritto romano cristiano, III (Milan, 1954), 339–41. For earlier Eurician discrimination against the unmarried daughter and the grandchildren ex filia, see J. Lalinde Abadía, 'La sucesión filial en el derecho visigodo', AHDE, XXXII (1962), 113–29, and King, pp. 218–27.

[3] IV. 2. 2. Although IV. 5. 4 talks of the right of grandchildren who have lost a parent 'cum patruis aut avunculis equales succedere' in an aval estate, IV. 2. 18, guaranteeing such children the full inheritance due to the parent if he or she had lived, makes it clear that equal shares per stirpem are meant.

[4] IV. 2. 2.

[5] Arg. ex IV. 2. 3.

[6] IV. 2. 6. On this and the hitherto mysterious CE 328, see the convincing suggestions of J. Lalinde Abadía, 'Un enigma jurídico visigodo', AHDE, XXX (1960), 631–41. But note that when a parent, A, inherited from his child, it was A's relatives rather than those of the parent from whom the child had previously itself inherited who succeeded on A's death sine prole and intestate: IV. 2. 18.

248

probably the case that rights were then continued in the persons of their descendants and only if these were lacking in the ascendants,[1] when the truncal principle was again applied.[2] Inheritance by nephews and nieces alone was certainly *per capita*,[3] and this may have been the general rule for succession *a latere* when brothers and sisters – who inherited equally[4] – were absent. The testamentary disposition of property inherited from a relative was itself subject to the restrictions described earlier.[5] We may mention also that half-brothers and half-sisters had equal claims to the estate of their common parent, but were wholly excluded from succession to each other.[6] No right of intestate inheritance existed beyond the seventh degree of kinship: after that point, husband and wife succeeded to each other's possessions, while the Church took the estate of a cleric, monk or nun.[7] *Bona vacantia* fell to the fisc.[8] The simplicity of these rules is as striking as is the further concern for children shown by the occasional royal provisions that property should not be forfeited to his victim by an offender with a family.[9]

Family law is among the most intractable of historical topics, and in no period more so than this, when the manifold provisions and principles of Christian teachings, Roman and Germanic traditions, vulgar practice and natural law philosophy intermingled and influenced one another to a bewildering degree. It must be frankly admitted that more of what has been said above is controversial than is not, even if attempts to stamp a wholly Roman character upon Visigothic successory and matrimonial regimes essentially *sui generis* can safely be attributed to apriorism. Enough is clear, however, to indicate the fundamental themes and, particularly, the strength of those two singled out at the beginning of this chapter, regard for the

---

[1] *Arg. ex* IV. 2. 8.

[2] See Zeumer, XXVI, 102–4, arguing from IV. 2. 7 as an exception.

[3] IV. 2. 8: see Zeumer, XXVI, 94–5.     [4] IV. 2. 5.

[5] Cf. IV. 2. 18, dealing with the *luctuosa hereditas*.

[6] IV. 2. 5, 5. 4. But differently Zeumer, XXVI, 100–1.

[7] Cf. IV. 1. 1–7 (= *LRV.PS* IV. 10. 1–8), IV. 2. 11, 12.

[8] Zeumer, XXVI, 107–9, is convincing: see now also F. Tomás y Valiente, *AHDE*, XXXVI (1966), 201–4. See IV. 5. 7, and cf. VI. 5. 18, XI. 2. 1: a special case in III. 2. 2.

[9] Thus, e.g., an adulterer was delivered into the power of the husband with all his property unless he had children, when it passed to them (III. 4. 12). Similar reservations in III. 3. 1, 4. 1, 2, VI. 2. 1, XII. 3. 8. For a different attitude altogether, see above, p. 86, n. 4.

interests of children and enhancement of the legal condition of women. One is justified in doubting whether the members of either of these two groups, granted knowledge of the past and of the immediate future, would willingly have exchanged places with their counterparts of either epoch.

# THEFT AND ROBBERY

In VII. 2. 13, a law entitled *De damno furis*, Chindasvind declared the liability of the freeman-thief to ninefold restitution and that of the slave-thief to sixfold restitution of the property stolen, whatever its type and value, while every thief was to receive one hundred lashes:

'Cuiuslibet rei furtum et quantalibet pretii extimatione taxatum ab ingenuo novies, a servo vero sexies ei, qui perdidit, sarciatur, et uterque reus C flagellorum verberibus coerceatur'.

The penalty of ninefold restitution decreed here for the freeman is found also in other laws: in the *Antiquae* VII. 1. 1: 'Quod si rerum causa est, et ingenuus est [sc. index qui non potuerit probare quod indicavit]... novecuplam...conpositionem exolvat', VII. 2. 10: 'Si quis de tesauris publicis pecuniam aut aliquid rerum involaverit vel in uso suo transtulerit, in novecuplum eam restituat' and VII. 2. 14: 'Fur, si captus fuerit, perducatur ad iudicem, ut ingenuus in novecuplo sublata restituat', and in the Reccesvindian laws VII. 2. 23: 'Si quis...quodlibet animalium genus nocte aut occulte occidisse convincitur, novecupli conpositionem dare cogatur...tamquam fur novecupli conpositionem inplere cogatur' and VIII. 6. 3: 'Si quis ingenuus in appiaria furti causa fuerit conprehensus, si nihil exinde abstulerit, propter hoc, quod ibidem conprehensus est, tres solidos solvat et L flagella suscipiat. Ceterum si abstulerit, novecuplum cogatur exolvere'. But despite the explicit and unqualified nature of VII. 2. 13, and the further evidence of these other provisions, it has been maintained that only in special circumstances was the thief obliged to ninefold restitution. This point of view is based essentially upon VII. 2. 9, an *Antiqua*, which deals with the man who knowingly buys stolen property and which allegedly evidences twofold restitution as the penalty imposed upon thieves:

'Si quis rem furtivam sciens a fure conparaverit, ille, qui emit, suum representet autorem et postea tamquam fur conponere non moretur. Si vero furem non invenerit, *duplam conpositionem, que a furibus debetur*, exolvat; quia apparet illum furi esse similem, qui rem furtivam sciens conparasse cognoscitur'.

# Appendix I

One suggestion for the resolution of the apparent contradiction between this and the texts cited earlier is that we have in twofold and ninefold restitution the respective compositions for what Roman law had known as *furtum nec manifestum* and *furtum manifestum*; another is that twofold restitution was the normal penalty for theft and ninefold that imposed for 'aggravated' theft.[1]

Neither of these standpoints is justified. Late vulgar law had not maintained a clear distinction between *f. manifestum* and *f. nec manifestum*, and a single penalty of fourfold restitution had become usual in all cases of theft.[2] Against this background it is impossible to explain in terms of Roman law both the alleged appearance of the distinction in Visigothic law and the massive increase in the penalty for *f. manifestum* – especially when it is remembered that this penalty would have been higher than that imposed by the Romans for robbery. Germanic tradition might supply the answer, for it knew a similar distinction.[3] But the truth is that the distinction is not witnessed in Visigothic law. Not only does no law ordering ninefold restitution unquestionably allude to the capture of the thief in the act rather than to his arrest or capture later, but *f. manifestum* is quite clearly not envisaged in VII. 1. 1, where an *index* is required to satisfy ninefold for laying false information, for it was of the essence of *f. manifestum* that proof was rendered unnecessary by the capture of the thief red-handed.[4] 'Aggravated' theft as the explanation for the ninefold penalty is hardly more appealing, however. Again, one might be inclined to reject it simply upon the strength of the vulgar law background. But there are other reasons for rejection. Not only is it difficult to see why the furtive killing of animals should be regarded as an 'aggravated' offence,[5] but VII. 2. 9, with its *dupla conpositio*, still requires explanation: why *dupla* rather than *dupla aut novecupla*? – for the circumstances of the original theft might well have been 'aggravated'. If it is answered that twofold restitution is referred to because it is the normal penalty, one has still to explain

[1] The respective views of L. G. de Valdeavellano, 'Sobre los conceptos de hurto y robo en el derecho visigodo y postvisigodo', *RPH*, IV (1949), 219–22, and G. Rodríguez Mourullo, 'La distinción hurto–robo en el derecho hist. esp.', *AHDE*, XXXII (1962), 54–8. The suggestion of Valdeavellano (echoing that of E. Mayer, 'Das altspanische Obligationenrecht in seinen Grundzügen', *Zeitschrift für vergleichende Rechtswissenschaft*, XXXVII (1920), 53, n. 43) that part of the ninefold payment went to the fisc is conjecture confounded by VII. 2. 13: 'Novies...ei, qui perdidit, sarciatur' – as he himself recognises.

[2] Levy, *Obligationenrecht*, pp. 316–19.

[3] Brunner, *Rechtsgesch.*, II, 830ff.

[4] Thus already Rodríguez Mourullo, p. 57, n. 108.

[5] Ib., p. 57, would see aggravation in the nocturnal timing. But the law has 'nocte aut occulte' – and simply 'furtive' in the title.

why there is no mention of special circumstances in VII. 2. 13 – which in fact reads naturally as a general statement of the normal penalty – and why the malicious informer in VII. 1. 1 is required, without allusion to the character of the alleged theft, to compose ninefold.

It may be suggested that these solutions to the problem of reconciliation fail precisely because no problem exists. We are sure that a ninefold penalty existed: are we sure that a twofold penalty co-existed with it? Quite the reverse: we are sure that it did not. The *Antiqua* VIII. 4. 1 is of key significance here. The man who took away someone's animal and used it for his own purposes was obliged to restore the animal to its owner and to give another of the same value – that is to say, to restore *in duplo*[1] – if the animal was discovered by its owner within three days. Was this man then a thief? No: for the law continues by declaring that it is only when the beast is not found within the three days that the man who has taken it is to be treated as a thief:

'Quod si tertia die animal inventum non fuerit, ille, qui animal alienum presumserat, pro fure teneatur'.

The *Antiqua* conclusively excludes the possibility that the thief was obliged to restore *in duplo*: his obligation was clearly more onerous.

But how then to explain VII. 2. 9? As it stands, that law certainly makes little sense. A man who knowingly buys from a thief is required to present the vendor and then himself to compose as a thief. If he cannot find the thief-vendor, he is obliged to pay 'duplam conpositionem, que a furibus debetur', because he who knowingly buys from a thief appears similar to a thief. On the assumption that twofold restitution is required of the thief, in other words, and that this is indicated by the quoted phrase, the receiver is ordered here to compose in precisely the same way whether or not he produces the thief-vendor! The law clearly says more than this![2] The most satisfying explanation that has been put forward is

---

[1] See II. 2. 7: 'Ingenuus...duplam, id est amissam rem cum simili re, in satisfactione restituat'. For this view of restitution *in duplo*, see also d'Ors, *Código*, p. 101, Levy, *Schriften*, pp. 250–1.

[2] Rodríguez Mourullo, p. 55, n. 107, interprets the law to mean that the receiver paid the composition himself if he could not present the thief-vendor: if he could, the payment was shared between them. VII. 2. 4, 14, admittedly show that when a freeman and the slave of another acted together in a crime each had to pay half his normal composition. But VII. 2. 7: 'Non solum ille, qui furtum fecerit, sed etiam et quicumque conscius fuerit vel furti ablata sciens susceperit, in numero furantium habeatur et simili vindicta subiaceat' is more easily understood to mean that each individual concerned was required to pay in full. Certainly in VI. 4. 2 accomplices in a crime were each required to pay the full composition: cf. also VI. 3. 7, VII. 5. 2, 3, 7, 8 etc., though elsewhere helpers are treated distinctly. In any

that in the Eurician version of the law the first sentence was followed by the 'quia...cognoscitur' clause, and that Leovigild introduced a further element, in the form of a provision dealing with the consequences if the thief-vendor was not presented. Through bad drafting this interpolation was introduced before, rather than after, the 'quia...cognoscitur' clause. The innovation consisted in the imposition upon the receiver who did not present his *auctor* of a composition double that which was demanded if he did. 'Duplam conpositionem', that is to say, means not 'the double composition' but 'double the composition'.[1]

This explanation is the more convincing for having been propounded by an author who nevertheless retains belief in twofold restitution as the normal penalty for theft in early times. But what evidence is there of this? The only law citable in support is v. 4. 8, which deals with the sale or donation of something owned by another:

'Quotiens de vendita vel donata re contentio commovetur...ille, qui alienam rem vendere vel donare presumsit, duplam rei domino cogatur exolvere'.

But there is no word of reference to theft here, and the law's final sentence: 'Similis scilicet et de mancipiis vel omnibus rebus adque brutis animalibus ordo servetur' suggests that land rather than movable property is primarily in mind: so too does the earlier allusion to the right of the deceived purchaser or donee to receive compensation for what he has expended upon the improvement of the property.[2] The law should be considered to deal not with the thief disposing of his loot but with the man responsible for the occupation by another of property rightfully that of a third. But

case, a receiver is not the same as an accomplice in the crime: the legislator may well have been concerned to strike at the fences whose activities encouraged the thieves. Above all, Rodríguez Mourullo makes the law say very much more than it does.

[1] D'Ors, *Código*, pp. 227–8. The same view of *d. conpositio* already in Dahn, *Studien*, p. 258, and E. Wohlhaupter, *Gesetze der Westgoten* (Weimar, 1936), p. 179, who translated: 'So soll er doppelte Diebsbuße leisten'. Differently, Levy, *Schriften*, p. 254, who yet offers no solution to the internal problem presented by vII. 2. 9. Both Levy (*Obligationenrecht*, p. 319) and d'Ors (*Código*, pp. 101ff.) hold twofold restitution to have been the Eurician penalty for theft (with fourfold the penalty for 'aggravated' theft in d'Ors's eyes: but the texts alleged are in my view concerned with robbery) and ninefold to have been introduced later, by Leovigild (d'Ors) or Chindasvind (Levy). But neither essays explanation of the (alleged) appearance of all these penalties in Ervig's code.

[2] See also A. Schultze, 'Gerüfte und Marktkauf in Beziehung zur Fahrnisverfolgung', *Festgabe für Felix Dahn*, 1 (Breslau, 1905), 5–6. The point is denied by Levy, *Schriften*, p. 250, n. 16, but, if accepted, does not invalidate his argument for a Visigothic *Anefangsverfahren* (ib., pp. 248–57).

the law looks at the matter mainly from the point of view of the innocent recipient, providing that he should receive back from his *auctor* the purchase price as well as compensation for expenses and any *pena* fixed in the document of the transaction, and it says nothing of the question of the possession, as opposed to the ownership, of the property at the moment of the conveyance, although property in the possession of the alienator is perhaps chiefly in mind, for v. 4. 8 would then stand in appropriate juxtaposition with v. 4. 9, which forbids the alienation of property in contention (that is surely to say, voids the transaction) but provides no penalty. In all respects, v. 4. 20 appears in a complementary relationship to v. 4. 8. Here, the concern is with the alienation of property in the possession of another, and there is no mention of the rights of the deceived recipient – rights clearly deemed by the legislator to have been sufficiently established in v. 4. 8. Quite in accordance both with v. 4. 8 and with the general laws on *invasio*, the possessor of land alienated by a second party and consequently occupied by an innocent third (the term *invadere* actually appears here) was entitled, if he was the true owner, both to receive back his land and to gain another parcel of equal value, or the price of this, from the alienator: if, on the other hand, the alienator had a rightful claim to the property, this was simply forfeit, and the land returned to the possessor who had suffered *invasio*. v. 4. 8 and v. 4. 20 belong naturally together, in other words: just as the second is concerned with *invasio*, so is the first.

Only if one expects a consistent adherence by the Visigoths to the principles and provisions of the Roman legal regime does the swingeing severity of the penalty of ninefold restitution cause surprise. The fact is that in the matter of theft and related offences, crimes with which the barbarians had had as long an acquaintance and as urgent a need to deal as had the Romans, Germanic influence was very strong. This is not so much witnessed in the Visigothic notion of theft as the subtraction of movables from the rightful possession of another,[1] with a view to more than temporary appropriation,[2] for although this subtraction was described in (Germanic) terms of physical removal,[3] vulgar law had already moved

---

[1] Theft of one's own property: v. 6. 2, VIII. 5. 3.

[2] See VIII. 4. 1, above in text.

[3] See Brunner, *Rechtsgesch.*, II, 826. *Auferre* is the verb normally used in the code. The significance of removal is well brought out in VII. 2. 16: 'In furtum, dum res furtivas secum portare conatur' and even more so in VIII. 6. 3 (above, in text). Unconvincingly, Rodríguez Mourullo, pp. 51–2, holds that *contrectare* was meant when the legislator used *auferre* in the latter law: even if the thief was caught 'in appiaria' (not a necessary assumption!), removal – from one of the hives – might, of course, have taken place.

away from the classical notion of *contrectatio* as the physical basis of the delictual act.[1] On the other hand, the treatment as a thief of the metal-worker who appropriated some of the material he had been given to fashion,[2] of the depositary who in fact retained property which he alleged to have been stolen,[3] and of the man who neglected to inform the authorities of goods he had found,[4] cannot be used as evidence of predominant Roman influence,[5] for such individuals were in Germanic law guilty of *Unterschlagung*, which bore the same financial penalties as did theft.[6]

But Germanic traditions were dominant in the distinction which appeared in the code between theft and robbery. To the Romans, *rapina* had been nothing but *furtum* aggravated by the use or threat of violence, but the tendency in post-classical times had in fact been towards a blurring of the line which marked it off from simple theft.[7] To the Germans, on the other hand, the two offences were quite distinct, with the characteristic mark of theft seen as secrecy, that of robbery as openness.[8] The very appearance of the two crimes as distinct in the code points, therefore, to Germanic influence:[9] but Germanic also are the concepts.[10] In the nature of things, of course, an open act of robbery is normally accompanied by force or menace, and it is not surprising that an element of violence is in fact involved in all the particular circumstances dealt with in those laws concerning *rapina*.[11] Stealth, on the other hand, rather than non-violence, distinguished the act of the thief: 'furtive' in the title of VII. 2. 23 is

[1] Rodríguez Mourullo, pp. 44–5. *Contrectatio* (but *clandestina*) still appears in Isidore's definition of theft in *Etym.* v. 26. 18, where also reference to fourfold restitution: but Isidore relied upon older sources, as shown by A. Tabera, *SDHI*, VIII (1942), 30–47.     [2] VII. 6. 4: cf. VII. 6. 3 (adulteration).

[3] v. 5. 3. Composition for the theft of deposited articles went to the depositary, not the owner.

[4] VIII. 5. 6: cf. VIII. 5. 8.

[5] See Valdeavellano, 'Hurto y robo', pp. 227–30.

[6] Brunner, *Rechtsgesch.*, II, 840–1.

[7] Levy, *Obligationenrecht*, pp. 320–1, d'Ors, *Código*, p. 103.

[8] Brunner, *Rechtsgesch.*, II, 826–7, 837–8.

[9] The distinction is explicit in VII. 2. 4: 'Ut furtum forsitam faciant vel aliquid rapiant'.

[10] Differently, Valdeavellano, 'Hurto y robo', pp. 222–7, who identifies Visigothic robbery with Roman (thus also Rodríguez Mourullo, pp. 61ff.). But in Roman terms his suggestion of fourfold composition for robbery, ninefold for *f. manifestum*, makes no sense.

[11] It is tempting to see Germanic 'openness' alone in v. 5. 3 (robbery from a burning house, where the robber goes brazenly in) and VII. 2. 18 (robbery 'ex incendio, ruina vel naufragio'), but Roman law regarded these offences as founded in circumstances of violence and thus treated them as cases of *rapina* (Rodríguez Mourullo, pp. 36–7): VII. 2. 18 is, in fact, based directly upon *LRV.PS* v. 3. 2.

significantly rendered as 'nocte aut occulte' in the body of the text.[1] Again, it would not do to overstress the contrast of the two notions, but a real distinction did exist: taking a man's belongings after killing him was theft if the actions were committed insidiously.[2]

Precisely because of the underhandedness of the act of theft, the Germans regarded it with repugnance as the most despicable of crimes and invariably treated its perpetrators with great harshness.[3] There is nothing astonishing about the ninefold penalty of the Visigothic law when it is remembered that the death penalty was elsewhere imposed for certain cases of theft and that ninefold restitution itself appeared as a penalty for the offence in the laws of the Lombards, Bavarians, Alemans and Chamavi.[4] Remarkable, indeed, would be a penalty of twofold restitution, for this would oblige us to believe that the Visigoths actually decreased the fourfold composition usually imposed in vulgar practice. Quite unsurprising also is the more lenient punishment attached to robbery, for which fourfold restitution was normally demanded:[5] other barbarian peoples similarly treated robbery less severely than theft.[6] But it should be borne in mind that the robber would frequently also have been required to make satisfaction for damage or injury caused.[7]

While ninefold restitution was thus the norm for theft and fourfold that for robbery, particular cases of one or the other were treated on their merits and punished in distinct fashion. There was little point, for example, in requiring the thief who stole the warning bells from animals to compose ninefold: the significance of the theft lay in the possible loss of the animal as a result, and satisfaction therefore took the form of a sum of money, varying according to the type of animal.[8] Ninefold restitution was clearly also out of place when theft from a grave was in question.[9] Direct Roman influence can be seen in the provision that trees cut down and carried

---

[1] And in VIII. 5. 3, 'furto' = 'occulte'.

[2] VI. 5. 12: 'Quecumque...persona...propter furti rapacitatem...quemquam insidians occidisse detegitur...'. For 'treacherous, underhanded' as the meaning of *insidians*, see VII. 2. 6.

[3] Brunner, *Rechtsgesch.*, II, 825, calls it 'die schimpflichste, eines freien Mannes am wenigsten würdige Missetat'.

[4] See ib., 828ff., for details. I do not understand VII. 1. 4: 'Si autem talis sit fortasse condicio, ut necesse sit illum, qui fur probatur, occidi...'.

[5] Thus, VIII. 1. 9 (depredations by campaigning soldiery), VIII. 1. 12 (robbery from a traveller or field-worker), V. 5. 3 and VII. 2. 18.

[6] Brunner, *Rechtsgesch.*, II, 838–9.

[7] Cf. VIII. 1. 12: 'Qui...violenter...abstulerit, quadruplum restituat, aut si aliut aliquid cedis vel damni fecerit, legaliter satisfaciat'.

[8] VII. 2. 11: see d'Ors, *Código*, pp. 104–5.

[9] XI. 2. 1, 2 (above, pp. 148–9).

away were to be restored *in duplo*[1] – in the form of standing trees, naturally, or of money. The particular offence, related to theft, of neglecting publicly to announce that one had taken possession of animals belonging to another, when these had mingled with one's own, was punished by twofold restitution – no doubt on the not unappealing grounds that the culpability of the offender yielding to the temptation of a situation which he had not himself brought about should be rated less than that of the man who deliberately chose to assume the charge of strays, but concealed the fact.[2] When firewood or wood for cooperage was taken the offender forfeited his cart and oxen[3] – for more wood would be of no value to the woodowner and its money equivalent negligible. For similar reasons, the diversion of waters was punished with a fine, the amount of which depended upon the quantity involved and the time for which it was appropriated.[4] A fixed fine penalised the man who took back his animals from their lawful impounder – although the damage also had to be made good *in duplo*.[5] Particularly harsh penalties, on the other hand, awaited certain types of robber. The man who formed and led a band of robbers or rustlers had to pay elevenfold restitution:[6] so too did the *servus dominicus* who misused his position as enlistment officer to appropriate the property of those whom he summoned to arms.[7] And Germanic notions of the sanctity of the house[8] provided that robbery committed after forcible entry be treated in the same severe fashion.[9] In all these cases, however, the penalties were, so to speak, circumstantial. They in no way affect the basic rule that theft was paid for by ninefold restitution and robbery by fourfold.

[1] VIII. 3. I. Lengthily on the Roman and Byzantine regimes see O. Carelli, *SDHI*, v (1939), 329–413.

[2] VIII. 4. 14.                     [3] VIII. 3. 8.

[4] VIII. 4. 31.                    [5] VIII. 3. 14.

[6] VIII. I. 6: cf. VIII. I. 10.        [7] IX. 2. 2.

[8] Present also in other provisions. Armed entry into another's house was punished by one hundred lashes and a composition of ten *solidi*, even when no damage was caused (VI. 4. 2). The man responsible for preventing a householder from leaving his home was flogged and had to pay thirty *solidi*, while to prevent his entry was treated as *invasio* and involved the offender also in a flogging (VIII. I. 4). *Invasio* of a house *domino absente* was treated more severely than *invasio* otherwise was (VIII. I. 7). Note also the provisions concerning sexual misbehaviour in the house: above, p. 178, n. 5, and p. 240. J. Orlandis, 'La paz de la casa en el derecho esp. de la alta edad media', *AHDE*, xv (1944), 107–61, refers in passing only to VI. 4. 2 (pp. 113, 142–3).

[9] VI. 4. 2. Elevenfold payment (ignored by Valdeavellano, 'Hurto y robo') is exceeded in the code only by the eighteenfold composition sometimes required of receivers.

*Appendix II*

# KILLING AND MISUSE OF
# THE PERSON

Germanic traditions were firmly rejected in the rather sophisticated and detailed treatment which the code afforded to killing.[1] The early Germans had distinguished only in a haphazard manner between the deliberate, the culpably negligent and the wholly accidental killing of a man. It was the act of killing with which they were primarily concerned, not the will of the killer: it was the immediate agent of death to whom they attributed liability.[2] Such crude ideas had also informed early Roman law but had soon yielded place to more advanced notions. These distinguished between the killing committed with malicious intent, *malo dolo*, that committed as a result of negligence, *culpa* or *negligentia*, and that committed by pure, unavoidable accident, *casu*.[3] It was upon the basis of these more developed concepts that the law of the Visigothic code was founded.[4]

No specific term for murder was employed in the code: *homicidium*, man-killing, frequently denoted a blameworthy killing, but not consistently so.[5] But the concept itself was accepted. Murder was that sort of *homicidium* which came about as the result of a deliberate and malicious act: its punishment was death, although it is likely that murderers sometimes at least had the opportunity of purchasing their

---

[1] The following comments assume freemen as both actor and victim unless indication is given to the contrary.

[2] See the full account of Brunner, *Forschungen*, pp. 487–523 ('Ueber absichtslose Missethat im altdeutschen Strafrechte'), especially pp. 487–9, but cf. E. Kaufmann, *Die Erfolgshaftung* (Frankfurt am Main, 1958), pp. 23ff. Examples of a similar approach in post-Visigothic times are to be found in J. Orlandis, 'Sobre el concepto del delito en el derecho de la alta edad media', *AHDE*, XVI (1945), 114ff.

[3] T. Mommsen, *Römisches Strafrecht* (Leipzig, 1899), pp. 85ff.

[4] But negligence was now subsumed within *casus* (so occasionally in Roman law: ib., p. 89, n. 5) and in Visigothic law *culpa* regularly denoted criminal culpability as opposed to negligence: see V. 4. 18, 5. 1, 2, VI. 4. 10 etc.

[5] Compare, e.g., VI. 4. 6: 'Talis mors pro homicidio conputari non poterit' with VI. 5. 2: 'Si...nolens homicidium amiserit...securus abscedat'.

lives by the payment of composition.[1] An *Antiqua* stated the position succinctly:

'Omnis homo, si volumtate, non casu occiderit hominem, pro homicidio puniatur'.[2]

The culpable act might be one of omission as well as commission: thus, the judge who maliciously permitted an accuser to torture his adversary to death was himself executed.[3] Equally, it might consist simply in the order, later executed, to kill, as when a slave-owner instructed his slaves to murder on his behalf.[4] Moreover, the intention might be to injure rather than to kill.[5] But intention not followed by action by, or at the orders of, the intending killer involved no liability for murder if this should take place: the death penalty did not await the man who conspired with others to murder but left the killing to another.[6]

In contrast to these killings were those where malicious intent played no part. All these were classed by the Visigoths as accidents, *casus*,[7] but the law in fact drew a clear distinction between the unavoidable and the unintended but avoidable accident. The general rule was that the unwitting (*nesciens*) or involuntary (*nolens*) killing of a man was not punishable: biblical precept coincided with Roman precedent in the establishment of this principle.[8] The extent to which this rule departed from Germanic tradition is clear: less clear is the extent to which it succeeded in practice in driving out the older Germanic notions. For the provision that a killing, to be without penalty, must have been unintentional was coupled with the

---

[1] There is no doubt but that the offence was capital: see VI. 5. 17: 'Cum nullum homicidium volumtate conmissum nostris legibus relinquatur inultum, et illum *magis* oporteat mortem excipere, qui consanguinitate proximum presumsit occidere...', VI. 5. 7, 12, 16, VII. 3. 3 (later in note) etc. Death was expressly prescribed for certain killers in VI. 1. 2, 2. 3, 3. 1, 2, 3, 7, 4. 2, 5. 17, 18 (cf.19), and VII. 4. 5. But payment in lieu of execution is indicated by VII. 3. 3: '[Plagiator] parentibus in potestate tradatur; ut illi occidendi aut vendendi eum habeant potestatem, aut, si voluerint, conpositionem homicidii ab ipso plagiatore consequantur, id est solidos CCC; quia parentibus vendidi aut plagiati non levius esse potest, quam si homicidium fuisset admissum'. (For the sum see below, in text.) Note also *damnum* in VI. 5. 1 (n. 5).

[2] VI. 5. 11.          [3] VI. 1. 2.                    [4] VI. 5. 12.

[5] VI. 5. 6: cf. VI. 4. 8 and for a related text VI. 4. 10. *Voluntas nocendi* (thus VI. 5. 7) would have been better in VI. 5. 1: 'Non enim est iustum, ut illum homicide damnum aut pena percutiat, quem volumtas homicidii non cruentat'.

[6] VI. 5. 12. But he was severely punished nonetheless.

[7] Cf. VI. 5. 9, 10, 11, 20 etc., and note that killing in self-defence is 'casu' in VI. 5. 19. For the *casus/voluntas* contrast in other connections see VIII. 3. 6, X. 3. 2.

[8] VI. 5. 1 (cit. p. 37, n. 2) – where Numbers 35. 22ff. and Deut. 19. 4–6 are doubtless in mind – VI. 5. 2, 3.

stipulation that there had been no bad blood between the killer and his victim:

> 'Si nulla occasio inimicitie ante cum eo fuit, et ille nolens homicidium amiserit adque ante iudicem hoc potuerit adprobare'.[1]

Are we to assume that – presumably in the absence of independent witnesses – the defence of lack of intention was not acceptable if the killer had borne enmity towards the dead man?[2] Or is it rather the case that the involuntary killing of a man to whom the killer was hostile was equated with murder without further ado? If the second alternative is correct, we would be justified in recognising here the vestigial influence of the Germanic idea that the act reflected the will of the actor.[3]

But the general rule was in fact stated in too absolute terms, for even involuntary and unwitting killings involved liability for their perpetrators when they came about as the result of negligence. The notion of negligence underlying the Visigothic laws was that of the Romans: negligent behaviour was that which might or must lead to the injury of another. No doubt decisions as to the degree of culpability and the character and extent of remedy were, in the great majority of cases, in the discretion of the judges. But enough laws deal directly with the matter of negligent killing to allow us a fairly good idea of the likely consequences. Penalty regularly took the form of composition: on only two occasions was a corporal sanction inflicted, and on only one of these did it take an extreme form.[4] The full *conpositio homicidii* was the enormous sum of 300, later 500, *solidi*.[5] In two cases we find this amount demanded of the negligent killer: it had to be paid by the judge who without malicious intent allowed a man to die under torture and by the man whose animal killed another person after he had neglected to heed warnings of its viciousness.[6] But it was no doubt this same sum which was required in composition when a man failed to give adequate warning before cutting down a tree which then killed someone in its fall.[7] As common to all

---

[1] VI. 5. 2: cf. VI. 5. 1.
[2] D'Ors, *Código*, p. 113, n. 275, suggests that prior enmity operated as a presumption of malice.        [3] See Brunner, *Rechtsgesch.*, I, 213.
[4] XI. 1. 6 (above, p. 87, n. 1). For the other case see p. 262, n. 3, below.
[5] VI. 1. 2, 5. 14, VII. 3. 3, VIII. 4. 16: cf. IX. 2. 3.
[6] VI. 1. 2; VIII. 4. 16. The *Antiqua* version of the latter (on which see Melicher, *Kampf*, pp. 74–5) had an elaborate tariff of charges, with 300 *solidi* as the maximum composition, imposed for the killing of a man aged between twenty and fifty: a woman of childbearing age (fifteen to forty) was rated at 250 *solidi*. All distinctions disappeared in Ervig's revision, with 500 *solidi* as the universal composition.
[7] VIII. 3. 3: 'Si, dum cadit, arbor aliquem occiderit…pro occiso homine tamquam homicida teneatur' (not *puniatur*).

three cases can be seen an element of wilfulness in the refusal of the guilty party to take simple and proper precautions to avoid putting others at mortal risk, and it is clear that the composition was regarded as providing punitive as well as compensatory damages.[1]

In certain other cases, the consequences were less severe, although still daunting for the ordinary man.[2] Negligence is a common factor of all these cases, but the line of thought of the legislators is not always easy to justify or even to follow. It was reasonable enough that the man who, without evil intent, pushed a second and thereby caused the death of a third should have been held liable, and understandable that a death-blow struck in carelessness or fun should have involved the striker in penalty.[3] But why should the man who started a fight in which his adversary accidentally killed a third man have been held more to blame than the actual killer? The law's unsatisfactory answer was that the killing was committed through his agency because he precipitated a situation in which death could occur.[4] Why, equally, should the actual killer have been required to pay a larger composition if his victim had interceded with the object of stopping the fight?[5] It is difficult to see what the intentions of the dead man, however laudable, have to do with the matter of the killer's culpability. Most of all, why should a teacher or patron administering what is absurdly called 'fitting and moderate discipline' to someone under his control have been held free from penalty if the chastisement led to death, 'cum nihil ille, qui docet aut corripit, in hunc invidie aut malitie habuerit'?[6]

The basic law on misuse of the person, Chindasvind's VI. 4. 3, helps to allow a more precise understanding of the concepts of ill-will and negligence referred to above, for the law takes similar account of the state of the mind of the offender, but distinguishes between the action committed 'ex priori disposito' and that committed 'subito exorta lite et cede

---

[1] The message of VIII. 4. 16 (p. 261, n. 6), where if a slave was killed the payment of two others was ordered. Nevertheless, the judge negligently allowing a slave to die under torture had only to replace him (VI. 1. 5), although for a freeman he had to pay the full composition. Cf. also XI. 1. 6.

[2] VI. 5. 9, dealing with the consequences of the following cases when the victim was a slave, should have been revised in the light of Ervig's new version of VI. 5. 12, for it provided for payments (half the compositions payable when a freeman was the victim) sometimes higher than those for intentional killing (above, p. 172), if the slave-prices suggested above (p. 175) are correct.

[3] VI. 5. 3 (a pound of gold 'quare lesionem vitare neclexerit'); VI. 5. 7 (a pound of gold and fifty lashes 'quare...indiscrete percussit nec vitare casum studuit').

[4] VI. 5. 4: 'Ambo damnum habebunt, quia ille volens aditum mortis dedit, iste nolens mortem iniecit'.  [5] VI. 5. 5.

[6] VI. 5. 8, where the justification is: 'Qui disciplinam abicit, infelix erit'!

conmissa aliquo casu...se nolente'.[1] Premeditation is shown by this to have been an essential element of *mala voluntas*, while an offence perpetrated in the heat of the moment was treated as a sort of *casus*, although one involving liability.[2] A detailed tariff of financial compositions was provided for payment by the man guilty of such an 'accident'. These sums were extremely high – one hundred *solidi* when a nose, eye, ear, lip, hand or foot was lost or a hernia suffered, from ten to fifty *solidi* for each digit, twelve *solidi* for a tooth and so on – but no doubt willingly enough paid by an offender able to show lack of premeditation. For the general rule followed in cases of the premeditated misuse of the person – and this covered offences like putting a man in chains or imprisoning him as well as scalping, amputation and other physical assaults and injuries – was the primitive one of retaliation in kind.[3] This represented in effect the legal consecration of one of the concepts underlying feud, but one for which powerful and explicit support could be found in the Old Testament.[4] The private character of the offence of wounding is laid clear by the provision that composition in the place of talion should be acceptable at the discretion of the victim and at the amount fixed by him. But retaliation in kind was forbidden in the case of injuries caused by a slap, punch or kick or by a blow to the head on the grounds that it might cause greater injury than had been inflicted on the original victim: floggings, of from ten to thirty lashes, were provided for blows which were not severe enough to cause bruising or injury to limbs, while a scale of compositions ranging from five *solidi* for a bruise to one hundred for a broken bone was established for blows to the head causing visible damage.[5] Noteworthy is the fact that the floggings were administered by the victim himself.[6]

[1] The contrast is not taken into account by d'Ors, *Código*, p. 117.

[2] See above, p. 177, for the case of slaves killed by provoked freemen.

[3] See also VI. 4. 5 (where *talio* was decreed for criminal offences to the person not specifically dealt with in the laws, along with other penalties) and XI Tol. 5. *Talio* for wounding was a Chindasvindian innovation: in the (obviously unrevised) *Antiqua* VI. 4. 8, compositions for wounding were fixed at judicial discretion.

[4] Exod. 21. 23–5, Levit. 24. 19–20, Deut. 19. 21. No more than any other was Visigothic society able (if willing) to erect Matt. 5. 38–9 into a legal principle.

[5] The compositions appear in VI. 4. 1.

[6] For the elaborate provisions governing cases where non-freemen were involved, see VI. 4. 1, 3, 9–11.

# BIBLIOGRAPHY OF
# WORKS CITED

### I SOURCES

Agobard of Lyons, *Liber adversus legem Gundobadi*, PL, CIV, 113–26.

Augustine, *Ep.* XCIII, PL, XXXIII, 321–47.

Braulio, *Epistolae*, ed. J. Madoz, *Epistolario de S. Braulio de Zaragoza*, Biblioteca de antiguos escritores cristianos esp., I (Madrid, 1941), 71–206.

Cassiodorus, *Variae*, MGH.AA, XII, 1–385.

*Chronica Regum Visigothorum*, MGH.LL, sectio I, *Leges nationum Germanicarum*, I, 457–61.

*Chronicorum Caesaraugustanorum reliquiae*, MGH.AA, XI, 222–3.

Cixila, *Vita s. Hildefonsi*, PL, XCVI, 43–8.

Claudian, *De bello pollentino sive gothico*, MGH.AA, X, 259–83.

*Codex Euricianus*, MGH.LL, sectio I, *Leges nationum Germanicarum*, I, 3–27.

*Codex Theodosianus*, ed. T. Mommsen, *Theodosiani libri XVI cum constitutionibus Sirmondianis et leges novellae ad Theodosianum pertinentes*, ed. T. Mommsen and P. M. Meyer (2nd edn, 2 vols in 3, Berlin, 1954), I, part II.

*Codicis Euriciani leges ex Lege Baiuvariorum restitutae*, MGH.LL, sectio I, *Leges nationum Germanicarum*, I, 28–32.

*Concilia Hispaniae*, PL, LXXXIV, 301–626.

*Concilios visigóticos e hispano-romanos*, ed. J. Vives, España cristiana, textos, I (Barcelona–Madrid, 1963).

*Confessio vel professio Judaeorum civitatis Toletanae*, ed. Dahn, *Könige* (q.v.), pp. 650–3.

*Continuatio Hispana*, MGH.AA, XI, 334–68.

*Crónica de Alfonso III*, ed. Z. García Villada (Madrid, 1918), pp. 53–85 (redacción primitiva).

*De fisco Barcinonensi*, PL, LXXXIV, 608–10.

*Edictum Theoderici*, MGH.LL, V, 150–68.

Ennodius, *Vita Epifani*, MGH.AA, VII, 84–109.

*Epistolae Arelatenses genuinae*, MGH.Epp., III, 5–83.

*Epistolae Wisigoticae*, ib., 661–90.

Eugenius, *Carmina*, MGH.AA, XIV, 231–70.

*Excerpta Valesiana*, ed. J. Moreau, rev. V. Velkov (Leipzig, 1968).

*Exemplar judicii inter Martianum et Aventium episcopos*, ed. Dahn, *Könige* (q.v.), pp. 615–20.

Felix of Toledo, *Vita s. Juliani*, PL, XCVI, 445–52.

*Formulae Visigothicae*, MGH.LL, sectio V, 575–95.

*Fragmenta Gaudenziana*, MGH.LL, sectio I, *Leges nationum Germanicarum*, I, 469–72.

Fredegar, *Chronicae*, MGH.SSM, II, 18–168.

Fructuosus, *Pactum*, PL, LXXXVII, 1127–30.

*Galliae concilia*, PL, LXXXIV, 237–302.

Gregory I, *Registrum epistolarum*, MGH.Epp., I and II.

Gregory of Tours, *Hist. Francorum*, MGH.SSM, I, 31–450.

 *Liber in gloria martyrum*, ib., 484–561.

Hidatius, *Continuatio chronicorum Hieronymianorum*, MGH.AA, XI, 13–36.

Ildefonsus, *De virginitate perpetua sanctae Mariae adversus tres infideles*, PL, XCVI, 53–110.

 *De viris illustribus*, ib., 195–206.

 *Liber de cognitione baptismi*, ib., 111–72.

*Inscripciones cristianas de la Esp. romana y visigoda*, 2nd edn by J. Vives, Monumenta Hispaniae Sacra, serie patrística, II (Barcelona, 1969).

Isidore, *Chronica*, MGH.AA, XI, 424–81.

 *De ecclesiasticis officiis*, PL, LXXXIII, 737–826.

 *De fide catholica ex Veteri et Novo Testamento contra Judaeos*, ib., 449–538.

 *De laude Spaniae*, MGH.AA, XI, 267.

 *De natura rerum ad Sisebutum regem liber*, PL, LXXXIII, 963–1018.

 *De viris illustribus*, ed. C. Codoñer Merino, El '*De viris illustribus*' de Isidoro de Sevilla, Theses et studia philologica Salmanticensia, XII (Salamanca, 1964), 131–53.

 *Epistolae*, PL, LXXXIII, 893–914.

 *Etymologiae*, ed. W. M. Lindsay (2 vols, Oxford, 1911).

 *Historia Gothorum*, MGH.AA, XI, 268–95.

 *Sententiae*, PL, LXXXIII, 537–738.

 *Synonyma*, ib., 825–68.

*Iudicium in tyrannorum perfidiam promulgatum*, MGH.SSM, V, 529–35.

John of Biclar, *Chronica*, MGH.AA, XI, 211–20.

Jordanes, *Getica*, MGH.AA, V, part I, 53–138.

Julian of Toledo, *De comprobatione aetatis sextae*, PL, XCVI, 537–86.

 *Hist. Wambae regis*, MGH.SSM, V, 501–26.

 *Insultatio in tyrannidem Galliae*, ib., 526–9

 *Prognosticon*, PL, XCVI, 453–524.

Leontius, *The life of St John the Almsgiver*, ed. E. Dawes and N. H. Baynes, *Three Byzantine saints* (Oxford, 1948), pp. 207–62.

*Lex Burgundionum*, *MGH.LL*, sectio I, *Leges nationum Germanicarum*, II, part I, 30–116.

*Lex Romana Burgundionum*, ib., 123–63.

*Lex Romana Visigothorum*, ed. G. Haenel (Leipzig, 1849).

*Lex Teudi*, *MGH.LL*, sectio I, *Leges nationum Germanicarum*, I, 467–9.

*Lex Visigothorum*, ib., 35–456.

*(Le) Liber Ordinum en usage dans l'église wisigothique et mozarabe d'Esp. du cinquième au onzième siècle*, ed. M. Férotin, Monumenta Ecclesiae Liturgica, V (Paris, 1904).

Marius of Avenches, *Chronica*, *MGH.AA*, XI, 232–9.

*Novellae Valentiniani*, ed. P. M. Meyer, *Theodosiani libri XVI* (see above, under *Codex Theodosianus*), II, 69–154.

Orosius, *Historiae adversum paganos*, ed. C. Zangemeister, Corpus Scriptorum Ecclesiasticorum Latinorum, V (Vienna, 1882).

Paul, *Ep. ad Wambam*, *MGH.SSM*, V, 500.

Procopius, *Hist. of the Wars*, trans. H. B. Dewing, Loeb Classical Library (5 vols, London–N. York, 1914–28).

Prosper Tiro, *Epitoma chronicon*, *MGH.AA*, IX, 385–485.

Salvian, *De gubernatione Dei*, *MGH.AA*, I, part I, 1–108.

Sidonius Apollinaris, *Carmina*, *MGH.AA*, VIII, 173–264.

*Epistolae*, ib., 1–172.

Siricius, *Ep. ad Eumerium*, *PL*, LXXXIV, 629–38.

Tacitus, *Germania*, ed. J. G. C. Anderson (Oxford, 1938).

*Testamentum Vicentii episcopi*, ed. F. Fita y Colomé, 'Patrología visigótica. Elpidio, Pompeyano, Vicente y Gabino, obispos de Huesca en el siglo VI', *BRAH*, XLIX (1906), 137–69, at pp. 155–7.

Valerius, *Ordo querimoniae*, ed. and trans. C. M. Aherne, *Valerio of Bierzo, an ascetic of the late Visigothic period*, CUA studies in mediaeval hist., new series, XI (Washington D.C., 1949), 68–109.

*Replicatio sermonum*, ib., 114–51.

*Vita Eligii episcopi Noviomagensis*, *MGH.SSM*, IV, 663–742.

*Vitae sanctorum patrum Emeretensium*, ed. and trans. J. N. Garvin, *The 'Vitas sanctorum patrum Emeretensium'*, CUA studies in medieval and renaissance Latin language and literature, XIX (Washington D.C., 1946), 136–259.

*Vita sancti Fructuosi*, ed. and trans. F. C. Nock, *The 'Vita sancti Fructuosi'*, CUA studies in mediaeval hist., new series, VII (Washington D.C., 1946), 86–129.

*Vita Viviani*, *MGH.SSM*, III, 94–100.

# Bibliography of works cited

II SECONDARY WORKS

Abadal i de Vinyals, R. d', 'À propos du legs visigothique en Esp.', *Sett.*, V (1958), 541–85.

*Del reino de Tolosa al reino de Toledo* (Madrid, 1960).

'La monarquia en el regne de Toledo', *Homenaje a Jaime Vicens Vives*, I (Barcelona, 1965), 191–200.

*Dels visigots als catalans*, I (Barcelona, 1969).

Adams, T., *Clementia principis*, Kieler hist. Studien, XI (Stuttgart, 1970).

Aherne, C. M., 'Late Visigothic bishops, their schools and the transmission of culture', *Traditio*, XXII (1966), 435–44.

Aldama, J. A. de, 'Indicaciones sobre la cronología de las obras de S. Isidoro', *Miscellanea isidoriana* (q.v.), pp. 57–89.

Altamira y Crevea, R., 'Spain', *The continental legal hist. series*, I: *General survey* (London, 1912), pp. 577–702.

Amira, K. von, *Germanisches Recht*, 4th edn by K. A. Eckhardt, I: *Rechtsdenkmäler*, Grundriß der germanischen Philologie, V/I (Berlin, 1960).

Anné, L., *Les rites des fiançailles et la donation pour cause de mariage sous le bas-empire* (Louvain, 1941).

Anton, H. H., *Fürstenspiegel und Herrscherethos in der Karolingerzeit*, Bonner hist. Forschungen, XXXII (Bonn, 1968).

Arenillas, I., 'La autobiografía de San Valerio (siglo VII) como fuente para el conocimiento de la organización eclesiástica visigótica', *AHDE*, XI (1934), 468–78.

Arnal, J., and Riquet, R., 'Le cimetière wisigothique des Pinèdes à Saint-Mathieu-de-Tréviers', *Gallia*, XVII (1959), 161–77.

Aubin, H., 'Stufen und Formen der christlich-kirchlichen Durchdringung des Staates im Frühmittelalter', *Festschrift für Gerhard Ritter* (Tübingen, 1950), pp. 61–86.

Bachrach, B. S., 'Another look at the barbarian settlement in southern Gaul', *Traditio*, XXV (1969), 354–8.

Baron, S. W., *A social and religious hist. of the Jews*, 2nd edn, III (N. York, 1957).

Barrière-Flavy, C., 'Le costume et l'armement du wisigoth aux Ve et VIe siècles', *Revue des Pyrénées*, XIV (1902), 125–43.

Bencyto Pérez, J., *Estudios sobre la hist. del régimen agrario*, Cuadernos de estudios económicos y sociales, VII (Barcelona, 1941).

Bethmann-Hollweg, M. A. von, *Der Civilprozeß des gemeinen Rechts in geschichtlicher Entwicklung*, IV, part I: *Der germanisch-romanische Civilprozeß im MA. Vom fünften bis achten Jahrhundert* (Bonn, 1868).

# Bibliography of works cited

Beumann, H., 'Zur Entwicklung transpersonaler Staatsvorstellungen', *Das Königtum* (q.v.), pp. 185-224.

Beyerle, F., 'Zur Frühgesch. der westgotischen Gesetzgebung', *ZRG.GA*, LXVII (1950), 1-33.

Bidagor, R., *La 'iglesia propia' en Esp.*, Analecta Gregoriana, IV (Rome, 1933).

'Sobre la naturaleza del matrimonio en S. Isidoro de Sevilla', *Miscellanea isidoriana* (q.v.), pp. 253-85.

Biondi, B., *Il diritto romano cristiano*, III (Milan, 1954).

Biraben, J.-N., and Le Goff, J., 'La peste dans le haut MA', *Annales: économies, sociétés, civilisations*, XXIV (1969), 1484-1510.

Blázquez Martínez, J. M., 'La crisis del siglo III en Hispania y Mauritania Tingitana', *Hispania*, XXVIII (1968), 5-37.

Blumenkranz, B., *Juifs et chrétiens dans le monde occidental, 430-1096*, Études juives, II (Paris-La Haye, 1960).

*Les auteurs chrétiens latins du MA sur les juifs et le judaïsme*, Études juives, IV (Paris-La Haye, 1963).

Bouchier, E. S., *Spain under the Roman Empire* (Oxford, 1914).

Braegelmann, A., *The life and writings of Saint Ildefonsus of Toledo*, CUA studies in mediaeval hist., new series, IV (Washington D.C., 1942).

Braga da Cruz, G., 'A sucessão legítima no código Euriciano', *AHDE*, XXIII (1953), 769-830.

Broggini, G., 'Retroactivity of laws in the Roman perspective', *The Irish jurist*, new series, I (1966), 151-70.

Bruck, E. F., 'Caesarius of Arles and the *Lex Romana Visigothorum*', *Studi in onore di Vincenzo Arangio-Ruiz*, I (Naples, 1953), 201-17.

*Kirchenväter und soziales Erbrecht* (Berlin-Göttingen-Heidelberg, 1956).

Brunner, H., *Forschungen zur Gesch. des deutschen und französischen Rechtes* (Stuttgart, 1894).

'Beiträge zur Gesch. des germanischen Wartrechtes', *Festgabe für Heinrich Dernburg* (Berlin, 1900), pp. 39-60.

*Deutsche Rechtsgesch.*, I, 2nd edn (Leipzig, 1906); II, 2nd edn by C. Frh. von Schwerin (Munich-Leipzig, 1928).

Brynteson, W. E., 'Roman law and legislation in the MA', *Speculum*, XLI (1966), 420-37.

Buchner, R., 'Kulturelle und politische Zusammengehörigkeitsgefühle im europäischen Frühmittelalter', *Historische Zeitschrift*, CCVII (1968), 562-83.

*Cambridge economic hist. of Europe, The*, I, 2nd edn by M. M. Postan, (Cambridge, 1966).

*Cambridge hist. of Islam, The*, ed. P. M. Holt et al., I (Cambridge, 1970).

## Bibliography of works cited

Cardascia, G., 'L'apparition dans le droit des classes d'*honestiores* et d'*humiliores*', *Revue hist. de droit français et étranger*, 4th series, XXVIII (1950), 305–37, 461–85.

Carelli, O., 'I delitti di taglio di alberi e di danneggiamento alle piantagioni nel diritto romano', *SDHI*, V (1939), 329–413.

Carlyle, Sir R. W. and A. J., *A hist. of mediaeval political theory in the West*, 2nd edn, I (Edinburgh–London, 1927).

Cassani, J. L., 'La medicina romana en Esp. y su enseñanza', *CHE*, XII (1949), 51–69.

Castán Lacoma, L., 'S. Isidoro de Sevilla, apologista antijudaico', *Isidoriana* (q.v.), pp. 445–56.

Checchini, A., *Scritti giuridici e storico-giuridici* (3 vols, Padua, 1958).

Clark, G., 'Bees in antiquity', *Antiquity*, XVI (1942), 208–15.

Claude, D., 'Zu Fragen der merowingischen Geldgesch.', *Vierteljahrschrift für Sozial- und Wirtschaftsgesch.*, XLVIII (1961), 236–50.
'Studien zu Reccopolis, II: Die historische Situation', *Madrider Mitteilungen*, VI (1965), 167–94.

Conrad, H., *Deutsche Rechtsgesch.*, I: *Frühzeit und MA* (Carlsruhe, 1954).

Courcelle, P., *Hist. littéraire des grandes invasions germaniques*, 3rd edn (Paris, 1964).

Dahn, F., *Westgothische Studien* (Würzburg, 1874).
'Über Handel und Handelsrecht der Westgothen', *Bausteine. Gesammelte kleine Schriften*, II (Berlin, 1880), 301–26.
*Die Könige der Germanen*, 2nd edn, VI (Leipzig, 1885).

Dalton, O. M., *The 'Hist. of the Franks' by Gregory of Tours* (2 vols, Oxford, 1927).

David, P., *Études hist. sur la Galice et le Portugal du VI<sup>e</sup> au XII<sup>e</sup> siècle* (Coimbra, 1947).

Davies, O., *Roman mines in Europe* (Oxford, 1935).

Diaz y Diaz, M. C., 'La cultura de la Esp. visigótica del siglo VII', *Sett.*, V (1958), 813–44.
'Un document privé de l'Esp. wisigothique sur ardoise', *Studi medievali*, 3rd series, I (1960), 52–71.

Dölger, F. J., *Antike und Christentum. Kultur- und Religionsgeschichtliche Studien*, VI (Münster, 1950).

Dupont, A., *Les cités de la Narbonnaise Première depuis les invasions germaniques jusqu'à l'apparition du Consulat* (Nîmes, 1942).

Echánove, A., 'Precisiones acerca de la legislación conciliar toledana sobre los judios', *HS*, XIV (1961), 259–79.

Eckhardt, K. A., 'Die Nachbenennung in den Königshäusern der Goten', *Festgabe Harold Steinacker* (Munich, 1955), pp. 34–55.

Bibliography of works cited

Ehrhardt, A., 'Byzantinische Kaufverträge in Ost und West', ZRG.RA, LI (1931), 126–87.
Eichmann, E., 'Die rechtliche und kirchenpolitische Bedeutung der Kaisersalbung im MA', Festschrift Georg von Hertling (Kempten–Munich, 1913), pp. 263–71.
Ensslin, W., Gottkaiser und Kaiser von Gottes Gnaden, Sitzungsberichte der Bayerischen Akad. der Wissenschaften, philosophisch-hist. Abteilung (Munich, 1943), no. 6.
Esteves, A., 'O germanismo de S. Frutuoso na profissão monástica do século VII', Bracara augusta, XXI = Actas do Congresso de Estudos de Comemoração do XIII Centenário da Morte de S. Frutuoso, I (1967), 258–76.
Ewig, E., 'Zum christlichen Königsgedanken im Frühmittelalter', Das Königtum (q.v.), pp. 7–73.
'Das Bild Constantins des Großen in den ersten Jahrhunderten des abendländischen MAs', HJ, LXXV (1956), 1–46.
'Résidence et capitale pendant le haut MA', Revue hist., CCXXX (1963), 25–72.
Fernández Alonso, J., 'La disciplina penitencial en la Esp. romanovisigoda desde el punto de vista pastoral', HS, IV (1951), 243–311.
La cura pastoral en la Esp. romanovisigoda, Publicaciones del Instituto Esp. de Estudios Eclesiásticos, monografías, II (Rome, 1955).
Fernández Espinar, R., 'La compraventa en el derecho medieval esp.', AHDE, XXV (1955), 293–528.
Fichtenau, H., Arenga. Spätantike und MA im Spiegel von Urkundenformeln, MIÖG, Ergänzungsband, XVIII (Graz–Cologne, 1957).
Ficker, J., 'Über nähere Verwandtschaft zwischen gothisch-spanischem und norwegisch-isländischem Recht', MIÖG, Ergänzungsband, II (Innsbruck, 1888), 455–542.
Fontaine, J., 'Isidore de Séville et l'astrologie', REL, XXXI (1953), 271–300.
Isidore de Séville et la culture classique dans l'Esp. wisigothique (2 vols, Paris, 1959).
'Conversion et culture chez les wisigoths d'Esp.', Sett., XIV (1967), 87–147.
Gagé, J., Les classes sociales dans l'empire romain (Paris, 1964).
Gama Barros, H. da, Hist. da administração publica em Portugal nos séculos XII a XV, 2nd edn by T. de Sousa Soares (11 vols, Lisbon, 1945–54?).
Gamillscheg, E., Romania Germanica, I, Grundriß der germanischen Philologie, XI/I (Berlin–Leipzig, 1934).
Gams, P. B., Die Kirchengesch. von Spanien, II, part II (Regensburg, 1874).
Garaud, M., 'L'occupation du Poitou par les wisigoths', Bulletin de la Société des Antiquaires de l'Ouest, 3rd series, XIV (1945), 548–63.

García, H., 'Notas para unos prolegómenos a la hist. del notariado esp.', *Estudios hist. y documentos de los archivos de protocolos*, II (Barcelona, 1950), 121–47.

García Gallo, A., 'Nacionalidad y territorialidad del derecho en la época visigoda', *AHDE*, XIII (1936–41), 168–264.

'Notas sobre el reparto de tierras entre visigodos y romanos', *Hispania*, I (1940–1), no. IV, 40–63.

*Curso de hist. del derecho esp.*, 7th edn, I (Madrid, 1958).

'San Isidoro, jurista', *Isidoriana* (q.v.), pp. 133–41.

García Garrido, M., 'El régimen jurídico del patrimonio uxorio en el derecho vulgar romano-visigótico', *AHDE*, XXIX (1959), 389–446.

García González, J., 'El incumplimiento de las promesas de matrimonio en la hist. del derecho esp.', *AHDE*, XXIII (1953), 611–42.

García Villada, Z., *Hist. eclesiástica de Esp.*, II, part II (Madrid, 1933).

Garnsey, P., *Social status and legal privilege in the Roman Empire* (Oxford, 1970).

Gaudemet, J., 'Survivances romaines dans le droit de la monarchie franque du V^{ème} au X^{ème} siècle', *Tijdschrift voor rechtsgeschiedenis*, XXIII (1955), 149–206.

*La formation du droit séculier et du droit de l'église aux IV^e et V^e siècles* (Paris, 1957).

'Les ordalies au MA: doctrine, législation et pratique canoniques', *Recueils de la Société Jean Bodin*, XVII: *La preuve* (part 2) (Brussels, 1965), pp. 99–135.

*Le Bréviaire d'Alaric et les Epitome*, IRMAE, part I, 2b *aa β* (Milan, 1965).

Gibbon, E., *The hist. of the decline and fall of the Roman Empire*, 6th edn by J. B. Bury (7 vols, London, 1925).

Gibert, R., 'El consentimiento familiar en el matrimonio según el derecho medieval esp.', *AHDE*, XVIII (1947), 706–61.

'El reino visigodo y el particularismo esp.', *EV*, I = Cuadernos del Instituto Jurídico Esp., V (Rome–Madrid, 1956), 15–47.

*Hist. general del derecho esp.* (Granada, 1968).

Giese, W., 'In Iudaismum lapsus est', *HJ*, LXXXVIII (1968), 407–18.

Gómez-Moreno, M., 'Documentación goda en pizarra', *Boletín de la Real Academia Esp.*, XXXIV (1954), 25–58.

*Documentación goda en pizarra* (Madrid, 1966).

González Gallego, I., 'Apuntes para un estudio económico de la Esp. visigoda', *Archivos leoneses*, XXI (1967), 89–109.

Goubert, P., 'Influences byzantines sur l'Esp. wisigothique', *Revue des études byzantines*, IV (1946), 111–22.

Grassotti, H., 'La *ira regia* en León y Castilla', *CHE*, XLI–XLII (1965), 5–135.

Grierson, P., 'Election and inheritance in early Germanic kingship', *Cambridge hist. journal*, VII (1941), 1–22.

'Visigothic metrology', *Numismatic chronicle*, 6th series, XIII (1953), 74–87.

Review of Miles (q.v.), ib., pp. 183–5.

'Commerce in the Dark Ages: a critique of the evidence', *Transactions of the Royal Hist. Society*, 5th series, IX (1959), 123–40.

'Coinage and money in the Byzantine Empire, 498–*c*. 1090', *Sett.*, VIII (1961), 411–53.

Guarino, A., *Storia del diritto romano*, 4th edn (Naples, 1969).

Guilhiermoz, P., *Essai sur l'origine de la noblesse en France au MA* (Paris, 1902).

Gundlach, W., 'Der Anhang des III. *Epistolae*-Bandes der *MGH*: *Epistolae ad res Wisigothorum pertinentes*', *NA*, XVI (1890), 9–48.

Halban, A. von, *Das römische Recht in den germanischen Volksstaaten*, part I, Untersuchungen zur deutschen Staats- und Rechtsgesch., ed. O. Gierke, LVI (Breslau, 1899).

Heymann, E., Review of *AHDE*, XIII (1936–41), *ZRG.GA*, LXIII (1943), 360–6.

Hillgarth, J. N., 'La conversión de los visigodos', *AST*, XXXIV (1961), 21–46.

'The East, Visigothic Spain and the Irish', *Studia patristica*, IV, Texte und Untersuchungen zur Gesch. der altchristlichen Literatur, LXXIX (Berlin, 1961), 442–56.

'Visigothic Spain and early Christian Ireland', *Proceedings of the Royal Irish Academy*, LXII (1961–3), section C, pp. 167–94.

'Coins and chronicles: propaganda in sixth-century Spain and the Byzantine background', *Historia*, XV (1966), 483–508.

Hinojosa y Naveros, E. de, *Obras* (2 vols, Madrid, 1948–55).

Höfler, O., 'Der Sakralcharakter des germanischen Königtums', *Das Königtum* (q.v.), pp. 75–104.

Honig, R. M., *Humanitas und Rhetorik in spätrömischen Kaisergesetzen*, Göttinger rechtswissenschaftliche Studien, XXX (Göttingen, 1960).

Houston, J. M., *The western Mediterranean world* (London, 1964).

*Índice histórico esp.*, ed. by the Facultad de Filosofía y Letras, Univ. de Barcelona.

*Isidoriana*, ed. M. C. Diaz y Diaz (Leon, 1961).

Jones, A. H. M., 'Were ancient heresies national or social movements in disguise?', *Journal of theological studies*, new series, X (1959), 280–98.

'Slavery in the ancient world', *Slavery in classical antiquity* (q.v.), pp. 1–15.

*The later Roman Empire, 284–602* (4 vols, Oxford, 1964).

*The decline of the ancient world* (London, 1966).

Juster, J., 'La condition légale des juifs sous les rois visigoths', *Études d'hist. juridique offertes à Paul Frédéric Girard*, II (Paris, 1913), 275–335.

Kamen, H., *The Spanish Inquisition* (London, 1965).

Kantorowicz, E. H., *The king's two bodies. A study in mediaeval political theology* (Princeton, N. Jersey, 1957).

Kaser, M., *Das römische Privatrecht*, II: *Die nachklassischen Entwicklungen*, Rechtsgesch. des Altertums im Rahmen des Handbuchs der Altertumswissenschaft, X. 3. 3. 2 (Munich, 1959).

Katz, S., *The Jews in the Visigothic and Frankish kingdoms of Spain and Gaul*, Monographs of the Mediaeval Acad. of America, XII (Cambridge, Mass., 1937).

Kaufmann, E., *Die Erfolgshaftung*, Frankfurter wissenschaftliche Beiträge, rechts- und wirtschaftswissenschaftliche Reihe, XVI (Frankfurt am Main, 1958).

*Aequitatis iudicium*, ib., XVIII (Frankfurt am Main, 1959).

Kern, F., *Gottesgnadentum und Widerstandsrecht im früheren MA*, 2nd edn by R. Buchner (Münster–Cologne, 1954).

King, P. D., 'The character of Visigothic legislation' (unpublished doctoral dissertation: University of Cambridge, 1967).

Kleffens, E. N. van, *Hispanic law until the end of the MA* (Edinburgh, 1968).

Klein, J., *The Mesta*, Harvard economic studies, XXI (Cambridge, Mass., 1920).

Koebner, R., 'The settlement and colonization of Europe', *CEH*, I, 1–91.

*Königtum, Das. Seine geistigen und rechtlichen Grundlagen*, Vorträge und Forschungen, III, ed. T. Mayer (Lindau–Constance, 1954).

Köstler, R., 'Raub-, Kauf- und Friedelehe bei den Germanen', *ZRG.GA*, LXIII (1943), 92–136.

Kottje, R., *Studien zum Einfluß des Alten Testamentes auf Recht und Liturgie des frühen MAs*, Bonner hist. Forschungen, XXIII (Bonn, 1964).

Lacarra, J. M., 'Panorama de la hist. urbana en la península ibérica desde el siglo V al X', *Sett.*, VI (1959), 319–55.

'La iglesia visigoda en el siglo VII y sus relaciones con Roma', ib., VII (1960), 353–84.

'La península ibérica del siglo VII al X. Centros y vias de irradiación de la civilización', ib., XI (1964), 233–78.

Lalinde Abadía, J., 'Un enigma jurídico visigodo', *AHDE*, XXX (1960), 631–41.

'La sucesión filial en el derecho visigodo', ib., XXXII (1962), 113–29.

Larraona, A., and Tabera, A., 'El derecho justinianeo en Esp.', *Atti del Congresso Internazionale di Diritto Romano, Bologna II* (Pavia, 1935), pp. 83–182.

Latouche, R., *The birth of Western economy* (London, 1967).

Lauria, M., 'Accusatio–inquisitio', *Atti della Reale Accademia di Scienze Morali e Politiche*, LVI (1934), 304–69.

Lear, F. S., 'The public law of the Visigothic code', *Speculum*, XXVI (1951), 1–23.

'Contractual allegiance vs. deferential allegiance in Visigothic law', *Treason in Roman and Germanic law* (Austin, 1965), pp. 123–35.

Leclercq, H., *L'Esp. chrétienne* (Paris, 1906).

Leicht, P. S., Review of García Gallo, 'Nacionalidad' (q.v.) et al., *RSDI*, XVII–XX (1944–7), 203–7.

Lemaire, A., 'Origine de la règle *Nullum sine dote fiat conjugium*', *Mélanges Paul Fournier* (Paris, 1929), pp. 415–24.

Levy, E., 'Vom römischen Precarium zur germanischen Landleihe', *ZRG.RA*, LXVI (1948), 1–30.

*West Roman vulgar law. The law of property*, Memoirs of the American Philosophical Society, XXIX (Philadelphia, 1951).

*Weströmisches Vulgarrecht. Das Obligationenrecht*, Forschungen zum römischen Recht, ed. M. Kaser et al., VII (Weimar, 1956).

*Gesammelte Schriften*, I (Cologne–Graz, 1963).

Lewis, A. R., *The northern seas. Shipping and commerce in northern Europe, A.D. 300–1100* (Princeton, N. Jersey, 1958).

Lombardía, P., 'Los matrimonios mixtos en el derecho de la iglesia visigoda', *AHDE*, XXVII/XXVIII (1957/8), 61–107.

Lopez, R. S., 'Byzantine law in the seventh century and its reception by the Germans and the Arabs', *Byzantion*, XVI (1942–3), 445–61.

López Rodó, L., 'Distinción entre los patrimonios de la corona y del rey en la monarquía visigótica', *Colección de estudios en homenaje al profesor Camilo Barcia Trelles* (Santiago, 1945), pp. 345–67.

Lot, F., 'Du régime de l'hospitalité', *Revue belge de philologie et d'hist.*, VII (1928), 975–1011.

Lowe, E. A., *Codices latini antiquiores*, V: *France, Paris* (Oxford, 1950).

Loyen, A., 'Les débuts du royaume wisigoth de Toulouse', *REL*, XII (1934), 406–15.

Lynch, C. H., *Saint Braulio, Bishop of Saragossa (631–651). His life and writings*, CUA studies in mediaeval hist., new series, II (Washington D.C., 1938).

Madoz, J., 'El florilegio patrístico del II Concilio de Sevilla', *Miscellanea isidoriana* (q.v.), pp. 177–220.

'El primado romano en Esp. en el ciclo isidoriano', *RET*, II (1942), 229–55.

'La teología de la Trinidad en los símbolos toledanos', *RET*, IV (1944), 457–77.

*El símbolo del Concilio XVI de Toledo*, Estudios onienses, series I, III (Madrid, 1946).

'Tajón de Zaragoza y su viaje a Roma', *Mélanges Joseph de Ghellinck*, I (Gembloux, 1951), 345–60.

Magnin, E., *L'église wisigothique au VII<sup>e</sup> siècle*, I (Paris, 1912).

Mans Puigarnau, J. M., *Las clases serviles bajo la monarquía visigoda y en los estados cristianos de la Reconquista esp.* (Barcelona, 1928).

Mañaricua, A. E. de, *El matrimonio de los esclavos*, Analecta Gregoriana, XXIII (Rome, 1940).

Maravall, J. A., *El concepto de Esp. en la edad media*, 2nd edn (Madrid, 1964).

Martínez, G., 'Función de inspección y vigilancia del episcopado sobre las autoridades seculares en el período visigodo-católico', *Revista esp. de derecho canónico*, XV (1960), 579–89.

Martínez Díez, G., *El patrimonio eclesiástico en la Esp. visigoda*, Publicaciones anejas a 'Miscelanea Comillas', serie canónica, II (Univ. Pontificia, Comillas (Santander), 1959).

'La tortura judicial en la legislación hist. esp.', *AHDE*, XXXII (1962), 223–300.

Martínez Gijón, J., 'La comenda en el derecho esp., I: La comenda-depósito', *AHDE*, XXXIV (1964), 31–140.

Martins, M., *Correntes da filosofia religiosa em Braga dos séc. IV a VII* (Oporto, 1950).

Mateu y Llopis, F., 'Las fórmulas y los símbolos cristianos en los tipos monetales visigodos', *AST*, XIV (1941), 75–96.

'El arte monetario visigodo. Las monedas como monumentos. (Un ensayo de interpretación)', *AEA*, XVIII (1945), 34–58.

Mayer, E., 'Das altspanische Obligationenrecht in seinen Grundzügen', *Zeitschrift für vergleichende Rechtswissenschaft*, XXXVII (1920), 31–240.

*Hist. de las instituciones sociales y políticas de Esp. y Portugal durante los siglos V a XIV*, I (Madrid, 1925).

Mayer-Maly, T., 'Das Notverkaufsrecht des Hausvaters', *ZRG.RA*, LXXV (1958), 116–55.

McKenna, S. J., *Paganism and pagan survivals in Spain up to the fall of the Visigothic kingdom*, CUA studies in mediaeval hist., new series, I (Washington D.C., 1938).

Melicher, T., *Der Kampf zwischen Gesetzes- und Gewohnheitsrecht im Westgotenreiche* (Weimar, 1930).

'Das Tötungsrecht des germanischen Hausherrn im spanischen, französischen und italienischen Recht', *Zeitschrift für vergleichende Rechtswissenschaft*, XLVI (1930–1), 379–409.

*Die germanischen Formen der Eheschließung im westgotisch-spanischen Recht* (Vienna, 1940).

Menéndez Pidal, R. (ed.), *Hist. de Esp.*, III: *Esp. visigoda* (Madrid, 1940).

Menéndez y Pelayo, M., *Hist. de los heterodoxos esp.*, 2nd edn, II (Madrid, 1917).

Merêa, P., *Estudos de direito visigótico* (Coimbra, 1948).

'Sobre a precária visigótica e suas derivações imediatas', *RPH*, IV (1949), 287–303.

'Le mariage *sine consensu parentum* dans le droit romain vulgaire occidental', *Revue internationale des droits de l'antiquité*, V = *Mélanges Fernand de Visscher*, IV (1950), 203–17.

'Nota sobre a *Lex Visigothorum* II. 1. 23 (juramento subsidiario)', *AHDE*, XXI/XXII (1951/2), 1163–8.

'*Edictum Theodorici* e *Fragmenta Gaudenziana*', *BFD*, XXXII (1956), 315–24.

'A lei IV. 5. 5 da *Lex Visigothorum* e o poder paternal do direito visigótico', ib., XLI (1965), 63–81.

Merk, W., 'Der Gedanke des gemeinen Besten in der deutschen Staats- und Rechtsentwicklung', *Festschrift Alfred Schultze* (Weimar, 1934), pp. 451–520.

Merschberger, G., *Die Rechtsstellung der germanischen Frau*, Mannus-Bücherei, LVII (Leipzig, 1937).

Merzbacher, F., 'Römisches Recht und Romanistik im MA', *HJ*, LXXXIX (1969), 1–32.

Messmer, H., *Hispania-Idee und Gotenmythos*, Geist und Werk der Zeiten, V (Zurich, 1960).

Miles, G. C., *The coinage of the Visigoths of Spain: Leovigild to Achila II*, Hispanic numismatic series, monograph no. II (N. York, 1952).

Millas Vallicrosa, J. M., 'Una nueva inscripción judaica bilingüe en Tarragona', *Sefarad*, XVII (1957), 3–10.

Minguijón Adrián, S., *Hist. del derecho esp.*, I (Buenos Aires, 1927).

*Miscellanea isidoriana*, ed. by the Jesuits of the Province of Andalusia (Rome, 1936).

Mitteis, H., Review of Merêa, *Estudos* (q.v.) et al., *ZRG.GA*, LXVIII (1951), 529–33.

Mommsen, T., *Römisches Strafrecht*, Systematisches Handbuch der deutschen Rechtswissenschaft, ed. K. Binding, section I, part IV (Leipzig, 1899).

Montesquieu, C. L. de Secondat, Baron de, *De l'esprit des loix*, ed. J. Brethe de la Gressaye (4 vols, Paris, 1950–61).

Monzó, S., 'El bautismo de los judios en la Esp. visigoda. En torno al canon 57 del Concilio IV de Toledo', *Cuadernos de trabajos de derecho*, II (1953), 111–55.

Mor, C. G., 'La *manumissio in ecclesia*', *RSDI*, I (1928), 80–150.

Müller, E., 'Die Anfänge der Königssalbung im MA und ihre hist.-politischen Auswirkungen', *HJ*, LVIII (1938), 317–60.

Mullins, P. J., *The spiritual life according to Saint Isidore of Seville*, CUA studies in medieval and renaissance Latin language and literature, XIII (Washington D.C., 1940).

Mundò, A., 'Il monachesimo nella penisola iberica fino al sec. VII', *Sett.*, IV (1957), 73–108.

Murphy, F. X., 'Julian of Toledo and the condemnation of Monothelitism in Spain', *Mélanges Joseph de Ghellinck*, I (Gembloux, 1951), 361–73.

'Julian of Toledo and the fall of the Visigothic kingdom in Spain', *Speculum*, XXVII (1952), 1–27.

Orlandis Rovira, J., 'La paz de la casa en el derecho esp. de la alta edad media', *AHDE*, XV (1944), 107–61.

'Huellas visigóticas en el derecho de la alta edad media', ib., pp. 644–58.

'Sobre el concepto del delito en el derecho de la alta edad media', *AHDE*, XVI (1945), 112–92.

'El cristianismo en la Esp. visigoda', *EV*, I = Cuadernos del Instituto Jurídico Esp., V (Rome–Madrid, 1956), 1–13.

'La reina en la monarquía visigoda', *AHDE*, XXVII/XXVIII (1957/8), 109–35.

'En torno a la noción visigoda de tiranía', ib., XXIX (1959), 5–43.

'La iglesia visigoda y los problemas de la sucesión al trono en el siglo VII', *Sett.*, VII (1960), 333–51.

*El poder real y la sucesión al trono en la monarquía visigoda*, EV, III = Cuadernos del Instituto Jurídico Esp., XVI (Rome–Madrid, 1962).

'El elemento germánico en la iglesia esp. del siglo VII', *Anuario de estudios medievales*, III (1966), 27–64.

Ors, A. d', 'La territorialidad del derecho de los visigodos', *EV*, I = Cuadernos del Instituto Jurídico Esp., V (Rome–Madrid, 1956), 91–124. (Also in *Sett.*, III (1956), 363–408.)

'El capítulo 327 del código de Eurico', *EV*, I (as last reference), 127–41.

'Varia Romana', *AHDE*, XXVII/XXVIII (1957/8), 1164–5.

'Dudas sobre *leudes*', ib., XXX (1960), 643–7.

*El código de Eurico. Edición, palingenesia, índices*, EV, II = Cuadernos del Instituto Jurídico Esp., XII (Rome–Madrid, 1960).

Otero, A., 'La patria potestad en el derecho hist. esp.', *AHDE*, XXVI (1956), 209–41.

'Liber Iudiciorum III. 1. 5', ib., XXIX (1959), 545–55.

'La mejora del nieto', ib., XXXI (1961), 389–400.

'La mejora', ib., XXXIII (1963), 5–131.

Palol, P. de, *Arte hispánico de la época visigoda* (Barcelona, 1968).

Pange, J. de, *Le roi très chrétien* (Paris, 1949).

Paradisi, B., 'Critica e mito dell'editto Teodericiano', *Bullettino dell'-Istituto di Diritto Romano*, 3rd series, VII (1965), 1–47.

Parain, C., 'The evolution of agricultural technique', *CEH*, I, 125–79.

Parkes, J., *The conflict of the Church and the Synagogue* (London, 1934).

Pérez de Urbel, J., 'Caracter y supervivencia del pacto de San Fructuoso', *Bracara augusta*, XXII = *Actas do Congresso de Estudos de Comemoração do XIII Centenário da Morte de S. Frutuoso*, II (1968), 226–42.

Pérez Pujol, E., *Hist. de las instituciones sociales de la Esp. goda* (4 vols, Valencia, 1896).

Perrin, O., *Les burgondes* (Neuchâtel, 1968).

Phillpotts, B. S., *Kindred and clan in the MA and after* (Cambridge, 1913).

Piel, J. M., 'Toponimia germánica', *Enciclopedia lingüística hispánica*, ed. M. Alvar et al., I (Madrid, 1960), 531–60.

Piganiol, A., *L'impôt de capitation sous le bas-empire romain* (Chambéry, 1916).

Pirenne, H., *Mahomet et Charlemagne*, 3rd edn (Paris–Brussels, 1937).

Pommeray, L., *Études sur l'infamie en droit romain* (Paris, 1937).

Raddatz, K., 'Studien zu Reccopolis, I: Die archäologischen Befunde', *Madrider Mitteilungen*, V (1964), 213–33.

Reinhart, W., 'Sobre el asentamiento de los visigodos en la península', *AEA*, XVIII (1945), 124–39.

'Sobre la territorialidad de los códigos visigodos', *AHDE*, XVI (1945), 704–11.

'La tradición visigoda en el nacimiento de Castilla', *Estudios dedicados a Menéndez Pidal*, I (Madrid, 1950), 535–54.

'Über die Territorialität der westgotischen Gesetzbücher', *ZRG.GA*, LXVIII (1951), 348–54.

Reydellet, M., 'La conception du souverain chez Isidore de Séville', *Isidoriana* (q.v.), pp. 457–66.

Riché, P., *Éducation et culture dans l'occident barbare, VIe–VIIIe siècles*, Patristica Sorbonensia, IV (Paris, 1962).

Rivera Recio, J. F., 'Cisma episcopal en la iglesia toledana visigoda?',
  *HS*, I (1948), 259–68.
'Encumbramiento de la sede toledana durante la dominación visi-
  gótica', *HS*, VIII (1955), 3–34.
Roberti, M., '*Patria potestas e paterna pietas*', *Studi in memoria di Aldo
  Albertoni*, I (Padua, 1935), 257–70.
Rodríguez Mourullo, G., 'La distinción hurto–robo en el derecho hist.
  esp.', *AHDE*, XXXII (1962), 25–111.
Roels, W., *Onderzoek naar het gebruik van de aangehaalde bronnen van Romeins
  recht in de Lex romana Burgundionum* (Antwerp, 1958).
Romero, J. L., 'San Isidoro de Sevilla. Su pensamiento históricopolítico
  y sus relaciones con la hist. visigoda', *CHE*, VIII (1947), 5–71.
Rubin, B., *Das Zeitalter Iustinians*, I (Berlin, 1960).
Rubio, J. A., '*Donationes post obitum y donationes reservato usufructu* en la
  alta edad media de León y Castilla', *AHDE*, IX (1932), 1–32.
Ruggini, L., *Economia e società nell'Italia annonaria*, Fondazione Guglielmo
  Castelli, XXX (Milan, 1961).
Russell, J. C., 'That earlier plague', *Demography*, V (1968), 174–84.
  *Population in Europe, 500–1500*, Fontana economic hist. of Europe,
  ed. C. M. Cipolla, I, sect. I (London, 1969).
Sánchez-Albornoz y Menduiña, C., 'La caballería visigoda', *Wirtschaft
  und Kultur. Festschrift zum 70. Geburtstag von Alfons Dopsch* (Baden bei
  Wien–Leipzig, 1938), pp. 92–108.
*En torno a los orígenes del feudalismo*, I: *Fideles y gardingos en la monarquía
  visigoda* (Mendoza, 1942).
*Ruina y extinción del municipio romano en Esp. e instituciones que le re-
  emplazan* (Buenos Aires, 1943).
'El aula regia y las asambleas políticas de los godos', *CHE*, V (1946), 5–110.
'El senatus visigodo. Don Rodrigo, rey legítimo de Esp.', *CHE*, VI
  (1946), 5–99.
*El 'stipendium' hispano-godo y los orígenes del beneficio prefeudal* (Buenos
  Aires, 1947).
'El gobierno de las ciudades en Esp. del siglo V al X', *Sett.*, VI (1959),
  359–91.
'Pervivencia y crisis de la tradición jurídica romana en la Esp. goda',
  *Sett.*, IX (1962), 128–99.
'La *ordinatio principis* en la Esp. goda y postvisigoda', *CHE*, XXXV
  (1962), 5–36.
*Estudios sobre las instituciones medievales esp.*, Univ. Nacional Autónoma
  de México, Instituto de Investigaciones Hist., series de hist. general,
  V (Mexico City, 1965).

'"La pérdida de España." El ejército visigodo: su protofeudalización', *CHE*, XLIII–XLIV (1967), 5–73.

Schäferdiek, K., *Die Kirche in den Reichen der Westgoten und Suewen bis zur Errichtung der westgotischen katholischen Staatskirche*, Arbeiten zur Kirchengesch., XXXIX (Berlin, 1967).

Scharf, J., 'Studien zur Smaragdus und Jonas', *Deutsches Archiv für Erforschung des MAs*, XVII (1961), 333–84.

Schlunk, H., 'Relaciones entre la península ibérica y Bizancio durante la época visigoda', *AEA*, XVIII (1945), 177–204.

Schmidt, A. B., *Die Grundsätze über den Schadensersatz in den Volksrechten*, Untersuchungen zur deutschen Staats- und Rechtsgesch., ed. O. Gierke, XVIII (Breslau, 1885).

Schmidt, K. D., *Die Bekehrung der Germanen zum Christentum*, I: *Die Bekehrung der Ostgermanen* (Göttingen, 1939).

Schmidt, L., *Gesch. der deutschen Stämme bis zum Ausgange der Völkerwanderung*, I: *Die Gesch. der Ostgermanen* (Berlin, 1910).

Schramm, P. E., *Herrschaftszeichen und Staatssymbolik*, I, Schriften der *MGH*, XIII/I (Stuttgart, 1954).

Schultze, A., 'Gerüfte und Marktkauf in Beziehung zur Fahrnisverfolgung', *Festgabe für Felix Dahn*, I: *Deutsche Rechtsgesch.* (Breslau, 1905), pp. 1–63.

*Über westgotisch-spanisches Eherecht, mit einem Exkurs: 'Zur Gesch. der westgotischen Rechtsquellen'*, Berichte über die Verhandlungen der Sächsischen Akad. der Wissenschaften zu Leipzig, philologisch-hist. Klasse, XCV (1943), part IV.

Schulz, F. H., *Principles of Roman law* (Oxford, 1936).

'Bracton on kingship', *EHR*, LX (1945), 136–76.

Schwerin, C. Frh. von, 'Notas sobre la hist. del derecho esp. más antiguo', *AHDE*, I (1924), 27–54.

Séjourné, P., *Saint Isidore de Séville. Son rôle dans l'hist. du droit canonique* (Paris, 1929).

Sharf, A., 'Byzantine Jewry in the seventh century', *Byzantinische Zeitschrift*, XLVIII (1955), 103–15.

Sharpe, W. D., *Isidore of Seville: the medical writings*, Transactions of the American Philosophical Society, new series, LIV, part II (Philadelphia, 1964).

Shaw, R. D., 'The fall of the Visigothic power in Spain', *EHR*, XXI (1906), 209–28.

*Slavery in classical antiquity*, ed. M. I. Finley (Cambridge, 1960).

Smith, R. E., 'Medieval agrarian society in its prime: Spain', *CEH*, I, 432–48.

Solomon Ibn Verga, *Schevet jehuda*, German transl. by M. Wiener (Hanover, 1856).

Sousa Soares, T. de, 'Essai sur les causes économiques de la ruine de la monarchie wisigothique d'Esp.', *RPH*, VI (1955), 453–61.

Sprandel, R., 'Über das Problem neuen Rechts im früheren MA', *ZRG.KA*, LXXIX (1962), 117–37.

Stein, E., *Hist. du bas-empire* (2 vols, Paris–Brussels–Amsterdam, 1949–59).

Steinwenter, A., 'Der antike kirchliche Rechtsgang und seine Quellen', *ZRG.KA*, LIV (1934), 1–116.

Stevens, C. E., *Sidonius Apollinaris and his age* (Oxford, 1933).

Stroheker, K. F., *Eurich, König der Westgoten* (Stuttgart, 1937).

'Leowigild: Aus einer Wendezeit westgotischer Gesch.', *Die Welt als Gesch.*, V (1939), 446–85.

*Der senatorische Adel im spätantiken Gallien* (Tübingen, 1948).

*Germanentum und Spätantike* (Zurich–Stuttgart, 1965).

Tabera, A., 'La definición de *furtum* en las "Etimologías" de S. Isidoro', *SDHI*, VIII (1942), 23–47.

Thibault, F., 'L'impôt direct dans les royaumes des ostrogoths, des wisigoths et des burgundes', *Nouvelle revue hist. de droit français et étranger*, XXVI (1902), 32–48.

Thompson, E. A., 'The settlement of the barbarians in southern Gaul', *Journal of Roman studies*, XLVI (1956), 65–75.

'Two notes on St. Fructuosus of Braga', *Hermathena*, XC (1957), 54–63.

'Slavery in early Germany', *Slavery in classical antiquity* (q.v.), pp. 191–203.

'The conversion of the Visigoths to Catholicism', *Nottingham mediaeval studies*, IV (1960), 4–35.

'The Visigoths from Fritigern to Euric', *Historia*, XII (1963), 105–26.

*The early Germans* (Oxford, 1965).

*The Visigoths in the time of Ulfila* (Oxford, 1966).

*The Goths in Spain* (Oxford, 1969).

Tomás y Valiente, F., 'La sucesión de quien muere sin parientes y sin disponer de sus bienes', *AHDE*, XXXVI (1966), 189–254.

Torres, C., 'Mirón, rey de suevos y gallegos, y los últimos monarcas suevos', *Cuadernos de estudios gallegos*, XIV (1959), 165–201.

Torres López, M., 'El estado visigótico', *AHDE*, III (1926), 307–475.

*Lecciones de hist. del derecho esp.* (2 vols, Salamanca, 1933–4).

Ullmann, W., 'The Bible and principles of government in the MA', *Sett.*, X (1963), 181–227.

'Der Souveranitätsgedanke in den mittelalterlichen Krönungsordines', *Festschrift Percy Ernst Schramm*, I (Wiesbaden, 1964), 72–89.

*A hist. of political thought: the MA*, 2nd edn (London, 1970).

*Principles of government and politics in the MA*, 2nd edn (London, 1966).

*The individual and society in the MA* (London, 1967).

*The Carolingian Renaissance and the idea of kingship* (London, 1969).

Ureña y Smenjaud, R. de, *La legislación gótico-hispana* (Madrid, 1905).

Valdeavellano, L. García de, 'El apellido. Notas sobre el procedimiento *in fragranti* en el derecho esp. medieval', *CHE*, VII (1947), 67–105.

'Sobre los conceptos de hurto y robo en el derecho visigodo y post-visigodo', *RPH*, IV (1949), 211–51.

*La comunidad patrimonial de la familia en el derecho esp. medieval*, Acta Salmanticensia, derecho, III, no. 1 (Salamanca, 1956).

'La moneda y la economía de cambio en la península ibérica desde el siglo VI hasta mediados del siglo XI', *Sett.*, VIII (1961), 203–30.

*Curso de hist. de las instituciones esp. de los orígenes al final de la edad media* (Madrid, 1968).

Vázquez de Parga, L., 'Studien zu Reccopolis, III: Die archäologischen Funde', *Madrider Mitteilungen*, VIII (1967), 259–80.

Vega, A. C., 'Una herejía judaizante del siglo VIII en Esp.', *Ciudad de Dios*, CLIII (1941), 57–100.

'El primado romano y la iglesia esp. en los siete primeros siglos', ib., CLIV (1942), 23–56, 237–84, 501–24.

'El primado romano en la iglesia esp. desde sus orígenes hasta el siglo VII', *RET*, II (1942), 63–99.

'La venida de San Pablo a Esp. y los Varones Apostólicos', *BRAH*, CLIV (1964), 7–78.

'De patrología esp. San Ildefonso de Toledo', ib., CLXV (1969), 35–107.

Ventura Solsona, S., 'Noticia de las excavaciones en curso en el anfiteatro de Tarragona', *AEA*, XXVII (1954), 259–80.

Vercauteren, F., '*Cataplus et catabolus*', *Bulletin du Cange*, II (1925), 98–101.

Verlinden, C., 'L'esclavage dans le monde ibérique médiéval', *AHDE*, XI (1934), 283–448.

'Le grand domaine dans les états ibériques chrétiens au MA', *Recueils de la Société Jean Bodin*, IV: *Le domaine* (Wetteren, 1949), pp. 177–208.

*L'esclavage dans l'Europe médiévale*, I: *Péninsule ibérique–France*, Rijksuniversiteit te Gent. Werken uitgegeven door de Faculteit van de Letteren en Wijsbegeerte, CXIX (Bruges, 1955).

# Bibliography of works cited

Vicens Vives, J., *An economic hist. of Spain*, trans. from the 3rd Spanish edn (Princeton, N. Jersey, 1969).

Vigil, M., and Barbero, A., 'Sobre los orígenes sociales de la Reconquista: cántabros y vascones desde fines del imperio romano hasta la invasión musulmana', *BRAH*, CLVI (1965), 271–339.

Vismara, G., 'La successione volontaria nelle leggi barbariche', *Studi di storia e diritto in onore di Arrigo Solmi*, II (Milan, 1941), 183–220.

'Romani e goti di fronte al diritto nel regno ostrogoto', *Sett.*, III (1956), 409–63.

'El *Edictum Theodorici*', *EV*, I = Cuadernos del Instituto Jurídico Esp., V (Rome–Madrid, 1956), 49–89.

*Edictum Theoderici*, IRMAE, part I, 2b *aa* α (Milan, 1967).

*Fragmenta Gaudenziana*, IRMAE, part I, 2b *bb* β (Milan, 1968).

Voigt, K., *Staat und Kirche von Konstantin dem Großen bis zum Ende der Karolingerzeit* (Stuttgart, 1936).

Wallace-Hadrill, J. M., *The long-haired kings and other studies in Frankish hist.* (London, 1962).

Wenskus, R., *Stammesbildung und Verfassung. Das Werden der frühmittelalterlichen gentes* (Cologne–Graz, 1961).

White, K. D., *Roman farming* (London, 1970).

Wohlhaupter, E., *Gesetze der Westgoten*, Germanenrechte, XI (Weimar, 1936).

'Das germanische Element im altspanischen Recht und die Rezeption des römischen Rechtes in Spanien', *ZRG.RA*, LXVI (1948), 135–264.

Wolfram, H., 'Methodische Fragen zur Kritik am "sakralen" Königtum germanischer Stämme', *Festschrift für Otto Höfler* (Vienna, 1968), pp. 473–90.

Woodward, E. L., *Christianity and nationalism in the later Roman Empire* (London, 1916).

Wretschko, A. de, 'De usu Breviarii Alariciani (etc.)', *Theodosiani libri XVI* (see above, *Sources*, under *Codex Theodosianus*), I, part I, cccvii–ccclxxvii.

Yver, G., 'Euric, roi des wisigoths', *Études d'hist. du MA dédiées à Gabriel Monod* (Paris, 1896), pp. 11–46.

Zeiss, H., *Die Grabfunde aus dem spanischen Westgotenreich*, Römisch-germanische Kommission des archäologischen Instituts des deutschen Reiches, II: Germanische Denkmäler der Völkerwanderungszeit (Berlin–Leipzig, 1934).

Zeumer, K., 'Über zwei neuentdeckte westgothische Gesetze', *NA*, XXIII (1898), 75–112.

'Gesch. der westgothischen Gesetzgebung, I', ib., 419–516.

'Zum westgothischen Urkundenwesen', *NA*, XXIV (1899), 13–38.
'Gesch. der westgothischen Gesetzgebung, II' and 'Gesch. ...., III', ib., 39–122, 571–630.
'Gesch. der westgothischen Gesetzgebung, IV', *NA*, XXVI (1901), 91–149.
Ziegler, A. K., *Church and State in Visigothic Spain*, Universitas Catholica Americae Washingtonii, s. Facultas Theologica, 1929–30, XXXII (Washington D.C., 1930).

It is to my shame – and loss – that the brilliant essay on the Visigoths added by J. M. Wallace-Hadrill in the 3rd edn of his *The barbarian West, 400–1000* (London, 1967) escaped my attention until it was too late to be of service.

# INDEX TO CITATIONS
# OF THE LAWS

# Index to citations of the laws

# Index to citations of the laws

# INDEX

# Index

Asses, 211, 215
Astrology, 146, 147 n. 5
Asturias, 194 n. 4
Athanagild, 191
Athaulf, 2, 50 n. 1
Audemundus, 57 n. 1
*Auditores*, 99, 100
Augustine, St, 48, 144
*Aulae regalis officium*, 56 n. 3, *and see Officium palatinum*
Avitus, 3, 8 n. 5

*Bacaudae*, 1
Baddo, Queen, 26 n. 3
Baetica, 11, 53 n. 3, 196 n. 4, 201, 215
*Balthi*, 23 n. 1
Baptism, 15, 130 n. 4, 144 f., 233 n. 3, 247, *and see* Jews
Barcelona, 69, 205 n. 6
Barcelona, First Council of, *see De fisco Barcinonensi*
Barcelona, Second Council of, 126 n. 7, 150 n. 4, 151 n. 1, 154 n. 1
Barter, 105, 106, 192
Basques, 17, 73, 76, 202 n. 1
Bavarians, 8, 159 n. 3, 257
Benedict II, 123, 124 n. 2
*Beneficia*, 187 n. 5, 210, 244
Betrothal, 192, 224–30 passim, 233–6 passim, 245. *See also* Dowry
Bible, Gothic, 5 n. 3; and justice, 37; protection of, 129; references, 27 f., 33 n. 2, 37 nn. 2, 3, 43 n. 3, 48 n. 5, 50 n. 1, 103 n. 5, 130 n. 6, 131 n. 1, 132 n. 1, 133 nn. 3, 5, 136 n. 1, 144 nn. 2, 6, 145 nn. 1, 4, 227 n. 5, 233 n. 4, 235 n. 6, 260 n. 8, 263 n. 4
Bigamy, 234 ff.
Birth, lying about, 111; and status, 55 f., 160, 161 f., 181, 183 f., *and see* Children
Bishops, act *ultra vires*, 17 n. 3; annual visitation, 154 n. 3; appointment, 124 n. 2, 126, 150 n. 4, 153 n. 1; attempt to profit from Reccesvind, 47 n. 2, 63 n. 2; crimes of violence by, 151; defamation of dead, 43 n. 3; dereliction of governmental duty by, 118 n. 7, 119 f., 127 f., 138 f., 153 f.; as electors, 46, 48 n. 5, 49 f.; and endowments by *servi fiscales*, 64 n. 7; as executive officers, 157; feuding, 151; Germanisation of, 150; and homosexuals, 157; and illicit unions, 153 f., 157; and infanticides, 157 n. 6; *invasio* by, 151, *and see* rights/failings, *below*; as judges in treason cases, 151 n. 7, 157; make grants

*in stipendio*, 60 n. 7; and metropolitans, 152 n. 8; and mutilation of slaves, 157; and *numerarii*, 70; and *palatini*, 41, 45 n. 3, 46, 47 n. 2, 56 n. 6, 57, 63 n. 2, 96 n. 2; payments to king by, 69; privileges of accused, 45 n. 3, 56 n. 6, 57, 96 n. 2, 114 n. 1, 152; represented in court, 43 n. 7: cf. 152; and reprieve of traitors, 41, 128 f.; rights/failings of, concerning Church property/personnel, 60 n. 7, 69, 78 n. 5, 128 n. 1, 151–5 passim, 156 n. 1, 160 n. 3; and runaway slaves, 127 f.; *saiones* of, 118 n. 3; sanctuary sought with, 96; schools of, 150 n. 4; and superstitious practices, 146 n. 3, 157; supervise/work with royal officers, 17 n. 3, 69 f., 78, 101, 110, 118 ff., 138 f., 146 n. 3, 153, 157; and testaments, 110. *See also* Church, Clergy, *and under individual councils*
Blasphemy, *see* Profanity
Blinding, 30 n. 7, 40 n. 3, 89, 90 f., 175 n. 4, 238
Bloodletting, 87 n. 1, 203 n. 6, 204
Bodyguard, royal, 54
*Bona vacantia*, 71, 249
Bordeaux hoard, 196 n. 8
Boundaries, 209
Braga, liturgy of, 123 n. 1
Braga, Third Council of, 150 n. 4, 151 nn. 1, 5, 152 n. 1, 153 n. 1, 156 n. 1
Braulio, 130 n. 4, 133 n. 4, 158, 165 n. 4; and laws, 19 n. 1, 25 n. 8, 30 n. 4; and papacy, 123; and royal authority, status etc., 28 n. 7, 123 n. 4, 126 nn. 2, 7; and succession, 50 n. 1
Breviary (*LRV*), 6 n. 4, 9 n. 7, 10 f., 19 n. 3, 112 n. 2, 146 n. 2, 161; cited, 10 n. 8, 14 n. 1, 26 n. 3, 82 n. 7, 86 n. 6, 103 n. 5, 249 n. 7, 256 n. 11; and councils, 10 n. 8
Britain, 197 n. 2
Bronze, 195 n. 7, 196
*Buccellarii*, 75, 187 f., 206, 231 n. 2: cf. 60 f. *See also* Patrons
Bullfighting, 202 n. 3
Burdunelus, 10 n. 1
Burgundians, 8 n. 5, 10, 121 n. 3, 204, 205 nn. 2, 5
Byzantium, 123 nn. 1, 2, 235 n. 6; commerce/maritime links with, 193, 197 f.; influence of, 12 f., 24, 53 n. 1, 56 n. 3, 73 n. 1, 90 n. 1, 121, 124, 133 n. 4, 196, 197: cf. 28 n. 2, 118, 120 n. 2, 125, 248 n. 2, 258 n. 1; in Spain, 11 f., 17, 193 n. 7, 197, 198, 201

Cadiz, 199
*Caelia*, 212

298

# Index

# Index

# Index

Hair-styles, 122 f., 130 n. 4, 164 f.: cf. 46 n. 6

Harvest, 98, 211

Heraclius, 90 n. 1, 133 n. 4, 193

Heresy, 18, 127, 129 f.: cf. 122, 125 n. 7. *See also* Arianism, Monotheletism, Priscillianism

Hermenegild, 12 n. 3, 13, 14, 15 n. 1, 24 nn. 2, 4, 207 n. 1

Hidatius, 3, 204 n. 2

Highness, of king, 26, 41

Hildigisus, 57, 58 n. 1

Hohenaltheim, 47 n. 5

Holographs, 109 n. 2, 110

Homosexuality, 91 n. 9, 127, 157, 235

*Honestiores, see* Nobles

'Honest men', 100 f., 113, 193

Honey, 202, 213 f.: cf. 195 n. 1, *and see also* Apiculture

*Honor*, kingdom as, 25

Honorius I, 123, 133 n. 4

Horses, 64, 71, 76 n. 2, 116, 195, 211, 215 f., 217, 226. *See also* Cavalry

*Horti, see* Kitchen-gardens

Hospital, 203 n. 6

Household, royal, *see* Court

Houses, 64, 202 f., 214; offences and, 88, 178 n. 5, 188, 208, 231, 240, 256 n. 11, 258

Huesca, Council of, 153 n. 1

*Humiliores, see* Nobles

Huns, 2

Hunting, *see* Trapping

Idalius, 143 n. 2

Idolatry, 128 n. 1, 145 ff., 157

Ignorance, clerical, 150 f.; and heresy, 130; and judiciary, 117 f.; of law, 34, 101

Ildefonsus, 135 n. 5, 145 n. 1, 150 n. 3, 158; *De viris illustribus* of, cited, 53 n. 3, 126 n. 7, 196 n. 2, 198 n. 1

Illness, 75, 77, 94, 99, 103, 109, 147 n. 7, 244 n. 6, *and see* Medicine

Imports, 194, 195 nn. 1, 2, 196 ff.: cf. 193

Imposture, 111. *See also* Slaves [posing]

Impoundment of animals, 191 n. 5, 200, 218, 219, 258

Imprisonment (and detention), 90 n. 4, 95–8 passim, 101 n. 4, 114 n. 1, 116, 147, 166, 176, 200, 203, 204 n. 1, 263: cf. 90, 154, 233 (confinement in houses of religion)

Incest, *see* Marriage/sexual relations

*Infamia*, 89, 102 n. 2, 103, 104, 111, 147, 148, 149 n. 3, 154. *See also* Testimony

*Inferiores*, 56, 75 (military), *and see* Nobles

Informers, 62, 89 n. 4, 91 f., 175, 194, 251 252, 253

*Ingratia*, 60, 61, 67 n. 5, 107, 156, 180 f.

Inheritance, 7 n. 4, 9 n. 7, 67 f., 86, 88, 108, 135 n. 2, 178 n. 2, 203 n. 2, 222, 223, 231 f., 233 n. 3, 236 ff., 241 ff., 244 n. 4, 245 ff.; accelerated by law, 233, 235, 249 n. 9; by Church, *see* Church; to clergy, *see* clergy; division of, 207; by fisc, 249; to fiscal acquisitions, 63; to founders of *Eigenkirchen*, 155; to freedmen, 67 n. 5, 170 n. 6, 180; to mandatories, 102; by slaves, 170; to *stipendia*, 61, 187

Injury, by/to animals, 97 n. 7, 148, 216 ff.; during arrest, 97 n. 7, 220; by bees, 220; by felling, 214 n. 4; by fire, 200, 203; resulting in death, 260; cf. 96 n. 1; by robbery, 257; by sorcery, 148; by torture, 113 n. 3, 163, 172, 176, 182; from traps etc., 200, 216 n. 6. *See also* Misuse of person *and under separate offences*

Inscriptions, African, 196 n. 4; dedicatory, of Reccesvind, 62 n. 2; funerary, 14 n. 2, 170 n. 1, 203 n. 6; Greek, 197; Jewish, 131 n. 1, 170 n. 1; in Merida, 197, 201 n. 8, 203 n. 6

*Institutio heredis*, 66 n. 2, 109

Intent, 86, 87 n. 1, 172, 218, 219, 259 ff.

Interest, 105, 192 f.

*Invasio*, 94 n. 3, 151, 155, 208 f., 254 f., 258 n. 8, *and see* Usurpation

Ireland, 195 f.

Irrigation, 212

Iruña, 202 n. 1

Isidore, and *curia*, 66 n. 2; on *defensores*, 83 n. 1; and economic matters, 190, 194, 195, 197 n. 6, 201 n. 4, 202 n. 1, 210, 211 n. 1, 212, 214 n. 1; on *economicus*, 156 n. 1; eulogises Spain, 190; evidence for anointing, 48 n. 5; and Jews, 133 n. 5, 135 n. 5, 138 n. 1; and kings (authority, duties, virtues etc.), 25, 30 n. 5, 33 n. 3, 38 n. 4, 41 n. 5, 44 n. 5, 47 f., 50 n. 2, 126 n. 7, 129 n. 2; known in Ireland, 196; and law(s), 6 f., 13 n. 5, 29 n. 3, 30 nn. 4, 5, 33 n. 1, 44 n. 5; on Leovigild, 12 nn. 3, 7, 13 nn. 3, 5, 15 nn. 1, 3; on matrimonial matters, 225 n. 2, 227 n. 5, 233 n. 4, 234 n. 1, 235 n. 6; on medicine, 203 n. 6; on military matters, 76, 198; on *millenarii*, 81 n. 4; and papacy, 123; presides at IV Tol., 133 n. 5; on Reccared, 12 n. 7; and Sisebut, 133 n. 5, 198; on status, 159 n. 4, 161, 179 n. 2; and succession, 50 n. 1; and superstition, 145 n. 4, 147 n. 5, 148 n. 1;

305

# Index

# Index

King (*cont.*)

transactions with, 44, 192 n. 5; translates divine justice/God's will into law, 29, 31, 35 ff., 44, 45 n. 1, 122, 153; voluntary obedience to law by, 29, 44 f.; votive mass for, 25. *See also* Court, Family, *Fideles regis*, Fisc, Law, *Officium palatinum*, Succession, Theocracy, *and under individual councils and kings*

Kingdom, last years of, 21 f., 121, 167 f., 170 n. 2, 199

Kitchen-gardens, 87 n. 1, 213

Lands, clearance/enclosure/new cultivation of, 190, 200 n. 7, 205–10 passim; division of, 7, 65 f., 204 ff.; held in common, 204 f., 206 n. 7, 207, 214; tax on, 64, *and see* Arable; travellers' rights to use of, 200; waste-, 190 204 f., 206 n. 7, 207, 214 f., 219; wood-, 190, 204 f., 207, 214, 219, 258. *See also* Arable, Pasturage, Viticulture

Language, Gothic, 4, 5 n. 3, 9 n. 1

Lashing, passim, but esp. 17 n. 3, 30 n. 7, 77, 87 n. 1, 89 n. 6, 90, 91, 94 n. 5, 98, 117, 118, 120, 147, 151 n. 5, 153, 157, 162, 167, 172, 175 n. 4, 177, 178 n. 5, 181, 184, 185, 186 n. 3, 187 n. 1, 191, 202 n. 5, 234, 263

*Latrones*, 168 n. 4, 199 n. 7

Law(s), abrogative, 38, 45 n. 1, 207 n. 4; canon, character of, 16 f., 125 f., and connection of with royal, 17, 20, 22, 40 n. 2, 45 nn. 3, 5, 63 n. 2, 128, 133, 151 n. 9, 152 ff., 235 n. 5: cf. 67 f.; concerned with generality, 29, 32 ff.: cf. 198; created, 36, 78; criminal, 87 ff. (distinction of private and public crimes), 36, 85 ff., 259 ff. (principles of): *see also* Lawsuits; customary, 7, 8 n. 5, 29, 38; *divalis*, 28; equality/inequality before, 33, 160, 172, 174 f., 181 ff., *and see* Nobles, Slaves, Women; eternal, 36 f., 44, 45 n. 1; ignorance of, 34, 101; as instrument of government, 28 ff., *and see* Public welfare; in Isidore, 7 n. 1; judgements upon, 21; and justice, *see* King [translates]; of late kingdom, character, 22, 121, 167 f.; national, 6–11 passim, 13, 18, 19 n. 3; natural, 30 n. 4, 35 ff., 248 n. 2, 249, *and see* King [translates]; obedience to, 29, 33, 44 ff.; post-Visigothic, 9 n. 6, 37 n. 2, 259 n. 2: cf. 21 n. 6, 40 n. 2; practical requirements of, 31 n. 5, 34 f., and actual characteristics, 21, 121, 220; preambles to, 21, 37; promulgation/publication of, 38, 57, 133, 138 n. 5; retrospective, 36, 45, 77 n. 2, 101; royal,

alone admissible, *see* King [judgement]; *sacra*, 28; and *salus populi*, *see* Public welfare; soul of public body, 34; source of, in king, *see* King [judgement]; territorial, 6 n. 4, 8 n. 5, 9 n. 7, 13 nn. 4, 5, 16 ff., 122; unattributed, 54 n. 5, 90 n. 1, 111 n. 6; unauthorised copying of, 90 n. 1; as vehicle of theocracy, 23 f., 122

Law codes, of Alaric II, 6 n. 4, 9 n. 7, 10 f., *and see* Breviary; Chindasvind, 18 f.; Egica (alleged), 21 n. 6; Euric, 6 ff., 13, *and see Codex Euricianus*; Ervig, *see* Ervig; Leovigild, 6 n. 4, 9 n. 7, 13, *and see Antiquae*; Reccared (alleged), 16 n. 5; Reccesvind, *see* Reccesvind; Theodoric II, 7; prices of, 20

Lawsuits, ch. 4 passim, 172–6; between nobles and freemen, 112 f.: cf. 152 n. 7; distinction of criminal and 'civil', 82, 84, 92 f., 95, 98, 100, 101 f., 104, 111, 116, and of private and public crimes, 87 ff.; hearings of, 102 ff., 111, 114, 173 f., 176, 181, 182 f.: cf. 22, 121 (evidence), 95, 98 f., 101, 189 (general rules), 87–98 passim, 114 n. 1, 152, 157, 166, 172 f., 176, 182, 189 n. 4, 203: cf. 204 n. 1, *and see* Accusation, Arrest (initiation/preliminaries), 100, 102, 189 (intervention of patrons in), 101 f., *and see* Mandatories (mandatories), 113, 114 f., 173, 174 (oath), 45 n. 3, 56 n. 6, 57, 99 ff. (publicity of proceedings), 99 f., 189 (seemliness), 92, 111 ff., 173, 176, 181 f.: cf. 121 n. 4, *and see* Torture (torture); involving clerics, *see* Church [jurisdiction], the fisc, 63 n. 1, 83, 102, foreign merchants, 194, 198, the king, 43; *palatini*, 45 n. 3, 57: cf. 96 n. 2, 152, n. 7, and women, 102 n. 5. *See also* Judgements, Judges

Lead, 195

Leases, *see* Tenants

Leatherware, 195

Legal vacations, 95, 98, 211, 212

*Leges Theodoricianae*, 7

Leo of Narbonne, 8 n. 5, 159 n. 3

Leontius, 197 n. 2

Leovigild, 11 ff., 24, 56 n. 3, 97 n. 3, 122, 168 n. 2, 179, 194 n. 3, 198 n. 2, 201 f., 205 n. 6; laws of, *see Antiquae*

*Leudes*, 58 n. 3, 243 n. 3

*Lex Romana Visigothorum*, *see* Breviary

*Lex Teudi*, 10 n. 8, 16 n. 5

Liability, principle of personal, 86: *but see* 43, 83, 95 n. 5, 166, 167 n. 1, 173, 174 f., 175, 189, 232 n. 2, 260; for animals' offences, 200, 218 ff., 261

# Index

# Index

# Index

# Index

# Index